A DANCE WITH SHADOWS

The Journey Beyond Sexual Abuse, Addiction, & Chemical Imbalance

Eric Bradford Adreon

A DANCE WITH SHADOWS

The Journey Beyond Sexual Abuse, Addiction, & Chemical Imbalance

Eric Bradford Adreon

ISBN: 148023740X
ISBN-13: 9781480237407
Library of Congress Control Number: 2012921039
CreateSpace Independent Publishing Platform
North Charleston, SC

1

WHO KNOWS WHERE THE NEEDLE came from? Its origin scared me less than becoming dope sick. The needle stung as it entered my flesh. Adding a small ball of black tar to the rotation, I ensured that I would have a hit like the rest of the junkies. The class of 94' T-shirt had long ago lost its colors. The filth of the city mixed with my own vomit gave it a look of abandonment, a sort of vacancy. Grey and putrid green—these were my new team colors. This worn shirt had become my letterman jacket. It allowed me to blend in with my new crowd. If I hadn't traded in a number two pencil for a syringe, I would have walked the stage to receive a diploma like the rest of my childhood friends. Instead, I found the shirt while dumpster-diving behind Goodwill. I first put it on in an attempt to disguise my pungent smell. It is now a bitter reminder of the things I sacrificed for any substance that could take me far away from my present circumstances.

Today as I walked the streets of Seattle, I am confronted by a minefield of emotions. I hadn't always been a teenage street junkie. The city once meant baseball games, Christmas photos with Santa and holiday gifts from Nordstrom's, but I had transformed from a child of light to a child of the shadows, and that change was complete. It was like gazing at an evening sky to point out when day gave way to night. At some level, my transformation was a seamless transition as well. I spent many years rotating from light to dark then back to light before realizing that there was no line of separation between them.

I lived in a world where those who traded morality for depravity thought they received more than they gave up.

"Hey," came a girl's voice. "Can I get that rig when you're done with it?"

It was never easy to decipher the age of those inside shooting galleries. Under a clouded haze, the girl looked just under fifteen. No matter how low a person goes, they never lose all of their former self. I searched for the compassion I had abandoned years ago. My lingering morality pressed hard against the person I had become. In my malevolence, I sought to chase away the young girl before her light dimmed to the state of my own.

"Don't you have a tit to go suck on, Betty?"

Even my sorry attempt at vulgarity did not send her running as I had hoped. Instead, it made her more stubborn.

"If I wanted to listen to my daddy, I would still be letting him suck on my tits at home."

She was as seasoned as I. With that sad realization, I handed her the needle then stumbled to a torn and soiled mattress in a corner of the room, hoping for dreams of things as they used to be. I sought the flagging of the syringe as my blood mixed with the heroine and led to dreams of the poppy.

There are many precipitating factors that may take a person from a life of reason to a life of obscurity. Molestation is one. It is a cruel betrayer of innocence that drives its victims to a world of hiding. The word itself elicits the most savage emotions. The very act is one that even those within the walls of prison disavow as the lowest form of humanity, hunting down the perpetrators as if hunting the haunting shadows of their past. Many people spend years behind the protective walls of a therapist's office discussing the violation they experienced, or the abuse experienced by a loved one. Public discussion concerning molestation was shunned except for lectures from elementary school counselors concerning inappropriate touch. Mary, the unisex rag doll, served as a buffer to any real discussion of what the act entailed and how it might affect the person experiencing it firsthand.

I was never told not to walk to the park, beach, or store out of fear of abduction or sexual assault. Either those scenarios didn't take place or, if they did, they were never discussed. I do not remember talks with my parents about "inappropriate touch" or "stranger danger." I did not fear strangers and I had no knowledge of pedophiles or rapists. It wasn't strangers who should have frightened me; I should have been wary of the people that I did know. Sadly, the perpetrators are often those who have already breached the walls of protection created by parents. They attack as acquaintances versus unknown monsters.

My sexual exploration started at a much earlier age than one might wish to acknowledge. I was five years old. Anna was in my kindergarten class and what we did was taboo. This created confusion and shame even though we explored each other in innocence. What we did felt good. How could anything that felt so good be so bad? The many declarations of how we should not and would not do that again solved one problem, but they did not answer the many questions that swirled in my head as a result of the experience.

Sexual abuse lectures did little to clear up the confusion. Instead, they confused me more. Mary, the rag doll, had a woman's name, but she did not have the body parts I had seen during my "what's in your pants game" with Anna. Further, the counselor described what a man might do to a little girl not what a woman did to a little boy. I had been Mary, the rag doll, to a babysitter. By the time I had spoken to the counselor, my babysitter had been molesting me for months. The community counselor was making her yearly rounds and it just so happened that I could relate to what was being discussed.

"Eric, you are not alone in this. Many kids have gone through what you have. I will do everything in my power to stop this from continuing." Her words came as a great relief. I had finally found someone who would help stop the humiliation. The counselor promised me an end—and I believed her.

Marlene had a way of mixing pleasure with humiliation. As our babysitter, she was well liked by my brothers. She was an island girl, in her teens, who by all accounts was seen as perfectly normal. What was later described as horrific and in need of immediate response seemed, to my young mind, just a matter of course. Until I was shown, I had no understanding that what she did to my body should not have been allowed by anyone. Marlene often humiliated me in front of my brothers and the neighborhood kids. If I was unwilling to do what she asked, she forced me to wear diapers made of dishcloths, as a form of punishment. "Eric's going to be a baby for us all today because he doesn't want to follow my rules." My brothers laughed, adding to the disgrace, so I laughed, too, as if what was happening did not bother me. As another form of punishment, Marlene would make me eat beef bouillon cubes or other disgusting and vile things. My brothers were young and had no idea that what was happening to me was abuse. They had no idea that the abuse continued behind closed doors.

Although some of my experiences with Marlene made me feel good, the acts of humiliation fostered an inner confusion that would haunt me in the years to come. To some, these acts might seem trivial; but to a developing child in the care of someone older, the damage is quite profound.

"Eric, if you tell your parents about this we will both get in a lot of trouble," Marlene would threaten. "If you think it's bad now, I can make things much worse if you tell."

I ask myself why I didn't say, "No," or run away. Why didn't I tell my mom immediately? Why didn't my brothers do anything to stop it? There are no easy answers, and although I spent many years blaming other people for what happened, how could they possibly have known what was actually going on without someone telling them? In cases of abuse, there is never anyone to blame other than the abuser. The abuser wields control over those entrusted to them; it is a power that seems impossible to break. They also understand the art of manipulation and use it to continue the abuse. In my case, manipulation mixed with intimidation worked until a counselor made it clear that I could confide in her and could do so safely and without repercussions.

What constitutes sexual abuse? Does reaching a particular age transition sexual abuse into sexual exploration? Thinking back, my experiences with Marlene felt like abuse. She was older and in a position of authority. Abusers use their power to gain control over their victims and then fulfill their own desires at the other's expense. I don't believe that age is a factor as much as the ability to dominate another human being through the abuse of real or perceived power. This abuse, which can manifest itself in many ways, affects the victim on a physical, emotional and spiritual level. Gender is of no concern.

I trusted that, as an older person, Marlene would hold my best interests at heart. Further, I believed that my parents would never put me in a position that could result in harm. My experience with Anna had not felt like abuse because there was no abuse of power; the experience was one of mutual exploration not one of domination. We were children trying to understand the universe through our bodies. Although that behavior may have been best left for later years, it did not make me feel as though I had no control over my body and my own safety.

I have often heard people call boys who are molested by older women "studs," as though the molestation was on some level less substantial because a woman did it. Because there is no penetration to the child, the impression is that it is not nearly as damaging. If the scenario is reversed such that a man performs the same act on a boy or a girl, the occurrence is viewed as repulsive, crossing every social boundary. Why is this? An abuse of power is always an abuse of power. The body of one human being is just as precious as any other; one gender is not more or less sacred than the other. The emotional confusion and violation that goes along with being abused is equal to either sex. My confusion, fear, loss of innocence, and humiliation was no less substantial because it came at the hands of a woman. In many ways, that added to the confusion and difficulty that I would experience in relationships with women later on in my life.

The abuse of men is more common than people realize. Discussing this abuse becomes more difficult as the years pass. Society teaches men that it is better to keep one's mouth shut than risk being viewed as tainted as a result of what happened. Men are also told that if they experienced abuse they may abuse in turn. Does that mean that if I share my experience, I will be tagged as a potential threat? That because I was sexually compromised I will do the same to others? These fears keep men like me from discussing such events, even with those who might help us work beyond the abuse. For years, I struggled with my decision to go to a counselor to describe what happened. Somehow I believed myself to be at fault because what Marlene did felt good. If she had not mixed physical molestation with public humiliation, I might never have said anything to a counselor in the first place.

I remember very little about what came next. Marlene continued to babysit then vanished from my life for a time, leaving invisible scars and haunting confusion. I wondered why I had not immediately received protection after my disclosure at school. The counselor assured us that any disclosure would be dealt with right away. The expression "We will protect you" eventually felt more like a taunt than a promise. The lectures with Mary, the rag doll, taught me that I wasn't alone. Why didn't the counselor tell my parents? Why didn't she follow through in her role as counselor? Had I done something to provoke this waking nightmare? Why didn't my parents come rushing in to destroy the first true antagonist of my youth? That was the great tragedy. The event was bad enough, but the lack of response from those who could have protected me compounded the grievance as they failed in their duties. Their job—above all else—was to protect me. Once I acknowledged the experience as abuse, every touch afterward took me from physical pleasure to emotional pain and shame.

I have no idea why my parents never spoke with me about what had happened once the counselor told them of my secret. This silence left me questioning the validity of a system established to keep me safe. Though I could not fully comprehend this as a six-year-old, the seeds had been planted and grew with the nourishment of life's experiences. Could I have expounded on those events then as I can now? Probably not. I did say words like "hurts," "scared," "sad," "alone," and "embarrassed." Regardless of the words used, I was relaying the same information then as I am relaying now. Though I used fewer words as a child, my message was no less profound. Because it seemed that nothing had been done as a result of what I had revealed, my voice felt silenced, my words meaningless. A tortured child mimed them.

Years later, I saw Marlene. Standing in the checkout lane with my mother, I saw her and felt an instant rush of panic. The power of an abuser is great even years after the events have taken place. Standing before Marlene, I felt like my six-year-old self. She smiled, unaware of or un-phased by my presence and the past we had shared.

"Mom, that's her."

She continued to check us out. My mother did not recognize her.

"It's Marlene," I whispered.

I had always assumed that my counselor had told my mother about the molestation, but that she had chosen not to act on the information. That was incorrect.

"Please don't say anything," I pleaded. "I just want to get out of here."

In therapy some time later, I discovered that my mother had dealt with Marlene in her own way. Though that cleared up some questions, it did little to rectify the outcome. Knowing that my parents had not swept the events under the carpet, as I had thought, eased some resentment, but it did not heal the pain that the perceived absence of action had created. Simply removing the abuser does not ensure healing; prosecution and forcing the perpetrator to face punishment does. In that moment, I could tell that my mother was fuming. Even so, she respected my wishes and we walked out of the store. Marlene maintained the power she once had, though now she held power over us both. She had never been held accountable for her actions. This gave her a power that would continue to abuse me even years later.

At thirteen, why could I not face a woman against whom I felt so much anger? Whenever my mother shopped at that store afterwards, I could not get out of the car for fear of seeing her again. Were men not supposed to bury this emotion and carry on? Physically I had become stronger. Why couldn't I muster some masculine bravado like I did at school? Looking back, I am glad a confrontation had not taken place. As I grew older and subsequently more angry and volatile, my actions became unpredictable. Violence would have done little in the way of closure or healing; instead, it would have given me brief satisfaction, and then re-opened the wounds again.

Abusing the abuser does not erase previous abuse; rather, it compounds the pain and suffering. I learned much later that forgiveness is the greatest healer of wounds inflicted by others. Though it goes against natural instinct, forgiveness leads to closure. Forgiveness removes the abuser's power and returns that power to the victim. That has been my experience. That has been the truth unveiled along my journey. I was not alone then and I am not alone now. In our country, one in six males are sexually abused before the age of sixteen. For whatever reason, the power of forgiveness is a lesson many of us share.

Though I felt the pain that came with understanding, I have gained more than I lost from the experience. Once I finally confronted the confusion and shame, I experienced a major shift both emotionally and spiritually. It was as though I had been deprived of the sun for so long that when I finally found my way into the light, I bloomed with a brilliance that forced the nightmare into the shadows.

Confronting these fears and shame gave me back the power that I had lost, motivating me to continue on. I discovered an inner strength, bred from survival and fostered by revelation. I found a way to turn a negative into a positive. This did not come through religious revelation or an instant emotional upheaval; instead, my inner strength came by way of many philosophies converging over time. The experience of this convergence allowed me to sort out the confusion of a battered past. The first step was a willingness to admit to and face the very things from which I had been hiding. Confronting the monsters of my past, knowing that legions of survivors and sympathizers stood eager to help me through the desolation of abuse and its aftermath, provided me with the strength I needed to move on. My greatest reassurance came from the support of others. This pursuit for inner strength did not manifest in grade school, middle school, high school, or the tip of a syringe. My journey manifested through self-reflection–the painful evaluation of the very scars that scared me so terribly.

2

KINDERGARTENS OVER *and we are going home.*
Goodbye, goodbye.
Goodbye, goodbye, goodbye.

As we lined up and waited for the bus, we sang the "Going Home" song. Children's voices sound like angels to me, and as a child, I understood these angels to be around us at all times. I knew this because I talked to them while playing alone in the woods and on the beaches. I knew that I was not alone and that there were other beings just out of sight. One of my first memories was of falling into a friend's pool as a two-year-old in Oregon. One of these entities picked me out of the water and set me safely on the edge of the pool. From that day on I have always felt the presence of something, especially at times of crisis and around other children.

As a kindergartener, I was pleased to be big enough to ride the yellow bus, yet small enough to crawl onto my father's lap to watch a ball game. At this age, and as I entered school, a whole world opened up before me. With my mother leading, my hand gently cupped in hers, I felt safe, secure, and whole. However, despite all that was good, my secret remained a constant irritation. Though it faded slightly, as good memories outweighed the bad ones, I could not shake the feeling that I was somehow different as a result of the abuse I had endured early on. The fact that I had buried those events in silence seemed to compound my isolation. I was, by most standards, normal. I had friends, played sports, and got into mischief just as any pre-teen might while trying to make sense of the seemingly senseless world. I followed most rules and respected authority, although I was never generous with my trust like the other kids my age. I felt suspicious of authority figures and believed they acted with a hidden agenda. Power still meant abuse, so those who wielded power held the potential to commit the crimes I had chosen to forget.

Just as I was learning to bury the secrets of my past, I was introduced to the very thing that would ensure that I did so thoroughly. Up to this point, imagination had served as my transport to a place free of the weight of the world. The innocence of imagination was replaced by something far more sinister. In the hands of one who sought avoidance, this new form of escape was quite dangerous, especially at the age of ten.

Mike lived just over the hill. We shared a love of adventure and found the thrill of escape through his father's liquor. Initially, the taste kept me away, but as curiosity met the "golden buzz," I was soon the oak liquor cabinet's greatest fan. Over the course of that summer, alcohol opened new doors and, without my knowledge, set a pendulum in motion. Ultimately, the pure enjoyment wore off and I found myself controlled by substances in varying forms. Alcohol, cigarettes, and marijuana were the most prevalent. They were easily accessible as society deemed them acceptable. I took smokes from my mother's cigarette pack without her noticing and watered down the liquor bottle after a few slugs from my parents' fifths. Marijuana was a little harder to come by. Still, every other week a friend from school shared a bud, which we smoked using a can pipe.

I showed signs of addiction the first time I used alcohol. I became obsessed with my friend's alcohol stash and was no longer as excited to race our bikes down the numerous Bainbridge Island trails. Instead, my mind locked on the bottles in the dark, oak cabinet. Our friendship, built from similar interests, no longer mattered. I became selfish. I no longer cared about what I could do for him as a friend; I cared only about the liquor and what it did for me. From what I can remember, he did not obsess the way that I did. He was not compelled to drink and seemed perplexed when our time together inevitably ended with a drink. When he asked me to stop, to avoid punishment from his father, I told him that I would. Although I wanted to respect our friendship, my desire to become intoxicated outweighed all else. I continued to break into the cabinet despite his pleas and despite my promises. In time, his calls to come over stopped.

Alcohol is recognized as socially acceptable. This acceptance invites children to do the same. I would have never used any of these substances had they not been accessible to me at that point in my life. Why would I? We are led by example. My parents smoked, drank and partook in other substances, setting the example I was to follow. The old saying, "Do as I say, not as I do" applied. Why would children heed the advice given by strangers if that advice contradicts the example set by their parents? Being chemically altered felt far too good for alcohol use to be as bad as they said it was.

Many people try various drugs without becoming substance abusers. They dabble without ever experiencing the almost instinctual drive that made me use until the substance was gone. I often searched for more with an obsessed fervor, one that forced me to sacrifice morals and self-respect to obtain a given substance. Despite losing many friends in the process, this behavior did not stop as the years passed; it became more powerful and uncontrollable. I sacrificed many of my early childhood relationships as a result of an entirely selfish and uncontrollable desire to alter my reality.

Middle school was a new and invigorating experience. The three island grade schools converged into one, and new faces surrounded me from every direction. Everything was larger: the older kids, the gymnasium where we played basketball before and after school, and the cafeteria where we ate lunch. The atmosphere felt electric. I began to thrive. Middle school also brought a strange self-confidence that I had not experienced in grade school. Along with my introduction to alcohol the previous summer, I had reached another milestone.

One morning I woke up quite early, which was unusual for my brothers and me on the weekends. Unless my father had a chore planned, or we had a game scheduled, we were dead to the world until the smell of pancakes and bacon rousted us from the sheets. I remember the previous night's dream vividly. The sensation I felt could only be described as ecstasy. The only sensation I had experienced that came close was from riding belly down on my skateboard, feeling a strange ticklish sensation in my groin. This was different—and it frightened me.

A mysterious, nameless girl had entered my dreams. I woke, my underwear sticky, and instead of being left in awe of this strange new gift, I felt dirty and ashamed by what my body had done. The confused pleasure I had experienced with Marlene returned. To erase the memory and the evidence, I needed to take a shower; doing so would wake my parents. If they woke, there would be questions. Though I was not aware of it at the time, they knew what happened under their roof; with two boys older, they would recognize the signs of puberty.

As I tiptoed into the bathroom and turned on the water, I could hear my father ask my mother who was up. My mother knocked on the door and I felt certain that she knew my secret immediately.

"Who is in there? Why are you up so early? You're going to wake up the whole house!"

I don't remember exactly what I said, but both of my parents knew that I had experienced my first wet dream by my fumbling response. To them, my silent admission seemed just a matter of course. To me, it was a somber occasion.

Shame should never be a part of one of the most important experiences in a boy's life. Given my history with sexual abuse, anything that seemed even close to the scenario I had endured with Marlene seemed wrong. The pleasure of my first ejaculation and entrance into manhood caused only confusion and questions, not enjoyment and wonder. How could I explain this to my parents if I didn't understand it myself? How could I seek the help that I so desperately needed without opening the door to my most guarded secrets? I wanted to share my burden but had no idea where to start or what the result might be. My safest bet was to internalize this experience like those that came before until I simply forgot. I knew exactly how to forget. Every tilt of the flask and every toke from the pipe had prepared me to forget.

My heart pounded in my chest, the pulse reverberating into my ears as though a helicopter hovered overhead. The bright yellow and green Scotch Broom surrounded me like a gnarled, endless maze. I knew I was supposed to be somewhere but my brain remained foggy, and my senses felt distorted. I loved how I felt in this new world of climactic sensation and desire. Everything seemed multidimensional. I had left an innocent world behind, exchanging it for one that beckoned for exploration. Had I eaten, or rather inhaled, the forbidden fruit of mythology or was this something far better?

She was the Eve to my Adam, yet how could I blame the problems of humanity on the blond bombshell two grades my senior who let me know I was no longer a pre-pubescent boy every time I saw her? If anything, my hormones were to blame for the temptation and innocence lost; they provoked the desire to explore the world in every way possible. She was nothing like the story from ancient texts. She was blond with budding breasts, the face and physique of a teen, stoner goddess, with a voice that summoned me like a siren's song. I knew very little about women other than my mother. Once, I had spied on my mother's friend Carol while she took a bath. Beyond little Anna and, of course, Marlene, I knew nothing more. I knew only that she lured me into her lair, smoked some buds in a six-bowled pipe she called, "The Revolver," had her way with me in the form of a dry hump, then disappeared as quickly as I climaxed. She left me spent, with a hell of a buzz, and late for an appointment at the barbershop.

· Two things were significant in that moment. One, I had come very close to losing my virginity. Two, I had not experienced the guilt and shame that I normally felt when I ejaculated. Thinking back, the only differences between this experience and those in my room were that I had smoked marijuana prior and that I actually had a living partner. Knowing that I could turn what was once a confusing and shameful experience into one of pure pleasure, I pursued chemical alteration during sexual pleasure to its furthest extremes knowing that I had found a potent combination for oblivion.

This intense experience with chemicals and sexual exploration had me from the very beginning. It was my own secret, which I chose not to share with anyone. What I did not understand, however, was that most people experienced the subtle or intense escape of chemical use as a luxury. I, in contrast, had no control over myself and would pursue any means to ensure a continuous flow of pleasure. For some unknown reason, maybe a cruel joke of the gods or a karmic debt I had yet to pay, I was one of the few who would ultimately destroy myself through the pursuit of ecstasy. What should have been one of life's most intimate and personal experiences, sexual intimacy, had become my ball and chain when mixed with chemicals. In time, I would pursue the feelings that I had experienced in that flowery paradise to the outermost edge of reality.

Aside from the various forms of chemical alteration I brought into my life, I loved sports. Sports fulfilled several things at once. My father and I bonded over sports. Although I rarely felt at home, I felt comfortable on the field. This was especially true when my father coached me in baseball. On the diamond, we found common ground; and through my talent, I experienced what felt like a true bond between father and son. At times, my success in sports allowed me to excel beyond and above others.

For a person who had felt less than for so long, this was a welcome byproduct.

Sports brought me praise from others and attention from girls. With each victory, I felt as if I was winning back a part of me that had been stolen years before. I was the dominant one now, and I would be damned if someone was going to take that away from me. Every hit on the football field had to be the biggest; every touchdown the winning one. Though I felt joy playing the game, that was not my priority; it was simply a bonus. This intensity on the field got me into trouble with umpires, coaches, and other players as I lost sight of the game's subtleties, blinded by my drive for praise and dominance. This type of drive often takes athletes to the very top of their game, carrying them through to a professional sports career. More than once, I was told that my talent could take me places. At the time, I was motivated by the very thought of such possibilities. Later in life, when sports glories echoed distant in the darkness, these promises turned to taunts of dreams unrealized. My talents ceased to represent a catalyst for bigger and better things. Instead, I burned briefly—quite bright—then faded into the shadows as others with more even temperament filled the gap I left behind. I had become the coach's example, the father's warning story, and a means by which to illustrate the failures that could come. "Don't do what he did." "That's what wasted talent looks like." No one had to tell me; I knew this was the case. I traded dreams for illusions repeatedly, ignoring the permanence in life that time cannot erase. My life was not unique in this. My story is one that has been lived many times over. Different actors take part in different scenes, but the lessons remain the same. One learns from the other, and that other endures far more difficult lessons having failed to heed the lessons taught in youth.

At some point in my transition, I had gone from victim to victimizer without realizing it. I may not have been creating victims of sexual or physical abuse, but I was creating emotional victims through my behavior. The victim becomes the victimizer. Though my actions were not those perverse behaviors that Marlene had used, it was abuse all the same. I fed on the fear of others, manipulated them, and sought emotional power and control. Is that not what Marlene was doing while she fed her perverse desires at my expense? Did I not do the same by trying to manipulate those around me?

For all the positive attention I received on the field, I experienced the opposite in the classroom and at home. Anger, rebellion, and depression all surfaced at once following puberty. No one emotion took precedence over the other; any of the three could rear up at any given moment creating confusion in those who had known me for years as a loving and compassionate boy. My teenage emotions, driven by hormones, were like those gopher games at the pizza parlor. You take the club and smack the gopher's head as soon as it pops out of the hole. Soon, they pop up all at once and it becomes harder and harder to hit them. The more they appeared, the quicker I hit, the less successful I became. It is an endless battle, one of frustration and torment.

My teachers began to spend more time policing my partners in crime and myself than they spent teaching the class. Causing frustration was my sixth-grade theme. In many ways, it became a sort of introduction for incoming fifth-graders. Hormones and emotions rose, then settled. As other students learned to change their behavior through discipline and maturity, I thrived on the negativity that my rebellion created. The frustration in my teachers' eyes was palpable, yet I remained unwilling to change my behavior. At times, I felt compassion for their position. Other times, it seemed like some unknown force gave neither them nor I a break from the destruction that drove me. This may sound dramatic, but I spent nearly three-quarters of sixth grade in noon detention and the other quarter under some alternate form of punishment. I am not sure how I made the transition from a boy who followed the rules to a boy who rebelled against them. I was not proud when other parents would not allow me to spend time with their kids. The battles that began at home were unpleasant. It was as though each negative experience fed the next until I was an uncontrollable source of frustration for those closest to me. I had no idea that the course I had set for my life would be terrifying. Regardless of what those who knew the story told me in an attempt to intercede, I was unwavering—I had chosen my path.

I felt a strange familiarity with the chaos I had created. Somehow in my misbehavior, I took the power. Every time a teacher threw his or her hands up in frustration, I took the power. Every time I stole a glass apple from the principal's prized collection on his desk and my classmates howled with laughter, I took a little more power. It was a strange compromise. I compromised my education, my dreams, and my reputation for the ability to illicit power through negativity. This power was, of course, a great illusion. For the abused, even the semblance of such power creates a false sense of having moved beyond the power exercised by their abusers.

This power struggle manifests itself in different ways. For some, it's like an invisible current, hidden just below the surface of a beautiful river. The current pulls the unsuspecting down in a quiet fury; it is a subtle force. Those who succumb to its force are unaware until they look up at the fading light, gasping for air, and wonder how something so calm could be so powerful.

The real trouble began when drugs, alcohol, girls, and rebellion combined with the onset of a Chemical imbalance. Each of these variables comes with a powerful set of characteristics. Every moment in my life at this point related to one or more of these things. If I was at a birthday party, I had to be the kid drinking alcohol downstairs or enjoying the intensity of a female body in an embrace. What I was doing didn't matter; feeling a rush of euphoria drove my every action. After a while, I found that mixing a buzz with the kiss of a sixth-grade crush made both experiences much more powerful.

Alcohol obviously impairs judgment and alters perception, but hormones do the same to a teenager. A teenager will throw all common sense to the wind in pursuit of sexual gratification, be it a hug, a kiss, or something more. I don't know how many times I risked the wrath of my parents to sneak out on a moonlit night for a rendezvous with other kids. Common sense would have told me to stay at home; hormonal sense said to sneak out and bring a condom. Although, the thought of a condom was a step in the right direction, its use in the sixth grade was not.

I found that I could take a journey of the body, mind, and spirit through these alterations and find relief from being human. In the bliss, I was both present and detached from everything around me, including my memories. I had many reasons to escape, or so I told myself. I had begun to live a life dominated by negative behavior, and though I was not proud of my actions, the things that I had buried needed to stay that way. Many of my childhood friends did the same things that I did, but they learned from the consequences. While they were preparing for life's future challenges, I was learning to avoid them. In retrospect, this is obvious. At the time, it seemed like the natural course of action. My judgment was clouded by emotions more powerful than caution.

People much wiser than I experience similar journeys through meditation versus chemical alteration. Rather than avoid things that frighten them, they embrace and face their fears. Things that initially seem large and intimidating cease to wield any power or control. These people enmesh themselves in a particular fear, and then they use that same fear as a source of empowerment. It would take me many years to understand this union of darkness and light.

My parents tried to steer me in a different direction. From suggesting meditation groups to church youth groups, they tried to talk to me on numerous occasions, but I was unwilling to reciprocate their gestures of compassion. My mother told me, "Talking will free you from your struggles." The harder they tried, the more I pushed them away. What I had wanted for so long I was finally getting: an opportunity to share with them my fears. Instead of embracing this opportunity, I gave them the cold shoulder. My rebellion intensified and sadness pushed me further and further into the darkness, away from others' outstretched arms. An emotional cloud had descended; I was unable to get my head above it.

Parents are ultimately held responsible for their children's actions, even when they have very little control over the circumstances that create the poor behavior. True, life at home was not perfect and it would soon get much worse, but my parents loved me. The various ways in which they tried to redirect me failed because I was unwilling to take the help. My parents attended countless parent conferences seeking solutions. With an unwilling participant, no consensus could ever be reached.

Halfway through my seventh-grade year, I began to see a fracture in my parents' relationship. What for many years seemed like an unbreakable bond began to show signs of stress and cracking. Fights became more serious, lingering for days. Resentment, far different from any ordinary anger or frustration, moves in and creates a cancer in its host. I saw this cancer develop in my parents. There is no description for what it did to me. An illness like cancer affects everyone in proximity of it. How can one not be affected while watching it ravage loved ones? I sank further and further into myself. Though I spoke with friends about this, they showed support and kindness with no solution.

The resentment between my parents had many symptoms, all of which were quite painful to watch. Whether it was my mother's drinking or my father's emotional distance I was at a loss for allocation of blame. At times, I felt hope as a smile passed between my parents, but these moments were dashed by a deepening decline. I watched helplessly as my false utopian world vanished before my eyes. I did not like the paradigm shift that I saw coming. At the very top of my pantry, my parents stashed a treasure trove of hard liquors. They were drinkers and kept a healthy supply. I braved the flimsy shelves to get to the sweet Kaluha and the head-shaking vodka. I sought anything that gave me the most immediate comfort. Painkillers only mask an illness, giving temporary relief by creating the illusion that pain is gone. This creates a risk for causing more damage.

One night, after a week of constant fighting, my parents decided that a movie might calm the waters. They were attempting to work on their marriage, which was quite commendable considering their symptoms. Their cool departure from a loving embrace and warm words had left me searching for a cure. Two or three times a week I climbed the shelves for my own private escape. I had done so for years unnoticed. This night was different. As I drank, I felt something deep within that compelled me to continue past the point of inebriation. I didn't want just a buzz. I wanted to forget. I wanted oblivion.

I remember hazy moments from that night, snippets like a slide show extracted from an actual experience. It was as if each slide held a lesson of its own. On the telephone, I told a friend goodbye...My brother entered the bathroom...Red dots covered the sink...The lights of an ambulance twirled in the driveway, the reflection caught in a puddle...My neighbor gave my brother instructions... My mother's hand ran over my forehead, as tears dropped from her cheek onto mine...Then, nothing. The slide show was over and the lights went out.

I woke to shame and regret. I felt ashamed that I had done this to my family. I felt regret that I had not finished the job. I was no stranger to shame, but regret was something new. Regret brought a gut-wrenching sadness that would follow me for years to come. I had given up on life before my life had truly begun; that hurt my family deeply.

Though some consider suicide attempts simply attention-seeking behavior, the attempt and the emotion that fuels it are real. Many so-called attention seekers end up in a casket as those who never took the attempt seriously, slowly lower the coffin into the ground. Believe me when I say that when a person chooses to harm themselves in an attempt to illicit attention, you had better listen; at that moment, there is something to listen to. Had I known which way the veins run in my wrists and how deep to cut, I am positive I would have finished the job that night. I sought attention for many reasons, but I blamed my parents for all of them. I could not endure their separation. Death meant relief.

My older brother, Ryan, reacted like a hero. He saw blood, a razor, and an unstable person inflicting damage. Without question, he acted immediately. That is what heroes do. They act according to the circumstances, pushing their own pain aside until the crisis has passed. After that night, a gap began to form between my brother and myself as a result of the scene he entered into. How can you blame a person for distancing themselves from someone who abuses themselves and those around them? He was just a child ten months older than myself, confused and conflicted. He faced the same uncertainty that I faced; yet his was far less messy.

My downward progression became a sort of spiritual experience. Each new tragedy brought revelation; each revelation fed into the next tragedy. Rather than working towards enlightenment, an emptiness devoured the negative consequences I had created. My life churned like a black serpent eating its own tail believing its stomach empty. I slowly replaced what remained of the innocence of youth with an understanding of far harsher things. These things have the power to turn a grown man's face downwards as he stares at an empty reflection in his beer glass—or a blood trail in a syringe. These experiences produce wrinkles on a child's face, replacing hope with despair.

Adolescent drug and alcohol treatment programs experienced a surge in the eighties and nineties. Generally, children who showed any sign of chemical use paired with emotional problems were sent to treatment. There are mixed feelings about this extreme approach, but at least it was a beginning to treat those things that brought pain and confusion into the lives of many. I think my mother was relieved when the chemical dependency counselor came back with a diagnosis of alcoholic/addict. A name could finally be attributed to the problems caused by my roller coaster of emotion, chemical use, and rebellion.

I don't remember ever seeing a psychologist. As most of my episodes included alcohol use, it was assumed that substances were the driving force behind my problems. If the counselors had looked a little deeper and if I had been a little more honest, the diagnosis may have been quite different.

There were two or three dual diagnosis treatment facilities in Seattle and Tacoma for people covered under insurance. During President Reagan's years in office, funding for mental health facilities was cut. Addicts with mild to moderate mental disorders flooded treatment programs. Adolescents who used multiple drugs, and therefore suffered from a mix of chemical imbalances, were nearly impossible to diagnose given the extent of their problems. The disease of addiction in its various stages is considered the primary disease, meaning that it must be treated first to clear the patient for further treatment. There were many who desperately wanted to help the kids recover; a series of issues and a general lack of funding complicated that desire.

My counselors fought to get me clean long enough to identify which problems were drug-induced and which reflected a legitimate chemical imbalance. The science was there, but I had to get clean and I had to trust the world of psychiatry, which I did not. Many psychiatrists at that time had no understanding of addiction as a disease; they thought that the right pill would solve my problems.

I felt like a pregnant twelve-year-old just beginning to show, being sent off to stay at relative's house. Although my transgression was already quite public, my parents followed the urging of the chemical dependency specialist who had evaluated me and sent me away. It must have seemed like the right thing to do. Our family's reputation was of little consequence compared to the life-threatening issues that my parents were trying to address.

New Beginnings was an inpatient adolescent treatment facility in Tacoma, Washington. Located in the west wing of a hospital, it had the look of an old folks' home though it hummed with unbridled energy. It was like no place I had ever been; it intimidated me. A thirteen-year-old is still a child in many ways. It must have been difficult to weigh the risks of keeping a child who abused himself, and others, at home. Sending me off to a world far different from my own must have been difficult. By inflicting self-harm, I had tied my parents' hands and forced them to respond. I had become an addict. As a result of my own exploration, I had experienced many things; but I was light-years away from these older teenagers in terms of life experience. The isolation of my island upbringing was stripped away leaving me fully exposed. I was forced to adapt in short order.

Teenagers tend to progress through the stages of addiction more quickly than adults. The progression from early stage to late stage may take just a few months or a few years depending on a variety of factors. First, teenagers are still developing emotionally and physically. Because of this they often experience brain, liver, and endocrine system problems. Teenagers who choose to use drugs and alcohol enter a world for which they are not fully prepared. Addiction is defined by a lifestyle of abuse. A cycle forms, abuse feeds addiction, and the cycle continues.

Excessive use also stunts emotional growth. While other adolescents are evolving naturally through the usual social channels, the emotional development of drug-addicted children is challenged and often stops after the first use. This makes addicted teenagers appear hardened and much older than they are. Other than experience, they are developmentally behind other children their age.

I spent my first three days of treatment in detox. Because this was a hospital, I was placed in a medical room where they could monitor my vitals to be certain I wasn't going through withdrawals. The doctors also wanted to monitor my mental state. Their main concern wasn't withdrawals; it was the possibility of inflicting self-harm again. My instability did not come in physical form; it was mental and emotional. It had only been a week since my suicide attempt, so the doctors were on high alert. I had no idea of the seriousness of my circumstances until a young, crack-addicted patient convulsed in front of me.

I had never been away from home. I had only recently felt comfortable sleeping at my friends' houses. More often than not, I chose to leave sleepovers before morning for fear that my friends' parents might treat me like Marlene had treated me. Separation from the safety of my home created an anxiety that I could not wish away. Some nights I cried into my pillow, not wanting anyone to know how frightened I felt. I had become accustomed to loneliness. Not the kind that comes from isolation, but the kind that comes from being surrounded by people, alone with my secrets. This was worst kind of loneliness, bred from a feeling of inferiority and absolute isolation.

The concept of the angel manifests within us all at different points in our lives. The transformation happens when the ego is set aside and is replaced by a genuine concern and true compassion for another. If you are like me, you believe that the Creator exists within us all; we reflect the Creator to those around us. At several points in my life, this reflection has occurred. These angelic beings, free of self and full of compassion, manifest at times of great need, exiting as quickly as they appear.

Need is sometimes quenched by the tenderness of another. My first human angel appeared one night as I cried into my pillow. Alfred, appearing monstrous, stood above me and stared down with blank, calculating eyes. After detox, I had been moved into his room. Alfred scared me. I had never known any African Americans other than Tyrell, my friend from grade school, and his mother. Alfred met every stereotype I had been taught. He was six feet four inches tall with dark, black skin and jerry curls under a shower cap to keep his pillow from staining. Alfred smelled of petroleum jelly. He had several scars on his chest. One was from a knife wound inflicted by his mother's boyfriend. The others were from gunshot wounds caused by rival gang members. Tattoos covered much of Alfred's hands and body. Many said, "... Crip." Another showed the footprints of a baby. That night, Alfred stood in front of the mirror throwing gang signs back at his reflection. He then did push-ups, a ritual that he performed every evening after brushing his teeth.

I thought my cries were muffled. Even then, I believed that showing emotion reflected weakness. Further, I didn't want to draw attention to myself. My father may have passed down this trait, or I may have simply grown accustomed to evading my emotions with chemicals. Either way, I hid my emotions the best that I could. That night, they burst forth like a flood. Alfred's presence, staring from the edge of his bed, paralyzed me with silent fear. It was the kind of fear I had experienced at the hands of Marlene so many years before. Alfred was far more powerful than I. As his giant hands reached for me, I knew I was at the mercy of a force far greater than my own. Alfred pulled me to his chest. I remember feeling confused by his gentleness. What I had presumed to be an oncoming assault was, in fact, an affectionate hug. His embrace released me from fears, past and present, allowing my emotions to flow unhindered. I am not sure how long I sobbed. Years of shame and guilt melted away as I bore my soul to a man I didn't know. In that moment, I experienced the same unobstructed release once offered by my childhood; I could be as vulnerable as I needed to be. Time was non-existent; time had no value. At some point, Alfred's embrace had become a cradle where I wept like a baby, soothed by gentle rocking and calming words, which put me on the edge of consciousness. When the stream of emotion had finally quelled, Alfred gently placed me back in my bed like my parents had after I fell asleep in their loving arms. I slept that night unlike any time before.

We never spoke about that night. The sunrise erased its existence. Alfred transformed from a midnight angel back to the crack-addicted gangster. Still, he imprinted on me an image of humanity that can't be erased. The stereotypes that society and the media paint about African Americans no longer held power over me. I experienced one of my first spiritual shifts in the arms of a gangster. In that experience, I realized that no matter how powerful a lie may seem, it is far less powerful than the single act of compassion that disproves it.

My relief did not last and, before long, my life returned to its previous state as an emotional roller coaster. In an attempt to harm myself, I began to punch the bulletin board in my bedroom. I gained instantaneous relief from the pain, pounding the board's course texture in a downward motion. After a while, my knuckles swelled and bloodied. Self-abuse gave me a sense of control over my situation. I could not control my circumstances, but I could control what I did to my body. That gave me relief.

I am by no means an expert on the psychology behind self-mutilation. It is a complicated issue. I am simply someone who engaged in it myself during a period in my life when I felt I had very little control. Though I didn't realize it at the time, the effects of substance abuse on my body were the same as the effects caused by cutting, only internal. The scars that tic-tac-toe a cutter's arms are like those that crisscrossed my heart and spirit as I abused others and myself. The external manifestation is simply an extension of the internal pain. A certain kind of relief comes as a substance enters the body and the effects begin to kick in. Worries diminish as a fog of euphoria sets in. The same physical and emotional change occurred when I punched those walls. My body produced its natural painkillers needed to suppress the pain. What followed was a satisfaction that no one could hurt me as badly as I could hurt myself. Again, this produced a false sense of power, which perpetuated the behavior. This behavior spread through the treatment facility like wildfire. It took many groups and dozens of suicide watches to settle us all down.

Over time, I had become everybody's token little brother. As the youngest, I welcomed the attention I received from all the older girls. The guys were fine, too, but they lacked perky breasts and an inviting softness. What was supposed to be a time of reflection and change became a sort of summer camp. I learned about the intricacies of drug addiction and survival. I heard things that I could never have imagined. With this information, I formulated my next plan.

I would do everything they had done but I would avoid all consequences. Listening to the stories, I didn't realize that each began with instant gratification and ended in consequences. The chance to experience the nectar of the gods came at a cost. The kids surrounding me were hard and experienced, and they were in treatment for chronic substance use. A few of the girls sold their bodies for crack and heroin. Many of the boys were hardened criminals, a necessity if you weren't willing to use your body the way that the girls did. Every pervert in the neighborhood had a taste for the young ones; as a result, girls and boys paid a heavy price for their next fix.

In the sixty days I spent at New Beginnings, I learned a great deal about others and very little about myself. After being released, I was given a big, blue book full of names and numbers of the kids I had met in treatment. The intent was to develop a support system. Instead, most of us would use the numbers for party connections, continuing in the same downward path we had all been following.

3

I F CIGARETTES, DRUGS, AND REBELLION were in their infant stages before treatment, they entered their adolescent stage after I came home. I was thirteen going on twenty—going on six. A hunger deep within had grown stronger in treatment. My curiosity peaked and I had every intention of reenacting the stories I had heard in such great detail over the two months I was hospitalized. Adolescent treatment is a double-edged sword. Kids are sent because their behavior is deemed so severe that commitment to an institution outweighs all other possible solutions. Parents hope that this last-ditch effort will bring about change, as outlined by licensed counselors describing the treatment process. "Don't worry," the counselors at New Beginnings told my mother. "Eric will leave with all the tools necessary to live a clean and sober life." They did not say that knowledge is only a small part of what is needed for long-term success.

For many, treatment serves as the catalyst for long-term recovery. For others, treatment is a springboard into far worse behavior. Teenage addicts must experience pain and consequence to justify change. This will motivate the addict to do the work necessary to give up substances and seek tools for recovery through a spiritual way of living. Producing long-term change is not simple; it often takes a series of relapses before the miracle will happen.

In my stay at New Beginnings, I met two people who exemplified the meeting of pain and consequence. One girl had turned tricks for drugs since she was twelve. Her father played pimp and lover until she ran away with a new man who promised a great deal more. He lied. At seventeen, she had become desperate for a way out. Alfred was the other. He had sold drugs and run with gangs since he was thirteen if not younger. He told me stories that left me breathless with battle scars to prove them. These two children had seen more in their few short years than many would over a lifetime. They paid their price in blood and tears. Their confessions in groups and their sincere need for recovery made me feel both compassion and a deep sadness. I watched them discuss their secrets in a way that I had yearned to do my whole life. Although I could not relate to the depths of addiction that they had reached, I could understand the abuse and the means by which they used chemicals to dull their memories.

There are those who say that pain is the touchstone to spiritual growth. By facing fear and the associated pain, we do not take dominion over it. Rather, fear becomes our ally and with it we learn how to face anything that comes into our path through hope and faith. I could relate to the raw emotion and the tears shared during those sessions. Alfred and the young girl spoke of a true desire to find another way to live, to leave the lives they had always known behind. They had the necessary ingredients that most did not. In their honesty, I witnessed humility; this humility gave them a chance. I did not want to experience what Alfred and the girl had seen and done. Their stories filled me with fear and loathing, though that did little to dissuade me from the inevitability of my future. The stories that peaked my interest were those that described what it felt like to smoke crack or to take an LSD trip. In bed at night, I fantasized about the sexual encounters recounted in hushed voices and giggles. I understand very little of what I heard, but the images gave me high hopes for trying things with the girls who had shared these stories.

When my parents brought me to aftercare on the weekends, I waded through the inevitable boredom of aftercare group looking forward to the real stuff discussed during smoke breaks. This is where I learned some of my most valuable information. Generally, those who joined our group of crazed teenagers depleting their oxygen levels were those who would talk openly about their conquests. Because of this, we were unhampered in our ability to make connections, exchange notes, and discuss what we would do when free from the prying eyes of parents and treatment staff.

I should be clear that this is my personal account of my first treatment experience. I do not pretend to paint a picture of what this experience is like for all kids who attend. The eyes of a thirteen-year-old are not always the best indicator of what actually takes place in adolescent treatment centers. Some, in the same circumstances as I, experienced the program in a way that I did not. They applied the lessons and information they received and distanced themselves from those of us who chose to continue in use.

Treatment was structured. Although I came out and continued my use, I addressed many things in the process. Family week offered a chance for patient's parents to share their perspective and to describe how their son or daughter's behavior had affected them. This experience demanded self-reflection. Patients shared feelings of shame and remorse, emotions that I knew well through my own experiences. Patients were placed in various levels of treatment. To move from one level to the next, the patient had to improve in all areas. Treatment specialists required that patients do a certain amount of work, attaining specific levels of self-awareness and understanding particular recovery concepts before leaving the program. New Beginnings armed me with the tools I would need to pursue recovery but I wished to move in a different direction.

The treatment process sought to provide information and begin transforming those at a younger age in the hopes that treatment would take hold before more consequences accumulated. The idea that abstinence will follow the first introduction to treatment is hopeful thinking. Realistically, it is a process that often takes years and multiple trips to such facilities to take root. A symptom of drug addiction is relapse. Many wish to avoid this topic as they hope, beyond all else, that the roller coaster of addiction will end after one treatment stay. Based on my own experience, recovery from addiction is a lifelong process, one that can be both excruciating and extensive.

Parents who enter the world of recovery with their children seek more than anything to avoid further pain. As they travel this road with their children, parents experience every consequence as if it were their own. If I were a parent facing the behaviors that I exhibited as a teenage user, I most certainly would have sent my child to treatment for help. Parents must try every option available when faced with something as serious as addiction. Kids die every day with needles in their arms; while parents sit at home believing such a thing could never happen to their child. The sad reality is that most parents know very little about what their kids are doing concerning drug use. Follow this simple formula: multiply what you know by a hundred and even then you may not know the full extent of their risk taking.

As recovering people, we don't avoid pain. Rather, we embrace it through family groups, intensive one-on-one counseling, group therapy, and other outside resources like twelve-step programs and Al-Anon. The idea that treatment provides a so-called quick fix to the problems faced by addicts and their families is a myth. This quick fix thought process mimics what addicts are looking for in substances. Recovery takes time. Treatment is only a small piece of the puzzle. Continued diligence and participation in recovery groups and cognitive behavioral counseling is key to long-term success.

I do not want to discourage parents from sending their children to treatment. I do want to caution them against resorting to treatment without first doing a thorough investigation of all behavioral factors. Weigh out what the counselor says and what your experiences show. Understand the dimensions of the program under consideration. Feel confident that any effort to improve the life of someone in need is not a mistake. Mistakes are often lessons in disguise. Simply putting energy into the betterment of another human being guarantees a positive outcome when the Creator so chooses. That may not be especially comforting to a suffering loved one, but it seems to be true in most instances. Life doesn't always go in the direction we dictate. Love given freely will distribute; it will not require persuasion.

Chemical imbalances often factor into our children's struggles. Addressing these and any other mental, emotional, or physical liabilities must be part of the treatment process. This may seem daunting, but the payoff is substantial. A "wait and see" approach may have devastating effects.

I was given information and insight at New Beginnings, whether I acknowledged it at the time or not. No matter how hard I tried to avoid learning while at New Beginnings, the information shared found a way to implant itself in my conscience. Over time, this knowledge germinated, then came in waves of spiritual experience unavoidable to those who are sensitive to such things. As an example, consider the seeds recently found in the Siberian permafrost, hidden in a burrow for over thirty-thousand years. Whoever, or whatever, hid the seeds knew that they had value. In time, the seeds would be put to use in the capacity for which they were intended. It did not matter if they bloomed in ten years or in thirty-thousand years. The end result would be the same: brilliance. The flower that germinated from a tattered, thirty-thousand-year-old seed bloomed petals a brilliant white that soaked in the sun and reflected its rays to all privileged enough to see. The Silene Stenophylla bloomed older than the holiest of holy books. Just because it did not bloom when it might have, did not detract from its brilliance many years later. Knowledge is the same. We never know when or how seeds of knowledge will be used in our lives. I consider the person or thing that placed those seeds in hiding to be like the many counselors who created change in my life by giving me spiritual concepts and ideas. At the time, those concepts seemed void of value; but when they bloomed, I understood that they were far more important than I had thought so many years prior.

When I returned home from treatment, I began to experience the type of ostracism that is bred from a fear of the unknown. As a result of my exodus and subsequent re-entry into the community, I was branded the island's troubled child. In many ways, I fit the role well. In others, I was still a frightened, teenage boy, alone and misunderstood by his teachers, peers, and their parents. I was suspended from the Pee-Wee football team as an added consequence of my substance use. Further, my school had organized a circle of trustworthy students charged with walking troublemakers from class to class in an attempt to discourage skipping. This may have eased the concerns of my parents, but it added to mine by further ostracizing me from my peers.

Those who straddle the fence live in two worlds at once. They must learn to use manipulation to appease expectations. I was a student, a smoker, a stoner, and a troublemaker. On one side of the fence, I was a student, an athlete, a brother, a son, a friend, a member of a youth group, and a child. I had to live up to the expectations of my parents, coaches, friends, and teachers. I sought exploration, a life that included behaviors vehemently rejected by the other side. Neither side complemented the other and I felt the subtle pull of each tugging at me internally. Like a man who tiptoes into his house well past midnight, the scent of another woman on his body, I knew that I would eventually be found out and would have to choose sides. For a time, I remained a shadow, slipping between both worlds. In this dishonesty the shame returned. I sought escape through chemicals, my natural alternative.

By the time my seventh-grade year ended, pot, alcohol, and cigarettes served as my main sources of entertainment. I still participated in sports, but my previous enjoyment lost precedence to the obsession that consumed me. My obsession for chemicals and sexual encounters had never gone away; instead, it grew stronger. Nearly everything I did centered on how to find my next buzz.

I had become somewhat of a celebrity with many of my classmates. After treatment, they received me with open arms, eager to hear news of the world beyond the island shores. They asked about New Beginnings and my experiences there. My response was always, "I met older girls and had the time of my life." I couldn't reveal the true emotional impact of my experience.

I felt somewhat relieved to still enjoy the admiration of friends I had had before being sent away. In some ways, I fed from their overcompensation, which fed my ego, which fed my addiction, which fed my ego... I found myself in a vicious cycle. Addiction is a biological disease with a very human component that feeds on the distorted emotion stemming from immaturity and ego. I was doomed.

Delivering punishment for the behaviors associated with addiction is not a new idea; this approach has been around as long as people have been misusing chemicals. The belief that this approach could lead to substantial change is a farce. Those who believe in punishing addiction, view it as a moral issue as opposed to a medical condition. In truth, addiction is complicated by moral deterioration, which is a symptom rather than the problem itself. Furthermore, addiction is often complicated by other chemical imbalances in the brain. This confuses an already complex issue. If the pain, suffering, consequence, and negative feelings associated with addiction were truly solutions to the problem, then many addicts would be clean. The physical, emotional, mental, and spiritual consequences of addiction are far worse than any consequence that society could inflict. "Pain is a springboard to spiritual progress" is only a half-truth. It is the catalyst. Spiritual progress is the springboard. There are many more catalysts than pain that help addicts to recover and those catalysts do not come from punishment. They come from compassion.

Some risked unmasking their own, long-buried problems through the act of recognizing mine. For others, my problems invited harsher realities into a sort of island utopia; they did all that they could to bury those realities by blaming the sick. My story destroyed the illusion that isolation and insulation would deter the inevitable. A side of humanity revealed itself that created a rift within the community. Misunderstanding, lack of education, and denial forced people to seek truth or continue with their blinders on. If you admit that there is a problem, then you are obligated to fix that problem. If this problem suddenly affects people you love, you might be forced to apply a solution you once rejected. It is not an easy situation.

I was not the first person to shatter the blissful ignorance that served to push the problems of a small well to do community into daylight. Off of Bainbridge, some of the young glided out from the nest until the reality of the world pulled them down into a heap of confusion. My oldest brother, as well as other island teenagers much older than me, began to enter treatment. Travis and I were in treatment at the same time. He also returned to an island confronting an epidemic that many thought didn't exist. I was not the only one being eyed by both sides of the issue. Despite the polo sweaters, Volvos, and large bank accounts, certain behaviors could only be masked for so long. Affliction follows humanity even to the most privileged of places. Eventually, people must admit that they, too, are a part of this large and confusing world.

At thirteen, I internalized the sideways looks from those who used to smile. I was aware that the birthday invitations that once flooded my book bag no longer came. Can you really blame the parents for wishing to avoid the liability of a drunken teenager? My shame grew as I saw how easily people turned their backs; feelings of isolation grew worse and worse. This rejection validated every negative thought I had about myself. The lies, once thoughts and now spoken, became real and then were sealed through repetition.

At some point, I chose to feed the image that I had unintentionally created. I did not do so hoping to lose friends. I didn't wish to lose the respect of people who had been in my life for so many years. I had not chosen alcohol and drugs over them. Addiction had chosen me. Through that selection, a barrage of misunderstandings and misconceptions followed.

My behavior with drugs and alcohol wasn't much different from that of the other island kids. My life was simply more public. My privacy had been violated in the hopes of educating others in the community. I was the example others used to deter their own children from the same traps I had fallen victim to. I could not seek recovery in support groups with anonymity. With every relapse or misstep came a reverberation of contempt for not following the process outlined by others. If I said, "I wanted" on the north side of the island, the south side heard, "to get high" before I could finish my sentence. The resulting frustration drove me into the city in search of anonymity and the drugs described by the other kids from New Beginnings.

Parents are in the business of protecting their children; instinctually, they will do whatever it takes to do so. As a potential threat to other children, I would be sacrificed to save many. Thankfully, not everyone felt the same. Thankfully, some believed that saving the individual was as important as saving one troubled child. It strengthened the community as a whole.

The community was not one of total ignorance. Many sought truth and wished to educate themselves to help those around them. Many supportive parents understood and felt compassion for the island teenagers who struggled. Teachers and other faculty worked diligently to find solutions. For every teacher who gave up, another stepped up to find a solution.

Mr. Miller entered my life right on cue. With bright red hair and brilliant, blue eyes, he had a kind spirit and showed a willingness to roll up his sleeves to delve into issues few would acknowledge. As my middle school guidance counselor, he began working with me when I felt the most alone. I liked him immediately. With big ears and a small mouth, he seemed more likely to listen than lecture. We met several times a week to discuss my struggle and frustration. The school put Mr. Miller in place to provide aftercare for those returning from treatment programs. Until then, very few island kids had been sent away.

Initially, I forced Mr. Miller to endure the hostility born from the slight I had experienced years before. It was not his fault that I distrusted counselors. He just happened to be my first school counselor since grade school. I would not be as open with him as I had been around Mary, the rag doll. Mr. Miller seemed to understand my distrust, as he never betrayed what little trust I gave him. I tested him constantly. If nothing else, our sessions gave me a reason to miss class a couple of days a week. In addition, he had candies on his desk that I could eat while he talked.

"Eric, your problems are compounded by your stubbornness," he said, his bushy eyebrows furrowed.

"I am not stubborn, Mr. Miller. I am confident." My smugness did little to divert his train of thought.

"Well, I'll tell you what," Mr. Miller said. "I am confident about one thing. If you don't find a way to heal that bruised heart of yours, you may have a tough road ahead of you. I am, and always have been, on your side. The problem is that you think this is a one-man show. The only place that idea gets you is alone and wondering where everybody went."

"Then I'll win the game myself."

With that, I exited his office. I felt sure that my arrogance would discourage Mr. Miller from ever calling me into his office again. My attitude didn't discourage him. A few days later, I was back in his office.

Mr. Miller had a way of helping me recognize my own importance. He never made me feel like I was less a person simply because I was dealing with what others viewed as demoralizing. Even when I feigned grandiosity, he called me out and brought me back so that we could discuss the issues at hand. I remember him telling me that compassion was my greatest attribute. "Why don't you build on that instead of your anger and false pride?" I could speak honestly and share my frustrations with being baby-sat at school. Mr. Miller simply listened and allowed me to vent. His objective was not to evoke shame, but to build on my strengths in the hope they would outgrow my liabilities. He saw self-confidence and a willingness to stay on track within me. He simply had to root it out through compassion. He did not fail. I just wasn't ready then.

I discussed mostly superficial topics with Mr. Miller. I kept my secrets hidden deep within. At a young age, I decided that some experiences in my life would never again pass my lips. Even Mr. Miller's compassion could not pull them from me. Though he assured me that anything I said would follow him to the grave, I had heard it all before. Though I desperately wanted to relieve myself of the secrets of abuse, I could not trust and would therefore never share.

Mr. Miller did stay true to his word. He carried the few secrets I entrusted to him to his premature grave. I am not sure of the date of his death. Bingeing on drugs, the years of my life began to blend. Still, it seemed a tragedy that he died so young. That one with such a large and compassionate heart could die from its failure is one of life's many great ironies. I guess when you use your heart as a means to heal others; its potential failure is a daily threat. The fact that he did it is a testament to his character.

The island's inhabitants filled the auditorium. I sat in the shadows reflecting on a man who had moved me in ways that few could know or understand. Mr. Miller helped me realize that despite the slights and broken promises, people are capable of holding true to their word. Regretfully, I never thanked him in person; I was unaware of the gift that he gave me back then. My stubborn nature and immaturity required that I maintain my distance. He held a thankless job in some respects, yet his passing filled an auditorium with students, parents, teachers, and friends who knew what he had done for the community. I wept quietly and from a distance while his loved ones spoke of what I felt but would not show.

Eventually, my life began to settle. I didn't stop using substances and my behavioral problems continued, but time passed. People began to focus on their own lives, so I was able to get on with mine. I write this as though my life had become the topic of every dinner table discussion. In my mind, my life was the center of the universe. That is typical of the teenage mind, even before chemicals are introduced. My self-centeredness was compounded.

When my eighth grade year began, I was voted class president. Socially, I had settled back in with my childhood friends. The election results didn't sit too well with various teachers and parents. Despite the various protests from teachers and parents, I kept my position. Even though Mr. McLaughlin, our principal, had the power to veto, he remained respectfully silent. I was told, however, to keep my grades up or I would lose the position and be kicked off of the wrestling team. In just a few weeks, I was forced to relinquish my presidency to another student.

I continued to play and excel at sports. I dated girls, experimented sexually with the willing, and felt about as normal as someone afflicted with addiction could. Whenever I felt anger, shame, inferiority, sadness, anxiety, or fear, I quickly found ways to alter my mood. My contacts from treatment provided me with a steady supply of drugs. I huffed gasoline or drank mouthwash to silence my cravings. The substance did not matter; I sought the effect above all else.

Also that year, I became aware of a transformation that had occurred, one which bothered my mother to no end. Older women from the island began to take notice of me. I found them fascinating; they appeared to feel the same. This fueled my sexual desire, a desire that burned as strong as my desire to use chemicals. At times, one yearning won out over the other, though I sought them both together. In a shroud of teenage passion and chemical oblivion, I found the all too familiar place where nothing could hurt me—or so I believed.

I always woke up feeling regret and shame, which propelled me to search for further escape. This vicious cycle grew until no one, especially me, had the power to stop the whirlwind it created. The swaths of upturned trees and churned-up soil following the addict's tornado, leaves many with their heads down, sifting through the wreckage of their lives, wondering how they could have allowed this to happen again. I had become the tornado, and even if I had wished to stop, I was at the disposal of a force far more powerful than myself.

It is insane to love a tornado, but many do.

4

MY PARENTS' RELATIONSHIP BEGAN to deteriorate quite rapidly. Fights escalated and lasted for much longer. Affection, the byproduct of love, no longer existed. Those who understood the symptoms could see the inevitable. I would not. Self-preservation can be blinding. As my parents distanced themselves from each other, I became more depressed and binged. I was not above the actions that had led to my suicide attempt the year before. I believe that my parents knew this and tried to hold their relationship together long enough for my older brothers and me to regain our emotional equilibrium.

Depression, chemicals, and emotional trauma led me to make decisions that, in retrospect, I wish I had not made. I sought to hurt myself worse than someone else could hurt me; that would lessen the sting of the pain that they inflicted. My angry outbursts and abusive verbal assaults proved inadequate to protect me from my parents' inevitable divorce. The people I loved most were in the throes of an emotional separation that had ended long before their physical separation on Christmas Day. The pain I felt after coming home to my father's empty closets must have been similar to the pain he experienced while packing his bags. In reality, the date didn't matter. The separation would have come to pass whether on Christmas Day or any other. To choose another day would not have lessened the sorrow I felt for the loss of our family as I had known it. What it did give me was a target for the sorrow that began to fester into rage.

Although my father could be harsh and unyielding at times, he was also loving and compassionate to me. The combination could be confusing, and it was not until I became a man myself that I understood how one person could possess both traits. The love he felt for his family was indisputable and his absence did not diminish that fact. That is what confused me most. We fished, hiked, and camped together. He shared his gift of music by playing his guitar. In retrospect the things he gave me far outweighed anything taken by his empty closets, though it didn't feel that way at the time.

For years, I used Christmas Day to elicit a specific response from those who heard my story. As a victim of life's circumstances, I fed off of the good intentions of others to survive. This is a form of abuse employed by addicts to manipulate and deceive. I had to find a way to keep my self-destruction going by turning anger to bitterness, igniting my deep sorrow into rage, and making my father's absence into something far worse—abandonment.

People internalize divorce differently. In a household with three boys, each of us responded to the same set of events in a different manner. Though I can only relay my own experience, my brothers all carried the pain of the separation into the years ahead, fueling their exploration into their own shadow. They chose to process their pain through avoidance; in time, they were forced to confront their own pain. For many years, I believed that I walked alone in much of this. I assumed that I was the sole inheritor of the pain associated with the divorce. As a result, I discounted the feelings of others in my family. In my self-centered and attention-craving behavior, I limited my family's ability to process their own pain. Like an emotional leech, I took whatever my family had left to offer. Now, I regret that I didn't allow my brothers to grieve. I wish that I had found a way to share their pain and taken a supportive role. Instead, I forced a wedge in our relationship, one that grew as our lives moved forward.

How do you describe your mother and ever do her justice? I will begin here. The remainder of my story will help to fill in any blanks I leave. My mother is an incredible human being. During my preschool years she was my greatest friend. As I grew older and my two older brothers began grade school, my mother and I spent our days running errands together and filling up on yogurt cones from the health food store. That was our daily ritual. Looking back, she seemed aware that these times would soon end. "I love you more than all the stars in the sky," she would say. "I love you more than all the sand on the beach," I would tell her, each of us looking to outdo the other. This was our game. There was no winner. She said things that made me think and wonder. We shared secrets, laughter, and tickles. My life was full of the love and affection that is thought to be a protector against life's savagery. If love and affection could solve every problem that parents face on behalf of their children, then I would not be writing this book. Love is just part of the solution; love helps children to heal from life's inevitable hardships.

My mom spent a great deal of time making everything on the outside look good, no matter how hard things were on the inside. She had a knack for this. She was organized, motivated, and made her boys her top priority. She kept us well-dressed and well-fed. My mother was gentle but showed a subtle fierceness that could only have come from a life of survival. She had been parenting since she was six years old, starting with her younger brother, Bill. By the time she had my oldest brother at twenty-two, my mother understood what was expected of her. My father brought home the paycheck, kept the yard manicured, kept the house in good order, and coached the boys' sports teams. My mother managed our home, filled the cupboards, cooked the meals, did the laundry, cleaned the house, bought school clothes and the sports gear, played taxi, and did just about everything else under the sun including work a job at a bank. She was a miracle worker. She bridged the gaps whenever they would appear; yet there were bridges in her own life that she could not close no matter how hard she tried.

Shortly after my father left, my mother made the decision to get sober. She attended a support group that dealt with codependency. That group led her to another, which focused on addiction. The guidance provided by these groups allowed my mother to draw some strong boundaries concerning my substance abuse. She had zero tolerance and would no longer allow even the slightest deviation from the rules she had created. The rigidity of her boundaries created both protection and the potential for greater harm.

One day when she was out grocery shopping, I decided to run away. I packed a small bag with clothes, food, my brother's knife, and the blue book of contacts from New Beginnings. I never considered calling a friend to pick me up. Hitchhiking seemed like the best course of action and I took little time to think it over. Writing the goodbye letter gave me a thrill like the one I had experienced as a young child running through the woods around my house. I felt free. I told my mother that I needed to reclaim something that she and the rules she enforced had taken from me. In the letter, I wrote:

Mom, I want to use. I understand you don't want me to do it while living in your house so I have decided to leave out of respect. Please don't come looking for me. You will not find me.

Although my mother's reasons were quite sound, they also seemed hypocritical. She had downed bottles of wine every night for countless years. Her liquor cabinet enabled my alcoholic benders. An alcoholic haze kept her from realizing what I was doing. Now, I believed that she had ruined everything. She quit drinking, and using her black belt codependency crap, she expected a choirboy to emerge as a result of her choices. In my teenage mind, I blamed her. As was my pattern, I made an impulsive decision. I was on my way.

Though leaving gave me a sense of freedom, it also gave me power through abandonment. Unlike when my father left, I was now doing the abandoning. It seemed that if I struck first, I would feel less hurt. My father had left the family, and I would not be caught off guard again. Although I had done a great deal to make both of my parents pay for what I felt they had done to my life, it was never enough. I couldn't get far enough away quickly enough. The freedom of the road would help me to avoid the unspeakable things in my life.

I never spoke of these feelings. Whenever anyone tried to bring them up, I retreated and closed the door tightly behind me. These emotions fueled a rage within and allowed me to justify the way I used and treated those around me. I convinced myself that the things I had seen and endured justified my substance abuse. My reality was distorted by emotion and this distortion provided justification, minimization, and rationalization. Had I known how much worse my life would get and how quickly that would happen, I might have heeded the advice of those attempting to help me. Instead, I moved forward, only looking back to justify looking forward again. Dreams seemed possible in the world ahead of me. The present became a liability because it meant taking responsibility for my actions and focusing on the now. The now is what I wished to avoid and there was only one way to do that.

A couple of do-gooders picked me up. Rather than minding their own business, as I would have hoped, they spent the whole ride lecturing me like my father or preaching like the youth groups I had attended. The sermons hadn't helped back when I was chugging pine whiskey and punching out church windows, so it sure as hell wasn't going to help now. I cut the ride short. Walking away from the car, they spoke words of warning with their windows rolled down, a final effort to convert the unwilling. They seemed to understand what might come next but I wasn't interested in any roadside prophecy. I found more hope in a fix than I did in any savior.

The next person to pick me up was a man in his forties with a bag of weed and a loud stereo. Now that was my kind of guy. As we made our way toward Tacoma, I felt things begin to change. I understood what it meant to be the object of someone's affection. Usually women showed interest in a sort of game of predator versus prey. Other older people tried to convert me to their way of thinking, but this man had other things on his mind. Dropping me off wasn't one of them.

"Do you want to come to my house in Renton and stay for a while? I understand how uptight parents can be and I am nothing of the sort. I assure you."

As the man spoke, his hand made its way from the stick shift to my knee then up my thigh. It was time to figure out how to get out of the truck. I told him that a few beers and a smoke would make my decision easier. He pulled over and went into the store to buy what he believed to be his price for my innocence. I jumped out of his truck and grabbed my backpack and his bag of weed. His misjudgment was my gain. I threw his keys as far into the woods as I could. Still, I considered how I might get the six-pack and smokes as well. This man scared me in a way that I had experienced from only one other. Throwing the car keys seemed to give me back the power he was trying to take away. He would not enjoy the same innocent boy that Marlene had abused. I was beyond that kind of treatment—or so I thought.

With relief and in greater proximity to Tacoma, I made my way to a pay phone to call one of the numbers in my big, blue book. Ironically, the support groups I attended after treatment preached that the answers to all of my problems could be found in the book. Yet the only time I had ever opened it was to call a friend to score drugs or get laid. Those were the only solutions in which I was interested. So I guess they were right in some respects. The answer to what I believed to be my problems at the time could be found in the book. Looking back, I didn't have any real problems. I had a mother who would not let me use at home and a dad who seemed to care more about his girlfriend and his job than he did his own kids. Leaving that truck, I had some cash, about a quarter of an ounce of marijuana, and my friend, Mike, coming to pick me up.

Mike should have been in his first year of college playing football, but he hadn't fulfilled the requirements of a contract he had made with the school. When I met him in treatment, he was trying to get back onto his high school team after being suspended for drug use. To do so, and to regain the interest of recruiters, Mike had to stay clean after treatment. He'd been clean for a while, probably longer than most of us, but eventually returned to his old ways.

Mike had a dual addiction: he smoked and sold crack. He picked me up in a dark-blue Cutlass Sierra with tinted windows and a stereo system that made my eyes vibrate. Though he claimed to hate attention, Mike drew attention to himself in every way possible. I loved it. He was a white guy who weighed about two hundred and twenty-five pounds, all of which was muscle, from his enormous thighs to his forearms. Mike seemed built to play football, so it was a shame that he wasn't. He wore two, massive diamond studs that reminded me of something from *Yo! MTV Raps*. I assumed they were real as Mike didn't do anything halfway. Even in treatment, he wore a different flight suit every day of the week.

In treatment, people hype themselves up as a distraction from their problems with addiction. Each person describes him or herself as the biggest dealer or the worst addict. I am no exception. I said and did anything to avoid the reality of who I was; to do otherwise required me to admit to the shameful truth. I was unwilling to do that as were most in treatment. Mike, on the other hand, described himself as he was. He had not over-or under-hyped himself in the slightest. He was exactly what he said he was during smoke breaks and exactly the opposite of what he said he was in groups. Mike knew just what to say to get what he wanted regardless of the situation. I learned a great deal from him. He was a hustler in the truest sense; no one knew when they were being hustled.

Mike and I made a quick stop by his friend's house, switched cars, and then we were off. Mike said that he never drove his Cutlass when he was packing drugs and guns. Instead, he drove a Ford Escort with no frills. The only extravagant items were his sky-blue, Nike jumpsuit, white, K-Swiss shoes, and two beepers, which went off constantly. As we drove through the neighborhoods around Tacoma, Mike made frequent stops at corners, stores, alleys, and people's houses depending on the codes he received from the beepers. At each delivery, people showed Mike the utmost respect. I don't think it had anything to do with the pistol resting in his lap. Plenty of people carried guns, but most didn't have the guts to risk a lengthy prison term. This didn't seem to be the case with Mike. I suspect he had used his before and would probably use it again. Mike knew his way around things and spoke in a language that was foreign to me. He worked quickly and paid me little notice during transactions. If customers sized me up or asked questions, he told them to mind their own business in a voice that elicited silence. To those he liked best he'd say I was his cousin.

I felt safe with Mike. I knew that alone in the places we had visited, I would not have lasted long. I had very little experience with street life. It both fascinated and scared me. The people who came out of the shadows to give Mike money had learned to survive the streets at a level I could not imagine. They were survivors in a world that cast them away like trash in a burning barrel. Only those whose pockets they filled, like Mike, recognized their worth. I realized that I was more like them than Mike.

After the last bars had closed, Mike took me home to his mother's house. He exchanged his car, gun, crack, and cash at the stash house. I tried not to pay much attention to his dealings. I knew enough to understand that some information was good—but too much information could be trouble. Even if I had wanted to go into the stash house, and to see the operation, Mike never would have let me. To be honest, I was ok with that.

Mike's house was modest. We smoked the weed I had scammed the day before and talked until the sun started to come up. Mike and I hit it off in treatment because he said I reminded him of himself at thirteen. We both excelled in sports. He tried in his own way to steer me away from what I was doing. Like other, older kids, Mike mixed stories of his own use with lectures on why I should clean up and get right. I found his advice confusing, another scenario of do as I say, not as I do. I tuned him out and heard only what I wanted to hear. This time, Mike wouldn't let me change the subject.

"I didn't want to come and get you when you called," Mike told me. "I have seen this too many times and I definitely don't want to see you on the other end of a crack sale."

I don't know if I believed that it would happen to me or not. Sadly, it would happen eventually. I would end up on Mike's end or the other. I didn't know enough about Mike's side of the story to know just how good his arguments were. There was no "both ways" when it came to selling and smoking crack.

As he rolled a blunt with the last of my weed, Mike said, "You can smoke and sell all the pot you want, but when you graduate to the white stuff, all the kindergarten crap has to go. You are in the big leagues then. Life and death. Stay on top by any means necessary."

His words helped me understand the respect and fear I had seen that afternoon. Mike said I could hang for a couple of days while we visited friends, but that would be it. I couldn't stay with him. He called me a liability and said he didn't want the responsibility. Though it was disappointing to hear, I was happy to have a few days with him. We smoked, drank, snorted, and picked up girls. To my great disappointment, most of the girls just called me cute. It was interesting to see how younger kids gravitated towards older people sexually and older men and women gravitated towards younger kids. I didn't understand it at the time, but in the days ahead, I would be introduced to the dark world of sexual addiction, which manifests in opposites.

Mike wouldn't let me smoke coke because I had never done it before. When I asked one of the girls to get me some, she said that Mike had told them not to and that was that. No matter how twisted this may seem, Mike spared me from a demon. The streets are no place for a child with a habit. No one wants to watch that habit start.

Who knows what might have happened had Mike been desperate enough to use me to his advantage. That is generally the story. The drug world devours the innocent. It feeds on them, leaving an empty shell, scarred from the inside out; ready to feed on the next generation. It is a never-ending cycle of abuse. Children are most susceptible due to the strong sexual perversions that accompany stimulants of this nature. They are also far easier to take advantage of, as children are naive to the ways of the shadow, much as I was. He honored our friendship and passed the torch to someone more desperate down the road. That day would not be my day. I wish I had thanked him.

Through my ignorance and naivety, I was simply unaware of what had transpired in our relationship. Not until I first put a needle into another person's arm would I look back and shamefully realize that Mike was a better man than I had become. When given the same opportunity, I had failed.

5

A T THE AGE OF FOUR, the buildings of Seattle appeared to be pedestals to the heavens. We had moved from Roseburg, Oregon, so my father could begin his new job as a mid-level manager for a telephone company. His promotion was the first major change in my life. Not that change was bad; it was merely the first of many to come. This was where my memories began, the beginnings of a tapestry that would ultimately become my life. Events so big that they stick in the memory of a toddler are indeed substantial.

I have hazy recollections of my family crossing the Puget Sound on a large, green-and-white ferryboat to Bainbridge Island. The seagulls sang their chorus to the blue skies. The dark, blue water glistened in the sun. A spring breeze filled my nostrils with the salty perfume of the ocean. I called the sea foam created by the boat's hull whipping cream, then pretended to eat it. This made my family laugh. Laughter seemed to be part of everything in those days. The pure love of childhood nurtured by the stability of family. I felt untarnished joy. Porpoises rose and dipped ahead of the ferryboat. Everywhere I looked seemed to teem with life.

At thirteen, I no longer viewed Seattle through the lens of an innocent four year-old. Though it still held unknown adventures, it was no longer pure. Jessica, one of the older girls from New Beginnings stayed at a loft near Pike Place Market. We had engaged in several sexual rendezvous after release from treatment, including one on my living room couch about four months prior. The shame I had once experienced as a result of sexual pleasure was replaced by a growing hunger.

When I saw Jessica coming down the street on the back of the moped, I knew something was wrong. The guy giving her a ride seemed displeased to be meeting. When Jessica stepped from the bike, I saw immediately that her body had changed. Her stomach was much larger and her face held more weight than it had before. Judging by her belly, I guessed that she was about four months pregnant. There were only two explanations: either I had gotten Jessica pregnant or someone else had. There had been no discussion of other guys when she and I were together. I assumed there weren't any. Though I had lived beyond my age in some ways, I was still a naive thirteen-year-old in others.

My intense sexual experiences began with a physical desire and ended with impulsive acts that could lead to a condition like Jessica's. What further complicated my sexual encounters was the absolute lack of communication concerning the emotional attachment and other intricate spiritual and emotional weavings that accompany such an intimate act. Something like an emotional condom would have been helpful; I chose alcohol, which failed more often than not.

The naivety and innocence of youth can be quite beautiful. A boy and a girl fumble in search of each other's hands while sitting in a movie theater. At the first dance, two bodies sway, stiff and self-conscious. In these delicate moments, the young learn the subtleties of sexuality. I never had these experiences. By passing up this natural process, trading it for the temporary relief of orgasm, I missed one of the most important lessons in adolescent development. In the confusion of hormones and youthful sexual encounters, life begins; an experience I was not ready for.

I seemed better suited for the instinctual, hormone-driven sexual encounter rather than the tender sensuality of a held hand or a gentle embrace. Marlene robbed me of a proper first sexual experience. Her behavior taught me that the goal was not intimacy but a perverse form of sensuality fed by physical obsession. This obsession drove me to seek relief in the very thing that refuses it. Looking back, I was no different from Marlene. This is not easy for me to admit; my natural instinct, even now, is to draw lines and create contrasts in order to remain the victim. The reality is that I sought the same means for satisfaction as Marlene. Though I did not take advantage of young children in a perverse game of sexual gratification, I fed the same sexual compulsion.

The transformation from prey to predator is not pretty. Mine began at the hands of my abuser. As years passed, my secrets festered, and I turned to self-abuse through suicide attempts, burning, cutting, and drug use. At that point, it became easy to abuse those around me, especially those closest to me. I forced any raw emotion inward as my habits solidified; my transformation was complete. When I looked in the mirror, I thought little of myself, recalling Marlene's words: "This will be our little secret."

The very thing that the abused wish to avoid had come to pass. I pursued each girl in an attempt to gratify my own desires; each girl had become my victim. In most cases, I didn't pursue the girls themselves; I pursued what they could provide me. I used one girl and then moved on to the next. They became victims of my need to feel loved and the misconception that love existed in pure physical contact.

One definition of abuse is to use to bad effect or to cause harm. My behaviors did just that. The emotional harm that I caused was the greatest, and in many ways, the most serious of my abuses. Human beings have a need to be loved and respected in the intimacy of sexual pleasures. My encounters were void of compassion but full of passion. This made for a night of escape, but did not allow for long-term relations.

Jessica created a new set of problems. I had never acknowledged the very real possibility that I could have a child at such a young age. Her pregnancy left me feeling like a sprinter just before the starting gun fires. To make matters worse, Jessica had a bruise next to her left eye. She looked panicked. The guy she was with outranked me in years, weight, and—I was guessing—aggression. If things got ugly, my tough-guy reputation and delusions of masculine superiority would not help me.

Instinctually, I recognized in Jessica a forced acceptance that only those who have endured abuse can understand. She had obviously decided that abuse was a fair exchange for being cared for in some other manner. I felt Jessica should have been spinning freely in a sundress and laughing at silly jokes with her friends. Instead, she stood with her head lowered, eyes averted. I am not sure how she managed to come and meet me. I hoped that her eye was not the price she had paid; looking at the brute, it seemed a likely assumption.

Our meeting was brief. As if she had practiced her explanation, Jessica described her living situation, then said I would not be able to stay with her as we had previously discussed. Apparently, the ape on the moped had claimed the couch, or rather, her bedroom. Instead of a warm night in the arms of an angel, I was in for a cold night in the back alleys of downtown Seattle. With a kiss on the cheek, a wad of bills, and change from her purse, Jessica passed me her half-empty six-pack and sped off. That was the last time I would see Jessica, speeding away with her arms wrapped around the waist of a brute on a moped.

I handled Jessica's rejection the same way I had handled many others: with alcohol and flight. You couldn't hurt me if you couldn't catch me. Alcohol suppressed the emotion waiting to escape; running ensured that no one would see if it did. I relied on this combination many more times in the years to come, leaving a wake of broken relationships and unresolved emotion. Had I learned this behavior from my mother and father? My mother's many upturned wine glasses and my father's empty closets. I knew that, "Do as I say, not as I do" did not work. I decided to try "do as I do, not as I say." The latter worked much better and would continue to do so until my problems ran faster than I could.

Huddled in a dark alley, it became apparent that I had come unprepared. A couple of changes of clothes and my brother's knife would not suffice. I didn't have the skills to navigate the urban jungle. The hardest ground I had ever slept on was at Crescent Lake, Oregon, where our family camped years before.

Passing buses and flickering street lamps made shadows that moved as if they were coming to take me. Like a man with no country, I was a boy with no home. I sought comfort in the beers left by Jessica. Fear did its best to engulf me, as the warming effects of the alcohol battled

63

against it. In time, one or the other would win. The victor ultimately depended on whether I drank enough booze to bring on a spinning cradle of oblivion. I could not call my mom at midnight in tears because I was unable to sleep. I had made my bed—rather, my doorway—and now I had to sleep in it.

When cold creeps into the flesh, the body cannot compensate. Concrete drains core heat, grating bone against bone. A night spent on concrete and steel leaves one feeling arthritic regardless of age. In the morning, I felt grateful for the sun. In daylight, the shadows disappear; my fears disappeared as well. Why is that? A shadow is a shadow despite where it comes from. Are we conditioned by an instinct from another age, one which tells us that the hunters emerge at night? They do. In the comforting confines of my home, I didn't realize as such. The shadows are nightwalkers, feeding on the fears of others. Night is both their cloak and their dagger. I would soon find that the only way to beat my fear of the shadows was to join them.

It had been almost a week since I left home. My father invited me and my brothers to a Sonics basketball game at the Seattle Center. He wanted us to meet his girlfriend, Cathy. I declined because I had been drinking, formulating my next plan of attack. I had no intention of going home and had exhausted all possible contacts from the blue book. I had grown tired of making calls only to receive a lecture and pleas to go home. Had wanted to go home, or even to get clean, I could have called one of the numbers given at a recovery meeting. The problem was, recovery meant facing fears and discussing my past. That was the last thing I would have done at the time.

I felt a strange satisfaction knowing that my parents were probably very worried, suffering as a result of my decision to leave. By that time, they must have exhausted all leads realizing that I had left the island or persuaded someone to lie about my whereabouts. In many ways, I was trying to punish them for their separation and their desire to control me. I punished them by punishing myself. It was a dangerous maneuver but quite effective, as I didn't care about hurting myself in the process. I never thought about consequences when I lashed out or acted out of resentment and anger. I just reacted then let the pieces fall where they may.

I spent the majority of the day drinking to spite my father and his faceless girlfriend. I intended to be good and drunk when they exited the game. After a while, it became apparent that I would never run into them in the flood of spectators leaving the arena. I sat against the south wall and drank until both the bottle and the arena were empty.

I recall meeting a man with an Australian accent who was drinking a Foster's. He was obviously drunk as well. We passed beers for the better part of the night and into the morning. I learned quickly that passing the bottle meant passing stories as well. Every time I tried to fabricate a story, he would say, "Live a little and then try again, sonny," as if he knew I was lying. Through slurred ramblings, I learned a great deal that night about vaginas, long-shoring, and Brisbane. After hearing my plight, this nameless sailor offered me a place to stay. He had been squatting for weeks in an abandoned house past the old Ivar's restaurant. As we approached the door, I could feel the hair on the back of my neck begin to rise. The man motioned to a lantern just inside the door and tried to herd me in. I thank the Creator to this day the he entered first after I refused.

Instinct is an amazing thing. Even though my senses were distorted from the alcohol, I could feel that something bad was about to happen. I wasted no time. I simply ran, allowed the self-preserving jolt to take hold and carry me away from the house and into the lights of the city. I don't remember how far or where I ran, but when I stopped, I felt wet from exertion. The man had reached for me as I was turning to run. Doing so, he tore my shirt and scratched my neck. His curses followed me into the night, confirming his sinister motives. When instinct warns that something is wrong, comply. In his attempt to take something from me, I learned that a drive for survival exists within all of us, one that comes not from experience or simple instinct, but from a source beyond reason and explanation.

For several days, I wandered the streets spending the last of the money I had in my pocket. I hoped desperately that I could find a way to subsist without returning home. When it wasn't raining, I found comfort on the rooftops of the city. Many of the buildings toward Lake Union had flat roofs so I was able to sleep without fear of other people sneaking up on me in the night. The rooftops also threw fewer shadows.

The rain, however, was not my friend. It refused to stop, destroying my rooftop oasis. A man I met and drank with told me of a shelter in a building downtown. He said I could find a cot there and a bagged meal. He warned that I would have to sing for the meal. This meant gospel music and prayer. I had no problem with that if it meant I could get out of the rain and sleep on a soft cot. I assumed there would be no shadows there either, which added to my motivation to arrive before nightfall.

As I approached the rotating doors, I saw many grateful people eating sandwiches and soup. Some of the cots held motionless shapes were covered in blankets of various colors. Others served as couches for those congregating to talk and share stories. I could see empty cots and there was no line in front, which meant there would be room for me inside. This was a relief, as I had nowhere else to go. Bad things happened at night and I did not want to fall prey to the shadows.

A man sat at the door and screened those who came through. As I approached, he sized me up like a bar bouncer then refused me entry.

"You have to be over eighteen to stay here at night. You're barely sixteen."

He sounded somewhat remorseful but also well-rehearsed; he had said the same words to many before and would do so after.

"Liability issues. We can't mix teens with adults."

I was confused. I did not know what could happen to me in a shelter that wasn't more likely to happen in some back alley. The man directed me to a youth center for homeless kids in the University District, though it was only open during the day.

"The streets are a more kid-friendly in that neck of the woods. You'll probably be a little safer there than downtown."

I wish I had heeded his advice and gotten directly on a bus. Instead, I threw caution to the wind and headed for the bowels of the city where the shadow walkers lived.

Kenneth stepped from the shadows, though I am not sure which one. If you have ever walked the streets of a large city, you have seen him. He has long, brown hair with a scraggly beard to match. Sometimes he smiles; other times he stares at the ground in passing. His clothing is stained and worn from many days without washing. His nose is a little larger than most, and red and blue veins are visible across his face. His skin is wrinkled and tan, not from age, but from the elements. I saw wisdom in

Kenneth's eyes, a knowledge that could only be attained through experience. Looking at him, it was impossible to determine his age. The bundle he carried may have looked worthless, but inside he kept everything he needed to survive on the streets. Kenneth watched his surroundings like a hawk. His survival depended upon an ability to emerge from nowhere, descending on his prey from just beyond its line of sight.

I met Kenneth when I was at my most vulnerable and in the greatest need of help. If Kenneth had not entered my life at that exact moment, I would have used the remaining change in my pocket to call my mother. He suggested seeking comfort using cardboard. Cardboard acts as both an insulator and a cushion against the cement. Although I was wary, I did as he suggested. Kenneth disappeared as quickly as he'd manifested. In the doorway of a shop near Pioneer Square, I settled in for the night. I looked around one last time to see if he was still there. My field of vision was limited; I was young, inexperienced, and desperate.

I woke to the pleasant realization that my bones did not ache as much. With newspaper for covers, this was a welcome turn of events. I actually felt warm. At once, Kenneth appeared with a bag of donuts, a jug of Carlo Rossi, and an invitation to eat and drink with him and his partners. If I had looked him in the eye, I might have seen the flash of satisfaction that comes with springing a trap.

In many homes, families meet around the breakfast table to discuss the day's plans and give directions to their kids. Our breakfast table consisted of a set of benches in Pioneer Square. Others congregated and I recognized numerous faces from the several days I had wandered downtown. Kenneth introduced me to the gruff parties that had gathered, and the jugs made their rotation around the circle. I imagined a plate of eggs passed by my mother, but settled on cheap wine and dumpster rations.

Although they were all quite friendly, they clearly maintained a hierarchy within which I fell to the bottom. My attempts at interjection were brushed off. They talked over me and listened only when I answered a question. Even then, they listened just long enough to hear my answer. They didn't exclude me. I simply had not yet earned their respect. On skid row, a code of ethics is strictly enforced. As in prison, the strong rule the weak and the weak protect the strong through their silence. I did not know it then, but I would find out later that I was brought into the circle for a specific reason; that reason was not for my stories.

Passing the food and wine around the circle ensured that all who sat at this urban breakfast table got their equal portion. Even those with nothing to bring participated. People passing by, cast judgment, looking through a lens of social bias. In so doing, they missed lessons of humanity taught by those whom society had rejected. Some even called them inhuman. I witnessed more humanity from that group of drunks in the park than I had from many of the people on the island, people who society deemed more worthy.

Sitting with these strangers, I experienced a sort of communion. The apprehension I had felt earlier began to fade away as the liquor and nourishment eased my desperation. I felt like I could sit for eternity listening to the stories told by these men and women. Rising voices and laughter replaced the initial rigidity. The effects of alcohol warmed their spirits as much as the sun that parted the clouds, giving us all a reprieve from the drizzle and our plight.

Pigeons massed in expectation of what moving hands promised. Shit, birdseed, and cigarette butts speckled the brick courtyard. In some areas, motionless bodies lay in a mass of wool and newspaper. In others, groups congregated. Only the emptying of jugs marked the passing of time.

As the others rose to depart, Kenneth eyed me like a jeweler might eye a diamond. In my own eyes, I held very little worth. To Kenneth, I held value. We were alone. In an awkward moment of silence, I abandoned myself to him in a way that only those who have relied on another for survival can understand.

"So if you're going to live among us, you have to learn how we do things," Kenneth told me, his voice low. "You're obviously not prepared for a life on the streets. Keep your mouth shut, and I'll help you through the worst part. Then you're on your own."

Relief! My protagonist had arrived and, with him, my thoughts of home disappeared completely.

The idea of raising a bottom so that an addict will become open to change is an important concept for those who wish to travel the road to recovery. Those who still hold some emotional, or material sway over the addict can manufacture consequences. When addicts have at least one remaining resource, they will generally continue on their existing path. Money, an occasional shower, the keys to a car, each represents the potential for the next fix. That is why the car is never returned on time, the pills go missing in the bathroom, and the loan is never repaid. When my mother drew the line at home, she was hoping to bring me in sooner. In Kenneth I had found my new resource. In an unspoken agreement, we planned to use each other, which is often the case in relationships formed in need and sealed in selfishness. We each believed that we had hustled the other. Only one of us was correct.

Growing up, I had seen panhandlers in Pioneer Square, but I was on the giving side. In the daylight hours, we walked through the square on our way to baseball games, asked by panhandlers for spare change. Though I felt intrigued, I also felt a deep sadness by what I saw. Even at a young age, I could relate to their sadness through an empathy bred from the abuse we shared.

Some in society say that people are responsible for themselves and must make their own way without the help of others. These same people argue that weakness lies in the compromise of morality that comes from an upturned cap. I understood little of what might drive a grown person to beg. I believed that all human beings deserved to be treated with dignity, respect, and compassion. Providing for those unable to care for themselves seemed reasonable. Are we not obligated as spiritual beings to ease the suffering of others? I understood that their condition was not always self-imposed.

Alcohol is far cheaper than the medication that would relieve the paranoia which keeps a person from sleeping indoors. The meth pipe may seem like the only thing that slows one's thoughts long enough to focus. Many of the people whom the normal observer would assume to be drug addicts are, in fact, mentally ill. The filth and tattered clothes simply reflect society's lack of care. It is far easier to label and condemn a person than it is to help find solutions. Casting judgment and assigning labels of immorality eliminates obligation. Removing obligation enables the individual to continue in a state of ignorant bliss.

It seems that at this point in history, our need is greater than our compassion. Humanity has been set aside in favor of comfort and power. If you believe that every homeless person is homeless of their own volition, ask yourself this: why would a human being trade comfort, love, and access to basic necessities for a life of discomfort, violence, and fear? People on the streets don't trade their most basic needs for a life of home-lessness. They are forced into it. Something beyond their control interrupts their ability to provide the most basic things.

It took me just a few hours to earn several hundred dollars. Kenneth definitely knew his trade and his little diamond had begun to pay dividends. Prior to turning my hat up, Kenneth taught me that truth mingled with lies would bring in more money than all lies or complete honesty. He told me that any lie should be backed by some truth; this would make me believable. Most people could read through lies then would go on the defensive and offer little. The goal was to draw them in using sympathy. On the other hand, if I told people that I was an island kid, fresh to the streets, they would probably haul me by the ear down to the ferry and send me home. Some place in the middle created enough illusion to bring in cash and protect me from being sent away.

As quickly as my pockets filled, they were emptied into Kenneth's. I never thought to keep some for myself. With my new trade, I blended into the crowd and could subsist until age forced me into a new profession. Kenneth used the money I generated to buy our greatest necessity: alcohol in its cheapest form. Next came smokes. Food was last on the list. As we sat down, people flocked like birds, coming to enjoy the spoils of victory. Strangers congratulated me on my collection. Others still dominated the conversation, but because of my midday exploits, my name became part of several stories. On occasion, I was asked to fill in the blanks. I assumed that this was how it worked. I earned my voice and position through what I could provide to the group.

Those who experience abuse and abandonment tend to gravitate towards others, forming unhealthy and inappropriate bonds. Abusers rely on this and exploit it when it enters their lives. Abusers are often creatures of opportunity. Some track their prey, while others wait patiently then lunge with blinding speed.

I was exploited and used by the streets just as many others had been before me. You do not have to sell your body to be pimped out to the streets. Exploitation at the hands of another creates the same painful bond. People are used for what they can provide; they are controlled through subtlety and aggression. I know now that Kenneth would not let me go home, even if I had wished to.

Kenneth, a master at his craft, knew that he could control me through promises and a semblance of trust. He used alcohol and other drugs to close his grip on me. A master of manipulation controls those around him without their knowledge. The respect he enjoyed in those circles was the by-product of his ability to produce for the whole group. By delivering to the whole group, he controlled those who partook of what he offered. Kenneth's generosity initially seemed innocent. Eventually, I recognized the signs of a master manipulator, predator, and victimizer—a shadow walker.

I am not sure how long I spent in downtown Seattle, panhandling, using, passing out, then doing it all over again the next day. I scanned the faces in the crowds heading toward the island ferry, praying I would see my father. My protagonist had become my antagonist. I needed a hero to save me from the shadows that surrounded me.

Memories of my father flooded my mind as I remembered waiting for him to come home from the city. A sea of people rushed towards me as I searched for his familiar smile in the crowd of commuters. Other islanders, family friends and or acquaintances, would nod or wave as I waited. Eventually, I would find my dad among the other tired faces, and in a rush, I would lunge towards him, yelling his name. He would kiss my head, ruffle my hair, and soon we would be headed home for supper.

My father never received a handout in his life. He endured a two-to three-hour journey by boat and by bus every day. Often times, forty-hour work weeks turned into sixty-hour workweeks as he tirelessly supported his family. My father's work ethic was topnotch. He had moved up the ladder rapidly and often the coins from his pocket filled the upturned hats of others. I remember him wondering aloud when he no longer saw a particular homeless person in their specific doorway or underpass.

Regrettably, my memories did not return my father to me. Instead, I found the old train yards south of the Kingdome. Our group spent a great deal of time in the yards when we were not working downtown. This was the artery that brought new people to skid row. The majority of men, and some of the women I met, tramped up and down the West Coast and across the high and low lines by rail. Each possessed the skill of catching trains and navigating the various train yards. People shared stories of near-scrapes coming to and from various locations. The idea was to move constantly. Staying in one place for too long created a potential liability. Many kept a low profile, careful to hide their faces and avoid unnecessary attention, to stay clear of local law enforcement. Heroin served as a source of commerce for some. People would travel by rail into the Border States to bring product back up north. Pot did not generate enough cash in smaller amounts to make rail transport lucrative. Packing light was a necessity. What could be made in a pound of black tar would take a railcar full of Mexican red to make the same profit.

Kenneth continued to teach me the intricacies of this lifestyle. I never knew if he was telling me the full truth, the half-truth, or simply lies when he discussed his past. One night over a pallet fire, Kenneth became quite drunk. Pacing my consumption of alcohol seemed next to impossible, but for some reason I felt suspicious of his change in spirit and drank accordingly. In an emotional monologue, he described being a teacher and a father. He told me that his children were three and eleven; though this was merely the age they had been when he left them with their mother. Kenneth had kept his back turned to them for many years now. There are times to ask questions, and there are times to remain silent.

At some point in life, the past catches up to the present. No matter how much alcohol or tar you have pumped into your system, it is impossible to avoid or erase the torment that the past brings. These feelings surface unexpectedly, and they cause suffering for time spent locked in the depths of the consciousness. Kenneth's demons caught up with him that night. He danced with his shadows on the walls of the warehouses surrounding us. He sobbed and screamed as the flicker of our fire marked the cadence of his deep sorrow. He did not stop sobbing even after he fell to the ground in exhaustion. The candle followed his fit. The spoon, syringe, and nods eventually chased away the past that had accosted him. I waited a long time before spreading out his bedroll and covering him with his blankets. I wanted to be sure that I would not re-awaken the beast I had witnessed. He slept until the following morning. I did not sleep until daybreak.

We never spoke about that night. I know that Kenneth remembered a portion because he began to sink into himself the way a person does when they feel ashamed of what they have done. As far as I was concerned, he had no reason to feel shame. Kenneth had only done what I had wanted to do so many times since I had buried my own past. Our relationship changed. The jokes and laughter stopped, not only with me but also with others. Where he had once practiced patience, he now had none. He pushed me to make as much money as I could, and he spent less. He began to store light, dry foods and other items in two bedrolls instead of one. When I asked about this, he shrugged it off as if it held little importance.

People suffering from post-traumatic stress disorder (or PTSD) describe things that happened in their past as if they are living that event in the present. PTSD may develop as a result of experiencing major trauma or other life-threatening occurrences that cause a person to feel helpless. There are certain experiences that we go through in life that, no matter how hard we try, simply cannot be erased. The memory of the events that led up to—or occurred during—will stay with us forever.

If you have a difficult time with the very real abuse that happens to children on the streets, then you may want to skip ahead to the next chapter. I will not bury this event in silence as I did previously. Silence protects the abuser but forces the abused to relive it. I have changed the name of every individual in my story because I wish to protect his or her privacy. Kenneth is the only name that I have not changed. If I knew his last name, I would publish it. For years, in therapy and in groups, I distorted the truth of this assault, making it more, or less tragic, as if this took the power from him and returned it to me. Endless times, my story ends with my brother's knife plunged deep into his genitals as I ran. I cannot erase the reality of what happened to me, even if I wished to do so.

This was to be my night of celebration. Kenneth told me that we would get up in the morning and I would take my first train ride to southern California. I had assumed we had made camp far from the prying eyes and ears of others for that reason. Trust can be a liability. On the streets, trust blinds you and reliance slows one's instincts. This is why the abuser works so hard to win both. Once they have succeeded, they are that much closer to what they came for.

Kenneth looked more serious than he had before. He took a great deal of caution in how he set up camp and exactly where the bedding was placed. Mine was placed against a warehouse wall parallel to a set of tracks, rusty from disuse. Tall grass surrounded us. Lying down, one could see only buildings in the distance. I remember thinking that it was the perfect place to go unnoticed. Kenneth had thought the same.

Kenneth forced me against the wall so I had nowhere to run. His fondling brought me out of my sleep. His actions soon moved to rape. I was a six-year-old boy all over again, unable to stop what was being done to my body. The only difference between then and now was that I felt no physical enjoyment. Confusion was replaced by a horror and filth that no shower could wash away. My mouth betrayed me, and what had been calls for help became sobs of defiance. I could not run as Kenneth maintained control of my legs.

Time distorts when you endure something like this. What takes minutes seems like hours. When it is done, you sense a reluctant gratitude for surviving the worst of it. I remained as still as I could so he would not notice me as he dressed himself and gathered his things. He did not take the bedroll he had used earlier in the night. All of his preparation from the previous days had been for that moment. He had taken the food, the money, and the second bedroll for his escape. He had acted in a sort of practiced movement that only experience could breed. I thought back to the stories of him as a schoolteacher and of his own children. Sadly, I knew that my tears were not the only ones shed as a result of his deviance. I watched from the ground as Kenneth walked through the grass, a shadow walker blending into his own shadows.

I did not sleep or move the rest of the night. I felt terrified that he might emerge from any shadow. I waited for the sun to rise to chase the shadows away. There is no way to compare abuse, to categorize some as better or worse. Abuse is abuse. I will say that what was done to me that night set me on a path of self-destruction. I fell to depths that few know, and with my fall came a rage born from terror.

The abuser's greatest talent is convincing his or her victim that they are at fault for the abuse. How is this so? Besides the act itself, the greatest damage exists in what we tell ourselves afterwards. Lies rise to the surface as we try to force away or rewrite the memories. When the tears ended, I felt numb and blank. I stared into the distance at nothing a million miles away.

I will give Kenneth credit for two things he left in that camp: my life and a half-empty bottle of Carlo Rossi. I returned to my previous ally, seeking to destroy and forget. It was obvious the amounts used prior would not suffice. I needed to run far and fast enough to keep what had happened behind me. I would use chemicals to erase what I had endured at the hands of a monster. The fastest running shoes would no longer suffice.

The Seattle police met me at a phone booth not far from the camp. I cannot remember our conversation, only their brief search around Pioneer Square and the rail yards. Every face I saw was Kenneth's. The realization that he was riding the rails, wind in his face, and his back turned, left me furious with his cowardice.

A feeling of self-loathing rose within. As the effects of alcohol wore off, the voices became louder:

You should have run.

You should have seen that coming.

You should have known better.

What kind of man are you? You didn't even fight?

You asked for that one.

That's what trust gets you.

Are you an idiot?

Men aren't raped; women are.

You're less of a man.

There is no God. If there were I wouldn't have had to go through that.

I have no one to protect me.

I am alone.

Over and over, voices whispered lies in a never-ending, internal mantra. Eventually, the voices silenced. The lies had become imprinted so deeply that to reverse their emotional damage would take years of counseling.

The officer looked bored as we waited for passengers to board the ferry. I understood that I was probably not the only runaway he had escorted to these docks. My parents had reported me once they knew of my intentions to use. Information is not always disseminated in the way that it could be. In an awkward moment, the officer waited for the ferry to dock then watched to be sure I stayed on the boat.

I went to the upper deck seeking the anonymity of evening's shadows. For some reason, the shadows no longer scared me. What could they do that had not already been done? Was there something worse than betrayal and violation at the hands of another man? The shadows and demons had danced on the walls and all the while I did not realize it had been my indoctrination. His sorrow passed into my spirit one night, and then it passed into my flesh the next. Our shadows danced, shedding the last innocence and delivering me into a world much harsher than the one I had known. Gazing down at the waves as they pounded the ferry's bow, a cold, dark void called my name from the depths. One jump and it would all be over.

6

I N JAPAN, WHEN SOMETHING AS FRAGILE and beautiful as pottery breaks, they do not cast it out as if its parts are less important than the whole. Instead, they repair the pottery using a process called Kintsugi, which means golden joinery. To the Japanese, pottery is precious; its intrinsic value outweighs the cost of rebuilding it. Gently gathering the pieces, they are careful not to overlook any parts that may have escaped. Each fractured piece is necessary to recreate the whole. Gold is used to solder the seams of each piece. Hours and expense are sacrificed in the process. When the new piece is complete, its value far exceeds what it was prior to being shattered.

When my mother picked me up from the ferry that evening, I was in pieces. My jaw firm, I met her eyes with a flat stare. She did not respond in anger or scorn, but with a compassion and tenderness that only a parent can show. She seemed to sense that her child had been injured in some horrible way.

I don't remember exchanging words, only an embrace that seemed to inflame my emotional wounds. The contrast between the soulless man who had left me beside the tracks and my mother's embrace with only a ferry ride between was too much for me to bear. The shadow walker had followed me home to my sacred ground; he devoured the only source of light left. To protect those I loved, I needed to lead the enemy away and keep the island sacred. I had to remove myself. I would become a shadow, one caught between the day's departure and the night's arrival. I was left in despair.

My despair confirmed that I had never been invincible. The games I had played as a child had lost their meaning. My naivety departed, replaced by an intimate understanding of the cruelty of human nature. Whatever innocence Marlene had left, Kenneth took from me tenfold.

At home, a fire blazed in the hearth. What had been lit so many times to chase away the night chill was now meant to erase the physical imprint of my assault. I watched the torn jeans caked with city filth and blood burn to ashes. If only I could have thrown my body to the flames, purging it of what had been done. I searched our living room walls, hoping to see my shadow dance so I could reclaim myself and become whole again. Instead, my mother and brothers watched me, wondering at the spectacle in front of them.

Suffering from PTSD, I relived every detail of the event. The way the dirt felt grinding between my teeth; the smell of sour breath, the sound of wind through long grass, and the sight of buildings in the distance, their backs turned. Though these memories transported me back to the event that tormented me, I was also protected from its aftermath. Although I remember the brutal assault in candid detail, I do not remember: words, friends, school, brothers, parents, meals, showers, beaches, ivy-covered cliffs, assessments, phone calls, tears, meetings, embraces, reproaches, my father, glove oil, cartoons, lucky charms, wrestling matches, or emotion.

My life became thick and muffled, lacking the emotion that should have overflowed. I didn't need substances to numb the pain. Feelings did exist; a sort of primal protection muted them. I had become the shell of a child, the contents devoured.

Parents are often criticized for placing their children in treatment at a young age. They are likewise blamed if they try to address the problems at home. Judgment is rendered without the slightest understanding of the variables involved. Those once called villains are later commended for their heroic actions. My family's difficulty with addiction was not unique; it was just a bit premature.

You should have given him more religion. You should have sent him away sooner. You shouldn't have sent him away at all. You should have kicked him out. You should have let him stay. You should have remained silent. You should have said more. You should have sent him to more meetings. You never should have let him go to any meetings. By now it should be abundantly clear that there are no easy decisions when trying to keep a child alive.

I try now to look through the eyes of my parents. They had a fourteen-year-old child who had been committed once for addiction and suicide attempts, continued to run away from home, refused to stop using, did not register emotionally, was physically and verbally abusive, skipped school, stole repeatedly...They also had two other children to support, work to attend, a house to save, their own recovery to tend to, plus all of life's other responsibilities. Just the thought is overwhelming.

There are no easy solutions. You trust those educated in addiction to guide you in the right direction and to help you do what is necessary to keep your child alive. There are those who thought they knew what was best for our family. If my parents had followed their advice, I might, or may not, be writing this book. I am not questioning the past. I am attempting to ease the suffering of parents who may be faced with similar decisions. My parents made life or death decisions with no knowledge of the outcome and no promise for positive results. To do so required courage, one that comes of faith, desperation, and blind trust despite the numerous voices that argued to the contrary.

At some point, my parents formulated a plan to get me back into treatment. My father's insurance package covered the care. Had that not been the case, I know that my parents would have done whatever it took to pursue the help I needed. They believed that treatment for a child who is unwilling to stop using is critical. They did not base their decisions solely on the input of those around them. They listened to the advice of professionals trained in the diagnosis and treatment of addiction. Being in recovery, or knowing people who are, does not make one an expert in the field of addiction. A misguided or undereducated suggestion can often create more problems. The illness of addiction is often accompanied by physical and psychological issues that are best addressed by those trained and educated in the fields of medicine and psychology. The risk is too great to take chances when dealing with a loved one who is unstable and has shown signs of self-harm.

As mentioned previously, addiction is considered a primary disease. It is reflected in an individual's pathology of pursuing reward or relief by substance use and other chemical responses caused by specific behaviors. The obsession and compulsion alluded to earlier provide examples of this pathological issue. Memory, the brain's circuitry, and motivation are all affected by addiction's progression. Brain dysfunction leads to deprivation in the areas of social, psychological, physical, and spiritual behavior. Like other chronic diseases, addiction often involves cycles of relapse and remission. The inability to abstain, impairment in behavior, incessant cravings, and the deterioration of interpersonal relationships, as a result of dysfunctional emotional responses, are common side effects. Society often avoids taking responsibility for these behaviors and, instead, blames those who suffer from the disease.

Though this form of blame makes no sense, it is unfair to blame those who hold to this archaic view. Given the many symptoms associated with addiction, it is easy to overlook the medical and psychological implications and focus instead on the symptoms that manifest as moral complications. The widespread imprisonment of addicts is one example of addressing the moral implications in an attempt to solve the larger problem. Hundreds of thousands of addicts are warehoused all over this country. Instead of throwing money at rehabilitation, money is poured into imprisonment. This is like throwing gasoline on a growing fire. In so doing, precious resources that could be used to address the core issue, and to potentially resolve the problem once and for all, are wasted.

I can't remember when I was finally told to pack my bags. Emotion began to surface as I prepared to go to a place I had never been. The excitement of treatment as a new experience had worn off. I felt abandoned. Like any child, I viewed my parents as the providers of my basic needs. In a perfect world, they would deliver love, food, clothing, and shelter as the basic necessities of survival. As we grow older, this dependence does not disappear, it simply evolves into a more emotional and spiritual dependence. When children do not get these basic necessities from their parents, the dependence shifts to someone who can provide them.

I had begun to realize that my parents could not protect me from the things that might damage me the most. No matter how hard they tried, and due to my unwillingness to conform to their expectations, I exposed myself to some of the world's most painful experiences. This made both my parents and me victims. They experienced everything that I experienced simply by loving me. We were all at the mercy of a disease that devastated our lives. I felt devastated to realize that my parents could no longer chase away the shadows. My mother's embrace and the bass of my father's voice still provided some comfort. Sadly, I knew that shadows loomed over her shoulder and beyond his words should I wander too far from their protection.

Unlike my first trip to treatment, I felt no excitement as my mother packed my bags for my second treatment. I was told I would be traveling to Montana to attend a treatment facility on a ranch. I did not protest or attempt to manipulate my way out of their decision. I felt beaten and had little vigor to oppose the forces that now directed the path of my life. I was at the mercy of two of the four people I now blamed for my life's circumstances. My silent indignation proved more powerful than screams in protest.

To travel by train added insult to injury. My parents had opted to send me to Montana by way of rail. I could see from my seat the old train yards, a reminder of Kenneth's promise of departure week's prior. Instead of feeling the wind on my face, I watched through a large picture window as the city receded from view. Images blurred through my tears and the rain, which streaked across the glass. I tried to leave the sight of my mother's pink nose and bloodshot eyes behind, but images of this kind are powerful. This was not the first or the last time I would see my mother fight off emotion in a show of solidarity, only to lose her composure once I had gone. I left her there under the confused and compassionate stares of passing strangers.

Midway through my trip, I noticed a beautiful blond sitting in the seat across from me. I had not been aware of her when I sat down, but when I surfaced briefly from the torment of my memories, she was there as a welcome relief. She began to ask me questions about my trip. "So where are you parents? Where are you headed? How old are you? Do you want something to drink?" Her questions seemed disguised as genuine interest. I answered them, just as I had with Kenneth. How could Kenneth have changed appearances so quickly? How had he manifested himself as a beautiful woman?

Conversations between a victimizer and a victim result in a lopsided exchange of information. The victimizer extracts a disproportionate amount of information. The victim is fed lies and half-truths. The victimizer protects him or herself, and then blends back into the shadows once their desires have been satisfied.

Becky pulled mini Jack Daniel's bottles from her pockets. She produced enough to get me drunk. Somehow, I had found my two greatest forms of refuge sitting directly across from me. Despite being three times my age, she gained my full confidence in no time. Our conversation turned to laughter as the alcohol she poured into my pop began to take effect. As always, the mix of sexual interest and alcohol erased the memories that haunted me. Life felt bearable. I no longer thought of the past or the future. I sensed only my altered state in a hazy present. It seemed I could live in that space forever.

We spent some time in the smoking car then found our way back to the passenger car, where instead of taking her former seat, she sat beside me. I felt both uncomfortable and excited as our bodies touched. When she placed a blanket over our laps, I knew that her hand would follow. Kenneth had used the same strategy. This woman fed from my innocence, as though in defiling a child, she gained rather than took something away. As the darkness of night passed outside, I did not feel the apprehension and fear I had experienced at the hands of Kenneth.

What started under the blanket ended in the privacy of a bathroom stall. I remember very little of the experience except that she guided me in and left me there when she was through. Refuse is treated better than I was; it is flushed, erasing all signs of its existence. I was left in a drunken heap, waking hours later to someone pounding on the door and the smell of vomit mixed with bathroom freshener. When I returned to my seat, Becky had disappeared much like Kenneth. A name—a story—an act.

Society has a strange way of looking at the sexual abuse of children. Once the male enters puberty, abuse administered by older women is seen as a conquest. Despite laws to the contrary, abuse prior to pubic hair and a cracking voice is not viewed in the same manner. I mentioned this briefly in my discussion concerning Marlene. The same holds true regarding Becky as well. Genitalia and age are of no consequence when discussing sexual assault endured by underage children. In both instances, I was assaulted by adults then abandoned once their perversions were satisfied. I felt no different waking up in the bathroom than I did beside the train tracks. A blow to the innocent spirit does not differentiate between genders.

When does it become appropriate for sexual activity to occur between people of differing ages? There exists a vast developmental gap between adolescents and adults. In this country, society accepts sexual activity between adults and children between the ages of sixteen and eighteen. This serves as a legal reference point for prosecution of those who cross the lines that were crossed in my experiences and in the lives of many others. Morally, these lines are quite different for many human beings. Some understand the developmental gaps and allow maturity to evolve before they approach.

The impacts of sexual abuse can manifest quite rapidly and in a variety of ways. Alternatively, the effects may take years to surface. Abuse causes both short-term and long-term emotional and psychological harm. Issues include, but are not limited to, depression, PTSD, eating disorders, poor self-esteem, dissociative and anxiety disorders, neurosis, sexualized behavior, and educational problems. Behavioral problems may include substance abuse, self-harm, and suicidal tendencies, among others.

Being sexualized, depressed, and pushed toward addiction are crucial elements to my story, as are many of the other manifestations described above. Because sexuality was introduced at such an early age, I did not develop emotionally as many others kids my age did. Ideas and images were inserted into my consciousness and I was left to sort out the pieces. My sexual education came through hands-on experience forced upon me by those who had no interest in helping me learn and mature. In the years that followed, sexuality and a drive to feel loved became drugs as much as any other. I have been spared pedophiliac perversions. In their place, I grapple with a form of sexual craving referred to as sexual addiction.

At fourteen, this addiction was in its infancy, but moved rapidly to become a full-fledged addiction. I would use others as a source of sexual escape. I would use many of the tools, that I had been introduced to by my victimizers, to manipulate others into consensual sex. The notion that the victim becomes the victimizer functioned as a sort of prophecy that would manifest itself in my life many times, regardless of how much I despised the idea. Genuine emotional attachment would dissipate. Love would intimidate.

The countryside of Idaho and Montana was the most beautiful I had ever seen. I marveled at the landscape that passed my window. The colors, textures, and patterns mixed in a way that only a master painter could have created on a palette then brushed onto canvas. I will never forget the transition into this part of my life. I felt as though the rugged land could protect me in ways that others could not. How could the inhumanity I had experienced breach these towering mountains and dense forests? Others could not see what I had endured if I blended into the falling snow. I would become an animal whose coat thickens then lightens to endure the harsh realities of a deep winter.

I longed to walk into the landscape, to enter the depths of the mountain winter, where I could avoid all else. I would invite Marlene, Kenneth, and Becky to follow me into the wilderness as they had invited me into their own. I would watch as the elements consumed them, leaving their lips blue and their hands blistered and black like their souls. I would howl to the moon as I fed on their corpses, taking back what they had taken from me pound for pound. I would leave their hearts knowing that they were poisoned.

The sadness and shock of my experiences had worn off. In their place, a rage burst forth from intense emotion long denied. This rage waited, prepared to attack the next person who tried to penetrate the fortress around my heart. I would never again allow myself to be used. I would not allow my heart to become poisoned. Instead, I would push away anyone who threatened me. I was no longer a child. Knowledge became my burden. My rage mingled with the loneliness and isolation of the abused, emotions that made me feel unique in my burden.

I did not understand my parents' intentions for sending me away. I did not understand how they could turn their backs on me at a time when I needed them the most. Though I screamed words to keep them far from the truth, I meant the very opposite. "I hate you! Leave me alone!" meant, "I need love now more than at any other time in my life." I needed the reassurance and protection of an embrace. I needed a silent walk on the beach picking up seashells. Abused and addicted children tend to speak in opposites. They refuse the help that they so desperately seek. Their refusal is the greatest indicator of need.

As the train slowed, I could see Whitefish Lake. This signaled the end of my ride. Skiers bustled, gathering their things for a weekend adventure. I grabbed my bags in preparation for something much different. The laughter of others dampened my spirit. A staff member from Wilderness Treatment Center greeted me as I exited the train. I don't know if he had been given my description or if I simply fit the part. He greeted me with a smile and a hug, which made me feel like I was suffocating. His name was Gerry and he would be taking me to the ranch.

As we made our one-hour journey to the treatment center, Gerry talked to me in a language that seemed foreign. I had heard bits and pieces in twelve-step meetings, but it seemed that Gerry knew no other form of communication. I usually enjoyed listening to people new to me; I pieced them together like a puzzle, but I hoped that Gerry would soon be quiet, so I could nurse my hangover and enjoy the images passing by the window. I tried to remember which way we had come so that I could retrace my steps back to the train station if the situation so required.

"You smell like vomit and alcohol," Gerry said. "Do you have any more drugs on you?"

My silence answered the question. Gerry's silence formed his reply.

We pulled off of Highway 2 and passed through the gates of the ranch. At the end of a long, dirt driveway, I could see cabins in single file on either side. Guys stood in different areas smoking cigarettes; others played basketball in the middle of a courtyard. I scanned the area for danger. In my hyper vigilance, I felt alarmed by the age of some of the men. Many were substantially older than I was. This was not out of the ordinary, as I had been the youngest at New Beginnings as well. Next, I scanned for a possible exit. There was none; mountains and forest surrounded the area, an impenetrable wilderness foreign to me. Finally, I looked for a way to feed my hunger for substances. Since drugs and alcohol were unlikely to be in great supply, I would have to rely on the satiation of my sexual needs through the prospect of female patients. Much to my frustration, I soon realized that this was a program for boys ages fourteen to twenty-four. This meant that I had no way to escape my hauntings.

In treatment, patients go through initial intake during which one's bags are searched. Patients undergo a brief examination, receive the rules and expectations, and are then at the mercy of the treatment community. When my belongings were returned to me, I no longer had the marijuana and pipe, which I had carefully hidden in the tips of my boots. To my consternation, I discovered that my most precious belongings had been added to Mrs. Brekky's collection. They would then make their way to the local sheriff's office. Rumor had it that Mrs. Brekky's desk was full of smuggled items. I made note of the potential stash in case an opportunity arose. The staff could not be considered greenhorns with respect to young male addicts and their attempts at use during treatment.

The only thing I remember of my first night at Wilderness was a large Native American man named Edwin. Edwin sat on me so that I would not pound my head against the wall in the cabin to which I had been assigned. Edwin told me, "The bears around here circle the place waiting for youngsters like you to run." He'd been assigned night watch as I had become erratic and tried to harm myself. His horror stories of wildlife did little to calm my nerves.

I became emotional as I sobered up; the unleashed suppression became too much to handle. The emotion, deep in the pools of my being, surfaced only when the sun was at its lowest point. My feelings rose with an unexpected violence, then receded into a hole, deep and hidden. The staff at Wilderness provoked my emotions, forcing it to rise to the surface when I least sought its presence.

Mornings felt crisp and fresh. As the sun began to appear to the East, the sounds of animals came from every direction. Although I had had my own early morning routine, it did not compare to what I experienced my first day at Wilderness. I had never risen to the sound of a rooster or the whinny of a horse. I remember the frost that covered every blade of grass and the mists that silently blanketed the surrounding hayfields. Despite sounds all around, there was also a silence. This may seem impossible to those who have never experienced country as such. I found the silence amidst sound comforting.

The dining hall smelled like a breakfast diner: freshly cooked eggs, bacon, toast, and cakes. It felt like home.

The ranch was not like the sterile hospital treatment center I had experienced before. Instead, it felt full of life—a mystery for those who had never experienced anything similar. The ranch cook, Marianne, took on a mother-hen attitude towards the boys who anxiously awaited her attention. She snapped at them, smiling, as they tried to sneak bacon before breakfast. Marianne's laughter and smile eased my apprehension and left me feeling as though all women possessed a mother's spirit within. She served love and compassion with those sunny-side-up eggs; as such, she lessened my fears and alleviated my anxieties.

Although surrounded by strangers, I did not experience fear as I had at other times in my life when I lacked control of my situation. The other boys in the program seemed friendly—maybe too friendly, for as early as it was. People engaged in constant motion, finishing meals and beginning chores around the dining hall and ranch buildings. A well-run institution such as this exhibited a kind of organized chaos.

Treatment consisted of a morning meditation group, in which we read from Narcotics Anonymous meditation books. The first readings generally covered one of the twelve steps or a spiritual concept intended to get us thinking in terms of recovery. Following meditation, we attended other groups, lectures, one-on-one sessions with counselors, recreation time, work crews, study time, and twelve-step meetings. Wilderness Treatment Center's program taught change through hard work, adoption of the twelve-step philosophy, and taking responsibility for one's actions. It focused on recovery from the disease of addiction as described in *The Big Book* of Alcoholics Anonymous. In the sixty-plus days I attended, I completed steps one through five and participated in a twenty-one-day wilderness trip in the wilds of Montana, where I applied what I had learned during the first weeks of treatment.

Though I did not think so at the time, the process followed at Wilderness was ingenious. The first phase of treatment consisted of the admission of my powerlessness and inability to manage my use of chemicals. This admission is one that many addicts never make. They succumb to the power of their addiction every day, but are unwilling to look at their powerlessness square in the face. Addiction convinces the user that there is no problem. As a form of denial, users lie to themselves to continue their deadly behavior. Addicts take this denial to absurd extremes, often changing their circumstances should they begin to reveal the actual problem.

When my counselor gave me my first assignment, I struggled. I found the idea of powerlessness and the notion of being unable to manage my own behavior difficult to comprehend. I understood powerlessness to mean weakness. Someone who could not manage meant a person incapable of taking care of him or herself. The world told me that addicts were weak human beings, and that they were flawed in some way. I did not want to be categorized as such. I was an athlete. I was good-looking and popular. I came from a white, middle-class community; being successful meant being powerful. The most powerful players on the field won the game; those people ended up in the newspaper and became the talk of the town. Those with the most powerful jobs had the biggest houses. Wasn't the very country we lived in forged from the power of steel, coal, and gunpowder? Powerlessness is not a part of our nation's vocabulary; this fact was well engrained into my conscience.

I was unaware that true power lies in surrender. Through surrender, I opened myself up to other things. I did not comprehend that paradox at the time. The beginning of my recovery came with the realization that I had no control over substances or myself when I used them. In this defeat, I would find a victory of sorts, a power that did not rest in myself but came through the divine. As long as I believed that I held the power, I would not get far in recovery, or in life.

When I thought of drug addicts, I thought of my Uncle Bill. When I thought of drunks, I saw the faces of those in Pioneer Square looking back at me with vein-covered noses and orange-tipped fingers. Addicts were those people huddled in the doorway of some building, the glow of a butane lighter casting a blue glow. In my ignorance, I did not realize that I was one of those people. I had passed the bottle in the bag, slept in doorways, and sacrificed everything for use. At fourteen years old, I had given drugs priority over all else, and in so choosing, I had crossed a line without notice.

Now my counselor wanted me to admit to power-lessness and unmanageability? I understood what powerlessness meant personally. My personal definition of the term had nothing to do with drug use. It had to do with adults who forced themselves upon me. In those instances, I became powerless in a way that few would ever experience. I could not admit to powerlessness concerning drugs; drugs didn't have Kenneth's iron grip or whisper threats like Marlene. Listening to the other boys talk about drugs and alcohol in the same way I thought about my abusers only confused me more. They described something that controlled them and made them do things they did not want to do. They talked about how, when they least expected it, drugs had brought them to their knees and humiliated them. They described a complete loss of control, a feeling of being at the mercy of the substance. Their sentiments of fear, panic, hopelessness, betrayal, mistrust, and anguish mirrored my own. I became increasingly confused.

How could chemicals do to these boys what my abusers had done to me? I had fallen into a trap familiar to many young addicts. Minimal experience with chemicals, and the resulting consequences, can easily be blamed on parents or other external life factors. Young addicts often protect that which gives them relief in the hopes it will not turn on them as they are told it will. They do not realize that in their fear, the enjoyment of chemical use will be lost as they move far beyond the type of use described as social. I believed that I was in treatment because I had an excessively protective mother, who because of her experiences with other family members' addictions had sent me to ease her fear. Her boundaries and zero-tolerance rules had created a problem; my use had not created the problem. If she had backed off and let me be, I felt I could use like any kid my age and there would be no problem.

I compared myself to young adults four and five years older than me. This made it easy for me to deny my own using problems, especially since many of the boys had been using drugs intravenously for many more years than I had been smoking pot and drinking. By blaming the circumstances in my life, including my family's strict rules around substance use, I could point fingers rather than looking at myself honestly. It was not my fault I was raped; it was my mother's fault for not allowing me to use like other kids. If I had not been forced to run away, I would never have fallen prey to the streets. I did not have an anger problem; I was upset at my father for abandoning our family. I clung to those beliefs and excuses for years. As long as I remained the victim, I could justify my actions. This self-justification enabled me to continue on a self-destructive path.

At Wilderness, my assignment was to make a list of twenty-five examples of powerlessness and unmanage-ability. As described by the twelve-step program, power-lessness is the inability to control the use of drugs once addiction had started. It referred to a total loss of con-trol over the amount used. In the addict, a compulsion to use is awakened after ingesting chemicals; when the addict is not using, an obsession beyond the instincts of most people propels the addict to find more drugs. As such, a cycle begins and will continue until the addict dies or is forced to abstain as a result of institutions like the Wilderness Treatment Center. People often wonder why addicts spend their money on alcohol and drugs when they really need a bath, shelter, or food. The brain's chem-istry changes as a result of repeated use. The instinct to use chemicals begins to outweigh the instinct and even the need for other things. Use is no longer a choice. The addict succumbs to complete powerlessness, a lack of control that few but the addict, those who love them, and the medical world can understand.

Stories exist in which someone lost in a desert becomes so desperate for water that they instinctually resort to drinking urine to survive. Instinct drives that person to do whatever it takes to hydrate their body. In an attempt to stay alive, they are willing to make moral sacrifices. No one in their right mind would ever drink their own urine; yet in this case, sanity is set aside in favor of self-preservation. The addict experiences the same phe-nomenon. Reason is abandoned. Instinct dictates that the use of drugs is a matter of life and death.

I did not understand this concept even after it was explained to me. I could not make a connection between that idea and my desire to use. I did not want to see the similarities. I did not want to believe that I had become morally deficient as much of the world believed addicts to be. I believed that I used because I chose to use, not because I had to use. I used out of rebellion, not out of compulsion. I denied the truths that had mounted against my feeble defenses. I saw the differences, and not the similarities, in other addicts and myself.

The unmanageability aspect is part of the powerlessness. With the loss of control over use comes a loss of control in other parts of one's life. For instance, bills go unpaid and obligations are not met. People that the addict once adored become distant and detached. The addict sacrifices resources until nothing is left then breaks laws to support their habit. Physical, psychological, and spiritual problems emerge, and the cycle accelerates. This occurs at various levels. Many people, who have not reached these levels of desperation, point to things they have not done in avoidance. In reality, an addict at any stage of addiction needs help.

My list consisted primarily of finger-pointing. Although I did not include the sexual abuse I had endured, I did blame island parents, teachers, my parents, and anyone else by whom I felt slighted. My unmanageability list consisted of my parents' and my school's restrictions rather than the natural consequences I was given as a result of my use. By the age of fourteen, I had quit school, abandoned my family, used excessively, been suspended from school and sports, hurt the people I loved, compromised my morals, tried to commit suicide, blacked out, experienced craving and compulsion, stolen and lied to continue using, placed myself in danger to use, turned my back on friends, used illegal drugs, been institutionalized twice, engaged in promiscuous sexual activity while intoxicated, and on and on and on.

I was as advanced in minimal use as the older kids were in heavy use. It did not matter what or how much I used. What mattered were the effects of my use. When I used, I wanted more and would do anything to get more. People around me saw this even when I could not. The addict eliminates everything to use. Instead of learning from my poor choices, I used more and made my problems worse. I reopened my wounds over and over, never allowing them to heal; as a consequence, they festered.

I was no dummy in treatment. I understood that to progress, I had to play by their rules, but I tried to pull a fast one. I believed that by acknowledging some of what was said in the books, I could move ahead in the program. Little did I know that by reading the material and participating in groups, I was participating even if I thought I wasn't. Hearing truths—whether I knew they were truths or not—initiated change. In time these truths would reveal themselves.

Some believe that treatment is a waste of time for kids who have not reached certain levels of despair. These people rate the effectiveness of a treatment center according to its discharge statistics. Spiritual progress cannot be measured in numbers or by quantity. For some, spiritual transformation is immediate. For others, the transformation process is gradual. For every person, spiritual growth is different and it depends upon life circumstances, levels of pain, and a willingness to take part.

This understanding is part of what made the Wilderness Treatment Center so amazing. The counselors understood that they did not have all the answers. They could guide, teach, and instill in the participants ideas to be used in recovery once they were willing and able. The counselors are not the solution; they are merely a part of the solution. My time at Wilderness introduced me to a spiritual way of living upon which to build, one day at a time, beyond the ranch and in my daily life. The counselors I worked with did not pretend to have invented the twelve-step approach. Rather, they used it as an effective and proven form of recovery, one that produced some of the greatest results in recovery from addiction.

As part of the program, we worked on the ranch several days each week. This work went beyond our regular chores like making our beds and helping in the kitchen. Larry, a seemingly ageless man, wore a large hat and walked with a swagger that reminded me of the western movies I had adored growing up. Horses and cattle were new to me. Larry was silent save the directions he gave. This made him legendary. With Larry, there was never room for argument. I, like the others, did just what he asked me to do.

My favorite thing was when Larry brought out the Belgian horses to pull the sawn logs out of the mountains. Massive animals with intelligence in their eyes, they reminded me of storybook animals. The Belgians never complained as their harnesses were strapped on. They seemed as eager as I was to be on the move. Climbing those hills, I lived in the moment. In the moment, the past could not torment me. Smelling the pungent pine fragrance, I wondered how strong the pine limbs might be at the top.

I had never been afraid to work. My protests to my father were never because I didn't know how to work hard. Instead, I thought I might be missing something while I dragged the orange and yellow leaves to the burn pile. At Wilderness, I invited hard work. I felt a part of something important as we dragged each log out of the forest. My father introduced me to this work ethic, and I put it to good use at the ranch. Work gave me a sense of accomplishment and taught me how to interact with others to complete a task.

Once, in early spring, the calves were brought in for branding and shots. I watched as they burned symbols into the skin of these little animals. It produced a smell I will never forget. We branded each calf, snipped their testicles, injected vaccines, and then tagged their ears. Many would have laughed at the sight of us that day. Thirty or so young men from the suburbs, rolling around in their Nikes and Converse, covered in blood, cow shit, and dust. I was cowboy for a day. In the moment, I laughed deeply.

7

WHEN I SPEAK OF THE CREATOR, I have no particular gender or other classification in mind. I am simply assigning a name to an idea to enable related discussion. I wish to avoid defining the Creator as definition implies limitation. To be perfectly honest, I have no idea what the Creator is. I have been attempting to educate myself on the subject for years but it seems that the more I look, the less I know. I am not sure I am meant to understand. When I was a child, I tried to see the sun, and no matter how hard I tried, I could not see its true form. The deeper I looked into the brilliance, the more blurred the image became. Eventually, I was forced to look away. I've undergone the same experience in my attempting to see my Creator.

The idea of God has never been foreign to me. My parents understood the importance of allowing a person to form his or her own concept of a Creator. As a child, I did not understand the gift they had given me. My brothers and I were not isolated from other beliefs; our parents left the door open for exploration. I attended youth group at the Rolling Bay Presbyterian church and enjoyed the singing there almost as much as I enjoyed flirting with the girls. On weekends, my family gathered with our close, family friends to study the teachings of Paramahansa Yogananda, the hesitant yogi. We practiced yoga, doing asanas to prepare our bodies for sitting meditation then lazed in a circle imagining the things described to us by our teacher. At the time, I was as oblivious to other religions as I was to the great debates that had fueled my parents' separation.

As we sat focusing on the breath in an attempt to silence the mind, my mind raced. I thought of the beaches just below my friend's property. I wondered what might have been washed up by the tide. I was not concerned with God, the great mystery that has baffled humanity since our ability to reason. When I asked my mother if I could go to the beach, she remained silent, and focused on her breathing. I silently escaped to the sandy beach below, in pursuit of my true spiritual freedom in the waters of the Puget Sound.

Adults form belief systems to help them make sense of the senseless world around them. Why must they indoctrinate children with those beliefs so early in life? Why don't we allow them to develop before we lay the shame of humanity upon their shoulders in a vain attempt to shelter them from its ravishes? Why do we try to teach children concepts like life and death or good and bad when they already have a better grasp of the workings of the universe than adults? Children should be teaching the adults. We should listen as they describe the folds of a flower in early spring. We should watch as they show us how to love without condition. Divinity lives in their innocence and the short amount of time they have been separated from the Creator through birth into the physical form.

For as long as I can remember, I had a sense of something greater than myself. The world seemed to reflect the divine. From the crabs clustered beneath every rock, to the droplets that formed on the ivy from the morning's salty mists, enchantment prevailed. My innocence created a sanctuary everywhere I went. The doctrine preached in the churches, and what I endured in sitting meditation, seemed to limit the divine through human ritual. The angels did not congregate in the places where I was brought to worship; they hovered high in the branches, watching me play.

I remember eating at a mission in Seattle when I was a runaway. We were required to stand and sing before being allowed to eat our meals. The songs and prayer served as payment for the food, which was placed in front of our famished bodies and then called charity. Gifts are never free when conditions are placed upon them. To do so replaces the divine with humanism, thereby defeating the purpose of providing meals in the first place. I asked the shelter staff if I could take the food with me rather than eat there. "No," they told me. "Your salvation is far more important than your flesh." I had to disagree. I had missed several meals in the previous days. At that point, I was most concerned with the flesh they were serving between slices of bread. Unlike the subservient men serving the food, I was not willing to do whatever was necessary to eat.

As I lay upon my back cradled by the waters, the clouds drifting in the sky demanded nothing of me. My only requirements were lungs full of air and hands fluttering in the water to keep my body floating on the surface. The beauty of the world around me radiated divinity eternal. My every breath and thought felt in union with the Creator. Laughter was my mantra. My smile served as my holy communion.

As the year's cycles completed each rotation around the sun, this human experience seemed to separate me from my childhood divinity. To be indoctrinated into the world of the oppressed became the great injustice of my youth. The realities of the world, and the expectations of existence, dulled what had lived within me as a child. Earth and the heavens separated; the world reflected its emptiness as those around me sought to fill the void with distraction. In that separation, emptiness emerged that yearned to be filled. Chemicals, sex, war, greed, religion, and power are just a few of the ways in which society seeks to fill the hole created by a separation from the divine. These fillers only make the separation greater. A great lie was perpetrated by those enmeshed therein; they are blind now to what they once knew. I know of no greater tragedy.

On these cliffs and beaches, I learned what true freedom encompasses. I learned that the mind can transport a person from a sometimes-harsh reality into the soft folds of the imagination. I learned that I am capable of feats believed to be humanly impossible and that I am part of everything that surrounds me. I experienced the ultimate communion, a joining of the Creator, nature, and self. Unwittingly, I learned that the manifestation of the creative force rests in everything around me. Every drop of dew threw a reflection of the divine. Every grain of sand glistened with eternity.

During treatment at Wilderness, I was taught that a power greater than myself could restore me to sanity. To believe this second step, I had to first believe that I was insane. In much the same way that I struggled with being an addict, I struggled with viewing my use or the behaviors surrounding my use as insane. I remained convinced that others had caused my misery. If insanity could be a factor, it was in the insanity of the actions of others versus my actions. Internally, I denied this treatment step. Externally, I mimicked those around me to progress to the third step. Step three asked that I decide to turn my will and life over to a power that would restore me to sanity. I found this laughable and bordering on religion.

I had no problem with religion or religious people as long as they kept their beliefs to themselves. The counselors at Wilderness never told me that I had to define the Creator, but I still felt that the idea was being forced upon me. My response had more to do with feeling resentful for being told what to do versus how the information was presented. If someone had thrown me a life preserver in an attempt to save my life, I would have swum in the other direction. That is exactly what was happening. The counselors were fighting for my life, and I was resisting simply because they were adults. Authority figures represented those who had hurt and defiled me. I had a bad track record for placing trust in people who would eventually abuse me. I did not wish to repeat the same mistakes. The idea of trusting something greater than myself left me feeling more vulnerable not less so.

I had no difficulty playing the role to which I was assigned. I often felt that I could hide in the anonymity of my age. Those with more pressing issues received greater attention. The expression "the squeaky wheel gets the grease" rang true. I tried not to squeak, and for the most part, I sat and watched those around me dissect their past in an attempt to move beyond their demons. I recognized in many the all-too-familiar aura of one who had endured too much too soon. We belonged to a fraternity of those who understood that life is not as described in fairy tales. I, like many others, had slammed the book shut halfway through the reading. While the others kids laughed and applauded, we sat quietly aware that, "Happily ever after" did not exist.

I have been honored to experience the purging of my soul on several occasions. It is an experience more intimate than the embrace of a lover; it is more startling and powerful than an unexpected burst of thunder. Sitting in group therapy, Michael became the focus. He had a grandiose attitude and deflected attention through verbal sparring and diversion. Elk often divert a predator's attention by running away from their newborn calf. I, like many of my peers, viewed the counselors as predators who thrived on our secrets. They became stronger each time they discovered a previously untold morsel. The counselors asked questions like, "How does that make you feel?" and "How does that affect your use?" The answers seemed too personal to share with men I had never met before. I would know the others in treatment for sixty days, and then the wind would blow us in different directions.

Michael learned, like most of us, that he could not avoid revealing that which he wished to protect most. The history of his use, like the elk calf hidden in the tall grass, would not survive long. Michael's father had been sentenced to prison for many years for savagely beating his wife and son. The last beating left his wife concussed and Michael with a broken arm and collarbone. Michael's attempt to protect his mother during his father's drunken rampage did not end well. He shared with us his father's words: "Michael, you son-of-a-whore, get out of my way!" Michael repeated the words until he could say no more. When his tears began to flow, I forced myself to suppress my own. I had never been good at watching others experience such raw emotion. I wanted to absorb it into my own. I could not relate to the type of parental brutality he had endured, but I could relate to the pure sorrow and rage that surfaced. In therapy, Michael had nowhere to hide. His bravado, the tall grass in which he hid, fell at once. He could not stop the emotion that came from easing the bonds of his suppression.

A release of intense emotion brings a freedom from secrets deep within. The pain that users seek to avoid through chemical use is the key to freedom from the experiences that caused such pain. Michael was not aware that his willingness to address his greatest secret released him from the bondage thereof. As he spoke, I watched his face change. What had once seemed hard and impenetrable was now open for all to see. I was both in awe and uncomfortable. Michael could not have been more vulnerable, even if he had been stripped naked and placed before thousands of people. I felt respect for Michael. Yet I promised myself that I would not do as he had done. Secrets are safest left unshared. Mine had been shared with three people, people who would most likely carry those secrets to the grave. I hoped they ended up there, sooner rather than later.

I was also afraid that if I allowed my secrets to be found, I would never stop purging. In that act, I would hand myself back to those who had caused my suffering. In my fourth week at Wilderness, I began to prepare for the twenty-one-day trip we would make into Montana's backcountry. Excitement filled me as I made the necessary preparations. While others dreaded the unknown, I welcomed it. I wished to avoid emotion, not adventures. The stakes increased when I learned that my parents had signed a waiver of liability in case of injury or death. Growing up, my family camped, hiked, and explored many miles of wilderness in Washington and Oregon. I thought this prepared me for what I would soon experience. Those experiences gave me little advantage on this new adventure. I understood little of what backcountry survival entailed, especially in the context of therapy. Little did I know that going into the woods was intended to create an internal shift, one leveraged by physical discomfort, which would hopefully bring about the change needed for long-term recovery.

As part of my preparation for the expedition, I was asked to repel from the granite cliffs near the ranch. Repelling required practicing principles of surrender, faith, trust, and willingness. Although I felt excited to repel, I was unwilling to place trust in anything other than the ropes anchored to the rocks above. Watching the wilderness guides tie each knot, I felt relieved to not go first. Trust and faith are great concepts for those who cannot think for themselves. I would survive this experience as I had many others—applying caution and common sense. Placing faith in oneself seemed much better than placing faith in others.

I am not sure the Wilderness staff had ever seen a patient double check the ropes. I assured them that it would take me only a moment to inspect their work. "Being tossed off the cliff head first will only take a moment as well," quipped one of the counselors. I suspected they were joking, though they did not smile. When my turn came, I stepped off the ledge and felt I had suddenly gone against my natural instincts to survive. I demanded to be pulled back up. My heart raced. I surged with the power of adrenaline, felt at times of extreme danger and rage. Rather than pull me up, Joe, my counselor, urged me on. "Eric, you are capable of anything, even overcoming your fear." My senses sharpened and I began to yell with each successive spring of my feet against the cliff's face. "Screw you! Screw it all!" This was my way of letting go.

Just as the fear began to dissipate, Joe informed me that Jeremy would keep me from falling as I practiced a test of faith by letting go of my breaking device. I protested, holding onto the ropes, thereby keeping this other treatment member from controlling my fate. I liked Jeremy, but I definitely did not trust him to hold my life in his hands. I remained in defiance, parallel with the rocks below. Looking at Joe looming above me, and then the sky beyond him, my arms extended outward. I let go of the ropes in defiance and in so doing, let go of my fear of allowing others to help and support me. Joe shouted, "At the top of your lungs, shout one thing that has held you back, one obstacle that stands between you and a relationship with a higher power." Before I could think of something to get this guy off my back, my own voice escaped me, rising through tears: "Myself!" My voice cracked, echoing through the canyon, then inside my head.

The experience lasted no more than a few minutes, but it seemed like a lifetime. If I could live in the feelings created by that experience, I would die a humble man. I had again affirmed that, in an altered state of being, I found my greatest escape. I had discovered that altered states of consciousness were not always negative. I could create a natural state of euphoria that mimicked what I evoked using chemicals, and this experience produced far fewer consequences. I had unwittingly allowed others to hold my safety in their hands, something I had not allowed for quite some time. Although I still grasped for control, the hands of another ultimately held me as I embarked on a journey of faith. This experience was an unconscious attempt to regain my being from a life that had taken a desperate turn to the shadows.

The excitement mounted for all those who prepared to embark on the backcountry expedition. If all went as planned, we would cover nearly one hundred and twenty miles in twenty-one days. This may seem a short distance to the seasoned hiker, but for a group of five teenage boys with no confidence and a desire to be anywhere else, one hundred and twenty miles felt more like one thousand. We would sleep in tarp shelters and bring only the bare necessities. Changes of clothing were not an option, although at resupply we would be provided with essentials, including more food. We received gorp, beef jerky, and dry rations. We would forage all other food along the way.

Horns honked as the van moved down the long, ranch driveway. Well-seasoned staff and ranch workers simply went about their business as the cycle of treatment continued around them. To them a new batch, of drug-addicted young men, was going off into their backyard to be molded by the wilds. Some waived as a matter of course. To the passengers in the van, a new adventure had begun.

Montana is a place of sensual pleasure. We drove through the heart of The Swan Valley, an expanse bordered by mountains snowcapped in defiance of the changing seasons. As we drove, many slept, grateful for the opportunity. I did not. I allowed the beauty of my surroundings to transport me to a place where my thoughts slowed to a crawl. Though I had no idea at the time, I was practicing a form of meditation. In this place, I found the relief I had sought through chemical use. By silencing my mind, I found a place to which I would return in the days to come. Thought often dictates emotion. Thoughts have the power to guide a person into success or ruin. For many years, I had acted according to impulsive emotional outbursts; alternatively, I had engaged in emotional outbursts formulated to manipulate those around me. I followed this pattern in an attempt to gain control, to get something I wanted, or to protect myself from perceived danger.

Often I would think about a situation, allow an emotion to fester, and then act according to a set of rules I had unconsciously formulated throughout my life. As an abused child, much of my emotion became an attempt to push those around me away to avoid future injury. I could not be hurt if I were isolated from those who might pull a heartstring. As a consequence, I cultivated a long list of superficial friendships. I moved on a regular basis, therefore roots would not form. My grandfather, speaking of my need for constant motion, told me I had rabbits in my boots.

We arrived at our destination, the northern edge of Yellowstone National Park, well into the morning. The trailhead was alongside the Yellowstone River. In the nineties grizzly bear populations were quite small in Montana, but our guide left nothing to chance. He discussed bear safety and how to handle possible sightings. We carried no bear spray and our guide had no sidearm. This left me feeling exposed. Since my first night when Edwin shared stories of the bears, I had been apprehensive of the dark and surrounding woods, especially at night. I imagined Kenneth transformed into a bear, living among the shadows. Every forest sound was him.

Late in the morning, we began our journey. The first day served as a brief summary of what we would experience in the next twenty days. My pack was quite heavy, but I was able to handle it myself. Our guide, Glenn, had this down to a fine science. He moved constantly, assessing those for whom he was responsible. Joe followed close behind, urging those who already wanted to quit to continue.

Our first camp was a place of intense beauty. The moment I saw the peaks reflecting off of the river, every sore muscle gave way to jubilation. We had passed the point where most would ever travel, both in terms of our physical surroundings and our physical exertion. Most people would not give up life's comforts for the discomfort associated with entering the backcountry.

Something about hiking makes food, that would otherwise be subpar, a delicacy. We devoured our dinner and ended our evening group long before the moon made its grand entrance. Early spring in the mountains can be quite deceptive. A chill descends quickly once the sun exits behind the curtains of the Rocky Mountain peaks. Unlike places void of a rocky spine, the sun does not linger in encore. Instead, the mountains usher it away allowing the creatures of the night to join the stars and the moon, sharing their sounds amid the evening's frostiness. The smell of river water is distinct, with an organic fragrance quite different from the smell of the ocean. I would have described it as stale had I not seen how clear the river was.

High above the ground and nearly a hundred yards away, we hung our rations in the trees out of reach of those who might steal it. Backcountry etiquette is based on common sense and a respect for the environment. Though bear populations were small, I felt convinced that bears surrounded us and could see us more often than we could see them. I figured that if I ended up in the intestinal tract of a grizzly, at least my suffering would end in a heap somewhere beautiful. This would make for a fitting end: becoming a pile of what I believed myself to be.

We practiced zero-impact camping and followed the "leave no trace" idea. This included using something soft from our surroundings in place of toilet paper. Digging a sort of cat hole to crap in seemed like no big deal; but using grass, leaves, or witch's hair left me feeling as organic as the river that we camped near. Zero-impact also means no fires, as fires leave rings that diminish the beauty of the surroundings and increase the risk of forest fires. This area had been ravaged by wildfires not long before, as evidenced by the charred remains through which we hiked for many days.

I felt in awe of the force of the fire that had destroyed such a place. Trees, countless years old, remained upright in their death. With death came life, and out of the charred remnants of a once green, lush forest, came shoots of grass, saplings, and pink flowers called Fireweed. Glen told us that many of the region's trees, like the Lodgepole Pine, had cones that are serotinous, meaning their seeds are released by an environmental trigger such as a forest fire. The resin coating seals the cones; an intense heat is required to crack the bond, allowing the seeds to release onto the forest floor.

Unhindered fire creates fear in most. Our natural response is to harness the flames and to seek control over its power. The notion of control appeared an obvious fallacy based on what I could see around me. Glen told us that wildfires served a natural purpose. "Fire clears the forest floor and allows growth that would not normally occur due to overcrowding. Although the surface is charred, below the surface the seeds which hold the key to the forest's regeneration spring forth life unhindered and untouched." Glen seemed to hold all of nature's secrets deep within; he had answers for the many things I asked him. Even when I thought I had him stumped, he would come up with some explanation as to why something behaved as it did.

The forest taught me many lessons as I looked beyond the distractions of my own self. Comparing what I saw to my own life, I realized that the things that had ravaged me were not powerful enough to destroy the wilds of my soul. I began to understand the fundamental pattern of my spiritual being. Like the seeds of the Lodgepole Pine, the intense heat and destruction had given more than it had taken. The seeds of myself burst from the limbs of the ancients then fell to the forest floor in preparation for a glorious reunion of old and new. Though the charred remains of a child stood lifeless aboveground, the seeds deep within remained untouched by the fire. Those seeds waited to spring back to life given time, patience, and nourishment. Even one of the most powerful forces on Earth could not end the cycle of life that surrounded me. Rather than destroying me, it enhanced me. This was a profound realization. A full understanding would require further exploration in the years to come. As a fourteen-year-old seeking to understand why life burned so hot, the regeneration of the forest gave me reassurance.

Could this renewal be applied to abuse and life's various tribulations? Are we born into the physical world to experience the good with the bad and the light with the shadows? Are the things that we wish to avoid the very things that we must embrace to move beyond the physical and into the spiritual? A person should not start the fire. Rather, I believe that a person should be as brave as the forest, standing firm to embrace the natural cycle of life in preparation for what lies ahead.

In my use of substances and pursuit of sexual gratification, I ran from the fire, fearing its fury. I did not realize my avoidance diminished the natural process of cleansing and growth that comes from perceived destruction. I did not escape the flames; I simply postponed them. It is a spiritual law that pain is inevitable; it is as necessary as joy.

In the backcountry, our days blended as the schedule of one day mirrored the next. Our mornings consisted of breakfast, morning meditation, then packing up a camp that had just been unpacked hours before. Joe and

Glen charted our next move with the leader of the day. They discussed possible water sources and camp spots. I offered up silent prayers without any knowledge that I was doing so. Every time a thought entered my mind then exited, I was praying. When I thought of my family, I attached the feelings of freedom and love evoked by the intense beauty of my surroundings; in doing so, I blessed them.

Motivation levels varied from day to day. A plan of action was set in place to get everyone onto the same page. Joe and Glen addressed the shifts in mood of those around me. I felt grateful that I did not dislike being there as much as the others, for their disgust seemed a miserable way to spend twenty-one days. Although I handled the journey well, I was not so naive to believe that I had the skills necessary to escape the backcountry on my own. Whether I realized it or not, I was practicing a form of faith by trusting Joe and Glen. They were kind men who made me laugh. I tested them to the best of my ability. Both showed a level of knowledge and understanding that made me feel more comfortable than I had felt in quite some time.

Ten days into our trip, a string of mules carried in new supplies. Larry, from the ranch, led the team. Montana seemed built around him. I admired Larry's quiet wisdom. He didn't have to talk a lot to be heard; one of his words held as much value as a hundred words from a 'babbler.' As the mules nibbled the grass, I considered the days remaining. I felt unsure of my three-day solo. A few of the guys bragged that it was no big deal, but I had been around people in compromising situations enough to see the fear. "I am not scared of anything that's in these woods!" This overused mantra did little to reassure those who puffed out their chests while they said it.

For thousands of years, tribes have used vision quests to prepare their young for adulthood. It is believed a spiritual shift takes place away from perceived protection and distraction. For my solo, I received a tarp, basic food rations, writing materials, a poem about God, and a change of socks. To say I was not fearful or intimidated would be a lie. I would remain alone, in the middle of nowhere, for seventy-two hours. I had never grown out of being afraid of the dark. If anything, I had grown more afraid as I came to understand the dark more intimately. Even though I understood that those who had hurt me could not get to me here, the night still gave me a fright that I could not shake no matter how many prayers I offered to the stars above.

The packet of treatment work consisted of the poem and papers called a "personal inventory." This was the fourth step in treatment. Leaning back against a tree, surrounded by wildflowers and grasses, I began to read the poem.

You weep for your childhood dreams that have vanished with the years. You weep for your self-esteem that has been corrupted by failure. You weep for all of your potential that has been bartered for security. You weep for all your talent that has been wasted through misuse. You look upon yourself with disgrace and you turn in terror from the image you see in the pool. Who is this mockery of humanity staring back at you with bloodless eyes of shame...?

I could not or would not continue to read it. How was it that this prayer had been written just for me? I felt warm tears run down my face. It seemed as though the author of my betrayal looked upon me from a distance. Was this some joke?

"I want to go back," I protested as soon as I saw Joe. I knew that he would want to remain unseen, so I found where the grasses had been beaten down over previous solo checks then awaited his return. "I don't want to do this anymore. I want to go home. I quit." The words stung as badly as the tears touching my cracked, parched lips. "Eric, if you quit now, you will never experience the miracle of self-searching." The fourth step said, *fearless and searching moral inventory.* I was not sure I could do either. The things I had been asked to dredge up promised to bring back the nightmares, and I was surrounded by shadows at night. Joe had never met Kenneth or Marlene. He had never seen the shadows rise from the grates of the city and manifest themselves in the soulless that preyed upon the innocent. I had. I would not invite them back into my life, even through the written word. Joe's words, as if reading my thoughts, came in waves of empathy.

"My life was consumed with fear before I inventoried and faced the things that scared me. I had been abused, rejected, and spit out by those I loved and trusted. I see in your eyes a boy much like myself who has carried burdens no child should have to carry. You cannot hide from those who have also lived through the horrors of abuse. In disclosing the things that fracture our souls, we find what we need to mend them. We need to move beyond punishing those who have betrayed us, as well as our own poor choices." I was not convinced of Joe's theory, but I believed he understood what I was experiencing.

"Would you like to say a prayer with me?" Joe asked. "A man who is very important to me once prayed this prayer when I was afraid and uncertain?"

Feeling I had nothing more to lose, I agreed to join Joe in his prayer.

"God, hear my prayer and let my cry come to you. Do not hide from me in the day of my distress. Turn to me and speedily answer my prayer. Eternal God, source of healing, out of my distress I call upon you. Help me sense your presence at this difficult time. Grant me patience when the hours are heavy; in hurt or disappointment, give me courage. Keep me trustful in your love. Give me strength for today and hope for tomorrow. To your loving hands I commit my spirit when asleep and when awake. You are with me; I shall not fear."

His prayer was beautiful; I could not stop the words that fell from my mouth. I had been flushed from the brush much like Michael had.

"I was raped when I ran away from my home before I came here. I can't sleep through the night without being high. I can't look into the darkness of night without thinking the man is there, even though I know he couldn't be. My nightmares wake me. I scream into the darkness, thinking I am being dragged away to be raped again."

I waited for Joe to turn away from me in disgust. Instead, he reached out and brought me into his arms. I could feel his tears on my forehead. I had rarely felt so safe or relieved.

"That was a Jewish Prayer for healing," Joe told me. "A friend taught me when I told him that I had been abused as a young man. I, like you, told him the very things that kept me closed off from those who could help me. Through faith in the recovery process, I was able to move beyond my experiences. You'll recover, too, if you don't sink back into yourself. No matter what you think, your trauma is written all over your face. It will make you as hard as the rock we're sitting on if you don't remain open."

We sat on a slab of stone half-submerged in the stream. As the sun fell behind the mountains, an eagle appeared.

"Do you see that?" Joe asked me. "It is your spirit, soaring and riding the wind. It is not controlled by the wind.

You must do the same in your life. By surrendering, you will use your spirit to your advantage. By remaining rigid and fighting, you will be blown in any direction it desires. The winds are neither good nor bad, they simply are— much like your past experiences. You will either use those experiences to your advantage, or you will let them drive you from what sustains you."

In that moment, the eagle dove and brought out a trout, carrying it to a perch far above us. I watched in awe as it tore flesh from bone. In time, the bones were stripped, then the eagle soared high into the sky, carried by the wind.

Over the remainder of my solo, I wondered how nature could have met my prayers and pain so perfectly. My pen flowed freely as I wrote my inventory and filled my journal. It no longer seemed impossible to explore the events that had made me who I had become. Joe had shown me that, despite my fear, I was capable of facing the many difficulties of my life. I could move beyond them and soar like the eagle. I had entered Wilderness Treatment Center a boy and left a young man. I saw things quite differently than before coming to Montana. Beyond the darkness I could see light.

8

THE EXCITEMENT OF MONTANA REMAINED with me following my return to civilization and all of its pressures. My mother followed through with her portion of my aftercare plan, sending me to an island outpatient treatment center. Marcus opened Intercept on the island in 1991. He'd been the director at New Beginnings when I attended. When the staff requested that I attend a few more weeks to deal with further issues, our health insurance provider declined payment. My parents could not cover the extension, so Marcus said they would try to find additional funding elsewhere. Remaining true to his word, Marcus found the money, and I was funded for the extended stay. When my mother found out that Marcus was the owner of the new outpatient program, she offered to volunteer at the center in gratitude for what he had done for our family.

As it turned out, Marcus needed the help, but my mother was not in a position to quit her job cleaning houses. The suggestion was made that she return to college to become a counselor. My mother responded that she did not have the time, the money, or the desire to go back to school. Marcus saw through her hesitancy and offered to pay for one class. If she did not like it, he said he would never bring it up again. My mother loved her class. As a result, she went back to school, continued cleaning houses, and completed her counseling internship all at the same time.

My recovery seemed contingent upon the recovery of others in my peer group. Adolescent recovery is often a minefield in which any number of variables can lead to hard-earned freedom from use or the disaster of relapse. I was easily pushed in many directions. One of my greatest struggles in recovery was how to enjoy a social life while avoiding social situations that might compromise recovery. Kids in my age group used chemicals. In my biased view, I believed that the only way I could socialize with them was to use with them. I could not picture a social life that did not incorporate the use of social lubricants like alcohol.

The mind of the addict tends to paint the world in generalizations. This is especially true when addicts wish to convince themselves that self-destruction is a sound course of action. *All my friends use. No one understands recovery. I'll never have any friends if I am sober.* I believed that maintaining my social life justified the self-destruction brought on through chemical use. In my eyes, my social life took precedence over all else, even continued abstinence.

I believed that to be like other kids, I had to do what they were doing—despite the consequences I had already suffered, and despite the knowledge I had gained attending two treatment centers. My list of justifications to rationalize continued use began to grow longer: my parents, abuse, and now social disconnect. I needed these excuses. Without them I would be forced to see that others had not created my problem. It was I.

Spending time with other recovering kids carried me through several months of recovery. The island had joined the movement of the nineties; adolescent treatment was in full swing. I found myself surrounded by kids experiencing the same lessons around use that I experienced. We joined in a waltz of abstinence and relapse, dancing together, circling, turning, and struggling to find our equilibrium after intense upheavals of emotion and circumstances.

As one kid came to group to discuss recovery, the next sat, eyes to the ground in disappointment over a failed drug test. As one came clean, another would offer experience to help them further along. A kid offering advice one week might be the one receiving advice the next. A month of clean time seemed like an eternity. A kid who'd been clean for several months became a recovery guru to the rest of us.

Influence has many currents; it can push a person closer to shore or pull them further away. By the end of my eighth-grade year, I had finished aftercare and attended a recovery support group as a means to stay clean. Our home became the local hangout for kids in recovery. I do not blame my mother for what happened next. Faced with considerable odds, she did what she had to do to support us and improved our lives in the process. She could not be at four places at once, though it sometimes seemed like she could. She sacrificed a lot to gain very little. Although I felt proud of what she was doing, my mother's new vocation as a chemical dependency counselor, threatened my behavior and my use of chemicals. There were many days during this time when my only contact with my mother was hearing her yell from down the hallway, asking for quiet so that she could study or sleep. We would go quiet just long enough to deflect her attention, then we picked up where we had left off.

After the separation, my brothers and I were given the choice to live with our mother or our father. All three of us chose to stay with our mom. Doing so meant that we remained in the home where we had grown up. My father moved into a house about a mile up the road, but it could have been a thousand miles given the minimal time I spent with him. We were able to spend as much time with him as we wished. My brothers took him up on the offer a great deal more than I did. My resentment had created a rift in our relationship; my teenage stubbornness widened that gap yet further.

Although my father and I had our problems, I didn't allow those problems to keep me off the ball field. I picked up where I had left off and played my last year of baseball. What had been a relationship of affection in my early years became icy; my father's authority became a target of my anger. This played out publicly. The other players watched in silence as I raged at my father on the diamond. I told him that he was harder on me than the other boys simply because I was his son. He worked to keep his composure despite the great pain and disappointment that he must have felt.

As my anger grew, the last thing that had brought us together—our mutual love for baseball—ceased to exist. The sand of the diamond and the grass of the outfield seemed to degrade and become a dust bowl as our personal struggles progressed. Our bond diminished. He understood that any control he once exercised as a parent and coach had faded, and then disappeared. "Get off of the field," he told me. "You are finished with practice." I was finished for good. He had tried to rebuild our relationship, but I had begun a pattern of trying to pay him back for his betrayal in any way that I could, even at the expense of my own dreams.

I have very little knowledge of my father's involvement in the lives of my brothers. I built a wall of defiance, rage, and isolation that kept him from playing the role he wished to play in my life. Blaming his new wife for my parents' divorce, I kept my distance and never tried to know her. I never tried to know her.

This was a difficult time for us all. We each sought our place in the new dynamic of our family. The process was not smooth. My poor behavior did not stop when I returned to the island; instead, it grew more intense. My angry outbursts became more savage. I went from reasonable to unreasonable in the blink of an eye. My bedroom walls took the brunt of my physical abuse. At times, I would scream at my mother or anyone trying to give me direction. My unresolved issues fed my rebellion, and I began a new pattern of parental and authoritative abuse.

Anger holds the power of intimidation. It is a raw emotion that elicits a different response from person to person. At that stage of my life, most people tried to avoid my angry outbursts rather than confront them. One yell led to a louder yell until the issue at hand was forgotten. Later on I experienced what being a victim of this kind of anger felt like. I stood in the shoes of those against whom I had raged, and I did not like how it felt. As a teen, anger gave me a sense of euphoria. I felt an adrenaline rush during angry outbursts. I felt powerful. This became another paradox in my life. My loss of control provided a sense of power. I knew how each outburst would end. My actions were not always conscious decisions; at times, I made decisions driven by habit. The euphoria I felt from loss of control was just another drug I could add to my arsenal to use as both defense and offense against others. The fight-or-flight instinct provokes a powerful set of emotions.

Those emotions have the power to bind those who abuse them, knowingly or inadvertently.

The abuse of my early years, which had finally surfaced in treatment, produced a well of rage and shame that could not easily be addressed over sixty days in treatment. The kinds of emotional problems that I was experiencing would have been better dealt with in a long-term treatment center for adolescent abuse victims. No one can be blamed. One cannot find a solution if one cannot identify the problem. Most people believed that the recovery groups were intended to solve all of life's problems. In many ways, that was true. My issues had been attributed to the disease of addiction. Thus, the solutions provided focused on addiction alone, but they did nothing to address my other issues.

It's easy to look back and talk about "shoulda, woulda, coulda's." I know that my parents and friends made their best attempts to help using the resources available to them at the time. How could they have known that along with addiction, I suffered from a set of emotional problems and chemical imbalances that would escalate my issues surrounding drug use and abuse?

I began to jog great distances. One of my mother's friends, who mentored me for a short time, introduced me to the world of endorphins. I ran on the island roads thinking about my life and feeling grateful for the numbing effect of the natural chemicals. I ran the equivalent of many half-marathons on wet asphalt, my tears blending with the drizzle. It was easy to view the disease from which I suffered as a moral issue because the aftermath was always treated with consequences. As I internalized this belief, the resulting rage propelled my body mile after mile. It was as though I could earn back what I had lost through physical exertion. I raced towards a finish line that would never appear.

As a teenager, I personalized every rebuff, keeping a silent tally in my head. Every sideways glance and every negative comment added to the poor perception I had of myself. The frustration, distrust, and disfavor felt by others as a result of my actions justified my low self-worth and negative self-image. I continued to act out attempting to match my behavior with the way I felt about myself. I simply could not win.

I believe I passed the eighth grade because the faculty at my middle school had simply had enough. I had fallen so far behind in my studies that I should not have passed. Aware, I felt grateful to be going to high school. Sadly, this victory would be short-lived as this was the last grade I would complete.

My everyday pursuits reverted to drugs, alcohol, girls, or any other means to create excitement. I did not let financial limitations restrict my behavior. I became quite thrifty at resources. I stole from my mother, father, brothers, neighbors, strangers, and even stores.

During the summer, tourists traveled to the island aboard yachts, while many local families left to summer elsewhere. As a result, many resources were left unattended. The thrill of stealing provided the same escape I found through chemical use. I spent the summer after eighth grade pursuing this rush and the inebriation it enabled. While others played ball or enjoyed the beaches, I became entrenched in addiction. All the things that I had found fulfilling in the past lost their appeal. I had progressed from an adolescent in the beginning stages of chemical addiction to an adolescent in the mid to late stages of addiction. Well beyond a loss of control, my life was dictated by sometimes subtle, and other times painfully overt, changes in the chemistry of the pleasure centers in my brain.

Death's timing is never good for those closest to it, yet for me, it could not have come at a worse time. When my great-grandmother died, my mother flew to Florida to attend the funeral. As usual, my friends congregated at my house to party while she was gone. When I could not find anything else, I used inhalants. They were easy to find around the house, and unless I got caught red-handed, my parents never knew. After huffing gas with my friends all day, I began to lose touch with reality. As my friends loitered in the yard, I pulled my father's loaded hunting rifles from the closet. For some reason, he had left them when he moved out. In my mind, the scene played out like a video game, my friends in the yard being a strange set of targets.

As I raised the rifle to begin firing from my mother's bedroom window, Joseph screamed. "He's pointing a gun at you!" I fired the gun once. My friends believed that my shot was directed at them, a reasonable assumption as I aimed the gun in their general direction. People ducked for safety. I turned the gun on myself. For the second time, my brother, Ryan, was forced to play the hero. He wrestled the loaded rifle out of my hands, potentially saving several lives. Minutes later, the police and an ambulance arrived at our house.

The hallucinations did not end right away. As the ferryboat made its way across the water to Seattle, the island looked to be coming closer rather than receding from view. I was strapped to a gurney and feeling agitated. I knew that the only way I could relieve myself of the discomfort was to get loose and dive into the depths of the ocean. As I attempted to un-strap myself, I felt the warm waves of sedation roll over me. I no longer needed the cold waves of the ocean. I had been given something much better. As my eyes got heavy and my body relaxed, I imagined never again waking from sleep. All went black.

Waking felt like punishment for the havoc I had created over the summer. Death would have been merciful considering my circumstances. Fairfax Hospital did not compare to Wilderness Treatment Center. I had entered the world of the insane—the chemically imbalanced. Despite my arguments, the staff reassured me they had not brought me to the wrong place. I was told that I had to be there for a standard, seven-day evaluation. Based on the results, I would either be sent home or sent elsewhere for treatment.

There are times in one's life when it is best to put on a game face and play the cards presented. This was one of those times. I knew that if the doctors thought I would harm others, or myself I would be kept there longer. Fairfax was the last place I wanted to be. If I could convince them that the gas was the cause for my behavior, then I might be able to go home at the end of seven days. That was the course of action I chose.

Put through assessment after assessment, I answered each question in the way that best complimented my plan. I brought discussions back to my drug and alcohol use and my experiences at the treatment centers. When they questioned me about depression, I answered the opposite of how I felt. When they read off a list of symptoms, I lied about the majority. My one issue was minimizing my history of self-harm. I could not dispute that I had attempted suicide on two occasions. To my benefit, I had been under the influence of chemicals when I had done so.

In truth, chemicals were not the reason that I had tried to commit suicide, but I was not going to tell them that. Chemicals gave me the courage, or better yet, the lack of fear necessary to follow through with the act. They dulled my instinct to survive just enough to allow me to go against what we are programmed to avoid. People call suicide the greatest act of cowardice. Having attempted it more than once, I know that it requires either a great deal of courage or a great deal of chemical alteration. Either way, courage can be defined in different ways. Those who call suicide an act of cowardice most likely have never endured those experiences that lead to the act itself.

My thoughts of suicide had built up over time. In the months after I ran away, a dark cloud began to form over me. The only thing that saved me from that darkness was the use of chemicals or other means of elation. When the cloud gathered, I felt plagued by intense feelings of low self-worth and insecurity. I isolated myself and spent many hours under my bed listening to music and contemplating ending my life. This was a very difficult time. I struggled, for the emotion that haunted me was both justified and unjustified. This left me confused. As the self-loathing increased, so did my grandiosity. I began to run for days at a time, using, engaging in sexual encounters, and avoiding my family. The mix of these emotional and chemical binges inevitably ended in another trip to a treatment center or institution.

At Fairfax, I believed myself to be on to the doctors. I would not let them tell me that I suffered from depression. A young girl, who had also tried to kill herself, described to me the symptoms of depression. Though I realized that they fit, I chose to use her symptoms list as a guide to avoid that diagnosis. When I asked if she suffered from depression, she told me, "No, I suffer from not having enough drugs." I felt the same.

Up early each morning, I participated in every activity appearing charming and motivated. It was an attitude I exhibited only on the ball field or while attempting to score drugs. Despite the urge to run off, I pulled off a masterful performance and was released seven days after being committed. They diagnosed me with final-stage addiction. I felt relieved that they could not keep me locked up with this diagnosis. I had to be mentally ill to remain and I had done everything I could to disprove I had symptoms of mental illness, even those I actually experienced. It never registered to me that in lying about the symptoms, I acknowledged to myself that I experienced the issues for which I was tested. I had acknowledged my problem with chemicals. Though I had done so purely to manipulate my outcome, I had been honest about my use. I was an addict.

My father picked me up from Fairfax when I was released. I had seen very little of him in the days leading up to my episodes, but he was always there to pick me up afterwards. Teenagers suffer from a strange duality. They want to be freed from their parents but they also need their parents. At the time, I fought against my parents' involvement in my life. As a result, my parents entered my life in times of crisis. It was only then that they could insert themselves as legal guardians. Anytime they tried to intervene, I would act out emotionally or disappear to avoid having any relationship with them.

My freshman year in high school began with the excitement of a new experience. I played football and attended all of my classes. I felt committed to starting out on a good note. I even stayed ahead in my classes to avoid the shame I had felt before when I had fallen behind. Coach Goodman was my favorite teacher and coach. He never reproached me the way that the other high school teachers had. He coached as he taught: exhibiting the desire to bring out the best in his kids. To do this, Coach Goodman treated each of us as though we were critical to the team. He convinced us that despite our flaws, we were important in the bigger scheme of things. I left his lectures, and my time on the field, feeling like a better person. "Character," he would tell us, "is built on how we act despite our shortcomings. None of us are exempt from human nature. It is how we work with this nature that sets us apart."

I had a very different relationship with the other coaches. They lectured me on several occasions about my alcohol consumption and use of inhalants; they told me that those behaviors would not be tolerated. The coaches knew that I had been in treatment. I believe that I was the only player to be lectured before breaking any part of my sports contract. In reality, I was on athletic probation for having a reputation. Despite my desire to rage when placed under a spotlight, I held my tongue in an attempt to remain on the team.

I lived in a small town. In time the coaching staff found out about my visit to Fairfax Mental Hospital the previous summer, and before long, I was told I could not play football for the remainder of the year.

"Why?" I asked.

"Because you stole alcohol from a store this summer and were sent away for inhaling gas."

To my knowledge, the sports contracts were not retroactive. I had just signed mine a few weeks before. Since signing, I had lived up to the requirements described therein. I had stopped using drugs, alcohol, and even cigarettes in an attempt to be healthy for football.

Instead of my normal run back to the locker room after a great practice; I walked alone off the field, head down. I would never walk onto a playing field again. Humiliated, I had been cast to the shadows. Those charged with helping me to become a better person had given up on me. This experience exemplified sacrificing one to save many. Coach Goodman, on the other hand, taught that saving one empowered others to rise to their full potential. As opposed to football jerseys, the gift of his lectures could not easily be stripped away.

Nearly every practice, I vomited from extreme exertion. In every game, I left my heart on the field. Playing football allowed me to regain a measure of self-confidence, and for the first time in many years, I felt like a normal teenage kid. I felt free from my experiences. In sports, I had found a release from my pain, much like I did using chemicals. Rather than suppress my feelings, I dealt with them through exertion. My emotions fueled my desire to do the best that I could. For the first time in many years, I used my emotions to fuel success rather than allowing them to dictate my behavior.

I didn't fight against the politics that had removed me from the team. I believed that I deserved my punishment. I had grown used to feeling shame, so I did what came naturally. I left my dreams on the field along with the promises of many who had told me that sports would take me places. My dreams had been traded for a desire to use, which was far more powerful than any commitment I could have made. My resignation came from an understanding that the shadow within me would surface again. When that coach turned his back on me, my understanding was confirmed. I would become the best loser I could be; that would become my victory. Within weeks, I put myself in a position to be suspended from school. My drinking and drug use escalated, as did my self-destructive behaviors.

My freshman year reverted to a familiar state. I was once again a kid under the influence. I was constantly suspended and assigned detention. My obligation to attend a recovery class kept me from running away. Afterwards

I experienced brief relief, and then the inevitable return to use and depression. My life was in turmoil. One day I attended a support group, and the next day I passed a pipe with my friends. This pattern was indicative of chronic addiction. I used great quantities over short periods of time. I was a binge user.

Jail time became a part of my cycle through relapse and institutionalization. My brother, Ryan, was the victim of many of my adolescent misdeeds. I used his name to get out of trouble with the police, and I stole his car at all hours of the night to drive around with friends. One night when leaving a party, my friend Mario and I passed a cop. The cop turned immediately as a game of cat and mouse began. I had learned that the best way to dodge island cops was to turn off the lights and to avoid using the brakes while driving down side roads. This time I made a high-speed turn into a dark driveway and waited for the police to pass. My heart seemed to beat in my temples while I waited as howls of laughter ensued. In the past, my brother had threatened to call the police if I continued to steal his car. That night, Ryan followed through with his word.

I coasted down my street, pulling into the driveway in silence. The police officer, who we had outrun earlier, was parked in my driveway. I knew what would happen next. Mario ran. I often took the brunt of the consequences because I was so used to them. This made me feel like a hero, even though I stood in the driveway a thief. The officer read me my rights and arrested me for vehicle theft. I was taken to the island jail. I had never been arrested before. It was a humiliating experience. They used handcuffs more for show than for restraint.

The jail housed two barred cells. In one, an intoxicated man stared at me in silence then erupted in a drunken tirade. He had been in the process of wrapping his cell bars with toilet paper up to the ceiling while singing some Depeche Mode song. Midway through the song, he stopped and asked me what I was in for. When I told him that I had stolen my brother's car, he returned to his singing and wrapping. I heard little else when the song finished. He had completed his privacy wall just in time for the jailer to come rip it down. "If you continue to destroy city property," the jailer threatened, "I'll have you hogtied." The drunk fell silent. Soon I heard the soft, obnoxious gurgle of a sleeping drunk.

Over the course of the winter, my friends and I had been casing cars that slid into ditches during ice storms. We broke into the cars then stored their contents at my house. Eventually, island cops raided my home and the stolen property was returned to the owners. I received a citation for stolen property and vehicular prowl. The eighteen-year-old whose idea it had been received a more serious sentence. I faced over thirty charges for car prowl. As a result of stealing my brother's car plus the other thefts, I was sentenced to several months in juvenile detention.

There is nothing fun about being locked up. Once the thrill wears off, the day-to-day monotony begins. Inmates spend much of their time searching for ways to escape the boredom. My cell walls were covered with names and dates of those who had spent time staring at them. I added my own name. I had always used writing as a means to relieve emotional pressure. I added my part to the stream of sorrow expressed by kids experiencing the shame of societal separation. My literary graffiti confirmed my inclusion in the fraternity of the abused and the abuser. It is amazing how many words can fit on the walls of a twelve-foot by eight-foot cell.

The fear that I felt when I entered did not wear off. I saw the violence that broke out between the other boys. Though not a regular occurrence, it was quick and meaningful when it happened. The assaulter had little time to inflict as much damage as possible. I felt grateful that I was not the recipient of the beatings I witnessed. Silence and shadows would protect me. I learned a great deal from those around me and began to predict when things were going to happen. A properly placed question often disclosed more than constant prodding. Though I was no stranger to criminal enterprise, I was unfamiliar with extreme and irrational violence. I asked questions in an attempt to understand why people did what they did. If I could understand the thought process behind their violence, then I might be able to predict the next outburst.

My conversation with Marcus, a teenager two years older, felt light, relaxed, and free of the weight that often accompanied discussions concerning crimes committed. With an air of dispassion, Marcus described attacking an elderly woman during a burglary. I sat back, acting as if the violent description had no effect on me, He walked me through the events, which ended in a brutal assault with a frying pan. I remember laughing to divert the attention from myself. This would be the first of many moral compromises I would make to survive. I could not even begin to imagine what might fuel the type of attack he described. I could not imagine acting against another human in that way.

I had developed a reputation for being able to take care of myself. I held an undefeated record in wresting and had emerged from a couple of scuffles at school on top of the pile. My experiences in treatment centers and institutions added to the mystery, allowing me to bolster a reputation built more on legend than reality.

This reputation served me well in my attempts to manipulate and bluster. On the other hand, when challenged by those who wished to usurp my reputation, the stories worked against me. I had very little fear of the scrapes in which I found myself. On more than one occasion, I found myself hugging the person I had just been fighting. I did not like hurting others. My ego pushed me on like a cheering, bloodthirsty crowd. Then I would be left with my conscience and compassion, urging me to amend my wrongs as the crowd dispersed.

I knew that Marcus and I were on very different levels. Going with the crowd earned me a certain level of respect. Knowing that I would lose in a battle of brutality against most that surrounded me, I protected myself in the flock. I lived by the saying, "Keep your friends close and your enemies closer." While I despised violence, it exploded all around me. My survival required that I participate through assent.

After many weeks of detention, my departure felt awkward. Movement, sound, and color seemed different, of a different world. As the doors closed behind me, I felt a relief that only distance could provide. I felt grateful that a few of the detainees would never leave the confines of detention. I would never have to face them again. Every negative experience etched itself deep into my conscience. The images lived in me like a cancer, eating away at my moral fiber, and bringing me closer to the brutality and victimization I witnessed in others. The shadows were within, and without the balance brought by light and power through choice, they would grow to consume me.

9

I BEGAN TO GIVE UP ON THE VERY THINGS that might have helped me salvage a life dangerously out of control. My addiction, resentment, and failure to keep up in classes pushed me towards poor decisions. I maintained a false perception of how others viewed me. My own insecurity and unprocessed resentment fueled my drug use. I perceived authority figures as enemies, judging me on my past.

When approached by the vice principal for previous poor behavior, I lashed out and got kicked out of school. Breaking the social bonds of respect for elders gave me a sense of empowerment, especially when I felt disrespected by them. I believed that lashing out verbally preserved my reputation.

When my academics continued to slip, I chose self-sabotage due to the potential for embarrassment and disappointment through failure. My former academic and athletic success had once framed my identity prior to drug use. The loss of this identity destroyed my sense of self-worth. I was at a turning point. I could either put in the effort required to catch up and address my addiction and emotional problems, or I could continue on a path of self-sabotage.

North Kitsap High School was not far from the island. After registering me my mom said she could not guarantee being able to give me a ride every day. She could not, and would not, change her schedule to accommodate my needs. I had chosen to behave in a manner that forced me to go to another school. My mom was exhausted.

When I began at North Kitsap, I was clean for a time. I enjoyed the popularity that comes with being the new kid, though I had already established a base of friends there. I had played sports against many of the kids from North Kitsap. Longtime rivalries developed into lifelong friendships.

I had honored my friendship with Marti through abstinence, both chemical and sexual. She affected me in ways that only a true friend could. In our closeness, I felt safe from the side of myself that caused the most damage. A part of me wished to keep the purity of our relationship intact; for that reason, I had not used her in the way I had used others. With Marti, I backtracked to a time when, as I played catcher on the baseball team, my greatest priority was getting the attention of the girls on the bleachers. Marti seemed to admire me in a way that I could not admire myself. In her fondness, I could almost believe in what she saw. This type of relationship had been rare for me. The absence of sexual contact reflected my deep respect for her. When we held hands, I felt fulfilled and content in a way I had not previously experienced.

Though I was sexually driven and used sex as a form of escape, I was not incapable of loving others. I could respect the lines others drew with regard to sex. At times, I pursued healthy and morally sound relationships with women. Those times were always characterized by my abstinence from drugs and alcohol, as well as my pursuit for emotional balance through therapy and recovery groups. I found intimacy with others to be easier in a state of chemical alteration. Otherwise, intimacy felt awkward and nearly impossible. Much of the awkwardness stemmed from the sexual abuse I had experienced; but some was simply a result of my age and feeling uncomfortable in a maturing body. Intoxication removed my inhibitions and allowed me to exhibit behavior that was otherwise uncommon to me.

Some of my fondest memories are of times I spent with Marti. She had shown a tender heart from the beginning. We met in grade school at the skating rink. As years passed, our friendship developed until Marti became a welcome reprieve from the dysfunctions of my life. Sitting on the edge of the dock, we dipped our feet in the water and I felt safe from the things that haunted me. The laughter we shared is what I remember most. We exchanged kisses, held hands, and passed notes full of secrets and drawings. I remember touching toes in the water and feeling perfection in the sweetness. In many ways, a lasting love and respect had formed in the innocence regained—not lost.

Marti helped me feel normal. The pressures of my life could not touch us; our friendship provided insulation and protection. I chose not to use around Marti for fear that I would lose her from my lack of control. I knew that if my other life infiltrated this oasis, I would have to leave and she would never be allowed into my life again. By protecting Marti, I also protected the part of myself that remained tender and compassionate. The self I believed to be tainted by abuse, sexual assault, poor choices and consequences, loomed like a shadow waiting to appear. I was afraid I could not survive a fall from such heights. My denial was an act of self-preservation.

Marti's mother did what she could to protect us from ourselves. She did not show concern when we spent time together. Instead, she expressed her boundaries and expectations openly. I never felt judged by her, and a result, I respected her expectations. I did not feel challenged in the ways I had felt challenged before. She never approached me with finger pointing and contempt. I did not feel I had to protect myself from her authority. Marti reflected her mother's kindness.

The innocent moments shared by teenagers are often those carried in our memories the longest. I remember sneaking into the woods for my first kiss. I attended my first dance in the sixth grade and felt the female form as it touched my own in an awkward embrace. I remember holding hands in the darkness of Lynnwood Theatre, ignoring the movie as the other girls giggled and spread news of the exchange. These innocent moments allowed me to come of age and reclaim what had been taken from me at such a young age. Of course, such moments of intimacy were interrupted by the residuals of sexual abuse. I did keep a portion of my innocence. I am grateful that no matter the circumstances, a portion of my intrinsic self remained. I look back at those days and feel grateful for such memories. Because Marti and I maintained certain boundaries, I gained more from our relationship. I learned more during that first dance than I ever did through climax. Through pink cheeks and maturing bodies, I learned about the wonder of creation and the power of attraction.

My time at North Kitsap started well, but many of my previous issues resurfaced in no time. I was unable to get to school consistently and was issued tardy slips on a regular basis. My academic frustration continued as I struggled to complete the assignments I was given. I should have been held back a grade to catch up, but for some reason, there were no safety nets for kids in my position. In truth, I am not sure it would have made a difference. I began using again, which precipitated giving up on my studies and many friendships. In so doing, I traded possibility for known torment.

An altercation with one of the teachers at school eventually led to being expelled. In front of a group of cheering peers, I had shouted, "Fuck you and your smug attitude!" I did not have the self-respect or impulse control to ensure keeping my mouth shut when tempted to lash out. Feeding my ego and maintaining a certain reputation far outweighed the necessity of staying in the good graces of faculty. The argument served as the perfect opportunity for me to exit on my terms, much like I had on the island. Again, I sought control through defiance, which ultimately resulted in a loss of control.

If I have not said it enough, I will say it again: the moment I place chemicals of any kind into my body, I experience a spiritual shift that changes who I am as a person. I regress spiritually, morally, emotionally and physically. I barely resemble the person I was before use. Consider Doctor Jekyll and Mr. Hyde. Many of the behaviors I exhibited in the throes of a binge, do not surface while I am in recovery. While intoxicated, I have stolen, lied, and thieved. My conscience will not allow me to engage in such acts when I am clean.

I became more than uncontrollable. What little control my mother had possessed disappeared. Our relationship consisted of screaming at one another and generally ended with a slamming door as I left on another binge. I cannot begin to understand the frustration she must have felt watching her son self-destruct so rapidly. I lost all reason as a result of my use. My ties within the community, those intended to help guide me, had been severed.

I followed no schedule and rode the tide of chemical use from parties to drug houses all over Seattle and the Kitsap Peninsula.

One of my many binges brought me to my friend Sara's house. Her mother kept a large bottle of codeine pills, which we mixed with alcohol and marijuana. Though Sara did not have a license, her mother was not home and Sara had her car keys.

The sky reflected off the wet pavement. As we raced towards the curve, I could tell, even through my blurred perception, that we would not make the corner. We slid sideways down an embankment, towards a tree. My last memory is sliding unhindered to the far side of the back seat. My head took the brunt of the force as I hit the window and the tree that stopped us.

Sara cried as I was carried into the ambulance to be taken to the island clinic. Given the condition of the car, a severe concussion and mild bruising seemed a mild trade-off for what could have been much worse.

Whether by chance or divine intervention, I was alive. Once the codeine and alcohol wore off, I felt both gratitude and disappointment. This duplicity may be difficult to understand. I was stuck between a desire to be clean and an obsession with using. My life felt like reading a tragedy. You have no power over the story's flow, yet you can see the final scene.

I was told I had to return to treatment. This left me feeling relief and desperation. I had been in a treatment facility twice over the previous two years. On each occasion, my stay was justified by a progression of the disease, the consequences of use, and a fear for my physical safety. Because my mother was unable to assert her authority, she was again forced to send me to an institution. The accident was the final straw. It had become clear that

I would absolutely not be able to quit without being institutionalized.

There is a misconception that treatment facilities are in the business of making large sums of money off of their patients. In reality, treatment centers have a small margin of return. Facilities are full of individuals who do the kind of work that changes and saves lives, yet their pay will never reflect such efforts. Included in their compensation is the understanding that they have salvaged a life ravaged by a disease. These people are angels on Earth, and they live for the well-being of others.

I spent thirty days at Olympic Center. Although I complied with their requests and showed a halfhearted desire to remain clean, I did not do the work necessary to continue my recovery. I had suffered enough consequences to justify abstinence, yet I did not have the desire to make abstinence bearable.

The work I did in groups and with my counselor reflected a practiced approach to therapy based on previous treatment stays. When I talk about work, I am referring to discussion of the root problems of my use, such as sexual abuse, shame, and depression. I needed to address a long list of liabilities to be freed from their grip. I did not know where to begin to initiate real change. I did not understand that every relapse reinvigorated the shame and abuse felt previously. My past combined with more recent issues made treatment that much more challenging.

I finished my time at Olympic Center and left with little progress. I returned home, remained clean for a short period, and then returned to using—much to the horror of those who had worked so hard to help me.

A great tragedy comes from watching someone suffering from a terminal disease invite sickness back into their life. Having watched with hope as their body began to heal with life returning to their eyes, one's faith in the Creator multiplies leaving an appreciation for the gift of watching this spiritual transformation. So much of what had been gained is lost when regression enters. Such is the experience of recovery for those on the front lines. Nobody likes to watch a tree die; yet in its decay, many on the forest floor are nourished. It is the same in recovery.

Back at home I had to work much harder to hide my use. This ushered in a new era of dishonesty. I had never liked lying to my mother. Furthermore, I was never very good at it. Along with dishonesty came my resentment that she allowed my brothers to use while living at home. I did not understand how a parent could get away with abandoning one child under the pretense of being code-pendent no more.

Parents are responsible for their children regardless of the circumstances. At this time tough love perpetrated a feeling of abandonment. It didn't make sense to me that boundaries should be drawn. In many ways tough love can be viewed as abandonment if basic necessities are withdrawn for the child; it creates more problems. Eliminating my basic necessities forced me to meet my needs in other ways. This got ugly, especially when I looked to the using world to fulfill them. Boundaries may speed up the bottoming-out process, but at a great expense. Children do not always know what is best for them. Sadly, parents sometimes share this lack of understanding as well. Although healthy boundaries are necessary a balance of needs must be held into account as well.

As an added consequence, looking beyond the family to meet what they need enables the child to point fingers. He or she may blame outside sources rather than blaming the disease. I believed that if all social consequences—like my mother's boundaries—were eliminated, drugs would have never been a problem. I believed that the idea of addiction as a disease was created to control children like me, to keep them from enjoying the effects of use, though I had already proven the great flaw in this theory. With use came a set of unavoidable consequences that could not easily be blamed on others. They were physical, emotional, and spiritual consequences. Because my mother would not allow me to use in her home, I felt justified in leaving. My bitterness fueled a desire for vengeance through self-harm.

10

BY THE END OF MY FRESHMAN YEAR, I had given up petty theft in exchange for the lucrative drug trade. The way the trade is organized everyone from the top of the pyramid to the bottom is given an opportunity to fill his or her coffers. I was at the bottom in terms of quantity and capital. On the island, I was at the top because I had access to drugs that most could not get otherwise, and I had been at it longer then most of the other kids. With one phone call or a quick trip by ferry, I could acquire and then distribute drugs. While my childhood friends were enmeshed in their studies, I was locked in the progression of addiction. I entered a level of lawlessness that I had not known before.

Because of my connections in treatment, I met criminals active in other ventures. Their favorite hustle was infiltrating the suburbs. Though I would not describe myself as naive at that stage, I understood little of how the drug trade at this level operated. In my pursuit of drugs, I showed a level of fearlessness that enabled me to enter places that many would have avoided. Some might have called it insanity. Regardless, I was fueled by a hunger that could not be satiated.

The city and its wealth of resources were just thirty minutes away by ferry. I had numerous options to ensure a constant state of alteration. As in other parts of the country, the drugs found in the inner cities made their way to the suburbs where resources could be exchanged. With a shared understanding, both parties pursued their goal and the shadows emerged in droves.

I spent many hours in the apartment across the street from the high school, filling the pockets of numerous people with money. My role was to link the people on the island who had money with my connections in Seattle. Often, I assisted with transactions that made people at all levels of the drug pyramid, happy. My participation did not make me rich, but it did provide me with my basic necessities: cigarettes, alcohol, marijuana, and cocaine.

Peddling drugs gave me a false sense of power, elevating my sense of self. This made me feel like everyone's best friend, giving me the ability to manipulate the world around me. Drugs sold themselves. I simply had to play the part. To some, I was the hero; to others, the villain.

No one suggested recording the transactions. For most of us, it made little sense to do so. Logic is not evenly distributed. One arrest could place our whole hustle under the radar of local authorities. Logic is also lost when a false sense of pride outweighs right and wrong. Pete embodied this type of egoism. In placing his distorted view of himself above common sense, he revealed two networks of drug runners working the island and the peninsula. His parents caught him with drugs and a ledger full of transactions. They then turned him in to the authorities with everything they had gathered. Pete had recorded both sales and purchases with meticulous precision. The authorities began to round people up for questioning.

I happened to be in Pete's ledger, and when the police came for me, I was at the high school with several bags of pot and cocaine. The game of cat and mouse had finally caught up with me. It is not difficult to find someone on the island, and I was well-known given my previous run-ins with the law.

The police initially confused me with my older brother, Ryan, and had taken him in for questioning. Once they realized that I was the one that they were after, they had lost the element of surprise. When they found me, I had prepared a well-rehearsed line then discussed it with the others in my group. Adding to their frustration, I was unwilling to talk. I felt fairly certain it was against the law to question me without my parents present. When I brought this up, the interview ended and I was allowed to leave with the understanding that if I were ever caught on campus again, I would be arrested for trespassing.

My previous relationships, formerly quite lucrative, ended. Paranoia ran deep and my contacts from Seattle made several trips across the water to warn me against talking. They made a series of threats that left no doubt in my mind that I was in danger. Several men, guys I had not met previously, came to my house on two occasions, threatening to rape my mother if I talked. The third time, they told me how easily they could climb the telephone pole outside of our condominium and shoot one of my family members. The fourth and final time I saw these men, they drove me to the waterfront, threatened to shoot me, and then left me there in sheer panic.

For weeks, the blinds in our condo remained closed. My oldest brother, Travis, kept a baseball bat behind the door in case the men showed up again. When my family had finally had enough, they decided to move me to Florida.

Though my circumstances changed, I did not. Internal change does not come about through the reorganization of external circumstances. Change evolves through internal shifts produced by major emotional upheavals. Change is the result of consistent emotional and spiritual work. I had finally reached a point where I wanted to stop using to maintain the safety of my family.

As I waited for my departure date, I returned to recovery meetings to sit in a circle of chairs and listen for answers. I was an empty shell, longing for the changes such groups promised. I stared through those around me and into the surrounding walls. I had many disguises, none of which took away from my sincerity; instead, they erased any trace of the demons that lurked all around me.

Sadly, I continued to be haunted by the shadows. They tricked me into believing that they had the answers. The shadows mimicked what I sought in recovery, telling me I could only achieve the spiritual world through chemical use. These torments pulled me away from my attempts for emotional health, reminding me of the powers of chemically induced euphoria. The shadows mocked my every attempt to find serenity. My soul was torn in two.

11

AS THE JET FLEW IN THE ANONYMITY OF CLOUD COVER, I watched lights flicker from the towns below. The rain had begun hours before. I closed the window shade and tried to forget. If only things could be that easy. If only I could pull the shade on the storm of my life, then open it to an endless blue horizon. As conditioned as I had become to upheaval, saying goodbye to my life on the island was a painful moment. I never lost hope that relocation would make my life better. The problem was that wherever I went, I brought my problems with me.

The intense turbulence above Florida seemed fitting. I had met the southern half of my family on visits as a small child, but I didn't know them well. When they visited Washington, they seemed to be from another planet with their southern drawl and mannerisms. It was amazing how people from the same country could be so different in views and culture.

My uncles and grandmother greeted me at the airport. Love and affection was written all over their faces; they showed no sign of knowing my full story. As we drove home to Bradenton, an awkward silence replaced the initial adulation. I sat in silence, studying the faces of those who would be watching me from here on out. I felt unsure of everything.

My two uncles were my mother's half-brothers from her father's second wife, Shirley. They were southern in every sense of the word, and I could tell they were curious about having me in their midst. Tim was a skinny, dark-haired fellow with a hefty mustache. Terry, who was heavyset, reminded me of a Washington logger, minus the plaid shirt. Despite their dissimilar appearances, they were twins in every way. One would begin the sentence and the other would finish it.

My grandma, Shirley, loved her grandchildren as though that was her only purpose. Her kisses seemed to come from every direction. To receive so much attention made me feel awkward. "It is so good to have you, love," She said with a smile. I had grown accustomed to getting little to no attention; I could tell that would not be her style. I was disappointed to find out that I had to have a curfew and would be expected to follow the rules that she imposed. Her number one rule was that I would attend school and bring home good grades. In addition, she imposed a policy of zero tolerance regarding the things that brought me there, in particular drug use. She was adamant that I would not return to the same lifestyle and type of friends I had left back in the Northwest. "If you can accomplish these things, I will consider loosening the grip a little." My grandma ushered in a new world of root beer floats, glittering jewelry, and *The Golden Girls* on television.

I arrived in the summer and began taking long walks up the crushed-shell roads to explore my new world. My thoughts drifted to home and friends I had left behind. I soon realized that the best way to avoid the pain associated with many miles of separation was to forget about them completely. I began to live by the expression "out of sight out of mind" to avoid the torment of my memories.

It was not long before I met a couple of "good old boys". Brian was about my age. Danny was a year younger. We quickly established a friendship, and my summer filled with the exploration of this peculiar place. Water moccasins and lizards became our greatest foes. We honed our knife-throwing skills to eliminate as many as we could find. We took caution, though, as the water moccasin's bite is deadly. Had I known what lived in the murky depths of the streams and ponds we explored, I would have had second thoughts about following the boys into them.

Although my friendships with Brain, Danny, and others felt familiar, they were also quite different. I had not seen one person of color in the circles I ran with. My new friends acted as though anyone who was not Caucasian was subhuman. The neighborhoods in Bradenton were still separated, even though decades had passed since the integration of southern schools. I remembered stories my mother told me about school segregation when she was a child going to the same school I would attend. I found it strange that people could be separated because of their skin color. The idea seemed as foreign to me as types of abuses human beings in third-world countries endured. I remember feeling like black and white trenches had been dug by the past, and I was stuck behind enemy lines. The South was still heavily entrenched by years of fear and hatred.

Brian and Danny were good for me in some ways. They were adamantly against the use of drugs and alcohol. After drinking and running their mouths, they'd been badly beaten up by some African American boys. A related lawsuit had further divided the community, fueling the hatred that had been a part of their culture for so long. When most people think of Florida, they think Disney World and Busch Gardens. After living there, my notion of a postcard paradise with white shell beaches disappeared. Echoes of the past still rang out through old Dixie, dividing people through fear and ignorance. The people there seemed unwilling to allow the worst parts of their past to diminish, thus the better parts of their present could not take root.

I had experienced firsthand the convergence of past and present. "Tyrell is a nigger." The phrased came out of my mouth in kindergarten at recess. I had no comprehension of what the word meant, only that a relative who had visited from Florida the previous summer had used it to describe African Americans. He had used the word as though it was an acceptable thing to say. "I am not a nigger," Tyrell told me. "I am African American." Tyrell had been taught that the word "nigger" was a bad thing to say. I had had no idea. I learned a difficult lesson that day, one made more difficult after Tyrell kicked me squarely between the legs. My mom told me that I should have known better. "Have you ever heard anyone, besides your uncle, use that word before?" she asked me. Shamefully, I told her that I had not. The large bruise was a small price to pay, considering the damage that language had done to others. "Then I expect you never to repeat it," my mother warned me. "It is both unkind and offensive."

I had never experienced the type of racial separation I saw in the South. Back in the Northwest the islanders worked hard to provide a place where people exhibited respect for others. It was a place of rich history and deep roots. Families had worked together for generations, to overcome some of history's greatest challenges. This shared past created a strong racial bond, and the island flourished in diversity as a result.

This multiethnic community fostered an atmosphere of cultural respect and admiration. Apart from visiting relatives and what I learned through the media, I had never heard racial profanity. These types of verbal assaults were not accepted. In many ways I had little understanding of the power and deep loathing such words could provoke.

When high school began in Bradenton, I felt thrilled to break out of the neighborhood and to interact with people who had varying perspectives. Brian and Danny were my only friends, and although I was grateful for their friendship, I was more interested in developing relationships with those who honored diversity. Soon, I realized that racial divide also existed at Southeast High School. I decided that I would not be a part of it. I was excited to be around so many different nationalities: Haitians, Puerto Ricans, Peruvians, and Cubans. The prospect of new friends and experiences filled the hallways with possibility and promise.

Whenever I sat and talked with someone who was not white, I was given a hard time by some of the other white kids. By no means the majority, the portion of students who behaved as such made me feel like my choice to go against a social norm could catch up with me. When I asked why people felt so much distrust and opposition, I was told that things had always been that way. No one could put a finger on any specific cause. Once again, I felt like I was living in two worlds even though I was not using. To hang out with Brian and Danny, I had to remain quiet when they spoke negatively of others. By compromising my morals, I felt like I was dishonoring everyone I had ever cared for, those who had given me the gift of their differences. In silence, I took no stance at all, and in so doing, I approved their behavior. By not living up to the values with which I was raised, I was complicit in their hatred.

This was not easy for me to digest. In time, I realized that the majority of people I was around spoke in racial terms that I found offensive. In an attempt to be liked by them, I joined in on their jokes and laughed when I should have argued against them. I worked to reclaim my belief systems and myself. Because I didn't do so soon enough, I could not avoid the shame of going against them. In a selfish attempt to be accepted, I had dishonored my friendships with so many people I had come to know and love.

I remember feeling that it was unfair to be stuck in the middle of a debate that would ultimately make me look negatively on at least one group of people. Looking back, I understand why a culture of racial hatred has remained for so many years. The generational and social pressures associated with racial division are extreme. As I watched this play out, I gained a new respect for those who had sacrificed their lives and safety to fight for the freedom of others. I understood why my mother had recoiled from anything that resembled racial disrespect because she had to fight to eliminate it from her life. Standing up for my beliefs, I felt empowered by doing the right thing. Most people seemed to respect my stance—or, at least, to tolerate it.

I believe my grandfather was born with wrinkles and a guitar in his hands. After years of preaching and hard living he had retreated into the bottle. I often found him out on the porch playing songs, transported to another place and time. Though I did not know many of the songs he sang, I wished I could live in the ballads. As he sang, his eyes closed and I thought I saw tears fall. In these moments, he would tell me stories about my mother and my uncles.

He told me about chipmunk hats and drunken rides to the store on the riding mower. Although the stories were funny, I could sense that my grandfather felt a deep sadness when he spoke of my uncle Bill. I didn't understand it then, but over time I would piece things together. My mother had compared me to him at times, her nose turning pink with emotion. I sensed that seeing Bill in me sparked painful memories. It was as if she feared watching the same scenes play out in my life that had played out in his.

I noticed something peculiar about grandpa. When he was sober, he seemed uncomfortable and out of his element. He had grown so dependent on alcohol that he couldn't be comfortable—emotionally or physically—without it. He almost always had some sort of drink in his hand, and I found myself hoping he was half-drunk when I came to see him. It was not until a gloss of inebriation coated his eyes that I knew he would laugh and tell me, affectionately, that I had rabbits in my boots. I was grateful to experience my grandfather's fondness, if only for a short time. The rabbits he'd described would soon find their way back, and the songs on the porch would fade as I retreated to my own escape with eyes glossed over as well.

Laire had a gruff voice and a bowlegged walk that made me chuckle when I first saw him. He dressed like he was on an endless Hawaiian vacation. My uncle had dropped me off at a support group at Sacred Heart Church. Laire had approached me afterwards, telling me he would be my group mentor. "Anyone who can bullshit like you needs someone in their life who can bullshit better," he said. "I am that man." I liked that he swore a lot and smoked cigarettes that looked a half-foot long.

A retired Army Colonel, Laire had fought in the Korean and Vietnam wars. He had a no-nonsense attitude. Every time he dropped me off at my grandmother's following a meeting, he would ask, "Has anyone told you they loved you today?" "No," I would reply. "Well, I do." This made me uncomfortable at first, and then I came to appreciate it. In time, I realized that I wasn't going to the meetings just for the coffee and smokes. I spent almost every day with Laire, working my way through the suggestions of the group with his guidance. I did this out of respect and fondness for him. He had the qualities of a father, grandfather, coach, pastor, friend, mentor, and Colonel. He intrigued me. I began to trust him.

Though I was not using, many of my other behaviors remained the same. My relationship with my grandmother began to deteriorate. She would only allow me to go to Brian or Danny's house, meetings with Laire, baseball games, and school. When I asked if I could go to a Pearl Jam concert on a school night, she said, "Absolutely not." I became enraged. I am not sure why I told her to fuck off. Later, I wished that I had told her I loved her instead. Though I felt a great deal of remorse, it did not stop me from doing what I wanted. Eventually, she asked my Uncle Tim to watch me.

It was apparent that love and affection were not the solutions to my problems. I had disproven my own theory that abandonment was to blame. I continued to act out despite the love I received. My grandmother showed me a double portion of both love and affection, yet I continued to lash out at her.

Laire insisted that I create an inventory of past deeds, resentments, fears, and sexual conduct. He argued that doing so would lift a weight from my shoulders. The abuse I had exhibited towards my grandmother and my emotional deterioration made making an inventory necessary. I was given two weeks to complete it, though Laire appeared at the condo where I now lived with my uncle, a week early. I had the sneaking suspicion that he was more motivated than I was.

We sat in his red Mercedes on Bradenton Beach, watching the winds bend the palm trees. The power of the surging waves gave me the feeling that at any moment, I would be swept out into the churning waters. Although I had not taken the full two weeks, I had completed Laire's assignment and sat ready for his next suggestion.

I read him the list of things avoided for so many years. The experience reminded me of doing the same with Joe on the rock overlooking the river several years prior. With a hurricane approaching, the rain blew hard against the windows of Laire's car. My tears blurred my vision. He asked me about things I didn't want to tell him. In the trust we had built over several months, I practiced a level of honesty I had rarely experienced before. Laying the years of abuse I had experienced at his feet, I told him about Marlene, Kenneth, Becky, and my parents' divorce. I discussed the things I did while drinking that had created shame in my life. I discussed the many people I had harmed throughout my relapses and my search to be altered. The details flowed from me, and in so doing, a weight did lift, much like it had on my solo.

Laire told me, "In your addiction, you are just like this hurricane, but more powerful. You run through the lives of all those you come into contact with and do the same type of damage."

I cried, realizing that I had made many others cry as they watched me deteriorate. We read from several books and prayed. Laire told me that I would soon be starting the amends process, and that I should prepare myself through continued prayer for willingness. We ended our meeting with a hug and the standard routine: "If nobody has told you they loved you today, I do." In that moment, I realized that I loved Laire in the same way that I loved my father. My heart ached in a way that it had not since my parents' separation.

Living with my uncle suited me. I transferred to Manatee High, which seemed more accepting of others. Even so, I would attend this school only for a brief time, as I made all the wrong connections and returned to my old ways. It seems tragic to me now. Regardless of the support I received and my chance to start with a clean slate, I still returned to a place that had created so much pain for others and for me. I slipped back into duplicity rather than allowing the work I was doing with Laire to take hold. I practiced behaviors that turned my sincerity into hypocrisy.

This was one of many times I gave up on myself, compromising my beliefs and trading self-respect for shame. With one use, I exchanged happiness for misery, inviting the shadows back into my life. They don't always appear at once. Some move in slowly, ugly in form, a reminder of the existence of consequence.

Because my uncle drank regularly and was rarely home, it gave me the opportunity to live as I had in Seattle. I was free to come and go as I pleased, and this allowed me to use without fear of losing a home. This was a great relief. I still had to show that I was in recovery, but in time, this requirement also faded. My uncle began to spend more days at his girlfriend's, leaving the house open to me and my exploits: girls, marijuana, alcohol, and pills they called "trucker's speed." Trucker's speed had ephedrine in it, a potent stimulant that is used in the manufacturing of methamphetamine. It was very potent on its own and could be bought legally over the counter. At times, it was also called "cross tops," "Mr. Zogg's," in addition to various other names. Combined with alcohol and marijuana, these pills allowed me to feel something I had never experienced before. My whole body pulsated and felt as though it levitated. It felt like a constant orgasm without the release. The effects of it lasted for hours. My worries disappeared and the world took on a new hue. Cocaine had sometimes made me feel similarly, but never at the same level. The effects wore off quickly. I was hooked after my first use. In time, the pills would destroy my life, while telling me everything was just fine.

My days were filled with the white sand beaches and palm trees of Florida. The chemicals made me feel free. My friends at the time would load up in a Winnebago and travel inland to pick "purple haze" mushrooms from the cow pastures that lined the highway. We found it hilarious when farmers chased us off, with no idea why we would dig in piles of cow dung like kids on an Easter egg hunt.

Heading back to the beaches, we would make tea and spend the midnight hours tripping in the breaking of waves, watching patterns of seashells along the sandy shoreline. Again, I bonded with a social group focused on the use of drugs. In that bond, we held hands in the darkness like frightened children who gained strength through each other.

Although Shaun loved to take the speed pills, he recoiled when his older brother smoked crack. He said the habit turned his brother into an angry, paranoid psychopath. Their father had introduced them to the ins and outs of the crack world. When he went to prison several years before, he left Shaun's older brother in charge.

Though he was spared from foster care, Shaun was not spared from the strangers associated with his brother's addiction. I saw in Shaun the same pain of abandonment that I felt as a result of my parents' behavior. He spent many nights at my uncle's condo, crashing on the couch until his brother either ended up in jail or ran out of money.

In my own addiction, I crossed a line. Entering Shaun's brother's bedroom, I saw sunken, dark eyes staring back at me. A sweet aroma lingered as the butane lighters glowed and the cocaine sizzled and cracked in the rotating, glass pipes. In that moment, I left the relative innocence of beaches, mushrooms, and bong hits. I had entered a world of endless consumption. The faces that greeted me seemed to be telling me to run for my life. For most there was no return. The toll would be paid in flesh and innocence, a recurring theme in my relatively short life. Something shifted when I chose to enter that room. Abuse no longer felt like abuse. Instead, it became normal in my life; it served a purpose that it had not served before. Indoctrination lasted for the better part of three days, and it left me in the depths of a shame I knew too well. My only escape was further use. The spiral began anew.

Rather than suppress abuse, I now invited it into my life. The people in that room fed off innocence like vampires. I don't think it's necessary to explain what happened behind those doors to understand why it changed me. Every touch carried a thousand Kenneth's and a thousand Marlene's. I traded a shame I had endured for the better part of my childhood for a few minutes of a euphoria that surpassed anything I had ever experienced. In the rush of cocaine, I lived a lie, believing that my life was ok and that the sadness had gone. Each hit produced a chemical god in physical form.

Leaving the confines of the room, I entered a new world of the shadow walkers. Not only did they exist on the streets of Seattle, they walked the streets of Florida, where the promise of my new start had all but disappeared. My uncle had given me the keys to his van and a nine-millimeter pistol for protection. Previously, I had hid the gun beneath the seat of the van, doubting that I would ever need it. At once, my previous drug adventures seemed innocent. The areas I had been told to avoid were now my destination, and in the back of the windowless, work van sat several, eager crack-heads hungry for more rock.

This group of addicts had transitioned from users to criminals. Their plans confirmed that I was in way over my head. The idea of robbing dealers seemed insane. I had only ever used my uncle's van to drive to the beach with friends, to get groceries, or to take him to Key West to go scuba diving after he'd drank a case of beer.

The plan was to use me as bait to lure an unsuspecting crack dealer to the sliding-door side of the van. I appeared the least threatening and would not be able to manhandle anyone approaching the side of the van. The first several dealers we approached did not fit the criteria. They either had friends with them or no crack on them. Our offers to drive them to pick up more crack were turned down. Our methods were not new to the streets. The combination of an unmarked, white, work van and a young, clean-cut kid left many dealers uncomfortable. They feared a police sting. The dealers had no idea that our intent was much more sinister. Adding to our difficulty, intricate networks had been established to protect both the street-level dealers and their suppliers. Many of these networks proved invincible.

Who knows how many attempts we aborted, but in the early hours of the morning we picked up an unsuspecting teenager. His indoctrination was quite different from mine. He was severely beaten, his pockets emptied of several hundred dollars and enough crack to fuel our party for a couple more days. I found violence appalling, yet in the throes of a crack binge, things that I would have avoided otherwise became possible and even justified. This both horrified and excited me, as my uncle's nine-millimeter sat on my lap with the hammer pulled back; cold hard steel in contrast to my warm pink hands.

When we arrived back at the apartment, Shaun was waiting for me. After exchanging tense words, Shaun grabbed me. I could see the pity and anger in his eyes. I had run towards the very thing that he was running away from. In so doing, I had chosen what he despised and feared most, I vaguely remember feeling remorse for abusing Shaun in this manner. In his attempt to rescue me Shaun showed a depth of character far beyond my own. Though I had betrayed our friendship, he remained true and extricated me from something of which I knew little and which he wished to know less.

In the weeks that followed, we agreed that I would not go to Shaun's apartment again. When the urge to use crack arose, which it did on many occasions, we would appease that urge with pot, alcohol, and trucker's speed. We believed this to be a justified pursuit. Those involved with these lesser evils spent their time loitering on the beach and chasing girls, rather than kidnapping drug dealers. The pulls to use other substances were subtle in comparison, yet they accomplished much the same thing. In every drug lives a separate personality. By choosing pot over crack, we hoped to produce an outcome far better than those experienced by crack-heads, wandering the streets with burnt fingers and white lips.

Again, my addictive behaviors would prove this type of thinking flawed. I did not understand that while each substance had unique characteristics, I would not benefit from those differences. The type of chemical used was not the problem. The biology of the addict was the problem. For me, any mood-altering chemical produced the same life altering and damaging effects as crack. My body, mind, and spirit reacted the same way to all chemicals. No drugs could be referred to as less-addictive drugs considering my addictive behavior.

In the months that followed, I realized just that. In a dulled panic, I saw these softer drugs had the same hold on me as crack. I could not stop using. The voices of those in recovery and treatment rang through my head, chanting the mantra of powerlessness and unmanageability. I had cared little for their introduction into my psyche. The desperation of those who knew and loved me began to make sense. I felt like I was on a bridge looking down into dark waters that had claimed so many before me. I realized that I had begun to live in the moments after the plunge. I had passed beyond the point of no return. I inhabited a place where nothing could bring me back into the arms of those who had tried so desperately to pull me away from the railing.

More than once, my uncle reached out to Laire and asked him to intervene. I vaguely remember Laire grabbing me by my shirt collar, inches from my face, pleading and pointing at the heaps of passed-out kids I barely knew. He did not beg; instead, he made his case and then went silently, waiting for my reply. No matter how hard I tried, I could not kindle the rage I had used on so many occasions to push others away. The man before me had faced death in war and he knew how to face it now. I saw Laire's hands reach out, but I didn't respond. Instead, I let them slide from my own, and in that moment, I understood the love he had for me.

The last words Laire would ever say to me were, "If nobody has told you today that they love, know that I do, and always will..." Then he turned, stepped gently over the other teenagers, and walked out the door. I would never see Laire again. In the tumultuous years that followed, his words echoed in my memory. He sent letters that arrived at the most critical times of my life. Even when I turned my back on myself, he reminded me that I was worth fighting for.

My drug use created a distance between my southern family and me. The gap created by chemicals had taken its course. In a few short weeks, I looked down at my grandmother and uncle from my seat on the Greyhound bus. I was headed back to Seattle. I have no idea what my grandmother and mother discussed when the decision was made that I should leave Florida. I believe it came down to the understanding that if I was uncontrollable, my mother would take the responsibility rather than placing it on the shoulders of those who had done their best to help.

Returning to the island felt surreal. Kids, who were once shorter than me, now towered over me. I felt the gap of time and distance. I would never again feel that I fit in with the people I had known for most of my life. I came back a different person. Friends I once turned to for understanding became commodities. I focused only on how to remain at the level of intoxication that allowed me to feel comfortable. Unaltered, I felt awkward. In every toke, pill, or drink, I felt whole again; use kept my instability hidden.

The people I called my friends began to resent my incessant manipulation. Many turned their backs to me, which added to my feelings of isolation. One of the saddest symptoms of addiction is the way in which the addict uses other human beings, just like a drug, to get their selfish needs met. I brought with me the street tactics I had picked up in Florida back to the island. Eventually, I couldn't be trusted to bring back a bag of pot untouched. When drugs were available, that is all that I could focus on. I had no interest in seeing those for whom I had once felt genuine affection. Arriving at this point was not easy. It became clear that my progression and transformation into a chronic user had become complete. I surrounded myself with only those people who shared this misery. My heart ached for the types of relationships that helped to build a person's character. I was left with those who were still willing to be around me—a few out of respect for the old days, but most to get loaded.

I could not stop even though I knew I was destroying the things I held so dearly. I boomeranged between recovery groups and drug houses. In each, a war of words raged in my mind, leaving the split in my soul larger every time. I pitted one against the other. To apply all the things I had learned to lead me out of the darkness, I had to experience a level of pain that I could not feel because of my chemical use. I would not allow myself to reach the level of honesty needed to bring about the spiritual experience created by facing emotion and spiritual truths.

The story of a boy named Tim haunted our island community. Tim was an athlete, a joker, a tender heart, and a person who suffered from addiction. We had known each other through sports and would see each other around the island. When we were much younger, we shared a similar circle of friends. Though we weren't close, we were friends, and I remember him being the source of many smiles. Our relationship deepened when we ended up in the same recovery class at the high school. In recovery, I saw a side of Tim that many did not. We shared our struggles and an understanding that what we presented to those outside of class rarely reflected our internal battle. In that bond, a new friendship bloomed. We shared a mutual respect for our commonalities beyond the football field.

The social influence of those in our community was quite profound. Many teenage addicts returned home from treatment only to be compromised by those who ignorantly urged them to use to revert to the old days, a time when using was simple fun. Adolescent aftercare became a place to discuss failed attempts at recovery rather than a place to celebrate continued abstinence. Our mistakes were our greatest teachers. Each time we found ourselves with our heads hanging low, the others would rally in support. It felt like a game of Russian roulette. At any moment, one of us could experience the type of consequence that would leave a seat empty. Tim's hand often fell on my shoulder in understanding of the struggle we both shared.

The fire raged out of control. Those on the first floor yelled, trying to get Tim to come down the stairs and out of the smoke. Alcohol, cigarettes, and a mattress formed a lethal combination. When the fire was finally put out, Tim's body was found in the bathroom. Tragically, he had chosen the wrong door. My brother Ryan had the misfortune of being at the house when it burned that night. I am not sure how anyone recovers from the senseless loss of a loved one. Our whole community joined in sorrow over Tim's death. On many different levels, Tim had touched the lives of everyone who knew him. People spoke of the absolute shame and senseless tragedy that the fire had caused without recognition of the true factor.

Ultimately, the addiction from which Tim suffered was responsible for his death. In the circle of our recovery class, we tried to navigate away from the flames that enveloped him. It felt as though we were the only ones who fully understood that his death, and the death of others like him, did not come in the form of a bottle or even a flame, but rather in the very make up of his being an addict. The rationalization that somehow persuaded him that it was ok to use despite his disease, was the true villain. The treatment centers and the people who tried to help him in his life had very little bearing in the end.

It was taboo to point fingers when a death remains fresh in the minds of those affected by it. It took me years to realize that not one person was responsible for Tim's death; rather, one could blame the collective. Society portrays drinking as a rite of passage from adolescence to adulthood. Though it may not be expressed in words, it is expressed through silent assent. Every time a football coach allows his players to drink at his home, or a parent pours a mixed drink at a party, they may as well light a flame below a child's mattress. Though a horrific outcome may not occur right away, in time, these small events progress to the inevitable. These are things we do not like to consider. In taking responsibility, we honor those we love and have lost. Every time I smoked a bowl with Tim instead of going with him to a group, in my actions—I told him—that the path we were on was ok.

A comment made outside the Catholic Church before his eulogy remains with me even today. In both gratitude and resentment, a friend told me, "It should have been you in that coffin, not Tim." Given the extent of my drug use throughout my life, I believed I had earned the pine box more than Tim had. I listened, as someone else expressed what I did not have the courage to acknowledge myself. Whether it was fair to say or not, in many ways, I saw truth in his words.

I wished it were me whose anguish had ended that day. When I viewed his body, I saw myself in his ashen lifeless form. I had never seen a dead body, but when I saw Tim, I did not see the horrors that others had pointed to when they tried to get me to change course. Life could be unfair, a fact that I would hold the Creator accountable for if I ever had the pleasure of meeting him or her. All I could see in the death of my friend was a reprieve from the struggle I often heard him talking about in aftercare group, while wiping his nose with a tissue. It was easier for me look at Tim's form in the casket than it was to look at his grieving mother. In her, I saw a reflection of my own mother. The resulting pain brought home the finality of the experience.

Tim's funeral procession extended as far as the eye could see. As we moved passed the high school, teachers peered from windows. The whole island was in mourning. Tim returned to the dark soil of the island, surrounded by the woods that once echoed the laughter of his childhood. In death and memory, he would remain a seventeen-year-old boy. As I looked up at the hillside, I saw childhood friends whose tears fell onto the grasses covering the graves of the unknown. This shared pain formed a bond. The walls of social ranking fell and a collective compassion took its place. Upon our souls a memory was etched in pain and loss. We shared a tragedy from which mothers never fully recover, one which friends recount, then raise a glass of the very substance that sent him there.

12

I'S ALMOST IMPOSSIBLE FOR ME TO PIECE TOGETHER the places I lived after Tim's death. Even with the help of records and input from loved ones, it is difficult to sort through the whirlwind of addiction and institutions that followed my binges. I know that when I was evaluated for mental health problems in my twenties, we were able to count nearly thirty different places I had lived between the ages of thirteen and twenty-two. From this point forward, I'll piece together my circumstances as best I can.

My mother did not set boundaries out of a fanaticism born of misunderstanding. In my life, my mother witnessed the same kind of use that left her caring for her younger brother when she was just six years old. The adults in her life, who should have been doing the watching, were too preoccupied with themselves. The perceived abandonment I experienced as a result of my unwillingness to remain clean was but a spark in the furnace of what she experienced at the hands of others.

I could relate to what it felt like for her to be shipped off to other family members because her parents were unable or were unwilling to care for her. At times, my mother took a lashing from those she loved for setting boundaries similar to those she set with me. It is not easy for those who have not experienced the abuse inflicted by those driven by addiction to understand why self-protection is necessary. Isn't blood thicker than water? The reality is that addiction brutalizes not only those who use, but those who love the addict as well. A part of my mother's heart was bruised every time she was taken advantage of or lied to. To maintain her own sanity, she had to embark on her own journey of recovery, which taught her about co-dependency and her own struggles with use. Her love did not diminish as a result of the boundaries that she created. Instead, her love strengthened. To the addict who measures love in terms of what they can get, this seems impossible. To those who create boundaries in the hopes of protecting themselves and eliminating a source of enabling, it makes perfect sense. Boundaries are more powerful than the anger they create in others.

For me there was nothing worse than a loved one who enters a recovery program for codependency. I lost my last option when it came to being rescued from the consequence of my use. The safe harbor that is believed to protect against the storm, only prolonged the inevitability of the tumult. I don't know a great deal about my mother's path in recovery; however, I do know my mother sought some form of damage control in preparation for the inevitable consequences of my lifestyle. I did not realize that the boundaries she so hesitantly set were the very things that would, in time, help save both my life and hers.

I will deviate from my story to tell you a part of my mother's. In many ways, they are similar—or could be. Her story reveals the alternative to the painful boundaries she was forced to create in our relationship. My uncle Bill was diabetic. He was also an IV drug addict and an alcoholic.

For years, he wavered in and out of our lives, entering only when he was in good enough condition to do so. As a child, he was simply my uncle. His moral deterioration was largely unknown to me. In the ways that he knew how, he showed a love for us that was undeniable. Fishing was one of his greatest passions. To this day, I use the knots he taught me in kindergarten to tie my fishing hooks. Along with the good memories, I remember the intense emotion my mother experienced when he was around. On one occasion, Uncle Bill asked my mother for money. The exchange brought tears to her eyes and anger to his. I did not understand until much later what had happened. I had to live that moment before I could fully understand.

After years of heavy drinking, my uncle's health began to deteriorate. The boy my mother had raised since he was six years old exhibited the most horrible physical deterioration brought on by continued use. When Social Security finally released a retroactive check for several thousand dollars, he had only one leg he could walk on. His other leg had never healed after a terrible break from a fall. He had half a lung remaining as a result of tuberculosis and hepatitis C. His social worker, as she gave him the social security check, said, "Don't drink this up." She may not have understood that a check for that amount was my uncle's death sentence. He purchased a big-screen TV, a kitten, and paid rent on an apartment in downtown Portland, Oregon. He bought enough alcohol to fuel his last binge, then drank until his final breath.

When my uncle was found, he had aspirated his own vomit. Paramedics resuscitated him and took him to a Portland hospital and placed on life support long enough for his son, Billy, and the rest of the family to come to see him one last time. He looked like the living dead, awaiting his final release from the bondage of the physical. His eyes revealed recognition of the love that surrounded him and an understanding that he would be passing soon. I did not sense fear, only relief. I felt like I was watching a hero depart from a great battle. I saw in him the bravery that exists in those who endure the harsher realities of life. To the average person, my uncle appeared as any man on the street, passed by in pity or judgment. To me, he was a gladiator of emotional torment. The world he had been forced to endure for so many years was riddled with an abuse from which most of humanity is protected. From an early age, he had lived with sexual abuse the way that I had. His most traumatic abuse took place in a Missouri State prison. He had been sent there for stealing a radio from a parked car while hitchhiking from Florida back to Oregon. His son was born while he was behind bars. The violence of skid row plus his many years of daily abuse compounded his problems. In his eyes, I saw the very things that had brought me to my knees—yet multiplied by many years and many more tragedies.

When the soul leaves the body, the finality is visible. I knew that as he exhaled for the last time, he had finally found the relief he had been searching for in the bottle. In this relief came the perfection of complete surrender. I had searched for this same relief for quite some time. I wished that I could climb up on his bed and ride with him into the realm of the unknown. There was no doubt that at that moment I saw my future if I continued on my current path.

When my mother made the decision to take him off of life support, a debate ensued. A woman who should have been thanked for sparing others the very painful choice instead suffered the anger of those who, in that moment, felt it was not my uncle's drinking that killed him. My grandmother was the angriest because in his death a part of her died as well. Their relationship had consisted of a type of reliance that only those who live in daily abuse can understand. For years, they had helped each other survive the low-income world of the inner city where the strong feed on the weak. They fed one another's addictions. This lack of boundaries perpetuated a slow and painful death. Still, they found solace in one another.

A year almost to the day of my uncle's death my grandmother died. She was addicted to prescription drugs and overdosed. When a friend found her, she was kneeling at her bed, clutching a rosary she'd borrowed from a neighbor in prayer.

To attend her funeral, I had to be released from the group home in which I was living at the time. When I entered my grandmother's apartment, my mother was cleaning out the pipes and other medications. As we sorted out the property details, scavengers began to appear. My mother dealt not only with the tragedy of losing her mother, but also the strangers who came by the apartment looking for handouts. When my grandmother's drug dealer stopped by attempting to get the pills he had supplied, my brothers and I escorted him down the elevator.

I tell this story to demonstrate the sharp contrast between how my mother chose to handle my addiction and how my uncle and grandmother chose to perpetuate each other's addiction. Rather than feed it, my mother broke the cycle of abuse that had been in our family for generations. This made her both hero and villain. Those in recovery who understood her intentions applauded her. Family members, who did not understand, felt she was turning her back on them. I fell into the latter category: and, in my anger, I would provide many examples of what I considered to be forms of abandonment.

No, my mother was not perfect. Who is? She had my best interests in mind. While in numerous institutions and treatment centers, she always sent me letters and care packages. What she could not address directly concerning my use, she made up for by supporting me in my abstinence. She visited and showed me love that only a mother can give in the darkest of moments. She was my one person, that one person, who is always available in times of great need.

My mother did not abandon me; it was I who abandoned all of those in my life who tried so hard to reach me. I turned my back on them, because facing them meant facing myself. I simply was not ready. By pointing the finger at her and my father, I perpetuated my sickness. To garner sympathy I regret that I painted such a severe picture of my parents and tarnished their reputations in the process. Those who truly mattered, however, knew the truth. It is, in fact, the responsibility of parents and schools to create social boundaries to raise the rock bottom before a deeper chasm is realized.

Lynn was my best option at the time. I gravitated towards her, which led the treatment staff to separate us. After I completed treatment at Olympic Center, I was sent to a halfway house in north Seattle that housed kids. Our shared experiences with abuse formed the basis for our tight bond. Her life had been filled with abandonment, sending her on a constant search to fill the holes left by her mother, father, and brother. Her foster parents sent her to treatment as a last-ditch effort to prepare her for adoption into their family. When I first saw Lynn, every part of me cried out in gratitude. She fulfilled everything

I wanted in a girl: needy, beautiful, rebellious, and sexually active. She was also very bright and made me laugh. She used sarcasm to deflect the pain and anger that she carried deep inside.

As I moved through relationships, I carried a part of each previous relationship, thereby jading every one. Unbeknown to me, this pattern would create complication and confusion as I tried to relate to other individuals and not the group. In Lynn, I sought the comfort of a mother, the sexual pleasure of the various women I had been with, and the friendship of Marti. It seems strange to have such unrealistic expectations, to look to someone else to fill so many roles, but this was a byproduct of my experience with multiple partners and a premature separation from my parents.

The staff's attempt to keep us separated might have worked had Lynn and I not attended school together. At University District Youth Center, we both rode the bus and shared time in studies, which allowed us time to develop a mutually dependent relationship. I acknowledge that love and companionship are good things. In the early stages of recovery, while trying to work through the abuse in one's life, a relationship is distracting. By focusing on each other, we avoided the therapy we needed to get beyond our compulsive behaviors. We used each other to avoid the emotions that therapy is intended to provoke. Nothing else mattered and nothing else held the same weight; we bypassed everything else to focus on each other.

As soon as we got off the bus, Lynn and I would retreat into a doorway and kiss until our bodies ached. As we kissed, I forgot everything that had put me in treatment. I no longer remembered the touch of those who had abused me. Her touch erased my dark past. I found my escape, again, in the female form. Of course, our adventures did not end with kissing. In time, we took cover in the closets of the youth shelter, exploring exchanges far more progressive than a kiss.

In relationships, I avoided the very things that would allow me to experience an honest and true connection. This tragedy could be attributed to the abuse I had endured in my life. Those experiences precluded my relating in healthy and respectful ways to those deserving. Instead, my partners received only parts of me. When something went wrong, I protected myself by all means. I held the most vulnerable parts of me close in an attempt to protect them from the inevitable pain that followed the dispersion of trust and love.

The counselors were eventually forced to separate us, and I was sent temporarily to another group home. In order to continue seeing Lynn I realized I would have to avoid the staff's attention.

Group homes were unpleasant. Experiencing several fights added to my resolve to never return. Although the fights earned me respect from those in the new home, the notoriety they produced did nothing to quench my craving for the feeling of Lynn's flesh. To some, there could be parallels between what we felt and love. We did not know the difference. The staff's attempts to separate us seemed like a great injustice. The more they tried, the more we resisted.

When does reliance on a friend and lover cross over to dependence? I have been told that once we no longer look at ourselves and instead focus all of our attention on the other person, that line has been crossed. Once we are distracted from the things that we must do to take care of ourselves, the relationship has become one of dependence. Some might refer to that as selflessness, putting others ahead of oneself. This caused me great confusion. Others told me that dependence is evidenced by the avoidance of emotion and substance. I would learn much later in life that real love rests solely in the desire to nurture another's spiritual and emotional growth. This belief removes all fear from relationships. During my relationship with Lynn, I felt a spiritual and emotional void; however, what could I have brought to our relationship other than a past that still haunted me? If I did not love myself, then how could I love another in the way that we both deserved?

I don't remember a time when I went without the companionship of a woman. The majority of these relationships turned to reliance as opposed to establishing balance between two human beings sharing their life experiences. Through relationships of dependence, individuality blurred and became crowded.

My relationship with Lynn carried on outside of the halfway house and across the miles that separated us. After her foster parents adopted her, she moved with them to Idaho, which complicated our ability to see each other. In her absence, I experienced the same set of emotions that often followed my early days of abstinence. Emotions surfaced that I could have avoided when with her. So when she left, I left as well. I ran away again. I lived with various friends, fluctuating between clean and not so clean. In desperation, I left for Idaho before my mother could protest.

Whether I was manipulating her or we were manipulating each other, I moved in with her shortly thereafter. Though her parents were hesitant, Lynn had them wrapped around her finger. They were kind people. It seemed the natural course for them to help a kid in need. Had they known how engrossed we were in each other, they may have made a different decision. What began in treatment continued unhindered.

We attended recovery groups and she eventually returned to school. I floated for a while, working for her father at his car dealership and taking other odd jobs. I was under the impression that her adopted father did not like me much. I don't blame him for that. I relied heavily on their family and did very little to return the favor. I had always been entirely dependent on institutions and handouts from others. At seventeen, I had no understanding of what it meant to be self-reliant. Although I desperately wished to be a part of their family, I could not force myself do the things required to make that happen.

Lynn's parents requested that Lynn and I redefine our relationship to one similar to a brother and sister. This made no sense to me. We were in no position to deal with the emotions that accompanied our relationship. Further, we had long since crossed lines that would allow us to be siblings. We fed impulse and desire. When we failed to make the requested shift, I was asked to leave.

In my recovery group, I met a woman named Sherrie. She had an adopted son and invited me to live with them. I could tell that her son was resentful; I was not the first stray she had brought in. Her expectation was that I would stay away from Lynn so that we could focus on ourselves. I agreed then did the exact opposite. Within weeks, the neighbors called Lynn's father to tell him I had been parking Sherry's truck down the road from their house. This ended our midnight rendezvous; it essentially ended our entire relationship. Though we had mutual friends, we didn't see each other much. Once she left my life, marijuana entered. Shortly thereafter, I was asked to leave Sherry's house as well.

Homeless, I traveled to Arizona and back. Eventually, I found a basement with no rules and people like myself. This was no ordinary basement. It was a teenage meth den and had housed a number of homeless kids. Marcus's father lived upstairs. He was gone most of the time, driving his truck to the Border States, returning with what the congregating kids awaited. Although we understood that Marcus's father did not sell to kids, we knew that he gave the drugs to his son to sell for him. I am not sure how this approach justified his actions, but it was sound enough to other addicts in the meth world.

I had used meth a few times in my life and loved everything about how it made me feel. Others described feeling amped up, but Meth had the opposite effect on me. I felt calm and normal. I had not experienced this type of rush for quite some time. My last similar experience was with crack, but meth had something that crack did not. With a five-dollar line, meth could keep me high for twenty-four hours or more. It also could be addicting after just one use. The combination of euphoria and my addictive personality guaranteed that, in a matter of days, I would become a slave to this powerful and dangerous substance.

When Marcus's father's gun was found missing bullets, I took the blame. I was evicted in short order, an event that sent me into one of the darkest times in my life. There exists a progression of homelessness for a kid on the run. Homelessness refers to the inability to use a place's resources to stay clean, fed, and sheltered. In most places, I could rarely account for all three. At Marcus's house, I was allowed to sleep on the couch but could not use the shower upstairs or eat their food. The other houses were very similar. I was more of a transient than a houseguest. In time, all transients are left to wander. The helplessness of wandering leads to desperation and great compromise. Such compromise can be horrific.

My homelessness left me vulnerable to manipulation. Despite my promise that I would never allow myself to be placed in a position of abuse again, I did just that. Josh was everybody's friend. I had met him on several occasions. Each time, he offered a large bag of meth and promised to supply more if I wanted to buy it. As with most addicts, I sold drugs to stay high. Josh and I formed a partnership. My sales were going well, as I consistently had to restock my stash. On several occasions, Josh was accompanied by a couple of guys in their late twenties and early thirties. When they came around, others became quiet. I knew from past experience that these men were not to be messed with. When they looked at me I slowly lowered my gaze in submission, as animals do.

Growing up, my ego and my pride allowed me to exhibit a sort of dominance. My experience with these men felt otherwise. Because I was physically smaller, I believed that I was also less a man. In some ways, the tactics they used on me were the same tactics I had used on the field or on the wrestling mat. Having my own strategies used against me gave me a sense of what my future held. This was not the football field. It was a world where people preyed on weakness; it was a world that defied reason. It was a world driven by money, sex, drugs, and weapons—where respect is measured in fear.

Josh offered to take me to a trailer outside of town to crash. He told me several other kids were crashing there; one more would not matter. I was desperate and because I already liked him, I trusted him. Big mistake.

I am not sure why I did not listen to my gut when given the opportunity to change course. Besides feeling desperate, I was curious as to where Josh scored his meth.

The drugs seemed to be making decisions for me, taking away my ability to say no or act on my instincts to run. Whatever the case, this proved to be one of the worst of bad decisions I had ever made, and I had made many. As soon as I entered the trailer, I knew that I had reentered the den in Florida. A similar chemical smell reminded me of what I had put up my nose for the last several months.

The living space was filled with kids of all ages, from thirteen to nineteen. Couches, mattresses, and Harley Davidson parts crowded the living room. The windows were covered with aluminum foil and the shades were drawn. The only light in the trailer was artificial. The kitchen looked unused save a scattering of fast-food wrappers. We sidestepped a mass of kids, then made our way down the hall toward the back bedroom. Josh knocked and a voice yelled, "Just a minute."

In the moments that followed, I compared where I stood with where I had come from. Our island house was a one-story, three-bedroom, ranch-style home. Though it was not much bigger than the trailer, far more life resided within. Though fairly humble by island standards, my home seemed like a palace. The large yard held the possibility of tree forts, kickball games, and wrestling matches. Our property was surrounded on all sides by wooded areas that led down to the island's beaches. As a child, I crossed the patchwork of nearby properties forming paths that looked much like the wild game trails of higher elevations. In passing, one could hear the voices of children laughing and yelling, "Kamikaze!" or, "Ready or not, here I come…"

Within minutes of leaving my doorstep, I could be in the thick of the cedar forests chasing the creations of my imagination. Staircases descended from the tall cliffs to the sandy beaches below. The ivy-covered cliff walls, many feet above, offered a greater challenge. As I repelled down, a cascade of sand and clay accompanied me. I found clear, cold springs and wild berries. Mushrooms grew in the dampness and creatures, safe from most, braved glances at me as I scaled through their sanctuaries. These natural havens were shielded from the rest of the world. A boy's mind could create anything there; no external force could dictate the outcome.

"Pirates in the distance and coming straight at us, Captain."

"Then fasten the lines and load the canons. If it's a battle they want, a battle they will get!"

I shouted among the forest's cover, my words echoing back. An imaginary band of sailors awaited their next command.

What awaited me inside the bedroom resembled a band of pirates, yet they were in no way imaginary. The frailest woman I had ever seen stood before me. She could not have been older than fifty, and yet she looked ninety. Her hair wispy, she wore makeup in an unsuccessful attempt to hide the dark circles beneath her eyes. Val was the housemother of sorts. What she said went. This had as much to do with her aggressive nature as it did with the two men who stood behind her, enforcing her orders. She quickly invited us in and closed the door.

Val's room was immaculate. It was filled with scales, a gun, bags of meth, and piles of money. Harry sat on the bed behind her wearing a silk nightgown. His genitals fell from between the smooth folds of the robe onto his pale legs. As he looked me up and down, I experienced a familiar feeling of one being valued at market.

I should have run. Had it been possible to forget what I had seen, walk backwards down the hall, through the living room, and then out the door, I would have. I would have taken my imaginary shipmen, swung from the trees, and dropped onto the beach below. I would have fought for the children trapped in the holds of the pirate vessel. I would have destroyed that vessel, sending those evil pirates to the depths of the ocean where the crabs could feed from their flesh.

The curse of abuse, however, continued to direct me into the hands of those who would fulfill the endless cycle. Because of a pleasure center that drove my continued use, I was destined to return to places where people feed from the weaknesses of others. I was destined to return to trailers like this one.

It was quite simple. Josh had been watching me for some time and decided I would be a good candidate to be a part of their family. Josh and I met while I was staying on Marcus's couch. Over a period of weeks, Josh sized me up, then eventually brought Val's boys over to make the final decision. I am not sure what criteria they used when shopping for teenagers to enslave. The most important quality must have been dependence on and submission through chemicals. It was no secret that I was reliant on them. I also exhibited a desire to go beyond use. I had proven that I would go above and beyond to stay loaded. At seventeen years old, I was not intimidating. I was thin and clean-cut despite my use of chemicals. They must have assumed I was an easy mark.

This was the hustle. Kids ran the drugs that Harry and the older boys cooked in the shed behind the trailer. Controlling the kids was easy; keep them in the shackles of addiction. In every shot or snort of meth, the bond strengthened. In time, debt, paranoia, and Val's sons kept them in line and well within reach. On occasion, someone would yell down the hall. "Laramie, get in here." When the girl returned, either a couple of hours or even a couple of days later, she had the blank stare of those returning from war. Little was said. Most knew the price being paid when entering that room. Val and Harry mostly abused the girls, but on occasion, one of the younger boys would be asked back. They returned far different from before.

In the beginning none of this was completely clear. All I knew was that even without any money I seemed to have an endless supply of meth. After several days of using and the inevitable coma that followed, I woke up to the prick of a needle. I was not greeted with smiles, but rather the look of those who had a purpose in mind. My heart raced and my lungs released the chemical love of my life. The world took on a whole new meaning. In my groin, I experienced a feeling like orgasm, yet it continued for many minutes. Instead of panic, I was filled with euphoria, a pleasure that surpassed even the largest crack hit I had ever taken. I felt grateful for what had been done to me.

The kids on the couches around me stared in recognition of what had just happened. As I walked down the hallway, I wondered if what had befallen the others was about to befall me. In that rush of my first injection, I felt invincible. Not in terms of my strength, but in my ability to mask pain. Something told me that everything was all right. More, something told me that everything was perfect despite my circumstances.

The bedroom held none of the terror that I had seen on the faces of those who had returned from it. "As you know, we sell meth," Val said, her tone matter-of-fact. "You are one of us now. Shooting meth was your right of passage." That passage felt far greater than the solo I had been on at Wilderness. "You work for me now. Get it?" I did get it. The men standing behind her fumbling with guns of varying calibers punctuated her statement. I was enslaved to them. With the promise of more meth came the promise of violence if I went against their system. On many occasions, Josh and I were released to sell lemon-drop crank. We always returned with pockets full of money. At first, I made a profit and would provide for myself as well as some of the other kids who struggled with their end of the bargain. Not all of them had to sell drugs to continue to stay there. Their price was the abuse I had experienced earlier in my life. The shame of not doing anything to protect them began to build. I was powerless in the face of their brute force. I might have looked different, but I was in the same position. Sitting right next to any one of them, no one could tell us apart.

The pain of standing by as others are abused is almost as damaging as being abused. The feeling of complete powerlessness strips a person of any self-worth. Seeing their faces, I relived my own experiences over and over again. I offered as much compassion as I could muster considering my use of a drug that numbs a person to such traits.

Why did they put the needle in my arm when I least expected it? Intravenous use is extremely potent. Further, delivery with a needle can cause instantaneous addiction. Val and Harry understood that, given the amounts that we sold, we would be in debt in no time if the habit stuck—and they made sure of that. From that moment forward, I only used substances intravenously. I did not smoke it, snort it, or eat it. I lost interest in alcohol and only used pot when I wanted to come down a little. Even then, pot just made my mind bend and turn to mush. It didn't matter how I sold the ounces that were given to me. With time, I stopped making a profit. Eventually, I was shooting their product instead of my cut from the sales. If I got lucky, I would be set up with something much larger and would be able to pay down my debt. Just like credit card debt, I was only paying off the interest. I used more than I could ever hope to pay back. This made me as helpless and trapped as the rest of the pale faces.

On one occasion, I was called into the room and told a story by one of Val's sons. He was about six feet two inches and weighed nearly two hundred and fifty pounds. He rode with a motorcycle club from out of state and wore a Nomad patch that afforded him a great deal of leeway. In the story, a young girl had worn out her welcome by talking too much. Her fate had been sealed in a barrel, buried somewhere in the land surrounding the trailer. "Bitch in a barrel" was a common expression. Its use was followed by chuckles, then silence from the kids. Before hearing the story, I had not understood the meaning. Afterwards, I realized that I was fighting for my life.

The vilest kind of violence imaginable went down in that trailer. As bikers came in and out, the kids were passed around like property. They sent the kids to the bedrooms with one or a group of people. These were particularly difficult times for me; I tried to escape through injections and headphones. I drew pictures for days at a time, trying to control the paranoia that accompanied my highs. In the tiny drawings, I disappeared from my circumstances and was transported to a place insulated from the horrors of a drug that brought out the worst in humanity. I drew until the pencil was gone or my fingers were bruised, and then I would start again with a new pencil. The pictures came alive with faces telling stories as I fell to the effects of sleep deprivation.

With excessive use Josh came to believe that spaceships were coming for him, so he refused to make night runs with me. This stuck me with one of the brothers who didn't talk to me much. When he did, he gave orders. We were packed into the vehicle and instructed that if we were pulled over by the police, we were to run as fast as we could. They intended to speed off so that the police would pursue them and not us. We carried the drugs. If they caught us, their whole operation would unravel. They emphasized repeatedly what would happen if we were caught and ran our mouths. This made the slightest idea of talking to the police impossible. Their operation was clearly worth more to them than any kid.

Part of Josh's initial inspection was to gather personal information that they could use against me if necessary. The network was far larger than a simple meth house. The trailer was merely the cookhouse for a much larger group. Recognizing this, I felt a new level of paranoia. Once again, I had to protect others by enduring the poor choices I had made.

I never knew who did the actual cooking. Many people came and went from the shed; however there was one common denominator, Harry. When the meth was being cooked, the trailer was on high alert; no one was allowed in or out. One of the brothers would dress up in dark colors then disappear into the land around the trailer to watch for anything out of the ordinary. He would not leave his post until someone else relieved him or until the batch was done. Cameras were set up to monitor outside the trailer. A communication system was put in place to give warning if something seemed out of the ordinary. I had never experienced the type of paranoia that comes with the mixing of chemicals. A general understanding prevailed that if they were caught, they would rather die than go to prison. As proof of this statement, high-powered guns had been stashed all around the trailer.

After several days of vigil, everyone converged. High-level transactions took place as associates came and went. The meth was obviously being cooked for someone else.

They were paid in product as well as the right to deal part of the batch in the area. The kids were given the leftovers to sell in smaller quantities. Smaller quantities brought the most profit if enough of it was sold.

Many months had passed since I had communicated with either my mother or Lynn. I had never stayed silent for so long. The trailer had no phone, and when I went out, I was never left alone. I also had a healthy fear of going against the rules. I called my mother and Lynn from a neighbor's house a few times. I had been selling this neighbor meth, and she had some understanding of my situation. I snuck in through her window at night, safe in the knowledge that the brothers wouldn't follow me. The calls were brief. I have no memory of what I said.

The last call I made was from an outlet mall while the brothers were clothes shopping. During our conversation, I shared with my mother the desperation I felt. I told her about the gravity of the situation and that I did not think I could leave without my things. She told me, "Fuck your belongings!" In my meth-induced confusion, I couldn't comprehend leaving even the slightest hint that I had ever been there. In rushed words, she told me that a ticket would be waiting at the bus depot. Lynn was forming a plan to get me out with the help of other addicts in recovery. As I began to discuss the specifics, I heard the brothers drive up behind me. I hung up the phone.

Although I told them the story I had rehearsed—about a made-up conversation with Lynn—I couldn't avoid the beating I took back at the trailer. In the days that followed, the brothers seemed gripped by paranoia. It was as if that one phone call could topple everything they had created. Just weeks before one of the boys left without telling anyone. Even his girlfriend, who was still there, did not know where he had gone. The brothers, Val, and

Harry said nothing. I hoped that he had escaped. I hoped that he was not in a barrel somewhere.

In my final days in the trailer, Val asked me on several occasions to give Harry oral sex as a way to pay down what I owed them. "He won't touch you. He just thinks you're beautiful and wants to always remember you that way." I refused on both occasions. After the second visit to the back room, I knew things would get worse if I stayed. I would become one of the blank-faced kids walking down the hall. Worse, I could end up decomposing in a barrel somewhere. The words "want to remember you that way" stuck in my head, like the promise of my own demise.

I remember nothing about my escape. The paranoia of many sleepless nights awake blended with the very real possibility that I would be chased by two of the most sadistic men I had ever known. My prayers were answered. A five-foot-six-inch angel rescued me from hell. She arrived when the brothers were preoccupied with someone else. Lynn, who had been to the trailer on several occasions, sensed the very real danger that existed there. She knew she was facing horrible danger, yet despite her fear, she was determined to save the life of someone she apparently loved.

I could see the relief in her eyes as she drove away, heading towards a safe house. Apparently, she had been busy in the months since our last phone call. With a group of recovering addicts, she had devised a plan to get me out of Idaho and into treatment. A whole network of people had collaborated; a group of friends I did not know I had. The two women, who I believed had abandoned me, had actually been working together to arrange a rescue founded on faith. The mind of an addict is unpredictable; it will sometimes tell us lies in an attempt to kill us. Lynn and my mother could see through my mind's trickery. I could no longer claim abandonment. Support came for me when I was ready and willing to accept it.

When I arrived at Swede's house, I was gripped with a fear that I could not shake. In Swede, I sensed the understanding a fellow recovering addict. I appreciated being given my own space and not having to answer any questions. I do not remember sleeping. I do not remember eating. I do not remember conversation. I only remember fear.

I walked up to the ticket counter and told the attendant my name. From under the counter, the attendant pulled out the ticket that had been held for me. The man showed a tenderness and sympathy that I didn't understand. "I am very happy to be giving you this," he said. My mother had asked them to hold the ticket, warning that they could not allow me to cash the ticket in. This same story had played out many times before those who work in public transportation. Like every other seventeen-year-old junkie, my face showed the fear of the life I had endured.

How could I thank the person who freed me from a prison from which I could not free myself? Had I known I would never see Lynn again, and that her efforts were the last expression of affection, I would have pulled her close and never let go. In her unwillingness to give up on me, Lynn showed a type of humanity that is so often overlooked. I had always assumed that in her willingness to set our relationship aside, Lynn had invalidated our time together. The experiences we shared came at a time in our lives when companionship meant more than anything. In reality, her willingness to end our relationship, despite the great emotional pain that it caused us both, exemplified a love for her father, her family, herself, and for me. Situations that require consideration for many people can cloud one's expression of love. To choose one person may appear to be choosing against another person. At the time, I didn't understand that real love doesn't always feel good.

I have come to learn that Lynn expressed her love in her willingness to depart from my life. This choice was far more intense than all the butterflies I experienced kissing in doorways. She let me go once, and then gathered me up again like so many pieces of porcelain, releasing me a second time with the faith that someone could put me back together again. Like my mother, she refused to give up on the ones she loved and expressed her love in ways that were sometimes misunderstood. Her choices epitomized love in action. Without my knowing it she loved me when I could not love myself.

13

SOCKS AND MISMATCHED CLOTHING seemed like a fine tradeoff for my relative freedom. In my haste, I did not grab my shoes. Consequently, I endured a few funny looks. Although I felt relieved by the change of scenery, a deeply ingrained fear and paranoia convinced me that 'they' were watching me as the bus moved through the night towards Portland. The recovering addicts who had come together on my behalf had arranged for me to attend a treatment program in Portland, Oregon. They had never even met me, yet they set their lives aside in the hopes that another addict would recover from a seemingly hopeless state of mind and body. They were the silent heroes who had helped Lynn and my mother extricate me. They were not paid money for their help; instead, they received a spiritual payment—of greater value. Addicts are an amazing breed once they make the transition from hopeless to hopeful. Many use their street savvy and unyielding faith to bring about change in those around them. Often, they do not receive the credit that they are due. This is of no consequence to them, as they don't seek recognition. They simply wish to pass on the gift that was given to them, and in so doing, save themselves.

Several men greeted me at the bus terminal in Portland assuring me that I would be safe. Though they tried to assure me that I was not being tracked, I suggested they do what they could to shake a tail, just in case. I still felt hesitant, not entirely convinced that they were telling me the truth. Further, I wasn't convinced that they understood the gravity of what might happen if I were being followed.

Confusion and paranoia fueled my delusion. The chaos of my deteriorating mental state was made worse by an aggressive prayer that accosted me. I believe in a Creator and a spiritual world. People who are aggressive in their religious beliefs can, through their good intentions, worsen the problems of those suffering from mental illness. I suffered from symptoms that mirrored bipolar disorder and schizophrenia. When the kids in the shelter began the laying on of hands while speaking in tongues, I had a mental breakdown and lost all sense of reality. Gratefully, they chose caution over faith, putting me in a room by myself when my threats began to escalate.

Sleep did not come easily as I relied on chemicals to move me into a state of unconsciousness. Without pills or tar, I could not come down from meth. My mind would not let me rest. I felt afraid of what might happen to me if I fell asleep. It was not uncommon for one of the brothers to kick the nearest kid in the rib cage while walking through the trailer. Conditioning from pain and fear added to my anxiety. My body eventually shut down, forcing me to sleep; it simply could go no further. When I woke the next morning, some semblance of reality greeted me, although the feeling of still being high remained. I had enough meth in my system to keep me going for several more days. I was also quite embarrassed to find out that in the night I had lost control of my bladder and was still wet.

Between the time of my arrival and the morning hours, something had changed in the way people approached me. The staff who had greeted me at the bus station were gone; the new staff acted with an urgency the night staff had not. Phone calls had been made during the night to discuss my mental and physical state. The clinical staff had advised those at the safe house that they were in no position to detoxify me. Based on my symptoms, I would be taken to Hooper Detox Center downtown. No time could be wasted, as there were concerns that my kidneys and circulatory system could be failing.

More zombie than human I arrived at the detox center. I was second in line amid a few dozen. Patients were brought in based on priority. I distinctly remember the man ahead of me because he was bleeding from his face, the result of an alcohol-induced seizure. They gave me immediate medical treatment in an effort to stabilize me. The handful of pills and shots had a calming effect, one that my body had not experienced in some time. I was assigned a bed, and then slept for the better part of a week. I woke only for medication and food. I still remember the feeling of the IV in my hand. What I felt was my body being hydrated, and in that, a cautious vitality.

Food seemed foreign. I could not remember the last real meal I had eaten. In the final weeks before leaving the trailer, I had eaten pancakes made from flour and water. Because of the phone call to my mother, I was not allowed to leave. Drugs suppress the appetite. As I became sicker and sicker, the thought of food made me feel worse. During the last few days of my confinement, water was the only thing I could ingest. In time, I quit drinking water as well. I have no doubt that given a few more days starvation and dehydration, caused by the meth, would have killed me. When I arrived at the detox center, I weighed less than one hundred and ten pounds, down from the 165 pounds I had carried into Idaho

My physical deterioration was a blessing compared to what some at the detox center experienced. The man three bunks down from me believed that a guitar was growing out of his head, which allowed him to hear everything in music. From what I was told, his meth-induced psychosis was permanent, and he would be released to the State for more psychological treatment at a mental hospital. With sleep and food, I slowly returned to a bearable reality. I began to feel clearer, but to others, I was far from sane. This was evidenced by the nurses' questions and comments. I often heard, "Why don't you lie down until dinner," or, "no, they can't get to you in here." Still, relative sanity was better than none at all: and, although I questioned those around me about where they came from, I was in far better shape than when I arrived. The psychosis diminished with each meal, glass of water, and hour of sleep, but the paranoia took months to disappear.

I was eighteen, but despite my protests, everyone treated me like the boy that I was. Though I showed all the signs of a junkie, I was still green in many regards. Those who chose to be compassionate shared how to stay clean despite their own failings. Those who envied my relative naiveté simply avoided me or did not engage me in conversation. Had I raised my arms, the creases would have shown red pinpricks and sores. Those with stories beyond my own would show deep, dark grooves running over their veins. I am sure it wasn't easy to face one so young who had deteriorated so much. Although the years had changed their faces to masks unrecognizable by even their mothers, they still remembered the days when they had stood in my shoes—on the edge of a precipice, looking down.

I was the only high-school-aged kid at the center. As a result, I became a bit of a mascot. I would walk through the bunks, talking with the others, trying to hear their stories. I loved it when they called me "little buddy" or "green horn." The names didn't bother me because they reflected acceptance, not insult. The nurses brought me food they had made at home and shared stories about their own children my age. Deep pity filled their eyes as they walked away attempting not to cross lines of professionalism. One or two nurses would sometimes give me a kiss, one that reminded me of my mother. I would wonder how she was doing.

At night when I couldn't sleep, I walked between the rows of beds and looked into the faces of those who could sleep. They mirrored the way I felt about myself: beaten down, deteriorated, and terminal. When awake, they did not appear hopeful; they sat in silence and stared into the distance, reliving the horrors that had brought them there. For many of them, detox was both a blessing and a curse. They became well by going through withdrawals, the pain of which most humans will never know, and then were released back into the hell that led to use in the first place. From hell, to relief, and back to hell again, they traveled to a place from which no preacher could save them. It made the hell of any holy book sound like a paradise in comparison.

Although I knew I would never find him, as a way to pass the time I searched the sleeping faces for Kenneth's. In many, I saw an eerie resemblance that warranted a second glance. Of course, I never saw his face or heard his booming voice. I am not sure what would have happened had I seen him. I imagined sitting in waiting, then pouncing when he least expected it, inflicting as much damage as I could before I departed—as he had done to me.

Violence could not heal; laughter did more to bring back life. I found myself moving in the direction of any laughter I heard. In many ways, it seemed foreign to me, and in the shadow of the experience leading to detox, I could not put a finger on one moment of genuine laughter expressed by anyone nearby. At the center, I soaked up the sound as I had soaked up liquids that first day. I understood it held something as necessary as food and drink. The deprivation of love and laughter that I experienced may have fueled an unconscious move toward death. If I had been unable to break the bonds one way, I would break them in another manner.

After several weeks, I was released from detox and made my way back to the island. I cannot imagine what it must be like for a parent to see the shell of a human being—a child who they raised—walk through the door after months of intravenous drug use. For the first time since leaving, I experienced the all-too-familiar pain associated with bringing sadness into the lives of loved ones. My father's tears were silent. He remarked on the detail of the veins he could see through my translucent skin. If my father had maintained any reservations whether or not I was an addict, those doubts were smashed as we walked around the park with my mother. We had come together to formulate a plan for my long-term treatment. The two people I had spent so much time resenting had come together to salvage the life I had cast aside so thoughtlessly.

Insurance coverage had run out for my treatment stays and my parents did not have the money to pay for further treatment. To get me into another program would be nearly impossible. Thankfully, I was eligible for Title XIX funding through the state of Washington. Thanks to society's willingness to fund treatment, I entered Olympic Center Bellingham. The seriousness of my situation rested on my shoulders as it had never before. I finally realized that despite several treatment stays and every person I had ever worked with in recovery, ultimately it was up to me to do what was necessary to remain clean. I had finally reached a level of dependence and pain that had convinced me of the severity of my drug use. The desire that others had described in recovery groups now made sense. I was convinced that this time I would do whatever it took to remain clean.

My return to Olympic Center was bittersweet. Those who had known me before expressed great sadness at the progression of my disease. Yet, they believed that pain brings spiritual progress, and that progress leads to the kind of lasting recovery that keeps chronic users like me in recovery, one day at a time. I felt as though I had arrived home. The counselors had always shown me a great deal of love and compassion. I had grown up in various institutions. Between using and running from home, I had spent more time in institutions than at home with my mother, father and brothers.

From this recurrent institutionalization I had missed out on many parts of a normal childhood. At eighteen, when most people my age were completing high school, I was simply learning how to survive. I understood survival at 1st Avenue and Pike Street in Seattle, but I could not balance a checkbook or shop for groceries.

As the days passed and my body worked to rebuild itself after the trauma of IV use, my mental faculties began to deteriorate rapidly. They mimicked my mood and behavior when I had tried to take my life several times.

I listened to songs I had heard in the meth trailer and attempted to dissect some imagined mystery. I tried to piece it all together, to understand how I had allowed myself to fall into the trap. The voices of those still in the trailer echoed in my mind repeatedly. The relief of my escape had worn off. I was safe but the others were not. I experienced what has been described as survivor's remorse. One counselor asked me to write about the situation in great detail, which only made matters worse.

The taste of tears reminds me of the ocean. The rush of emotion that forces tears to the surface churns like sand in the waves. Each salty drop mixes a thousand emotions. It is difficult to understand how so much can fit into something so small. With each outburst came those things I had avoided. I could control my tears as successfully as one can dictate the tide. With every breath inhaled and held, the exhale worked against me. That flood of emotion overwhelmed me, eventually forcing me to act. Some might ride out such emotion, finding relief through the experience. Others might choose to act in a more ominous manner, simply making the emotional flood yet more powerful.

Returning from a meeting in town, I entered the facility with one thing on my mind. I could not shake the cloud that had descended. I felt perpetual shame and a hopelessness that those who suffer from severe depression experience. It only seemed natural to peel away the tiny razors from my shaver in preparation. As the blood-letting began, blood from the artery in my left arm began to spurt onto the shower and all over the floor. Treatment centers offer very little privacy. In the one place where I usually enjoyed solitude, someone decided to take an evening shower instead of a morning one. The kid entered a scene similar to that which my brother had experienced five years prior. He wrestled the razors from my hands as I cried out in anger. He had kept me from finishing a job I had had every intention of completing

At the hospital, the doctor giving me stitches delivered a lecture that fell on deaf ears. I had wished to recede into darkness, not listen to someone who had only seen one side of a needle. When I returned to the center, my belongings had been moved; I was placed on the adult side of the facility. I had been moved to further my chronic care, but also to protect the younger kids from my progression. Through pain and blood, I had graduated from the world of the adolescent into the world of adult.

Although I had experienced some level of depression for a good part of my life, I had never stayed clean long enough to be accurately diagnosed. The symptoms of chronic drug use, detoxification, and early recovery imitate the symptoms of clinical depression. This is true of paranoia, anxiety, attention deficit disorder, and schizophrenia, as well. When the psychiatrist finished his assessment, he prescribed an anti-depressant. For years, I had hidden behind lies to avoid this type of diagnosis; now I found myself eager for relief from the extreme emotions that prompted my pursuit of drugs and death.

Some disagree with giving medication to those who suffer from addiction, believing instead that recovery is the only thing needed. As a result of this approach, many people die and suffer every year. Treatment with medication is given for a reason. Those who disagree have never lived the tragedy of watching people like myself attempt to medicate their condition using illicit drugs. In a misguided attempt to even our playing field, we travel down a path that exacerbates a perceived-to-be singular problem; however, in reality, numerous factors are in play for those who suffer from addiction, depression, and other disorders.

To benefit from the help that I received, several factors needed to be treated in unison; I experienced multiple symptoms, which occurred simultaneously. Without an incident that sends off alarms, people with multiple conditions can sometimes spend years in misery without reprieve. They believe they are doing something wrong in recovery because they cannot experience the happiness and contentment that others in recovery experience. Sadly, many are treated as though their imbalance is a result of a failure to take action. This message often results in a return to addiction or other, more serious consequences.

Some who are in, or have gone through, recovery believe that this makes them experts. These people do not understand that by playing doctor, they are essentially signing death certificates. On the flip side, many addicts engage in drug-seeking behavior that leads them to doctors. In these instances, the addict evades the difficult work of eliminating those things that cause adverse emotional responses through resentment and shame. Rather than facing these issues head on, as is required in recovery, the addict seeks a solution through pills, hoping that they will bring relief. Sometimes, they do, especially when the relief they find is through the use of habit-forming medications. The addict then has come full circle and, sadly, may continue to further develop his disease.

I have been fortunate. My episodes of self-harm clearly indicated my need for something beyond what recovery groups offered. Clearly suffering from depression; the extremes of ups and downs formed a more complete image of my issues and needs. It had become evident that I needed long-term treatment. To accomplish this, I was sent to Girard Street Halfway House located in Belling-ham. Given my previous treatment stays, I knew many of the people in recovery groups around the area. Girard Street proved to be a place of rest in my recovery. I began my studies again at the local alternative high school. Many things remained the same; I found myself at noon recovery meetings on a regular basis. I was one of the younger people attending the meetings, but that didn't bother me in the slightest. I wasn't trying to meet people; I was going to remain clean.

For the first time in my life, I spoke with sincerity in support groups. I wasn't just giving lip service. In my open-ness, I developed a new kind of relationship with others. For once, I could look beyond myself and see their emo-tional struggles. I realized that I wasn't much different from any one else in the room. One woman in particular touched my heart. Ann had suffered a stroke during the time she'd been clean. Crossing the floor to give me a hug and a kiss, Ann had to drag her left leg while holding her left arm in her right hand. Her extreme compassion made me feel like a part of that group. Ann seemed to under-stand that I felt stuck between two worlds. By law, I was an adult. Emotionally, I was a twelve-year-old.

In time, the natural desire of any teenager to be a part of the social scene led me to a hotel room where a great compromise occurred. The other kids didn't understand where I had been while they were in school or sleeping in their own beds at night. Only those at the recovery house knew that I was a recovering IV addict. Girls flirted, yell-ing at me from their cars while I walked to the recovery meetings at lunch.

It was with them that I took my first drink since leav-ing Idaho. It wasn't their fault that I reentered the world of substance use despite the tragedies of my life up to this point. In their eyes I must have seemed like a well-dressed eighteen-year-old who held the excitement of the unknown. I suspect that a misunderstood depth in my eyes attracted them, too. Had they known what they were courting, they would have run for their lives. I could hear angels crying in the background as I turned my back on them. Loneliness followed that I knew far too well. The emotion drove me to drink another; I returned to a slow suicide.

I was a chronic relapser. Despite my sincerity, I could not string together any substantial time of recovery. Instead of feeling freed of chemicals, I experienced a kind of torture that goes with the inability to achieve what others enjoy with impunity. A feeling of extreme separation descended. I retreated completely. My pattern consisted of using and self-harm. Sharing the continuous heartbreak of those who believed in me, I experienced great frustration with respect to my powerlessness over chemicals.

For several months before my relapse with the girls, I had been working for a local auto shop after school. A guy named Erin had come by the shop on several occasions to meet with one of my co-workers. It was evident that their relationship went beyond the typical buddy buddy thing, and I realized that they were grooming me for something serious. In reality, the willing cannot be groomed; the willing volunteer themselves. Before they could ask, I asked them about their angle. Erin dealt in prescriptions. He kept a pad with names, signatures, and Drug Enforcement Agency (DEA) numbers that must be on the prescriptions in order for them to be filled.

Erin shared with me the details of their plan. I had never tried to obtain a prescription fraudulently. I felt the familiar surge of adrenaline that accompanies making poor choices of this magnitude. As I entered the store and approached the counter, a familiar voice in my head told me to turn around and leave. The same voice had warned me about the trailer. The same voice had spoken, then been ignored, on numerous other occasions during which I was about to compromise my morality or was headed towards grave danger. When I placed the prescriptions on the counter, my pleading conscience lost out to the excitement. Behind the counter stood a teacher who had substituted in my alternative school not two days previous. In her eyes, I sensed recognition, but in her body language, I saw the repetition that comes with performing any job. She walked back to fill the prescriptions.

The eyes are said to be the windows to the soul. I've always learned more by looking into one's eyes versus watching how one moves or listening to what someone says. Had I trusted my instincts, and believed what I first saw in her eyes, I might have run. She had walked back to the phone, not the pills. Within minutes, the police surrounded me. I did not struggle or argue; I knew I had been caught red-handed. My first night in an adult jail felt lonely and frightening.

I had very little knowledge of how the game worked; I had never played it at this level. The brothers in the meth trailer had told me how to keep my mouth shut if I was ever busted, but I had never been faced with possible conviction of a felony. When the agents from the DEA began to put pressure on me, I folded as quickly as a pyramid of playing cards near an open window. Threats of prison time and what would be done to me there led to thoughts of Kenneth. The DEA men played me perfectly. They left me in detention for the three days, just to think over my charges. After a three-minute conversation, I had made a decision that I now wish I could take back a thousand times over.

I believe in taking responsibility for my own actions. I do not believe in making others pay the consequences on my behalf. Although Erin and his partner had far more experience, I was a willing participant. By pointing out one face in a lineup of eight, I had earned back my freedom at the expense of another. I had never made such a choice before, and I have never done so since.

As the agents congratulated one another, I walked out of the room, unsure of what had just happened. I had the feeling that prostitutes received better treatment than I had. They are often given a ride home and money for their services. I was simply released through the back door in disgrace. I walked home feeling ashamed of what I had just done, wondering how I had been turned so easily. Yes, I had been released, but at what expense?

As if on cue, I received my first letter of many that would follow. Laire refused to give up on me. In a positive moment, I had reached out to him and sent a letter. In his reply, Laire wrote:

May 6, 1994
Dear Eric,

Hello, hello, and once again hello! This is a direct steal from one of your recent letters, however, slightly modified to fit the prose of yours truly. So how about taking up pen and paper and bringing me up-to-date on what Eric has been up to? I am keenly interested in your educational plans for today, tomorrow, and on. Financial aid? Professional track you are most keen on, etc.

How is the quality of Eric's life today and in recent weeks? What are your joys, aspirations, and frustrations? What have you done recently to help another human being? I miss you son. Why? I don't know! God put you into my life for a reason; what that might be, I have no clear idea. However, I accept it for what it is. So I go with my feelings and also an attempt each day to do the next right thing, whatever it might be. I know I may screw up on this from time to time. So be it. At least I try.

I love you, son, and, yes, I do miss the havoc and consternation you caused me over our years together. It is my hope that one day, in the not so distant future, I may once again enjoy the pleasure of your company.

This old warhorse hasn't got too many years left before he joins his comrades in arms in "Fiddlers' Green". That's the final resting place: Arlington National. I have many good friends there already.

Keep in touch, son! If no one had told you today that they love you, know that I do. I do indeed love you!

I remain as ever,

Laire

In April of 1994, my life changed for the better thanks to the simple union of two people. My mother had been seeing Mick for some time, and they had finally decided to get married. Applying their parental calculations, they made a decision based on what was best for the whole versus the individual. In this case, and in many scenarios afterwards, their decision was right on. Although I had met Mick on many occasions, I was not sure how I felt about him. My parents' divorce still stung, even years later. Like a stinger left under the skin long after the bee has gone, the pain lingered.

I allowed the poison of resentment to affect how I viewed others in my life. Though I had not lived at home the majority of the time, I was still fiercely protective of my mother. I felt leery of anyone in a position of affection. To claim love for my mother was not enough to earn my trust; my trust had been broken too many times before. Though his smile and mannerisms showed genuine compassion, I was hesitant to put any stock in forming a relationship with him. I didn't test him as I had others; instead, I inventoried him every time my mother brought him to visit me in the institutions.

My emotional walls dropped sooner than I would have expected. In his visits with my mother, Mick never seemed to pass judgment on me. Accompanying my mother from place to place, and witnessing all the emotion that went into her continued support of my attempts to get clean, must have gotten old. Time passed and in place of judgment, I felt compassion from him. Further, his love and kindness for me, provided proof of his love for my mother.

It is obvious, looking back, that Mick's support enabled my mother to find the strength within to face one of her greatest fears: the possibility that I might never return from the throws of addiction. It is no coincidence that Mick entered our lives when he did. In him, I saw a father figure, a role I denied my own father. Mick's presence filled a gap I had perpetuated since my father's departure; he fit the role of stepfather perfectly. Although it would take many more experiences before I could fully warm up to him, the process left one less crack in need of repair.

As I witnessed their marriage, I felt a relief knowing that my mother had found the love of her life. Although I was still adrift, I experienced a reprieve. I had seen what the absence of love could do, even to the most unsocial person. I did not wish to see my mother grow old without a partner in her life. A hole exists for some adults that even children cannot fill. My mother's marriage brought with it a feeling of joy I had not known for quite some time, and although it was fleeting, it was added to a reserve from which I would draw in the days ahead.

An additional benefit came as a result of my mother's marriage: a wisdom to which youth is blind. This wisdom is built from many years of experience and is expressed through decisions that kids don't always understand. Many times while I was growing up, I didn't understand that my parents acted out of love. Though their actions seemed thoughtless, they were actually thoughtful. The impulsivity of youth had disappeared. In its place, my mother and Mick made a patient assessment of situations following any request. Mick seemed to provide a calm for my mother when she was dealing with me; and she provided it for Mick as he dealt with his own children. I recognize that my mother and father never lacked love when making decisions related to me and my brothers; at times, intense emotional issues produced a biased perspective, which impacted choices made.

As always, my mother transitioned from cautious pleading that I discontinue my use to consistent phone calls and communication when I was in recovery. In so doing, she allowed her vulnerability to show. She knew that at any moment I might choose an act of insanity. My hope of bypassing the symptoms of my disease relies upon the honesty of those I place around me, through recovery groups and healthy relationships. If I do not surround myself with the proper support, my distorted thinking returns and poor choices follow.

Although I was able to hold things together for a couple of months following my brush with the law, the thought of drugs, women, and oblivion eventually crept back in. Despite my near miss, I chose to practice the same behavior that had led to a point of compromise. I cannot put a finger on what might have led me to use again; I cannot think of even one valid excuse. My mother was an active participant in my life, going beyond phone calls and birthday cards by allowing me to return home. Yet despite the good, I slipped into a place of helplessness and despair. The math simply didn't add up. I saw improvement in all areas of my life—from school, to finances, to relationships, to recovery groups. By simply remaining abstinent, most addicts experience the beginning of a natural progression upwards.

Though the external parts of my life showed improvement, my mental faculties were diminishing. I began to avoid the very things that had helped me climb out of the hole I had created. I slept fourteen to sixteen hours every day. I either binged on food or ate nothing at all. I avoided phone calls from loved ones for no reason, and I stopped going to groups. I viewed life in grays instead of color, and my emotions followed suit. No matter how much I prayed to do otherwise, I spiraled down to the place that had led to my last suicide attempt. Before I could choose suicide again, I chose a slower path. Through drugs I might find at least a little comfort before the walls fell in and I found myself alone in the darkness of ruin.

Connie was a friend of my mother's, a medical doctor, and a mover of energy. She began working with me when I came back home in an attempt to help me remain clean. She also worked with me to address my impulse control, depression, and anxiety. I attended many sessions, and although I experienced some improvement, I did not experience the emotional relief that should have accompanied the work. Soon, social influences, mental deterioration, and the desire to use made the choice to use seem rational. Off I went again.

This pattern had been ongoing for some time. It began with desperation and ended in emotional turmoil. Typically, each crisis led to the desire to be clean, followed by several months of recovery, and finally, a dip in my mental faculties that led back to use. There were several deviations to the pattern, but it generally followed a progression that ended in mental deterioration and ignoring outside indicators. The boundaries in place had not changed. Use was not allowed at my parents' house. They never verbalized this fact; I knew that it was so. I didn't need any extra drama or a battle of wills. I was conditioned to understand that use brought shock, and though I didn't look like a lab rat, I sure felt like one. I desperately wanted to avoid even some of the tragedy caused by my use. I sought to alleviate a great anguish, one that the use of drugs could not take away. I wanted to leave before seeing my mother's tears and Mick's disappointment. I wanted a chemical that would finish the job for me.

14

SARA AND HER FAMILY WERE LONGTIME FRIENDS of my family. This caused her to feel some obligation to bring me in when I said I needed a place to stay. In part, I think her mother was still grateful that my parents had not filed a civil suit after the car accident. Sara and I attended treatment together afterwards, and we formed a relationship that went far beyond friendship. As a result of our shared experiences in treatment, we exchanged a genuine affection, more like siblings than simply friends.

While at Sara's house, I avoided IV drug use for a period. My abstinence was the result of my social influences versus a real desire to stay away from the needle. I spent my days searching for marijuana, alcohol, and anything else I could use to fill the ever-growing need to quench obsession and compulsion. When I wasn't looking, I was using; when I wasn't using, I was looking. I saved little time or energy for anything else. I used at the expense of my reputation, as friends grew tired of my manipulation. In essence, nothing had changed.

Lifelong friends became merely resources. The total selfishness of my addiction compelled me to set aside my values for substances. Although I understood that my morals had deteriorated, my sickness outweighed any perceived power of being able to fight it. I had no willpower. This was not because I didn't wish to have it. Willpower could not override the biological change I had experienced over the years of my use. Without spiritual intervention, I was doomed to the daily humiliation I brought on myself to obtain large quantities of chemicals so that I felt comfortable.

At times, I achieved small steps towards recovery. These attempts, though short-lived, showed a desire to stop. In these moments, I regained some dignity by paying a small amount of rent. This eased my burden, but it did little more. I set work aside to use. This put me in a position to be fired from a roofing job, which had provided justification to temper my use. Like any person, I was able to adjust my personality some, once I saw how it repulsed others. I learned that what was revolting to some was attractive to others, especially those who enjoyed the purity of the meth I got from California.

Many island kids used a variety of substances beyond marijuana and alcohol. Even so, I felt that I had tainted the island. I had seen things that surpassed what my most seasoned childhood friends had. This contrast brought the familiar pain of being different from those around me. This separation, plus the shame I felt, led me to view my drug use as a form of martyrdom. I sold in an attempt to support my own use. Once my habit surpassed my sales, I stole from others to compensate. This added to the lack of respect others had for me. My grandiosity returned, and my need to dominate others masked my insecurities, leaving me further ostracized.

Addicts often steal from those closest to them. For me, doing so had nothing to do with how much or how little I loved my family. Instead, I knew what resources my family had. More importantly, I believed that if my family caught me stealing from them, they would not turn me in to the authorities. Although this thought was not at the forefront of my mind, it was a thought nonetheless. It started with the theft of ferry tickets from my parents when they weren't home. When the tickets didn't bring the payoff I had hoped for, I stole items of greater value from my mother.

Stealing from family was a relatively common occurrence. As is the case in many inner cities, kids make their way to pawnshops, their loved ones' precious belongings in hand, hoping to cash them in. In Seattle, the brokers swore they had given me the best price, knowing full well I was unaware of the item's true value. Blinded by greed and habit, I walked out none the wiser. A whole layer of scavengers feed from this exchange. As things of value pass from one hand to another, no hand is less dirty than the previous. From the thief to the broker, the valuables belonging to loved ones are endlessly pillaged.

Walking down 1st Avenue towards the ferry, I felt relief knowing that I had enough money to fund my use for a considerable period of time. I didn't avoid those who peaked from alleyways as I walked. Instead, I courted them, knowledgeable in the language of the streets. "Tar...nugs...shards..." By the time I returned home, I had a healthy supply of black tar, meth, and pills I couldn't name. I didn't care what they were called as long as they did what was promised.

Though black tar heroin was not a major player in my life up to this point, it did play a minor role. That role would grow with time. My first introduction was in the trailer. I had become delusional on meth, so the brothers gave me a hit to calm me down. In that moment, I understood something profound. Drugs were tools. Not only tools to avoid things I wished to forget, but also tools to control and dictate the effects of other drugs. Obviously, this is very dangerous. Doctors spend years perfecting the delicate balance of drug interaction. For those whose self-worth is lower than the gutters they find themselves in, drug interaction is driven by the impulsive need to feel better at any given moment.

Black tar was like alcohol to me. When I used it, I hovered between unconsciousness and consciousness. When I was on it, I lacked awareness of my surroundings. The poppy-induced dream world was a fantastic place, but it did not protect me from the very real world outside of my body. With time and regular use, I became better at handling the highs and lows it created. It was best suited for the confines of my bedroom or the silence and anonymity of the island woods.

The woods provided the same solitude I had experienced as a child, though the shadows held a different meaning. I no longer focused on the beams of light filtering through the trees; instead, I peered into the shadows that the light had created. In the woods, no one would wake me from my nothingness. I felt safe in the crook of an ancient cedar, using moss as my pillow. I had found a soft gutter, one that protected me from the harsh realities of the city.

When the gypsies began to take over the city, I discovered a world that I had never known existed. The Grateful Dead stopped in Seattle during the last tour of Jerry Garcia's long career. I had been exposed to their music, but I understood little of the following they had amassed.

The shows brought with them endless drug possibilities. I easily blended with the crowds that gathered in order to experience all that was the Dead phenomenon. It was hard to believe that a whole culture could be mobilized and set up in the parking lots of various venues. Beautiful women twirled and danced to the rhythm of the drum; groups pulsated across the grounds.

The experience seemed unreal, especially after the white fluff (or LSD) took effect. Some Deadhead placed white paper on my tongue, which brought colors and patterns. Music bounced off of the surrounding buildings and wrapped around me. The illusions formed a potent elixir that changed the course of my life and how I viewed the world. I felt as though I had returned to some ancient memory. With every smile, I experienced warmth like I had never felt before. A scene of unrefined significance played out before me, at a time in my life when it seemed most important. The tide of the tour swept me from the three-day show in Seattle to Portland Meadows, where a large group of my friends gathered for a weeklong party, which ended with another two days of shows.

I experienced relief from the weight of my circumstances in the illusion created through drugs, colors, and the many fine people who made this their life. Their experience was far different from my own. I was just a tourist, whereas many of these Deadheads had created a life for themselves here, one that they had been living for more years than I had been alive. I saw in theirs, a life I wished I could experience. I understood that they lived with a balance of which I was incapable. Much of society, blinded by their own judgment, viewed these people as freeloaders. To survive in perpetual travel with the show, they had found a way to support themselves as many other nomadic people had. The great misconception is that drugs made their lifestyle possible. In fact, the great majority sold things that brought greater stability, and less risk, than the interstate transport of chemicals. They had found a way to capitalize on the crowds that flocked to "The Dead Experience." Many did use drugs as resources, but those resources had very little staying power. A T-shirt press held more value to most than a gram of raw LSD.

The shows reminded me of a beautiful flower, attracting insects to pollinate its folds to ensure survival for another season. In the intense colors and atmosphere, those who carried forward the lifestyle brought those resources necessary to survive at the next venue. Though I dressed as they did, I did not have the moral fiber necessary, or the respect needed, to be brought into the fold. In my path, I left destruction and a karmic debt that would not be paid for many more years. I tried to emulate what I saw on the outside, not realizing that kindness and spirituality does not exist in tie-dye, dreadlocks, or hemp necklaces. Their essence went beyond the physical and entered the realm of the spirit.

I have a difficult time describing the lessons I learned through hallucinogenic drugs. A thousand sages lived within every dose, flooding my senses and my mind with ideas for which I was not yet prepared. It was no wonder that medicine men from countless cultures had used this approach for hundreds of years. As I peaked, I had be drawn to the rhythm of the drum circles, my body giving way to a dance that reflected a tribal urge, one that surpassed the culture beyond the glow of the fire. The years that separated me from a time, which up to that point only existed in lore, now materialized in a culture that carried it like an ember in the wilderness; using it to spark the fire at the next stop.

Stumbling away from the rhythm and light, I traveled into a familiar darkness. I peered into a pit in which I saw an image of myself ingesting blackness that diminished the surrounding light. I was naked and gorged. The scars upon my body appeared black like the streaks I ingested. Around me, the bones of those I loved sat in piles of varying decay. I decided which to devour next. In repulsion, I could not look away as the shadows in the pit joined the feast, gorging upon the bones, and finally, me.

Turning away, I fell into the tree line that surrounded the camp. I had no point of reference. Every face that passed smiled in understanding of the darkness I was experiencing. Everything took on a sinister hue; permeating with the karmic energy I had created in choosing to use others as commodities rather than respecting them as teachers and fellow travelers. What was once a fun way to distort reality in my younger days became a dark corridor with many doorways. In each, a harsher reality presented itself. When I returned from the land of the spirit, I realized that much of what I had learned stayed with me. The things I had endured were not lost in the complexity of the hallucination. They stuck, and with them, a process of learning had sprouted.

I know this sounds crazy to those who have no concept of the potency of such experiences. Some will scoff and wave away the power of such things, calling the experience a chemically induced farce. The opening of the mind does not have to come through drug use; it may be achieved through natural alteration, like prayer or meditation. Others find it through intense debate or when feeling the winds upon a mountaintop. What I experienced in eight hours left a weight, one that I was not emotionally or spiritually ready to understand. This was merely my experience. I do not in any way, suggest that others follow in my footsteps. I recognize that every individual's spiritual path leads him or her to the places that they are meant to visit. I was meant to look within myself to see what I had been doing to others and to myself on a spiritual level. Perhaps this experience can be reasoned away by some other means, but I visualized a disassembled reality. The experience showed me aspects of myself that left me forever changed.

I continued to follow the Grateful Dead south to Oakland, California. My experiences remained the same in many regards; the only difference being that the money I had accumulated through theft, had been given to the show as an offering. This left me and my travel partner with our thumbs out, trying to return home to Washington. We left with nothing but a few T-shirts, pipes, patches, and a hell of a headache. I did not have the staying power of the others; even if I had wished to remain with the tour, I had nothing of value to give to the core traveling community. As a consequence, I was spun out like so many others and returned to the realities of a life I had no wish to revisit. It was no coincidence that I had started my tour the same year that it would all change. I remember hearing on the radio that Jerry Garcia had died as a result of detoxification from alcohol and heroin. He may have lacked the staying power that many others had as well. I was grateful for the opportunity to experience the shows, although I would have preferred to do so at my own expense. Not my parents'.

In the weeks following my return from California, I knew that I would be asked to leave Sara's home. They did not ask in anger, and I did not refuse to go. Instead, there was a silent understanding that her mother's obligation had been met and that I was grateful for what they had provided me. Sara's family had expected that I would find a job to eventually become self-sufficient, the same reasonable expectation I had met everywhere else. Usually my departure from a place was connected to some gross misbehavior that symbolized a breach in the trust that had been established upon my arrival. Though I could have helped a great deal more financially, I felt that in some backward, self-centered way, my payment consisted of not bringing the horrors of my past into their home.

The shame of decisions I had made at the beginning of the summer began to register, and I no longer had a veil of chemicals to hide behind. Although I still used, I agreed to begin meeting with Connie again prior to leaving Sara's. This helped to open a door into my soul; one, which I thought, had been sealed up tightly. The impacts of the most recent acts I had committed against others remained fresh within. The theft from my mother caused me great pain as soon as I acknowledged it. This brought a flood of emotion that I could not stop regardless of how hard I tried. All of my binges ended this way. Once my conscience caught up with me, I was forced to address the consequences. I am both blessed and cursed with a conscience that does not allow me to bury the acts I commit against others. As a result, I replaced long-term use with bingeing. In so doing, I caused as much or more damage in six months than most do over a lifetime.

In many ways, my sessions with Connie mimicked what I experienced on hallucinogenic substances. The movement of energy caused shifts in my body and mind that I could not begin to explain. To attain a certain spiritual wandering, I did not have to go through extreme self-loathing as I had before. Connie used a combination of Upledger Craniosacral and Somatoemotional Release. She also used other methods of energetic healing.

On one occasion, Connie warmed her hands to a temperature and an intensity I had only known in energy sessions. She moved her hands from my cranium, along my body's energy routes, clearing energy obstruction. At one point in particular, I felt a flood of emotion indicative of the type of release that typically signified my return to recovery, though this release was brought about through healing touch. In the release, I experienced a thousand words of shame that had collected since my last stint with using. In just a few months, a lifetime of self-directed ill will can accumulate. Every choice to use brings with it a spiritual shift, one that carries feelings of resentment, shame, and fear. These were emotional responses that I thought I had moved beyond in previous attempts to improve my mental health.

In a stream of words I released incidents I had tightly held. I described entering my parents' house and stealing from them. I expressed my shame that the two people who had honored me through their constant emotional support were the greatest victims of abuses. In that admission, a shame previously unknown erupted as a surge, overpowering the first. I understood that, through my self-centeredness, I had entered the world of the victimizer. Prior to each offense, a bending of morality took place; I rejected the emotional warning system put in place to keep me from hurting others. I was no longer the five-year-old at the hands of Marlene, or the fourteen-year-old shaking at the aftermath of Kenneth's offenses. I suddenly understood that in using others to fulfill my own desires, I had morphed into what I had always viewed them to be. This was not an easy realization. It left me huddled on the floor at Connie's feet. She listened as the secrets that kept me sick surfaced and subsequently lost their potency.

Connie understood the emotional and spiritual reorganization taking place within me. She knew that such raw power required direction and guidance over the days to come; this was a residual effect of the intense shifts that had taken place. When the soul turns in on itself, purging the negative energy that has been stored within, a person becomes susceptible to the things that left it that way to begin with. The cancer of addiction, self-harm, depression, or suicidal thoughts, as examples, can feed on the tenderness left in place of the putrefaction. Her invite was brief and to the point. She would allow me to stay with her and her husband for a short time while I amended my relationship with my parents. This was as much for them as it was for me, although I was not aware of the significance at that point.

There exists a misconception that those who are plagued by addiction and other disorders are bereft of spiritual insight, emotional depth, and mental fortitude. The truth is just the opposite. Addiction is forced to fight that much harder given the strength of these characteristics. Some of the most amazing people are those who have persevered through great difficulties. A second misconception claims that in the journey out of addiction, people gain a spiritual understanding to which they were not privy before. I would argue that those qualities or experiences earned or gained through self-improvement existed within all along. Addicts deny that they possess within that power or quality which could free them from their bondage. Allowing it to manifest destroys the image they've created that justifies the abuse of themselves and of others.

An internal light can equal, or surpass the darkness that lies within me–one balancing out the other. In times of turmoil, both aspects of my being fluctuate; leaving a void that must be filled. In many instances, the darkness fills this space, while the light fights to preserve what is left in the hope of restoration. At other times it is the opposite occurs. The balance is dependent upon my spirits condition.

I have heard a homeless man sing, the concrete of an underpass amplifying his voice. With his eyes closed in thoughts of a faraway place, every verse blends the perfection of music with his spirit. I have witnessed the lines of an unknown artist appear on the pages of their doodling pad, their talent better served on the walls of a fine art gallery. The creative power that lies within reflects the depth at which these people operate. Their one problem is the absence of the damper, which would enable them to balance the flames. Most burn out before they can find or be taught the equilibrium needed for their vast reservoir of spirit. Tragically, the musician finds at the bottom of the bottle a grave beneath the willows. The heroin addict finds a concrete pillow in an endless sleep. For reasons that I did not understand, I had been spared that ending. I might have invited it, but my inner desire to live overpowered my will to diminish. Drugs held veto power over my inner desire, an imbalance of power, which brought heartbreak to those who observed from a distance.

What I expected from Mick did not come to pass. His compassion and controlled anger made my transgression against my mother weigh more heavily upon my conscience. Our ferry ride left me thinking of the many things I had stolen from my mother that could not be replaced. Mick had been forced to pay an inflated price for those items that had not yet sold. The humiliation that I felt looking them both in the eyes did not manifest into shame as it typically had done; instead, it became something much healthier: remorse. I felt sadness as a result of how I had treated my parents. The realization that I had stolen from my mother left me speechless as we returned to the island with what could not be reclaimed.

In the end, my parents did not decide to press charges. Doing so would have left me facing numerous felonies. The scale had been placed before them as they weighed the various options, hoping that one would bring change without punishment. My mother's anger was suppressed, but only as a result of Mick's calm. It was decided that I would return to Connie's home where arrangements would be made for attendance at an adult treatment facility in Seattle. I was cast off, but not in ceremony. I held my head low, plodding forward along the path I had chosen for myself.

15

ONQUEST HOUSE MARKED MY ENTRY INTO a foreign land. When I arrived through the front doors, I was surprised—as were a majority of the occupants. This was not a place with many nineteen-year-old, white kids from the suburbs. I had grown accustomed to being the youngest in treatment centers. Being one of a handful of white men in a facility housing thirty or more African American men was new to me. I had never been in a place where I could be considered the minority; I wasn't quite sure how I felt about it. The reverend met us at the door, his gold teeth in clear view. He reminded me of a used car salesman wearing a polyester suit. I assumed that the black Cadillac parked out front belonged to him as well.

It is hard to give credit to those who do good deeds, while also committing bad ones. Does a good act balance out the bad? In my time at Conquest House, I saw a system of survival perpetuated by those who used the system to their advantage. In my first few days, I was given a questionnaire to be used at the welfare office. The shelter operated on donations, sales, and food stamps obtained by well-rehearsed applicants. I am not sure how far food stamps from forty people could stretch, but I am sure it went further than what appeared on our dinner plates. Four days a week, the food solicitation truck returned with food donated by local businesses. As part of kitchen duty, we were tasked with sorting through the moldy grocery bags to extract the food that was still edible. It was a thing of magic to see how the cooks managed to make edible food from society's garbage. I found myself eating light, or not at all, during my stay there. I was not alone.

Conquest House was a treatment center for addicts coming off the streets or out of prison. It was a place for those with no other options. For me, it was temporary housing until a space opened up at a facility in Seattle. We attended groups several times a week that were facilitated by a counselor and The Reverend. During the week, we were expected to attend the on-campus chapel, where those seeking extra attention from The Reverend became overcome by the Holy Ghost and convulsed on the floor in pretend elation. I might have believed the act had the men not returned, laughing at their own performances. I do not doubt the power of the Creator, but I had reason to doubt those who professed certain things in one breath and did the opposite in another.

The women lived upstairs and down the same hallway as Reverend. Some whispered that the hallway was his personal henhouse. Watching how the women were treated made it difficult to argue against the rumors. It didn't take much to see that the halfway house had been designed to stroke the ego of those who ran it. As the run-down treatment vans pulled into the compound, The Reverend pulled out in his shiny, black Cadillac with one of the lady patients riding in the passenger seat. God forbid that anyone got caught flirting with the women staying there. Salacious behavior would not be tolerated. The

Reverend's threats did not keep a steady stream of men from climbing the utility pipes and into the window of the women's rooms nearly every night.

Because most of the men came from prison, the treatment center maintained prison-like social protocol. I was excluded from many of the harsher truths of what this meant. Even so, it was understood that if anything happened, we would back our own races. "White is white and black is black," they told me. "Remember that when shit goes down. We set friendship aside. It's just the way it is." It seemed strange to me that men who were so grateful to be out of prison wanted to recreate the environment they had just left. Many nights, I heard fights in the rooms around me. I quickly learned to avoid conflict by turning my eyes. In my avoidance, I found myself shielded by the men who surrounded me, in particular when someone tried to give me a hard time. It seemed as though they had regained something lost in prison as a result of protecting another. I was the son, the brother, or the nephew they could not be around as a consequence of their choices. What the older white men experienced in day-to-day life, I was able to avoid because I was not a threat to anyone.

One man suffered from obvious mental problems. His problems kept him from adjusting socially. As a result, I became the victim of his hatred of white people. Regardless of what the others did to keep him from focusing on me, I remained the object of his resentment. On occasion, a game of dominos would escalate into a heated exchange. The man discovered that I wasn't quite the pushover he believed me to be; I was as good at banter as the rest of them. I was also unwilling to show any intimidation brought on by the twenty-year age gap. What began as his attempt to show dominance, ended with him verbally cut to pieces in front of the others.

I understood that I had to protect myself; the others couldn't protect me from everything. If I allowed myself to be pushed around, things would only get worse. After a few weeks, our altercations escalated and I found myself in a series of fights that left one of us on the losing side. This didn't end our dislike for each other. Ultimately, he pulled a kitchen knife on me. "I will slice you up, white boy. Try me! I will!" This act brought the weight of the men's floor down on him. What had been an amusement of sorts, had crossed a line that none of the elders would allow to continue. Pat was pulled into a bunk room. From that day on, his attention faded to muffled threats.

Part of our daily schedule included a door-to-door sales program, which dropped us in the wealthiest Seattle neighborhoods selling various items. Most popular were the cookies baked by the women from the shelter. They baked all day, then bagged the cookies, and added labels. The bags were then packed for us to resell for "donations." It was humiliating going door-to-door, sorting through any one of a dozen cover stories to sell a bag of cookies. We were taught the art of reading people's exteriors to predict their interiors. All we had to do was draw from our street savvy. We adjusted our stories to tug on their heartstrings in whatever way would benefit the shelter the most. For the religious, we told them about our religion-based program. For the politically left-leaning, we discussed a new program that integrated different approaches to bring about change in the addict. It was an ingenious hustle that exploited the resident's unsuspecting and tender heart.

Every time I made a sale based on a false pretense, I resented the shelter more. The shelter had been built on the lies of those trying to learn a new and positive way to live. Eventually, the cookies were replaced by a high-potency, all-purpose cleaner purchased in bulk from a local distributor and then repackaged for sale. I wasn't surprised when I saw the first finished bottle. The label included a picture of The Reverend, fists outstretched to show off his gold rings, grinning that million-dollar, gold-toothed grin. They called the cleaner Stomp Out, which brought more laughter than it got out stains. Discontinued after a short time, Stomp Out was used to clean the bathrooms at Conquest House, a fitting end, given the ego who had created it.

November 24, 1995
Dear Eric,

I had a most delightful surprise earlier today, just after the Thanksgiving meal. Your mother gave me a call from your grandmother's condo here in Bradenton. We had a most delightful conversation. She provided me with your most current address. She appears to be both very happy and content with her life.

It seems to me that you must've lost your ability to take pen to paper. In other words, get off your ass young man and write me a letter! If you were nearby, I had plant my boot where it might just get your attention.

Oh yes, first things first. If no one has told you today, and all days, that they love you, I do. Why? I don't know. I just do. It must be the Scotsman in me.

Life has been a bit hectic in my part of the world. I was at the Bay Pines, VA Medical Center for a routine checkup when I lost my balance. I was sent to an emergency room where an EKG and CAT scan were conducted. The latter was not good news. I was transported immediately to the VA hospital in Tampa, where I was given brain surgery to remove a clot. The lead surgeon told me that a large amount of sawdust was found in my skull cavity. He said I was a prime candidate for a brain transplant. I am still waiting for a suitable baboon donor to be located.

After many tests, the VA determined that I was bleeding internally. I am considered borderline anemic. They also found a spot in my left lung that a doctor at MacDill Air Force Base in Tampa will look at on the 29th. This is all speculation, but if you still pray, please keep me in mind.

Enough about medical conditions associated with old age. We all get old, God willing, and experience difficulties. It's a function of living, accepting, and dealing with the hand that has been dealt you.

Now for you. What have you done for your country today? Diane just returned from the mailbox and guess what she hand-delivered to me, a most unexpected and welcome surprise. I'll be damned! Apparently you do know how to put pen to paper. Progress. Keep working on it, son!

I know that school—better yet, college—remains a stumbling block for you. I can't help you confront whatever it is that's a problem for you in those regards, but I can assure you that a college education will be a very valuable asset in your life. Don't mess things up by letting whatever opportunity presents itself pass you by. Make your own opportunities and go for GOLD!

I love you, son. Why, I am still trying to figure that out. I simply love you and am worried about you. Don't keep messing things up. Do the best with what God has bestowed upon you, and that is quite a bit.

Love you,
Laire

I loved that man. I saw in him all the John Wayne bravado I had watched on TV as a child. Laire also showed deep compassion and simply would not allow me to succumb to this disease without having a say in it. We were many generations apart, but through the common bond of addiction, that gap diminished. Laire loved helping others; I loved whatever fit into a syringe. His love for me took away one of the many excuses I had used to justify my use. This was the gift. The large hole created by abuse and abandonment was slowly filling up.

On Christmas, my mother, Mick, my oldest brother Travis, and his wife Tanya came to visit me. Being clean left an open window of opportunity for those who loved me. They could come and spend time with the Eric whom they loved and missed. The patient's families were invited for a Christmas meal, one that left me wishing I had been raised in a different community. Though my mother was an amazing cook, something about the food served at Conquest House's Christmas party made me go back for seconds and thirds. The residents and staff treated my family with openness and a compassion that left me grateful. If only they had treated and fed us in that same manner the other 364 days of the year. When potential donors visited, they brought out their best linen.

The other days were not all bad. The scale tipped in favor of spiritual experiences, so Sundays made everything else bearable. The power of gospel music cannot be fully appreciated through a TV screen or a car stereo. The singing fills those who listen with a spirit and grace. I imagined angels perched high and listening. Revival was an all-day Jesus-a-thon. I attended my fair share of churches growing up, but those experiences did not begin to prepare me for the passion expressed in a black church. The style in which the sermons were preached made it seem like an unknown nemesis fought its way in through the church doors. Eventually, even the most energetic speaker could not compete with the singers lined up in rows and swaying to the music. Their songs lured the listeners, and the preaching drew people in like a good sales pitch. I wanted to tell them to quit sermonizing and just sing, to attract as many people as possible to hear the sound of the heavens.

On occasion, someone taken by the moment, would "jog for Jesus" around the church, only to be knocked to the ground by the preacher's touch. I never could figure out what the white covering stood for. My guess was it represented the Holy Ghost or death of the flesh. Whatever the case, I welcomed the reprieve from my daily routine at the shelter. I also liked how the older black women fussed over me afterwards. They fed me like their own, laughing and saying things like, "White folk don't feed their children enough. Look how skinny he is."

I began to see falsehood in the words spoken about the African American culture. The lies of my culture became apparent through my experience living among them. I never once felt fear or intimidation from them as a whole. Instead, they brought me into their world and showed kindness and compassion. Granted, I wasn't at 23rd Avenue and Cherry Street looking for crack rock. I also wasn't at a condo in Florida preparing to rob dealers with a group of white crack-heads. Conquest House allowed me to realize that the African American culture had been vilified by the other, more dominant cultures of our society. Some African Americans had furthered this image through perceptions in the media. I felt ashamed to be part of a race of human beings who had treated others with such prejudice and disdain.

I could see the abuses that the African American people had endured over time through the lens of one who had also endured the worst of humanity. Although I could never understand the hundreds of years of oppression that their people endured, I carried a ball and chain and the marks left by emotional lashings endured at the hand of my aggressors. Maybe that is why we related so well. We shared repression and the desire to overcome obstacles created by abuse. We shared a knowledge possessed only by survivors, and in this understanding, color disappeared leaving the spirit in its most raw form. That is why I stood in the last pew to dance and praise as one with them. Their songs brought the freedom I was looking for—hope's crescendo.

Eventually, I moved to Straley House, a youth home in the University District for homeless and transitioning youth. I fit both categories and felt grateful that I would not have to solicit to stay. As with any shelter, there were other requirements. At Straley House, the rules were intended to further respect for oneself and for others. Curfew fell between 11:00 pm and 1:00 am, depending on the day of the week. I participated in daily chores and house meetings, and was expected to find a job or go to school. I had no interest in school. With my high school experience as proof, I believed that I was incapable of finding success there.

When I made excuses to avoid the things that scared me, I jumped right to my worst experience; I glanced past those who might justify the opposite side of my argument. While living in another halfway house, I had taken and passed the General Education Development (or GED) test missing only two questions. Granted, it was not Harvard material, but passing did mean I was capable of academic success. My previous failures did not prove that I was stupid. I simply could not shake the idea that I was far less capable than others.

I started off well at Straley and found a job working for the Seattle Youth Garden Works program. I helped grow vegetables, herbs, and flowers in local green spots around the city. I had grown up with vegetable gardens and flowerpots at home, so designing a space where I could watch the miracle of growth begin and flourish excited me. Instead of digging through moldy grocery bags for food to eat, I grew fresh vegetables and brought them back to Straley House to become part of our group dinners. I was paid a modest sum, but the real payment came through work experience, kind people, and free organic food.

My momentum in this experience carried over into the house. I planted flowers and vegetable in the beds that I tilled. I felt as though I had finally found my place in the universe. I was no longer at the mercy of the winds constant change. I felt a part of the intricacies that make up the greater whole. This allowed me to shed some of my self-centeredness and emotional weight; I became a lighter version myself.

Only a few times in my life had I felt the way the way I did then. The first was as a child in the island forest. Those woods wrapped me in their embrace and balanced out my emotions without my knowledge. Those explorations amongst the ivy and ferns, light mixing with mist, allowed me to develop spiritually. The second was when I sat on the rock in the river valley on my solo, feeling for the first time that I was a part of every breath I took. I had existed—even flourished—by disassociating myself from my past and my future. In the garden, the dark soils and emerging buds, turned a city that had once scared me into a world both fresh and vital.

Along with the beauty of the developing flora, I began to develop relationships with others as my spirit sought to heal itself. To lead a child out of darkness to find his own light, validated and brought great pleasure to the staff at the house and Garden Works. They were saving lives. They did not have huge budgets but their gains were enormous. Capital came in the form of hugs and gratitude, not dollar bills and commodities

In protest to a world that placed material wealth before people, one of my counselors removed any advertisement she found on her clothing or things, from bikes, to hats, shoes, or coffee mugs. She eliminated any labels she felt fed a system that turned its eyes from the children she fought to protect. She despised the bank signs that lined every corner of the city, as pre-teen and teenage kids begged for change to meet their basic needs. How could businessmen and women walk past the soiled children of the streets, turning their noses up as they rushed home to their own children unaware of a fate they had escaped? She did not buy into the idea that if kids did not fit into their parents' social circles, then the parents no longer held responsibility. She felt that the community was responsible for the well-being of its most vulnerable members. In taking on this sacred responsibility, she hoped to create a future with fewer people damaged as a resulted of turned backs. She reduced the amount of suffering in the world around her, as many great healers have so successfully done.

As I prospered, my self-confidence reflected back to the people I met. I attended recovery meetings and met with the counselors, working to peel more layers away from the abuses I had experienced. To all appearances, it looked like I had found the balance necessary to continue on my path to recovery. I was still missing one ingredient, a symptom that had not yet been addressed. The unrelenting sadness and self-loathing began to infiltrate my refuge once again. Feelings that did not match my circumstances took hold. The things I had established as a barrier to fend off such feelings began to disintegrate. My biological and chemical imbalance cared little for the work I had done.

Depression deserves every profanity in existence. Chemical dependency, too, is darkness of the purest form. Like most junctures in my life, those who had fought so hard to eliminate the regression of both, witnessed my regression in stunned horror. I imagine it is like watching a movie backwards. The payoff at the end disappeared, each step coming undone, one after the other, until the only thing left to do was to wait until the process stopped, then to start again at the beginning.

The subtle call of the streets came from a block to the West. University Avenue provided all the necessary ingredients for me to continue my use. The constant influx of people ensured a new face every few seconds. The Avenue bustled with those who were simply passing through as well as those with a specific purpose. The homeless courted the tourists as they entered. They exchanged drugs such as heroin, LSD, mushrooms, ecstasy, and marijuana. Desires of the flesh brought kids more cash in an hour than they could have earned in days. Kids learned to turn off their emotions in order to emerge from a difficult or painful situation better able to provide for themselves. I must assume that the adults with a lust for children rarely, if ever, took into account the physical and emotional scars they left behind. The University District was no different from any area where human beings, controlled by addictive forces, placed their desires above morality; they are led by a force seemingly more powerful than any act of will to avoid it.

As I replaced one thing with another, I created a network within the University District of people who used as I did. Within a short time, I could procure anything the tourists wanted in a matter of minutes. In many ways, I had become a predator, seeking out those who could provide what I desired. I could fulfill any of the needs that binges required. This led me to alleyways, where I receded into the depths of the poppy, or high on meth, up for days at a time. I became a part of the city, like one who had returned to the hands of their abuser.

Through the moving traffic, I saw kids I had once worked with tilling the soil I had abandoned in favor of the concrete. My new land grew only cigarette butts and orange syringe caps. On some days, I hid in the sunflowers, shooting up and weeping over the fact that I was taking life, not nurturing it.

Ignominy is too simple a word to describe how I felt. Those who met me at the door of Straley House were no longer excited to see me. Instead, they presented me with alternatives to my current living situation. In my choice to use, I disrespected a space created for those who wished to avoid the hole I had fallen into. As a result of my choices, I had compromised all the kids who fought so desperately to rebuild their lives. I lived with a grandiosity that turned those with compassion to the role of protector, sheltering the others from the monster I represented. The people at Straley House were finished protecting me from myself; I had invited shadow back into my life. I was stuck, both longing to further what I had begun there, and longing to achieve the euphoria promised by the streets.

All of my worldly possessions fit into one suitcase. I had learned that having too many things meant leaving items behind or lugging them around the streets. Tears did little to change my circumstances. My heart ached as the doors closed behind me. I loaded my bag into my mother's car, and we headed to the next destination. As we drove away, I watched as one of the other kids tended the garden I had started. I had not left total destruction in my wake; this realization did little to soothe my regret. The staff at Straley House got me into a long-term, state-funded, adult treatment facility. I did not understand what that meant, nor could I blame them for making a life and death decision. They no longer sought to comfort me; they were hoping to save the life of a chronic, twenty-year-old junkie who seemed set on self-destruction.

The notion of punishing the addict versus treating the addict has been around for many years. It is a tactic often used and rarely questioned. The addict's actions make it difficult to decipher moral issues from symptoms of a disease. These symptoms take a very visible progression, one that often ends in death. People become so angry at the moral deterioration associated with drug use that they throw up their hands and allow forms of treatment that border—and sometimes cross over—the line of abuse.

It is hard for me to feel gratitude toward such places. Instead, their methods leave me with a deep sadness. They try to create change in the addicts who come to their doorstep in desperation. Though this is far better than returning to the needle, better options exist. A grey area may be preferable to a yet darker side. Behavior modification is one such grey area. The State of Washington referred me to a long-term program because it was one of several that offered long-term care to the chronic, low-bottom addict. I did not know that behavior modification programs are based on a philosophy that departs from the softer methods I had experienced. They tended towards punishment, the habit-breaking side of addiction treatment. The kindness and compassion fundamental to twelve-step recovery programs ceased to exist. Patients were forced to live in an environment where continuous, high-intensity confrontation was to be expected.

Instead of treating compulsion and craving, they chose to focus on a set of behaviors that they felt better addressed the problem of addiction. Tactics that were considered abuse to children two years younger than me became therapeutic tools. Screaming in groups by counselors, staff members, and clients was a daily occurrence. What would have seemed abrasive to most became routine and left me desensitized to the accompanying humiliation. Behavior modification supposes that an addict's behavior leads to use. Though behavior plays a substantial role in drug addiction, I believe it is not the key factor. The debate concerning whether or not addiction is a disease should have ended when the American Medical Association classified it as such. At that point, the obligation to treat addicts, as patients suffering from a progressive and fatal illness, should have taken precedence. Still, many cited moral deficiency, as justification for punishment of what they still believed to be behavior-driven.

I quickly learned that changing my behavior did not keep me from getting yelled at. I had to memorize, and then follow a particular list of rules. No swearing, no compromising, no reacting, no disregarding direction, and no talking bad about another person. This list was hammered into my consciousness to the point that I rarely found myself being screamed at. I avoided those who, when they screamed, sent spittle flying from their mouths or exhibited pressurized blood vessels popping from their foreheads. I also avoided having a toilet seat placed around my neck and getting my head shaved. Avoiding consequences did little to address the medical issues associated with my diagnosis. They did not address craving, tolerance, or progression. The program's one benefit was that it lasted two years. Some healing can take place in that amount of time regardless of circumstance.

There is very little work that has to be done to beat down the walls of an addict who has already been beaten down by addiction. At this level of care, it is rare to spend weeks working through the denial that many early stage addicts have yet to address. Breaking down a broken person simply worsens the shame from which the addict already suffers. Yelling and demoralization do little more than exacerbate a problem for which the addict is not responsible. Punishing behavior will not teach the addict to change their behavior. Emotional surrender and the development of a spiritual life generate emotional and spiritual shifts with staying power. Abuse begets abuse. I could not understand how the same type of abuse to which I had been subjected could help me stay clean. There are more compassionate ways to bring about change in the individual. The people I know who are the most balanced took part in spiritual, physical, and psychological components during their process of recovery. It is this holistic approach that addresses the many intricacies of the human condition.

Although religious activities were not allowed, I practiced prayer and meditation on a regular basis. I found that through the practice of breathing I could eliminate the stress of my environment. Through prayer, I could turn over my circumstances and accept them for what they were. Even though I was not allowed to study the philosophies I had learned through years of treatment, I could apply what I already knew; this allowed me to survive there, taking things day by day.

Monday through Friday I worked at the center-owned recycling facility. I went into the city to collect recycled paper from businesses. As I rode through the city, I imagined seeing my father on every bus. After being laid off from the phone company, he had become a city bus driver. I thought about what I would say if I saw him. We had not seen each other for some time. I wondered what a normal conversation between us would sound like. The Seattle route gave me the opportunity to feel normal again and to be separated from the micro-society of long-term treatment. My job also took care of the physical aspect of my recovery. At the end of every day, I felt good having accomplished something of value. Hard work taught me my limitations as well as my strengths. The systematic manner in which things were done taught me to view other work accordingly. These were firm lessons that I could apply to my life later on.

One evening at the treatment center, a counselor called me into the office. Whenever this happened, something out of the ordinary was about to happen. The evening staff consisted of a husband and wife who lived on-site with their six-month-old baby. The counselor, a tender heart named Catherine, treated everyone with respect and dignity. Entering the room, I knew immediately that something was wrong; I braced myself for whatever it might be. "Eric, your grandmother in Florida died from cancer." I began to sob. Because I suppressed my emotion for extended periods of time, I could not control myself once I let go. Sobs escaped my mouth, my chest expelling the pain of loss. Each inhalation carried a new, louder cry. People in the hallway turned, uncomfortable with witnessing my anguish.

In the moment that my pain peaked, I felt the tender embrace of Christian, the six-month-old, who was now reaching from his mother's familiar arms and wrapping himself around my neck. He did so tenderly, as his mother tried to pull him back. He would not allow her to pull him away. I have never seen a baby that young act in the way that he did. For at least twenty minutes, I was cradled in the arms of an infant, the pain of my loss echoing into silence through the hallways.

In Christian's embrace, I experienced the embrace of my grandmother. There was no doubt in any of the minds of those watching the scene that something profound happened. Through the innocence of a child, my grandmother was able to soothe me and to express the love she had shared so many times before. In my pain came the understanding that I could not take back the harsh words I had said to her, nor could I go back in time to take advantage of all she had done for me. In the miracle of that embrace, I knew all was forgiven. In the purging of my soul, I mended all that I had done to drive a wedge into our relationship. As I cried, Christian would pull his head back and look into my eyes. When a cry emerged, he would again bury his cheeks into my neck and hold me tight. When the crying finally ended and I felt the final surge of emotion dissipate, Christian reached back for his mother. He was again, a baby in his mother's arms.

Through the vessel of innocence, my grandmother gave me her last gift. Through the embrace of an infant, she reached out across the divide to soothe my great sorrow. In this final act, she left me with the understanding that, in death, we do not depart. We are still able to affect the hearts of those we love.

I left the office in a far better mental and spiritual condition than when I arrived. Catherine and the other staff members stood staring in recognition of what had just happened. In this facility I abhorred, I was gifted this most profound spiritual experience. The center took on a new light. In gratitude, I climbed the stairs to my bunk to sleep more deeply than I had in recent memory. I hoped that Christian would sleep well–oblivious to the gift he had given me.

16

January 7, 1997
My dear Eric,

Your mother must be in Bradenton attending to your grandmother. She called the other day, last Saturday I believe, and spoke with Diane for a while, explaining why she was down here. Apparently, your grandmother has passed on. I am sorry to learn about that.

1996 was not a good year for Laire. The doctors in Tampa determined that the remainder of my left lung had to come out. I lost half that lung while serving in Vietnam in 1967. Heavy Agent Orange exposure during both my tours (1965 and 1967) and heavy smoking have led to this inevitability. The operation went well. Unfortunately, a major infection developed and that put me in the hospital for another five weeks. Apparently that infection almost did me in; however, my higher power had different plans. I think he still has something he wants me to accomplish in this life. Anyhow, the wound would have to be reopened in order to have me heal from the inside out.

I was back in the VA hospital for most of October and a good part of November—post traumatic stress disorder. Seems like a good deal of what I experienced in Vietnam was still kicking around in my head, especially when I was sleeping. I was having horrible night dreams. The doctors decided I was not crazy. I just had too many nasty memories of years gone by. I don't know if they helped me, though I do have fewer dreams at this point, which is good.

I spent Christmas in Sarasota Memorial Hospital. I woke one morning and found my arm had swelled up about twice its normal size. I went to one of those walk-in clinics and saw a great lady doctor who referred me to a vascular doctor. They were concerned that a clot might be the cause my arm issue. Thankfully, with their help, it's gotten better.

I've gone on now for the better part of two pages about myself, and that's far too much. Now, let's get on with what is, is not, or should be going on in the life of Eric Adreon. First of all, if no one has told you today that they love you, remember, I do, Diane does, and even the dog does.

Let me hit on one of my major topics concerning you. I consider you exceedingly bright. You have a good mind that is apparently still being wasted. You are talented even though you might not know it, and have great potential for the future. Now, how does one go about putting all of this together? I offer a few thoughts and comments in the paragraphs that follow.

Let me start by telling you I was a teenager when I was sucked into the Korean police action. I was an uneducated kid that could not pour piss out of a boot with directions on the heel. I decided to become an officer and somehow managed to achieve my goal. The *lack of education would hold me back in the military environment, so I began night school. It took me nine years, nine colleges, 197 credits, a lot of time, and a lot of money to get my BS degree. Then I took on grad school. Another nine years of night and day school to earn my MBA. During this period, I served two thirteen-month tours in Vietnam and spent an additional eighteen months in a military hospital recovering from the damage that was done during the second tour. Darn it, son, if I could do it, why not you???*

I guess my main point is that I see, believe, and hope that you will at some point, hopefully soon, improve and exploit the natural talents that God has gracefully bestowed upon you.

I love you, Eric. Need I say more...?

Laire's letters helped me better understand the sacrifices he had made for his family and his country. Comparing myself to him—and to all the people who have entered and left my life—allowed me to see my own strengths and limitations. Learning of his accomplishments and the many challenges he had overcome, I began to realize that I was not the person I believed myself to be. His words "if I can do it" challenged me in a way that only he could. Laire did not pull any punches and I did not want him to. I needed a man in my life who would challenge me directly. Laire had faced death and survived three wars, the last of which was alcoholism. He had the physical and mental scars to prove it. Yet despite all the battles Laire had faced, he had improved his life and had accomplished things I never could have imagined.

Since his first direction as my mentor, Laire had proven to me that if he set his mind to something, he would never back down. In every letter, he showed unyielding love as a fellow survivor. Spiritual attraction is not always subtle. We saw in one another memories relived in the present. Spending time together, these burdens seemed to fade; we stood beside each other as survivors of tragedy. It is tragic when a child is raped and abused. It is tragic when a teenager must fight a war against men he has never known, expecting to either kill or be killed. Through our tragedies and common bond as addicts, we were brought together in a type of divine introduction that allowed us to heal through love and true friendship.

Each time I surrendered to my disease, longing to raise the white flag and give up the battle, I wrote to Laire, my mother, and sometimes my father. Laire would respond with words of encouragement and wisdom to apply to my daily life. His incessant prodding with regard to pursuing a formal education did not fall on deaf ears. It did however remind me of all the fear and insecurity I had regarding education.

Months later, I graduated from the treatment center on Queen Anne Hill and moved to a halfway house on Capitol Hill. Having been in treatment for a year, I had earned a small amount of freedom. I was given the opportunity to begin transitioning back into the community by either working a job off the unit or going to school. Though the new house made for a welcome change of scenery, the intensity and style of treatment worsened. One counselor in particular escalated my treatment in what I believe to have been an unprofessional and sadistic manner. I have always been able to feel appreciative of treatment in even the harshest setting. In this treatment, I felt thankful for being separated from the verbal assaults that all the patients endured returning to the center from our job searches and appointments. This experience mirrored how an abused child might feel returning to an abusive home. The cloud descended upon me once more. In the past year I had experienced several bouts of depression. I had been able to fight those bouts through willpower. I felt driven by a fear of what might happen if I allowed depression to take hold in a program that punished symptoms as "addict behavior." Constant prayer and meditation gave me the necessary balance to endure. The energy and euphoria brought on by activity gave me a reprieve from the excessive dejection, hopelessness, and feelings of inadequacy. I learned much later that many of my chemical imbalances occurred as a result of faulty neurotransmitters in my brain, essentially wires that were shorting out.

As is the case with mental illness and addiction, circumstances, outside influence, and relief through chemicals return the person to the pain and pleasure associated with relapse. Fate, karma, or destiny played no part in this end result. Feelings of resentment could also be blamed for my decline. I resented my living situation and the system by which it was governed, one that would not address mental illness. I was capable of conforming to the structure of each treatment center, but my resentment began to outweigh my desire to conform. My so-called addict behavior became the catalyst for the resurfacing of my real issues and an inevitable blow out. Through others in the program, I was able to take steps forward and make progress despite my limitations. Adversity forces a person to grow and adjust in order to overcome. My most difficult living situations have introduced me to some of my greatest spiritual teachers.

The shadow appeared in the University District barbershop just as I sought relief from the symptoms of an untreated addiction and chemical imbalance. I was on a pass from the halfway house. Entering the shop on the

Ave., I ran into an old friend. Emilio and I had been close in the months before I was placed in treatment. We met playing pickup basketball at Ravenna Park, an innocent circumstance. I had not yet begun to use heavily, and I took walks in the park to think about my life and reflecting on how I could make improvements to avoid spinning out of control again. The smiles and laughter on the court drew me to the game. I soon realized I could become good friends with Emilio and his sister if circumstances allowed it.

Soon we began to spend most of our free time together. I was the first friend they had made since moving to Seattle from New Mexico. As always, marijuana played its part and a progression began that I could not control. Emilio and I fed off of each other's addictions.

Emilio and I were alike in many ways. He came from the streets of Albuquerque and was only months removed from a crack addiction that he had come to Seattle to escape. Although some say that shared substance use disallows true friendship, I would have to disagree. Granted, our friendship could have been much healthier. Addicts who work the streets often form alliances with other dealers as a form of protection from other people in the drug trade. Shared harsh experiences create camaraderie, much like that experienced by those who go through war together. In many ways, the streets are like a war zone. Though some may debate this, the feelings associated with each share many similarities, an appreciation of which can result in bonds like the one I share with Laire.

I would never classify my relationship with Emilio as one of "using buddies." We did protect each other from the streets though. If I found myself in a bind, I knew that I could throw out Emilio's name as a so-called get-out-of-jail-free card and vice versa. Emilio had access to corners of the underworld I did not. He procured some of the purest powders and I peddled it to the college kids. I scratched his back and he scratched mine. We traveled to barter fairs, rainbow festivals, and parties together, both to capitalize on those looking for any of a dozen types of chemicals that we could provide, or to simply enjoy being chemically altered with someone trustworthy.

Emilio was privy to sides of me that I did not share with others on the Avenue. I had learned that personal information could be used against me. I wasn't willing to place my family in a position of compromise again. The streets took advantage of weakness; any emotion, other than anger, was considered weakness. Emilio and I tended to stay on the lighter side of the city, acting like hippie kids. This protected us from some of the harsher realities. Maintaining this image was not easy for either of us, because in the backs of our minds, sounded the ever-present voice urging us to use the drugs that would ensure our demise.

Pot, LSD, and hash are dangerous for the addict. In shooting galleries where heroin, coke, and meth are used, things manifest that in the world of relatively less serious drugs they do not. These things include sinister sexual behavior, the peeling of flesh, and sadistic violent behaviors, as examples. As an addict, if I could have remained floating in the world of milder drugs, I am sure I would have. I crossed a line such that I cannot physiologically differentiate between marijuana and crack. Over time, those milder drugs convinced me that I had the ability—with all of my knowledge and life experience—to use the more serious drugs that I craved. Emilio's life took another direction. Despite his warnings and pleading, I reentered the world of the shadow walker. He walked along the edge, calling my name. As is the case with the drug world, when feelings get hurt, people get angry. Emilio spent a good deal of time smoothing the chaos and drama that my use created. He still looked out for me, even when I made it hard for him to interact with people in his circles. He was a solid and loyal friend.

What Emilio had in his pocket at the barbershop changed our friendship permanently. Those small baggies of crystal began the waltz of the addict and the drug dealer. This relationship often disguises itself as friendship, especially when it began that way. I wish I could claim that our friendship endured. Instead, an alliance centered on drugs took it place.

While I was in treatment, Emilio was furthering his enterprise of distribution. In twelve months, he had become a well-known hustler in Seattle. It wasn't the quantity of meth he had that impressed me; it was his sophistication in sales. As we walked and talked, he spent the hour bouncing from me to his phone, directing a network of dealers that he was supplying. At the end of our conversation he had given me some kid's marijuana pipe, about a quarter-ounce of pot, and his sister's phone number in case I needed another place to live. Although he was proud of the fact I was not shooting up, Emilio seemed uncomfortable that I did not still smoke marijuana. We burnt one together as we'd done many times before as an expression of our commitment to the chemical world. It was a ritual shared between long lost friends, meant to recall the world we had shared together. As the blue-tinted smoke clouded my mind, I felt a shift in preparation for the inevitable. I had set off another downward spiral, one that would end far worse than the ones I had found myself in before.

For some reason, treatment became bearable. I was better able to avoid the frustrations, the resentment, and the depression by taking long walks and smoking pot. In group home settings, I found creative ways to hide the smell of drugs, like blowing the smoke through toilet paper rolls with fabric softener sheets wrapped around the end. Of course, recovery and addiction are like oil and water, and in time, people became suspicious. My thoughts returned to sedation, which made the decision to leave treatment easy. I knew that it was just a matter of time before I would be forced to leave, so I instigated a fight with the arrogant counselor and said all the things I had been afraid to say in the weeks prior. At least twenty people watched, applauding silently with smiles.

I turned twenty-one. Unfortunately, maturity did not come with the birthday. I regressed into a perpetual adolescent. Lashing out at the counselor was just a warm up for the great "Fuck you!" I had shout to my life, to society, and to those who had believed in me previously. I no longer desired to use. I longed to burn out as a result of use.

Emilio's sister, Mons, seemed the opposite of many I had known while using. Her kindness softened the effects of many months of rigidity. I felt a great relief that she allowed me to live with her, thereby eliminating the uncertainty of homelessness. The number Emilio had given me led me to the parking lot of a famous Italian restaurant where I waited for Mons to get off work. She lived in a three-story house in Ballard with four roommates. The moment I walked in it felt like a home rather than an institution. In the living room sat her other brother, Peter, along with Tracy, Marcus, and Carrie. As I looked around, I saw the typical debris of a twenty-something's life. Beers lined the tables and the smell of sweet leaf permeated the air. It felt as though heaven had descended. I had only dreamed of such a place. Their apparent balance gave me hope that I, too, could live this life.

Making a quick categorization based on superficial characteristics and standards, the roommates included five beer drinkers, four pot smokers, and two who experimented with cocaine; four who worked in restaurants and one office clerk; one lesbian, two bisexuals, and two straight people; two from Alaska, two from Albuquerque, and one from Seattle; two blonds and three brunettes; one nineteen-year-old, two twenty-year-olds, and two twenty-one-year-olds; two males and three females. Luckily for me, one of the females (blond, nineteen, Alaskan, worked in a restaurant, and experimented with cocaine) shared a similar interest in physical relationships. By the end of the night, the house offered both shelter and a lovely girl who would make my stay more interesting. As always, my intentions started in the purest form, then ended in devastation.

I entered the home with a job and the momentum of months of recovery, save my recent relapse. The impression I gave of responsibility helped me to win over the roommates. My use had not yet grown serious. For a few weeks, I was able to hold up my end of the bargain both financially and socially. I had been working at Nike Town in downtown Seattle for several months, traveling to and from my job on the city bus. There was an ordinary quality to my life that I had wanted for many years, but once I had it, it didn't give me the comfort I had anticipated. I felt confined to the daily ritual instead of the freedom I had been told came with responsibility. In time, I left the store never to return.

The Ballard house kept an active social life. We spent many nights dancing and drinking at Neighbors, a gay nightclub on Capitol Hill. While the others enjoyed the lifestyle of the city, I began the descent into addiction. While they snorted lines of cocaine with impunity, I sealed my fate like a contract that cannot be broken. I consumed significant amounts of alcohol; the desire that accompanied it propelled me to drink increasingly. While my roommates were able continue their lives without social and economic regression, I could not. My will played no part. In almost all other circumstances, my willpower was stronger than most; yet when it came to being altered, I had none whatsoever. It did not matter how much or what I used; my internal yearnings separated me from the rest.

Carrie had skin like porcelain with blue eyes and long, sandy-blond hair. She drew me to her like a thousand lines of ecstasy, and her touch sealed my fate. We spent many evenings and mornings in a passionate embrace that only those in their early adulthood can understand. Our bodies were at their prime, and with the help of chemicals, we elevated to a place of pure bliss. I was in heaven.

Carrie's embrace washed everything away and I became trapped in the moment. The combination of natural desire, chemicals, and a longing to break away formed a potent elixir that made time stand still. The experience was similar to the first time I felt the prick of the needle. It went beyond feelings of pleasure into the realm of obsession. Carrie could manipulate my very existence—as long as her desire didn't interfere with my primary dependency on chemicals.

When my binges began, they were sometimes subtle. The effects of my substance use seemed mild, but this mild behavior led me to believe that danger did not exist. As my use progressed, and the effects of varying forms of obsession and compulsions combined, reality and time distorted, leaving me with an unrealistic view of the world around me. This space borders reality and fantasy. When the two collide, enjoyment is replaced by torment.

Soon, the needle replaced the bong, and with it, the characteristics of habit returned. The power of addiction had entered my veins through a device originally created to save lives. At a party we threw at the house, a woman who lived at the end of the block stumbled in. It was apparent that she suffered from the same love of tar I did. We found ourselves in the bathroom, drawing up two hits from one spoon. Peter, Mons younger brother, loved new and uncommon things. He watched in curiosity as Jen and I drifted into semi-consciousness. As the scene blurred, then faded, I remember thoughts of how his curiosity was exempt from the type of behavior he had just witnessed because he chose not to use in the way we did. He left me in the bathroom, a form of entertainment for the remainder of the evening. I leaned against a woman I had never met, yet knew completely as a result of our shared bondage.

As is the nature of addiction, many addicts find themselves stuck in the torture of wanting to quit without the ability to do so. Their desire to stop is often hampered or influenced due to a lack of knowledge, which leads to faulty reasoning and failed attempts. Jen's notion of stopping, which included two hundred Valium 10s, made sense to me. The promise of a swift return ended as many drug transactions do. The drug runner uses the money that they were entrusted with to buy drugs to get high themselves. My promise to return in an hour with her Valium turned into a week.

At one point in the days that followed our agreement, I dreamt of red and blue lights pulsating on the blinds of the Ballard house. I lay on the couch, high on heroin. In another dream, a procession of cars filled every vacant spot around the block. People dressed in black paraded through the rain in silence. When my binge ended, and news of what had occurred in my absence found me, I felt a dull sense of failed responsibility.

Heroin withdrawals are hell. The body and mind scream for relief accessible only through further use. Along with the many physical symptoms, the addict endures mental obsession and depression. I am not sure what led up to Jen's overdose. My mind told me that it was my fault, the fault of anyone who had ever shot up with her. We fed our diseases together; in so doing, we both fed the monster that ultimately consumed her. My decision to take her money to get high on the very substance that she was trying to quit left me with a shame I anesthetized immediately.

I knocked on the door and a familiar face greeted me. Jen's husband had chased me, and many others, out of their home on numerous occasions. "Get the hell out, you filth." He fought a battle that many loved ones face. With the practiced tone of someone feeling great remorse, I said, "I am so sorry for your loss." In my compulsion for heroine I set aside any decency I may have had by pretending to be kind in the face of his tragedy. What I really sought was the stash of heroin Jen kept in the cushion of her couch. In her death, I had become the scavenger that my brothers and I had chased away after my grandmother's death. In his tragedy, Jen's husband confronted an emotionless scavenger. "Get out of here, you soulless bastard!" I felt remorse, not because I had deepened the wound of a man in grief. I had not achieved my goal.

I had entered a realm of darkness that fed off of others in a way that left them scarred, much like I had been. Again, my abuse had come full circle. Within this realization, I made my way to the heart of the city where the shadow walkers congregated. The streetlights no longer cast my shadow; I had become the shadow itself. I was a spiritual black hole, consuming light.

As I entered the bowels of the city again, I was no longer the fourteen-year-old boy observing from the outside. I looked from the inside outward through the eyes of one who knew a great deal more than he had a few years before. I told the youngsters to be quiet as I passed the bottle and told stories of my past. I passed to them the poison I had been passed years before. Instead of telling those who still saw their shadows in the streetlights to run while they could, I sealed their fate in silence, hoping to gain something from their demise. I was no different from the man I hunted in my alcohol-fueled rages. Had I looked in the reflection of a storefront window, I might have seen Kenneth's face reflecting back.

I had despised Kenneth for nearly six years. Although I never played a part in the rape of a child, or anyone for that matter, I did feed off of the innocent. Kenneth had done the same. I danced with the shadows, cursing their existence. This was a profoundly difficult realization, spiritual in nature, yet used to continue using. Pain from self-realization could have brought about change, but instead, I chose otherwise and my spiral continued.

Junkies provide a wealth of information for those wishing to gain information on the drug trade of the city. A junkie's daily route maps an accurate picture of whom and what influences the trade. Blinded by the hunger to stay high, an addict doesn't see those who track their path. Although paranoia is a very real symptom of amphetamine use, law enforcement uses that symptom to disguise their operations.

I have very little doubt that Emilio and I were watched on a regular basis. Although we weren't heavies compared to the many above us in the drug trade, we were part of the networks that supplied the city and could make calls that resulted in the kind of weight that made eyes turn. I can't recall every tail I recognized in the city. It's yet more difficult to explain how to differentiate between real and make-believe after being awake for many days. The city follows a current that one can begin to read. Inconsistencies arise and those who aren't a regular part of the flow stick out. The chase begins, and there is generally only one loser: the addict.

In my grandiosity, I invited the law into my life. My paranoia ensured that they would remember me. On several occasions, I asked if people I passed were Feds. Some would tell me yes. More than once, I avoided a tail, and then was cursed at as I drove away. The lines blurred, as I feared that cops, shadow walkers, and the demons that followed me, leaving me huddled in alleyways in hiding.

It was no less severe for Emilio. He would call me early in the morning, as he worked the streets, so that he would not be alone with his own demons. At first, his paranoia seemed contrived, but the more I listened and watched, the more I realized that some small part was identical to what I had experienced with the Feds. Emilio carried a gun and talked about using it regularly. "I am going to blast this fool," he'd say. It didn't matter if the person was real or imagined. On numerous occasions, a thin line of sanity kept him from drawing blood from an unknowing and unknown victim as they walked past.

I couldn't return to the Ballard house without bringing my paranoia along. I believed that the DEA lived in the vents of the house, men who Carrie had smuggled in at night. In the air ducts above my bed, I saw a remote camera that positioned itself so that it could document my sleep patterns and needle use. I looked in the furnace room to look for footprints in the dust on the floor. I wondered how these men got around without leaving marks. Through the laundry room window, the Space Needle turned into a woman in a white, fluffy coat dangling her feet and watching me with binoculars. Recounting the images of my insanity makes me uncomfortable even now. Those that I've not described carry a darkness I do not wish to relive for any reason.

I am not sure how Sam came to my section of the city and entered my circle of friends. One night, he sat in the living room drinking with my roommates. Sam played on my father's soccer team growing up. I had partied with him in the past. His grandiosity towered over my own, to the point that I searched for Carrie's car keys in an attempt to leave the house. This was not a new occurrence. I spent a great deal of time using her pink Ford Escort to make drug runs throughout the city. When I returned early the next morning, I entered the living room to find Sam and Carrie on opposite couches covered in blankets. I couldn't calm my suspicions that something had happened between them. Real or imagined their bare shoulders, my lack of sleep, plus a smirk on Sam's face convinced me that he'd been dipping into my bag, my woman. I am not sure what I would have done had I pulled off the covers and found them naked. To this day, I wonder if I made the best decision. Awash in paranoia brought on by use, I lived in a cloud of jealousy.

Emilio was in a hotel on Aurora Avenue. I headed there with the conviction of one willing to do whatever is necessary to relieve the rage and jealousy. Emilio didn't want to give me his gun at first, but he understood doing what you had to. We spent a couple of hours getting high during which he tried to keep me there with substance and persuasion. When I turned away from him, he snapped me around and said, "I'll do it for you if you want me to." I refused and the door shut behind me. I stood holding the gun. Pushing aside an impulse to turn the gun on myself, I turned toward Ballard.

When I reached the house, they were still there. My senses heightened by chemical use and jealousy, I knew that seven cigarettes had been smoked since my departure. They slept, unsuspecting of what awaited them. Their fate rested on a man who had been up for a week, exhibited extreme jealousy, and held a pistol. I stood above Sam and then Carrie, lacking all rational thought, trying to decide who should be awakened to face the consequences first.

This was a horrifying scene of insanity. I stood, unable to make the decision to pull the trigger. Was it their angels or my own? It didn't matter. A roommate returning home saved them, the sound of which sent me running for the basement door, then back into the night. I am not sure how long I contemplated using the gun on myself before I finally returned it to Emilio. I did not have to tell him what had occurred when I came back. He could see it in my eyes, which came as a relief to him. I returned inconsolable, and in that state, I left.

17

THE CITY IS DISSECTED INTO DIFFERENT sections by a grid of imaginary lines. These sections will not appear on any map or tourist guide. They are unspoken boundaries, understood by those who live in the subterranean world of illicit drugs. Along Aurora Avenue, one could get a bag of crack, meth, or indulge in the sex trade. On Capitol Hill, ecstasy, crystal, and heroin flourished. Many homeless gathered there with the hope of feeding their craving. Downtown included addicts and substances of all kinds. From 1st Avenue and Pike Street up to 3rd Avenue, a long list of illegal narcotics came in hefty supply. Of course, people crossed over into other sections; nothing was ever set in stone.

The University District provided a kind of oasis where youngsters could congregate and avoid the harsher realities of the city. The harsher realities existed there, but a culture had formed within which shunned most of what other areas had to offer. By disallowing amphetamines, heroin, and other hard drugs, they created a kind of neutral zone enforced through social pressure. The Ave. within the University District was full of shelters and food pantries for the homeless youth of the city. Kids congregated because they knew they could get their needs met.

This scenario complicated my needs and desires, because I wanted both the protection of the Ave. and the oblivion created by the drugs that were shunned there. The destructive nature of my disease did not allow me to fit into their culture; I had already crossed over to meth and the violence it brings. My addictive behavior, which lived alongside my peaceful heart, set me adrift in a sea of confusion and loneliness. An urban myth claimed that a person could not act the same way in the University District as in other areas of the city. The tribal community would gather to cast out those who had gone against their ways. This left me exposed. I felt ostracized from the graces of those who would have helped me survive there.

While living at Straley House, I had enjoyed the peace and safety of being a part of the University District's culture. I had something to contribute to the community at that time. That same community had turned their backs on me. I became toxic. In my veins, a poison circulated, diminishing my good within. It left in its place a ravaged spirit.

Meth was my great love. It's very molecular structure held a vile lie that changed the way I felt about myself, and the world around me. Through its use, all the shame and secrets I had buried for so long dissipated. Through smoke and mirrors, it lowered me further into darkness too awful for words. In the intense and immediate release of dopamine, the shadows introduced me to a power that mimicked the Creator. It became the medication my brain craved for balance, yet it gave none.

How could I stop this landslide once it began? Even in the revulsion expressed by those around me, I could not see myself, or my circumstances clearly. Every hit reinforced the delusion. My social gauge became nonexistent. I was a sociopath. My days consisted of floating from one shooting gallery to the next. It is difficult to describe the feeling of being possessed by something both inside and outside of oneself. The intense craving and a growing obsession dictated my every move. I became a creature of habit, spending multiple days in one place, then moving to the next as the drug lines dried up or circumstances forced me out. My face ashen, I trudged the sidewalks, with not a sign of life within. My eyes blank and void of passion, I had become a zombie.

On several occasions, someone I had known before my transformation, invited me to the tribal house across from Ravenna Park. The house was a gathering place for the most liberal aspects of the city. Dread heads, activists, and community supporters, all gathered there to celebrate solstices and other times of celebration. Each time I visited, I was exposed to a set of lessons in the gathering. The effects of my experiences there remain acute even now. The tribal house included various stages of testing and teaching. I understand now that my invitation to participate did not come from past friendship, but out of a deep sadness felt by those who had known me before. This humbling knowledge deflated my ego, and I moved silently through each sample lesson that they had planned for me. It did not matter that others had been gathered there for the same purpose; my tasks were catered to me and me alone. I would have taken a thousand beatings for one moment of reprieve. They were the ambassadors of a world that had turned away from me.

Drum circles are an ageless and sacred ritual. They bring communities together, surpassing memory and resonating within the consciousness. They come from a time before written word. The drums realize communication without the use of pen or tongue. Instead, the rhythm of hands upon animal skin merges the past and present resonating as a great rhythm of the earth. A lone drummer is incapable of creating this sense of community. Likewise, one drummer is incapable of creating a beat that matches the magnificence of the many who congregated. Many drummers converge as one, each drummer adding to the greater whole. Not singularly in selfishness, but in the humility of plurality.

I was given a drum ceremoniously and I joined the circle as I had on so many other occasions. I sought to join my individual beat with the rhythm of the whole. As I hit the drum, confusion reverberated throughout those nearby; it was obvious that my beat had thrown off the balance of the entire group. They had permitted my participation to tell me, non-verbally, that my single drumbeat had destroyed the rhythm of the whole. No words could have taught me more. Repeatedly, I attempted to join in, but the rhythm continued to fall into disarray. As I stepped away from the drum, I searched the crowd for any sign of recognition. Not one set of eyes met mine. Instead, they stared at the ground, unwilling to meet my gaze. People with whom I had smoked and attended other gatherings no longer acknowledge me. My ostracism was complete. The resulting shame shifted the way I viewed my actions. To the depths of my soul, I understood how the selfishness of my addiction could no longer blind me to the fact that my self-destruction affected the community as a whole.

I left the house and entered the darkness of Ravenna Park deeply affected by what I had experienced. As I looked into the night's sky, I yelled in an attempt to negate the reality of my experience. I would have left this world at that moment if given the option. Yet, for some reason, I understood that I was responsible for restoring the balance I had disrupted through use. My karma would not let me off easily. In death, I would simply be avoiding what I had avoided so many times before: a responsibility for and a recognition of the character defects with which I had naturally been endowed. I had a contract to fulfill and, up to this point, I had avoided my reason for being. What I had experienced as rejection at the tribal house was actually a form of love. It was a brutal honesty, not disguised by those things that would have relieved its sting.

That sting was exactly what I needed to break through the many layers of walls I had built and to release me from the numbing of chemicals. Truth bites to the depths of who we are as spiritual beings if we are not living up to our true potential. I would never be the same. What had begun in the meditation groups and youth groups continued in the rituals of the solstice and the reflection of the moon. I sat alone with no one to relieve me of my burden. I feel certain that at that moment, no chemical could have helped me escape the truth of who I had become.

I am not sure how long I spent in the University District, hiding in the currents of humanity. I do remember spending a full day at a busy bus stop on Northeast 45th Street knowing that in the constant flow of foot traffic, I could find relative anonymity. Tears had been shed; now they fell free of hindrance. I felt beaten, dejected and humbled. As I sat staring into the crowds, a woman approached me and wordlessly sat beside me. Once a full schedule of buses had passed the stop, it became apparent that she did not intend to catch a bus. She had chosen to sit beside me, shoulder to shoulder. I don't remember exchanging even one word—just a hand that reached out to my own. She held my hand for what seemed like eternity. Time passed and she eventually rose to join a group of travelers. I felt blessed and touched by her compassion. All hope was not lost.

Spiritual seeds planted through life lessons do not always take root immediately. They often require certain variables to manifest at times when they are needed the most. That need isn't for the individual; it is for the greater good. I entered the great circle of beating drums, and in so doing, understood that I do not set the beat—I join it. When I try to interject my own selfishness into the balance, the greater balance is lost. This opened me up to a series of lessons that would ensure my entry into the spiritual world. Although an outward change would not be apparent for some time, the emotional and spiritual friction took immediate effect. Those things that I believed to be my greatest hindrances in life were actually my greatest blessings. My disease progressed more rapidly due to my emotional imbalance, my age, and the boundaries created by my parents, all of which forced me to face harsh realities early on. The ostracism I experienced and the resulting spiritual shifts gave me a new outlook and enabled my conscience to work against my addictive behaviors in a very painful and profound way. Had I only opened my eyes, I could have seen the spirit world at work in the physical, directing those who were brought into its fold, to both teach and learn.

Some believe that those who do not appear to be on a spiritual path are void of the grace and knowledge that those who are, possess. Many gauge spiritual progress by material things like clean clothing and nice cars, or even the ability to phrase spiritual concepts in meticulous ways. Although these qualities are admirable, they are not accurate indicators of spiritual understanding and growth. I believe that spirituality is evident through joy, happiness, kindness and hope; but if that's true, then how should the most painful parts of the human condition be categorized? What purpose do the very things that bring us to a place of humility and self-realization serve? I have learned as much, or more, from harsh realities as from celebrations. In every shot of meth and in every song in the chapel, I pursued the journey for which I was destined. This does not mean that I don't strive for that which makes me feel happy, loved, and content. It means that I don't cast away my struggles as unnecessary elements within the larger picture.

Access into the world of the spirit is not difficult. It does not have to come through chanting or submersion into water. Access to the spiritual world is given simply by asking to be a part of it. Although a prayer or a shout to the heavens could be helpful, it's not required. My admission came prior to my birth, many lifetimes ago. In this I became a part of the greater whole, dropping away from the self, and actualizing the need for forces that work just out of sight and reason. The world of the spirit does not act in sequence with the winding of clocks; it is ageless, timeless, and formless. It cares little for categories. In all actuality, spirituality is most effective when it comes from a place with no labels whatsoever. Labels set limits and restrict spirituality to the confines of man's knowledge of the universe. Such knowledge is limited as has been evidenced through history and the evolution of understanding. On a personal level, the limitation of my knowledge and understanding becomes apparent when I look at how I have treated others.

Thus far, I have not touched on the many powerful friendships I formed at the Ballard house. Marcie had lost her husband just months before I met her at the house. She had just begun to socialize again. I can't begin to understand what came from the loss of a love of that magnitude. We met in the thawing of her heart. In her sorrow, Marcie was able to relate to my own, and for the first time in a great while, I was able to share the torment of my life. I related to her many experiences. In one observation, she was able to surpass all conversation. She had rarely seen me smile. In the short time I had known her, she could not recall one authentic smile. I had lost it along the way, and she brought the realization home. In time, she moved on to the next chapter of her life.

I pondered moving away from the city. The idea of returning to Montana would not leave me. I had become so accustomed to reliance upon others that I had no confidence in myself. I continued to binge and deteriorate despite the pleading of my mother and others, who I allowed into my misery for brief periods of time.

It is very difficult to act against the power of addiction, especially in an attempt to stop its momentum. Every part of my mind and body screamed against even the notion of abstinence. My mind had been warped into believing that with the loss of substances came the loss of my very being. The only way I knew how to survive rested in my understanding of the drug world and what I could extricate from it. If I was not using, I was living in institutions, allowing others to take care of me. I had not graduated high school, I had very little training in work, and I believed that if I did not have drugs, I would crack into a million pieces of porcelain that would scatter in all directions.

Just as the argument to leave began to lose out to the call of the streets, a gift was left at the front door. Marcie included a note to explain why she had returned.

Dear Eric,

I am writing to you today under the guidance that comes, not from my mind, but from the spirit within me. I understand the battle that you're attempting to face. A wise man once said, "Guidance comes when the horizon is at its blackest." How I find myself holding onto these words. I am not quite sure. Nor do I know why so many face the pain of life alone. I do understand that in this solitude, we find ourselves.

It is true that one must fight many demons in this search, and I have witnessed some that were unable to return from their battle. Despair has taken many. However, I believe that if we did not suffer, we could not understand. This may be the true beauty in life.

I also understand it may take some time for you to find the smile you seek. So be patient with yourself as you return to the mountain, sea, desert, or wherever your journey may carry you. Rest with the knowledge that this is why you were created to begin with. To bind with one's soul is a lifelong process.

We are blessed if we can find others that understand this. They listen when we are struggling. They comfort us when we are sad. They smile when we are happy. They let us go when we are searching, and they love us through it all. What a pure love this is.

Of the many things my husband left when he died was a backpack and traveling gear that he had used in the days he traveled in search of himself. I am not sure why I kept it as I gave many of his things away to those who needed them more than my dusty closet. I would like to share something about this backpack that is truly amazing.

Last night, my husband visited me in a dream. How I love it when his soul comes to visit mine. He *asked about the battles I've been fighting and about the people I've met along the way. As I answered, I looked into his eyes and witnessed such peace, love, comfort, and pure understanding. He took a great interest in the "seeker." He said, "May this seeker find peace in a world that at times seems so unforgiving." When I woke, I knew what I must do.*

The pack and the items in it now belong to you. Included is one of my most cherished possessions: a book that contains vast spiritual information. Its cover is made from the wood of an olive tree from Jerusalem. My husband carried this book with him for as long as I knew him. In its pages you will find many answers you've been looking for.

I take no credit for these gifts as they are not from me. No expression of thanks is needed. My Creator provided them all. Consider them gifts of the spirit. We are all just vessels by which God expresses love.

I do, however, have one request. When you do find your smile, share it with someone. I have no idea where the wind will blow either of us. If we keep the right outlook, wherever we go will be an adventure.

May you find in yourself the amazing person I see in you. I wish you well on your journey.

Marcie

Many have come and gone in my life. Marcie was also on a spiritual journey, and she recognized my search despite my many obstacles. At each juncture in my life, a person or a lesson has been placed in front of me enabling me to move towards my next destination. Laire, Connie, my grandmother, baby Christian, the eagle from my solo, my parents, the workers at Straley House, the drum circles—even Kenneth. They all contributed to the forward momentum of my life and my eventual spiritual evolution.

Marcie carried on the tradition of listening to the very real spiritual world around her. As a result, she passed on a gift while simultaneously receiving her own. In the gift she gave to me came the understanding that I was not alone. Despite my many flaws, some still rooted for me on this side and in the world beyond the senses. I am not unique in this regard; this is simply how the spiritual realm works. The entities from past, present, and future converge to bridge the river across which travelers must walk to continue their journey. I believe that we all play numerous roles throughout our lifetime. Every individual plays his or her part in the web of the spirit, crossing into many planes of existence. Each person's part is as important as the next—from the drunk under the bridge, to the moneyman on Wall Street.

With Marcie's gift, my future lay in front of me. I had never told her about my plans to leave. I thought of her husband, thanking him silently for thinking about the seeker when I needed a messenger the most. I decided to read his book while packing his backpack. Later in the evening, I tried to play the bamboo flute that I found in the side pocket. Watching the sun dip below the horizon, I fought the urge of the shadow walker to return to the city. The adventure of spiritual evolution is as painful as it is joyful.

18

DECISIONS ARE SIMPLY THAT: DECISIONS. For a decision to move beyond the mind, it must be followed by action. For several weeks, the backpack remained packed, waiting beside the basement door. I had been more than willing to leave when I had received the pack, but as I got closer to action, I was having a difficult time making the break from Carrie. She was good at stringing me along, making me believe that I was a priority. A longing to feel important kept me from severing my sexual and emotional dependence. I floated between euphoria and disillusionment, chasing Carrie around the city in the hope of spending time with her. I was no longer a secret. It appeared that she and her previous boyfriend had reached an agreement, because he was still coming around. When we were in the house at the same time, an undercurrent of tempered animosity showed signs of boiling over. She loved her little game, despite the many complications it created. She was equally dependent on the drama that she created, the cocaine that her former boyfriend supplied, and the sexual amusement I offered. She played a game of high-stakes emotional chess.

Eventually, the scales began to tip in my favor and she started to show me more attention and affection. I started to distance myself more. I finally held the number one position; and once I had it, my desire for her dissipated. I returned to the familiar love-hate relationship I had experienced with every other drug in my life. The initial use always produced the greatest high. From that point on, the highs diminished until the euphoria I once enjoyed, was replaced by need. The pleasure of touch diminished and our connection became habit, void of the passion we once shared.

In time, the white van that had picked me up many times before arrived. Inside sat my stepfather waiting patiently, willing to help me move on one more time. When I called to share my desire to stop using, my parents made themselves available to assist with the next leg of my journey.

I was not leaving as a healthy individual. I still suffered from the paranoia that had been building over the recent months. I regretted bringing my parents into the war zone that was my life. Although I had no debt in the drug world, I did have a karmic debt owed to the communities I had degraded by my presence. Those tended to be the most profound debts I carried, as well as the most difficult to pay back. Doing so required a complete change to my mental, emotional, and spiritual makeup.

The train could not move fast enough. My memories seemed to float outside the window as the train made its slow march away from the city. As I passed each section of Seattle, my recollection paired with remorse. Although I had enough marijuana to get me through about a week, I already felt an urge for the syringe. My prospects for a fix diminished with the receding city skyline. I had used up the remainder of my stash and threw away the rigs, cotton, and baggies several hours before Mick arrived to pick me. Aboard the train, I regretted having made such a decision. Short of jumping from a moving train, I was stuck, at least until I made it to the first destination. My mother and Mick had purchased my ticket, saving me from having to hitchhike across eastern Washington and Idaho. They knew that my direction could change as quickly as the wind. Recovery for IV addicts tends to be precarious. Safely aboard the train, I would return to Montana. What I did there was in the hands of the Creator.

In withdrawal, I relied heavily on miniature alcohol bottles. Though they did little for my constant paranoia, they awakened a hunger for more alcohol, giving me a short reprieve from the desire to shoot up. When the cravings came, they scrambled any good ideas I had, especially those that involved belief in myself. The insidious urge typically won out, which meant I was in a chess match with my addiction. I hoped I reached Wilderness Treatment Center before I was checkmated. In time and sobriety, normalcy would return. Until that point, the fog of intoxication took over.

Trading withdrawal from one drug for the effects of another is like paying off debt with a credit card. It does not relieve anything; it simply creates deficiencies and shifts reliance to other substances. Addicts do this all the time, believing that they can avoid the horrors of the drugs they use by using those believed to be less dangerous. I, on the other hand, had never had that issue. I knew from an early age that with any chemical I ingested, I didn't use it the way that others did.

The drug is not the issue; the addict's mind and body are. Anything that creates euphoria in the addict has the potential to do great harm. This covers the whole spectrum of substances from coffee to cocaine, and from doctor-prescribed painkillers to Mexican black tar heroin. Many alcoholics seem to believe that they are exempt from this truth. In reality, the same pleasure centers in the brain that dictate addiction for the addict, create a line of no return for the alcoholic as well. The belief system that alcoholics are not addicts has led many back into the throws of alcoholism—or active addiction, if you will. Alcohol is a drug, possibly the most potent and destructive of any I have experienced.

The mountains bordering Montana overwhelmed me the way they had when I was fourteen years old. I prayed that they could also keep the shadows, I had known in Seattle, away long enough for me to find a new beginning. Though I was skeptical I could remain clean, my hope remained. Hope can survive the harshest circumstances. If the hope for recovery diminishes, hope for a warm place to sleep replaces it. If hope in humanity disappears, hope in a bowl of soup on a cold day remains. As long as the spark exists in any capacity, hope may grow in the areas in which it is needed most.

Looking into the eyes of those who live without hope is like looking into a dark hole with no end. They are void of the spirit that fuels the desire to improve one's circumstances. Those who live with depression suffer from a loss of hope that saps them of all desire to move forward. A cocoon of sleep, food, sex, chemical, or suicide replaces it. They stumble seeking any relief to the hopelessness and despair that they endure.

I had only a gifted backpack, a bag of pot, and several pairs of shoes, evidence of the great imbalance in my life at age twenty-one. Since the age of fourteen, I could fit every belonging I owned in two bags. I sold anything of value for drugs to prolong a binge. My mother learned early on that sending me things of value was pointless.

It would end up in a syringe within hours. I had grown accustomed to receiving books that had some sort of recovery message in them instead.

As I hitchhiked my way toward Wilderness Treatment Center, I was picked up by a variety of people. Given my disgruntled appearance, I was lucky to be picked up at all. A guy named Michael picked me up for the last leg of the drive. He gave me an account of the surrounding area and told me that Kalispell was the closest town. As Michael pulled away, I walked down the driveway that my father and I had driven home from seven years prior. My hope rested in Wilderness Treatment Center and the miracle of possibility. I had not quite lost the spark, although one depressive episode could take that from me.

The sign above the entrance said "Don't drink. Go to meetings." This was sound advice that I had not taken. As a result, I walked back, humbled by my choice to go against those words. As I entered the campus, kids lined the driveway to my right. They looked confused to see a person walking, bag in hand, toward the treatment center. I would have been equally confused in their position. In a matter of moments, the staff appeared, immediately isolating me from the others in an attempt to protect the clients from the very real potential that I had drugs on me.

This was not the reception I had expected. They questioned me about why I had come. I realized that my hope of being readmitted depended upon whether or not they would be willing to cover or waive the thirty-thousand or so dollars necessary to pay for my stay. For some reason, I had never even considered having to pay for treatment when I decided to return. I still had the mentality of a teenager and gave little to no thought to how people paid for things.

I must have been quite a sight to see for many of the clients. They were eventually allowed to talk with me under the supervision of staff, bumming cigarettes and asking where I had come from. To many, the two-hour hitchhike from the train station seemed unfathomable. In their minds, they were stuck in the wilderness with no hope of escape. Their parents' resolve mixed with the vast expanse that surrounded them punctuated this thought. That combination established imaginary walls that kept them trapped.

In the office, Mr. and Mrs. Brekky watched me from their chairs. The counselors did their best to weigh out the situation, though they had no say in the outcome. Within minutes, my hope had been diminished by their refusal to allow me back into the program. "Please, I will work it off on the ranch or in any way that I can." My pleas went unanswered as they gave their intern directions to my drop-off point in Kalispell. They never gave me a full explanation for not allowing me back into the program. I have a suspicion that it had more to do with logistics than anything else. They were not driven by greed. Instead, they felt compassion and a sincere desire that I remain clean. They must have spent an hour or more giving me a pep talk. They told me that if I put as much effort into my recovery as I put into getting there, I would remain clean. Mr. Brekky said, "Asking for help is the most critical part of recovery. You showed the ability to humble yourself enough to get the help you need."

Although I felt disappointed by their decision, I was not defeated. I knew that I had come for a reason. Hadn't Marcie shown me that through her dream and her gift? The fact that I was going through withdrawals and still sought recovery meant a great deal. At the time, I didn't understand that their denial had given me perhaps the greatest gift I had ever been given by a treatment center—a closed door.

Their refusal of my request halted an unhealthy pattern of dependence on institutions. Doors had always been open. The presence of funding eliminated the work that I needed to do to further my recovery. Rarely had I been forced to put forth the effort to rebuild my own life, starting from the bottom of the hole I had created through use. I would need to learn that the very hole I had dug formed the beginning stages of a foundation. Pouring concrete into the holes we dig forms the foundation for any structure. Recovery teaches addicts to use their liabilities as assets. Why not learn to build upon my liabilities rather than avoid them? Why not learn to provide for my own needs rather than expecting others to do so?

This does not mean that treatment should be avoided, even for those who have experienced multiple stays. It means that those who do not have the resources to go to multiple treatment programs can find the resources needed within their community. There they will receive the help required to build their lives from the hole, to the foundation, to the framing and finish work. Going through the phases of rebuilding will help others to learn this process, thereby ensuring recovery for yet more people in need.

The intern dropped me off at the doorstep of an Alano club in Kalispell. Over coffee, I learned from one of the members that I could stay on the third floor of the Rose Briar Inn, housing that fell between an independent living facility and a mission. The inhabitants there were required to remain clean and get a job. The Rose Briar proved to be everything I had been told it was: Montana's version of low-income housing. I fit right in. I had little trouble adjusting since I had spent most of my life living in group settings. Fifteen men in a dormitory was not an issue and I was grateful to have a place to stay considering I had no money and very few options. Moving to Montana had been an act of faith; thus far, it had not gone exactly as planned.

Kicking dope was difficult. I used the group where I had been dropped off to provide the support that I needed. My withdrawal became severe. I walked to and from men's meetings on Main Street twice a week. I relied on those who had gone through similar experiences for support and suggestions.

Kalispell definitely did not look or feel like downtown Seattle. The pace moved slowly and none of the people I passed on the sidewalk seemed to be holding anything interesting. If I had wanted to score, I could not have done so on the corner of Main Street. Drug transactions happened behind closed doors because dealers couldn't hide in the current of the city—there was none. Inner cities are desensitized to the drug culture and look past its prevalence as if it did not exist. I felt relieved that Kalispell moved much slower.

I have never been able to verbalize fear, even though I lived with it on a daily basis. It seemed easier to avoid fear through substance use rather than face it head on. I felt afraid because I didn't know how to live on my own. I spent so much of my life running because to slow down, would allow people to know the extent of my limitations. They would not see me the way I saw myself: utterly hopeless and unworthy of help with learning the basics of getting by in the "real world." After a while, I took on an anti-society attitude, which made it easy to avoid the things I did not know. I thought that if people believed I was simply antiestablishment, they would avoid probing deeper into my circumstances.

The Rose Briar was perfect because I had very little responsibility. All I had to do was find a way to pay room and board. My work prospects were limited as I had very little experience. When I did work, the jobs had been short-lived. I had roofing and carpentry experience, but I had only provided manual labor. I worked hard, and I learned and excelled quickly when I was clean. The problem was that at each of my previous jobs, I eventually started using again, which took away any possibility of moving forward.

This frustration extended beyond the workplace. When I was sober, people seemed to find me likable, smart, hard working, as well as an asset to employers and the community as a whole. Those who believed in me expressed disappointment and deep sadness, as they were proven wrong repeatedly by my tragic return to using drugs. I was sincere when I gave my word that I was done. I truly believed that I was done. Sadly, sincerity alone is not the magic elixir for recovery.

One night, as I was returning from a recovery meeting, I heard church music emanating from a storefront on Main Street. I loved church music because it reminded me of the African American choirs I had heard as a teenager. Although this sounded altogether different, the music still drew me in. I walked into the makeshift church; I could feel the weight of many eyes descend upon me. A new face never seems to go unrecognized where Jesus' disciples gather. When the music ended, I did what I could to depart before the flock could become my shepherds.

I was not fast enough to avoid the pastor's wife. She stood waving a fan by the door. She asked me to get ice cream with her and her husband. What was it that either pushed people away or drew them to me? I was convinced that by asking the universe for help, I had become a magnet for every God-loving, spiritually minded person I came across. Or, maybe my newly acquired sense of the spirit while in recovery attracted me to like-minded people. Whatever it was, I found that my voracious appetite for drugs transformed into a desire for growth and development while clean.

Bill and Patty had spent the greater part of their lives sharing their love for God and carrying a message of hope in the best way they knew how. In their eyes, Jesus was everything. As a result, I had a double dose of him with my double scoop of sherbet. I have rarely looked down upon those of faith for being overbearing in their desire to spread their version of truth. How could I? If I believed that the well-being of those I loved and cared for rested in a certain philosophy, I would have proceeded with just as much zeal. People of all belief systems act similarly. They may take a different approach, but each pass on their experience with the hope of helping those who struggle. I never want to be so arrogant or self-righteous as to believe that my opinions and experiences are what is best for others or that my many answers and solutions negate the need to hear what has worked for others.

The idea of attraction over promotion shows a faith in a process that does not require a multitude of believers to push its belief system. I love the idea of being drawn toward the things that my Creator has in store for me as opposed to being pushed towards what others think the creator has in store for me. When the Creator's purpose is manipulated to serve the benefits of man, his or her message becomes diluted. When I sense this shift from the spirit to selfish motives, I turn away.

Bill and Patty did not suffocate me with their beliefs. They asked about my life and why I had come to Montana. Because I did not feel pressured, I shared with them my struggles. This was the beginning of a wonderful relationship. They shared a sincere desire that I would experience redemption from my conflicted past. I spent most of my evenings having ice cream with them, discussing God, baseball, and addiction.

I used faith as a way to manipulate those around me, either unconsciously or consciously. To claim to believe in something as a way of diverting attention, getting attention, or creating an image is manipulation all the same. What I wanted more than Bill and Patty's love of God was their undying faith. Their belief produced great happiness that was not tied to God. Rather, it was tied to the inarguable notion that what they believed in was their truth; in this, they found their sanctuary.

Throughout my life, I had seen others experience this very thing. I understood that the common denominator was not the religion itself or their specific spiritual principles. It was simply the faith people had in those beliefs. With hope comes the sprout pushing through the soil, and with faith comes the energy that pulls the shoot skyward. This combination binds all beliefs and creates the power to bring about even the most difficult change.

It did not matter that Bill and Patty were Christians. My manipulation was non-denominational and knew no bounds. It came from the hope that I could believe as they did, that I could get the same results despite our completely different life circumstances. One size does not fit all. Their faith was based in their own life experiences, not mine. I had to find my own way.

I spent many weeks with them in church, putting on a tie, and going through the motions of a man who came to Jesus in every way but the honest one. I must reemphasize that they could have been Buddhist or followed any other belief system. I would have done the same thing with anyone in my search for peace of mind, body, and spirit. I didn't realize that to form a bond with a Creator, I could not acquire faith and religion as I had acquired everything else in my life. My search required honesty, open-mindedness, and willingness. These words had been repeated for many years in recovery, and they applied to my search for faith as well.

Montana Conservation Corps gives kids the opportunity to do trail work, stream restoration, and other jobs to better the community and the environment. One of the church members knew an administrator in the program. Within a couple of days, I joined a crew designed to mentor teens in the youth system. There was a lot of discussion about my circumstances in recovery and how my position was contingent upon complete abstinence. I thanked them for the opportunity and conveyed appreciation at their interest in helping me remain clean.

I loved my new job and felt as if the reasons I had for coming to Montana were finally beginning to unfold. I had a job, had been clean for a couple of months, and had found a foundation of people who stood solidly behind me. My responsibilities took me into the mountains of northwestern Montana to do trail work. It had been years since I had experienced the coming together of nature, the Creator, and me. This union offered the possibility for balance delivered by way of an unforgettable experience. I felt transported to the days of my childhood when I was free from conflicting emotion and my life had not yet gone sour due to circumstance, poor choices, and my biological makeup.

I watched the insects interact with the vegetation and the sun cast shadows that did not scare me. Instead, beams of light filtered through the tree canopy, creating the impression that the mountains were alive, inhaling slowly and then releasing. Where the cement ends and the soil begins civilization slowly recedes. Only a few hand-made cabins, created and left by explorers of another era, remained. This place delivered a deep realization that I had taken things for granted. An old world revealed itself. In the fast-paced universe of injection, city lights, and club music, I had missed a place where the inhabitants had been in balance with their surroundings for hundreds of thousands of years. I had lost my way through distraction.

The sound of rustling leaves surrounded me and the blissful sway of their chorus caught my ears. Unlike the choirs of the inner city, this one had existed for centuries. I was in a state of perpetual praise for the one who had created it all. If I looked high enough into the canopy, I could see the angels that had gathered above the church pews and in the island forests. The wholesomeness of what I experienced made me want to dip into the glacial streams that descended the mountainsides. In the purity of the icy waters, I would enjoy spiritual union with my Creator.

The Creator's expression is not limited to the written word of man. Spiritual readings present a limited under-standing, rather than broadening the mind. In my vision, I saw women still united with the cycle of the moon, connected to the earth, moon, and all living things. They were still teachers, sharing gentleness and compassion to a world that would later turned away from them. In so doing balance and hope diminished as tenderness was replaced with bravado.

Wholeness came over me, birthed by the magnani-mous lands that surrounded me. The fragrance of a mountain wild flower seemed like a sacred secret, one that only my soul could translate. Butterflies danced from water to plant then back again. This was a holy place, one that held no judgment.

Every day as I dressed in my work clothes, I felt like I was dressing for a place of worship. I felt ready to experience the miracle of creation, a phenomenon that had spanned billions of years, never limited by the turned pages of a calendar. The Creator continued to breathe life into creation. This evolution went beyond man's arguments. I had a strange feeling that the authors of the natural world's demise had not seen things as I had come to see them. Otherwise, such men would not do things to destroy the earth. I began to have a deep compassion for them, not because I was better or different, but because we were the same. I, too, lived in ignorance of what I was experiencing. Separation from nature is man's greatest loss.

Roots seemed to climb my torso, forming coils around my body, and pulling me to the soil that nourished them. I began to see through the eyes of the earth—I became the earth. The rivers, clouds, and ocean became my circulatory system. I felt every slight of humanity as my resources were extricated and then used against me. It was as though my own hands strangled me, controlled by another. In humankind's desire to make technological advancements, it moved backwards, destroying through creation.

New creations of humankind made poor substitutes for the things they had to sacrifice for them. In that moment, I understood that I had done the same to my body as a result of every substance I had taken. The lessons from the tribe house and the drum circles returned to me. The rhythm of my own life shattered. In the selfishness of the human condition, I had failed to understand how each of us is connected in every decision that we make. Every time I poisoned my body in some back alley, the earth cried tears of mourning, knowing that in that tiny needle prick I chose death over life. I hacked away at my own roots.

I recalled people in my life whose belief systems had disrespected the earth as I had, yet instead of needles they held fists full of money. The children of the earth exploited me for their own gain, unraveling millions of cycles of creation. They replaced the Creator and dictated their own demise despite my warnings. I felt every fence built upon my spherical form as an attempt to further the idea that individual ownership overrides the collective good. Animals never staked ownership over my lands, save the instinctual need to protect their dens and areas of foraging. Now humankind claimed ownership as though I was their slave.

Even animals understood humankind's intent. What had been shared since a time before human memory was now apportioned. As nations disallowed the migration of people, a separatist belief came into fruition that went beyond tribal exclusion. Greed divvied up the wealth of the whole, enslaving my children, and creating a hierarchy of humankind that believed power could be gained through the building of resources and not the spirit. I began to realize that humankind was a cancer destroying my body. I felt warm.

Spiritual experiences never came as I expected. Coming out of my vision, I understood that the balance and love I experienced came in part from an understanding that the earth would right itself; it would eliminate the things that put the greater whole in jeopardy. Humankind, in its egoism, is unaware that this self-importance is simply perceived in the mind, and then perpetuated. Every time I came out of the woods, I emerged with a fuller understanding of the disrespect I had shown the very thing that fostered my spiritual experience. I came to understand that I was a guest here, and that the earth allowed humankind to use her as a place to learn and grow. Instead of thanking her, we exploited her. I became aware that the earth was part of the Creator.

These realizations left me feeling fiercely protective. I had been lied to my whole life by those who claimed to speak for the Creator and yet never taught what I had just experienced. While working with my other crewmembers in the woods, I formed profound relationships. I was able to share my circumstances without shame. Instead, I expressed simple statements of fact, which provoked discussions of hope, faith, and gratitude—three indicators that I was indeed living recovery through action.

I wish what I have just described had been enough to keep the thunderclouds from rolling in. Depression my nemesis, always surfaced when it might cause the greatest fall. It had a life of its own, the sole purpose of which was to merge with addiction and drive me to the depths of insanity, shame, and self-loathing. The addict and one who suffers from clinical depression experience hopelessness differently. For the addict, hopelessness can be found in the depths of addiction; from this place comes the possibility of hope. The addict doesn't have to be willing initially; but he or she must be clean long enough for the miracle to take hold. Hope is the counselor's greatest ally; hope allows for change with even the most stubborn patient.

In contrast, for those who suffer from clinical depression, hopelessness is not a catalyst for change. It is a place that makes depression worse, leading to even deeper despair. Once depression enters the realm of despair, horrific consequences may ensue. Medication supplies the brain with the substance it so desperately needs to restore balance.

Opposition exists with respect to the belief that hope is, in part, a result of a chemical reaction in the brain brought about by medication as opposed to a miracle described in the pages of a holy book. Although it is a miracle of sorts, it is a miracle of science brought about by years of study. A great travesty lies in the needless suffering of those who fall under the guidance of the many who will not educate themselves and instead restrict themselves to the dogma of faith.

Some chemical imbalances can be far more powerful than faith itself. To further a person's suffering rather than seek the benefits of psychological care is quite controversial, to say the least. My guess is that more people have been helped out of the abyss of depression through proper diet, exercise, medication, and therapy than from the laying on of hands, tongues, chants, incense, and holy water. Faith has a supporting role in this, not the leading one; this can be difficult for some of faith to stomach. I am by no means discrediting the importance of faith. Faith has its place. I am the first one to look to the beauty of the early morning sky, asking for guidance and direction, and praying for reprieve with the help of *all* things necessary to attain balance.

Depression is complicated by the use of methamphetamines. Such drugs leave many chronic users in a deep depression that mimics other mood disorders such as clinical depression or anxiety. As a result of the depletion of dopamine receptors in the brain, addicts are left feeling like a cloud has descended. This leaves them void of the emotions associated with enjoyment, well-being, and contentment. This may also affect states of being like gratitude, faith, and hopefulness. As a result, many addicts find themselves in the constant throws of depression. This leads them back to meth use as it simulates balance and offers a temporary relief. I suffer from a dual diagnosis. As a consequence, I suffered needlessly by believing that recovery and faith could restore me to a place of emotional balance. This lie—the result of misunderstanding and bias—caused me to continue to use and to suffer. I have led the charge to recognize that the brain is in need of help to attain balance. Coming to that point has taken a great deal of introspection free from all chemicals. Over time, I have realized that the fluctuation of emotions in early recovery has very little to do with the imbalance and everything to do with imbalance.

In my life, I have put on many masks in an attempt to find the answers I thought existed in others. In most cases, my desire for a reprieve was sincere, though I did not buy in completely to the philosophies of others. Without absolute commitment, hope and faith will not come about. Despite my best efforts to follow through with directions given in recovery groups, and despite the profound spiritual experience I had undergone, I was unable to keep deep depression from my life. As in the past, it followed my initial relief of getting clean again. No matter how hard I meditated, wished, cursed, or prayed for it to remain at bay, depression returned in full fury, dragging me back to the great lie that my only alternative was in the use of the chemicals.

Only addicts who have experienced certain levels of recovery and spirituality may be able to relate to this story. It is not one of the non-addict who cries into their beer after a fight with a loved one. It is the type of sorrow that comes after acting against one's conscience once again; trading the greatest gifts that the world has to offer for the misery of active addiction. As if watching from the outside, the substance immediately jades the spiritual experience, leaving the addict in an emotional and spiritual withdrawal that towers over everything else. I have sobbed many times as the needle pierced my skin. The only thing that could relieve me of that pain was further use of the very thing that caused it. As in abusive relationships, the abuser tells the victim "I love you" then beats him or her black and blue. The victim returns just to hear the words, knowing that a severe price will be paid in the process.

When I relapsed, I was staying at Steve's house. Steve and I had been working together for several months. He had entrusted me to stay at his small cabin in Marion while he and his roommate were on vacation. I had progressed far in several months. Friends who understood that I was an IV addict had enough faith, based on their experience with me in recovery, to entrust me to look over their things. I was being treated as a normal human being, deserving of trust because I had earned it.

I had convinced myself that I could handle using marijuana. When I had made that decision, a spiritual shift occurred. I entered the world I had exited months before as immediately as the spiritual experience came to me in the woods. The first puff produced an immediate desire to use more and more, until I eventually renewed my IV use. As an addict, marijuana changed me spiritually. Many who wish to justify its use argue otherwise. For me, marijuana had a negative spiritual effect, one which brought me further from my connection with the Creator—not closer to it. I felt this immediately. I was void again. I was alone with addiction and depression. I would have preferred to be on a battlefield rather than at war in my own body. Such might have increased my chances for survival.

19

MY RELAPSES RARELY OCCUR OUT OF THE BLUE. They are set in motion by a series of events that, in retrospect, present a detailed map of my many missteps before use. In this instance, my survivalist mentality led me to develop a plan B. This should have been my first indication that I was about to backslide into full-blown use. When the warning signs began to appear, I didn't reach out to those around me. I cast aside the recovery groups. At work, I became unreliable as my sleep patterns became unpredictable. Bill and Patty began to question my lack of attendance at church and my lack of willingness to spend time with them as I had before. I began to sink within myself, which was indicative of a depressive episode. Many of my behaviors relapsed as well; I became preoccupied, obsessed, and compulsive.

Those who tried to help me see the course I began to take, were eliminated in due order. Their care and concern felt like an infringement on my personal space or an invasion of my privacy. This left those for whom I cared wondering what they had done wrong, or why I had shifted from open and inviting to emotionally and spiritually shut down. No matter how hard anyone tried, once I reached this point, only medication or some spiritual intervention could divert my course. This is not a theory. This is a truth that I've proven to myself repeatedly through the cycles of depression, use, recovery, and relapse.

When I decided to use, I found a bud of marijuana within twenty minutes of the first craving. Within two hours of smoking, I had a needle in my arm and was pursuing injection as though I had never stopped. The idea that I could use marijuana as a form of damage control drug was a myth, one that I had destroyed repeatedly. It had led me back to the abyss.

How is it that an addict can sacrifice friendship to fill a perceived need? How was it that when placed in a position of trust, I put my self-centeredness ahead of things of value and substance? Several weeks later, I returned to Steve's house knowing that I could find things of value to support my awakened IV addiction. My role as victimizer allowed me to see the world in a different light. I sought potential weakness in those around me, and then stalked them like prey. It is not easy to admit that, at that point in my life and despite the progress I had made, I brought grief into the lives of those to whom, only weeks before, I had brought joy.

I had transformed into Kenneth and Marlene, people I swore I would never become. I never could victimize those I loved while in recovery. When I was at Steve's, I wasn't casing the joint or inventorying his belongings. Once the craving hit, I knew that I didn't have the resources necessary to satiate that craving. I was standing where I could easily acquire a means to satisfy my craving. It isn't that I believed I could get away with it. I simply didn't care about the consequences. I was driven by availability rather than loyalty.

For years, I played with the idea of eliminating close relationships altogether in an attempt to protect those I loved from my inevitable return to use. I liked to believe that this was my selfless side; in retrospect, it was still self-ishness. I wished to avoid the pain of my actions as well as the pain brought to those I loved. It was selfish for me to eliminate others rather than making the changes that would protect them in the long-run. They understood what I might do when I was using yet they embraced me. They lived in bravery and the shadow of potentiality.

Steve and his roommate were left blaming themselves for not seeing it ahead of time. Further, they felt saddened to see that trust is a precarious thing. Even after investing trust in those who have earned it, trust can be cast away as if it has no value. My former friends were introduced to a human being they had not known before. This someone may have caused them to lose some faith in humanity. It is easier to be victimized by a stranger. Otherwise, the personal element leaves a sting that lingers.

A lifetime worth of CDs brought a pitiful one hundred dollars or so at the pawnshop. The fact that I had stolen it resulted in emotional damage that far exceeded any monetary gain. I exchanged hard-earned trust and respect for an hour's worth of getting high. I pushed the shame of the act to the lower confines of my consciousness, which fueled further use. The people I used with never suggested I should act otherwise. Rather, they encouraged me knowing that in my sacrifice they would get high, too. The darkness fed itself. Shame permeated the ranks of addicts that congregated together—the like-minded leading the like-minded into the crowd of victims in search of their next sacrifice.

My first stop on my binge was to my friend Leaf's house. Leaf, a red headed, hippie kid from California, had come to Montana for the same reasons that I had. He sought reprieve from himself and the pace of the Los Angeles life. Growing up, he had been swept up in the drug culture and spent time in numerous treatment centers and recovery groups. We shared the same language and immediately hit it off. We spent weeks together, forming a bond through shared addiction. We hovered between consciousness and unconsciousness, nodding off for hours or tweaking into morning hours. A spark of humanity still existed within Leaf that full-blown use had not taken away. I believe he saw the same thing in me.

A striking difference separated us, however. Leaf did not take risks as I did. While I was out doing whatever was required of me to stay high, he worked a job and tried his best to participate in society on a level of which I was incapable—or unwilling. Leaf had no problem partaking in the fruits of my labor, or lack thereof, yet when it came to criminal acts beyond drug use and sales, he would not participate. I both respected and resented it. Leaf, like so many other people in my life, would ride the coattails of my risk taking, and then hide when it came time to take responsibility for those actions. Obviously, Leaf and the others like him were much smarter than I in this regard. I was simply desperate and because I had compromised on so many other occasions, the next compromise became that much easier.

As my use progressed, I began to make runs to Seattle for meth and other drugs. Although I moved only small quantities, I sometimes dealt in pounds of marijuana or ounces of meth and black tar. I found a way to stay ahead of my use, and although it was short-lived, I enjoyed a perpetual party. My life had returned to where I had left off in Seattle.

We spent most weekends in Whitefish, listening to music, and buying and selling drugs in the bars that lined the streets. On a night when I happened to have several ounces of marijuana and a teener of meth, my karma sought payment. I did not see it coming. I never did when my past, present, and future converged to present consequence. Pat, Leaf's roommate, drove that night, and one of his headlights had burned out. Paul wasn't a seasoned drug user and had very little reason to understand the consequences of leaving a bar at 2:30 am with a light out. In my stupidity, I failed to do the basic inspection I often did when carrying drugs.

I am not sure why I didn't eat the meth when the cop pulled us over. It would have changed the felony stop to a misdemeanor. Instead, I tossed my wallet onto the floorboard of the car then attempted to kick it under the driver's seat. We had been smoking marijuana, so when the windows opened, blue smoke rolled out. The patrol officer did not waste any time as he pulled us from the vehicle and lined us up against the side of the car. In searching the vehicle, he turned up numerous ounces of marijuana individually bagged. As my wallet and rolling tobacco were placed on the hood of the vehicle, I knew that in moments, the scene would get worse. As he looked through my tobacco pouch, he realized that the tobacco was mixed with marijuana. The cop shuffled through my wallet, then discovered the red-tinged meth. In moments, he called for back-up and the three of us were placed in handcuffs. My misdemeanor became a felony. As usual, I took the blame for everything once I realized I would get the heaviest charge. It made sense to claim the other ounces as my own since I was going to jail anyway. A backward pride comes with taking the fall for your friends. Physical possession makes up nine-tenths of the law, as the saying goes. In my grandiosity and limited understanding of the judicial system, I had no idea what I faced. I would have made the journey alone except that Leaf had a warrant for an unpaid fine. Together, we entered Flathead County Detention Center.

Processing was an arduous experience, especially since I desperately wanted a smoke, a hit, and my freedom back. The county deputies worked with a purposeful and systematic urgency that reflected the desire to get us into cells and out of their hair. Drunks are never fun to deal with; tweekers who have been drinking all night are worse. Leaf and I we were both loud and obnoxious, and from the look of it, we had awakened people who had been pleasantly unaware of their surroundings. We were unpopular guests. When we entered the group holding cell, a muscular man covered in tattoos stood and looked us both in the eyes. In four words, he had us humbled and silenced despite the chemicals that surged through our systems. "Shut—the—fuck—up!" His message was simple and he looked prepared to back it up as necessary. I spent the rest of the early morning hours staring at the ceiling and reading the graffiti that covered the walls by my bench.

Over the three years since my last drug arrest, I had grown. I was no longer a scared high-school boy, and I definitely would not point my finger in blame. I had made the decision to never make others take responsibility for my choices. Becoming an informant also eliminated the ability to live and operate in the drug world. I had become a seasoned drug addict, drug dealer, and criminal.

By using, this was the world I had chosen. When the inevitable invite came from the office down the hall, the first words that came out of my mouth were, "No, I will not cooperate." With that statement, I sealed my fate with the Judicial System of Montana State. An unwillingness to cooperate meant that my sentence would not be lowered. I would receive no sympathy from the Prosecutor's Office.

Leaf was released several days ahead of me. When my withdrawals started to take effect, I was brought before the judge and released on my own recognizance. I am not sure what led to my release other than my minimal adult record and place of residence. I was also a first-time offender as an adult, which made me a prime candidate for release. That decision brought me enormous relief, yet within an hour of my release, I had a needle in my arm with no plans to return and face my charges.

How is it that any non-addictive person facing similar circumstances would have returned to face the charges, learned from their mistakes, and then never repeated that mistake again? I was never a stupid person. I was capable of making some sound decisions while abstinent, but when I was high, afraid, or experiencing withdrawals, I acted impulsively and made already serious situations more serious. I pushed all reason aside and set a course from which I could never turn back. I made myself a fugitive of the law. This invited a new severity into my life. I ceased to be a boy in need of help; I became a man who needed discipline. The State of Montana would not rest until I was apprehended, brought to justice, and forced to pay the full price for my crimes—crimes of my past, present, and future.

Some try to glamorize life on the run, but I felt absolutely no enjoyment in looking over my shoulder and contemplating what would happen when the law caught up with me. Within weeks of my release and missing my court dates, I began to see flyers around town posted by Steve and Paul. I took down and destroyed as many as I could. I asked several friends in the area to do the same, which allowed me to remain under the radar for a time. I had to remove myself from the land of responsible citizens and sequester myself to places where I was least likely to get caught.

I was confined to the shadows of the early hours, fearful that in the light of the day, someone would recognize me. I was forced to avoid anyone who might turn me in for my own good, sinking further into the quagmire of drug use and the shadow walkers who thrived there. I existed but did not live. Although I presented a "who cares" attitude, I was concerned about where my life had gone. Despite my attempts to avoid emotional outbursts that might lead me to take responsibility for my actions, I was often consumed by emotion in private. As usual, I turned to drugs to avoid facing my own internal tug-of-war.

A network of friends helped me survive for the several weeks I remained in Montana. They provided enough drugs and capital to fuel a binge and to allow me to hitchhike across three states to Seattle. I knew I could live in the shadows there indefinitely if I could only get there. I would not return to jail. I decided that I would rather die than face the consequences I had created for myself. I was not the type of person who would intentionally take the lives of others. I was, however, the kind of junkie who could buy a couple of grams of tar and enter a dark alley never to return. Dying among the city's trash seemed a fitting ending, a reflection of how I now viewed myself. Forced into a corner, I could not fail.

I packed my belongings in garbage bags. The gifted backpack had disappeared along with most of my other belongings. When word got out that I was in jail, the feeding frenzy began. People assumed that I would not return. Thankfully, my diaries, old letters, and recovery books were of little interest to the thieves. I knew this from my own experience with thievery. Thank goodness my most precious items were not monetary. Not until later would I understand the significance of that fact.

With what little I had left, I made my way to a local sport shop looking for a backpack to carry on my journey. I had no money in my checking account, but I did have checks. I knew that the check would bounce, but my only purpose was to avoid facing consequences. Little else mattered.

I asked about different pack models as though my intentions were pure. The ability to sell myself had become a great asset; but for those I chose to victimize, my acting skills caused great frustration. I could play many roles at any given time. Doing so had allowed me to survive.

"Is this check good?" the cashier asked, taking it from me.

"Of course it is," I told him, feigning offense. "Should I take my business elsewhere?"

"Oh, no, no. I have to ask everyone that."

I receded into the lie. I packed my personal belongings into the backpack: five diaries, a large stack of letters, several books, and various pictures. I packed them with reverence. Had I shown the same respect for other peoples' belongings, I wouldn't have been in the mess I was in. That check was the first of thirty-four that would bounce in the surrounding states by my hand and the hands of those who had pilfered my belongings before I retrieved them after release.

Leaf and I had been planning to move to Seattle for some time. His girlfriend lived out that way, and I wanted to be near a big city with access to drugs again. I had a hard time entering into drug circles in Montana, which was frustrating since I had both bought and sold without suspicion before. One of my problems was how I looked. I appeared clean cut. Feeling as though I belonged nowhere, I lived between two worlds, neither of which would fully accept me. This put me in a position of being either the worst of the worse or the best of best. I had no middle ground. I could never be a regular, middle-of-the-road guy.

Leaf's house was already packed. For several weeks, we hung out at his empty house until his lease ended. Our destination was the Tonasket Barter Fair in northeastern Washington, where we would hook up with friends and get a ride back to Seattle. The journey took us the better part of the night and into the morning. By the time the sun rose in the eastern sky, we had arrived at our destination. We exchanged brief goodbyes. The people who had brought us there were friends of convenience, a relationship that extended both ways.

I loved the excitement of festivals. Thousands of people swarmed, offering many possibilities for provisions. I needed heroin, meth, coke, acid, mushrooms, ecstasy, marijuana, alcohol, or anything else that would dislodge me from reality. Needle junkies can't hide their use. I appeared to be damaged goods; others distanced themselves from me knowing I was unpredictable. I repeatedly ran into people I knew, mostly people I had grown up with then lost track of in my travels. Most were shocked by my appearance and I felt sadness in their prolonged embraces. Because of their concern, I avoided asking for a ride to Seattle. I did not want to ride home with people who had known me before, at a time when I was a far different person. I had nothing of substance to share with them, no self-esteem. My early years remained my prized possession; I did not share them with anyone. All I had left were my memories of being a boy who was loved, popular, talented, and bright. I had become the shell of that person, with nothing to show after many years of struggle other than scars, a few personal belongings, and a criminal record. I preferred to turn from their embrace rather than share with them the destruction of my life.

The Creator is always at work. Had I known that even a remote possibility existed that my oldest brother, Travis, and his wife might be at the fair, I would never have come. I was in no state to face those who could tug at my heartstrings. They were bartering sweaters, and when I saw them, I longed to turn and walk away. My brother's voice was like a beacon. His warm embrace thawed my icy core. He held on just a moment longer as my emotion forced itself free. I had known this release only a few times before. It was akin to working with Connie. No matter how hard I tried to pull it back, I could not. My entire ego disappeared. For the first time, I became aware of the things I would sacrifice through continued use and eventual death.

Memories of my brother mingled with the travesty of the years of separation from him. My brothers had always been my heroes. They represented everything I wanted to be and more: fast, strong, funny, and the purveyors of vast knowledge. As the younger brother, I always tagged along, then ran home to my mother the moment I felt slighted. "Crybaby's running home to mommy again," I would hear as I raced into the door of the house with tears in my eyes.

My brothers took part in a neighborhood gang that was comprised of the older kids in the neighborhood. I obsessed over joining them. I pleaded, offering to share new, secret hiding spots, but nothing ever persuaded them to allow me to join their secret order. Who really wants their little brother hanging around, especially when he's a loose-lipped crybaby? I had a knack for finding them when they least wanted me to, which led to savage dirt-clod fights, kamikaze attacks, and wrestling matches that left me in a crumpled heap on the lawn. They raced around the corner of the house in swift retreat.

It was lonely being the younger brother, always chasing those who I assumed did not want to be caught. Looking back I realize that in constantly trying to be a part of their group, I was a part of it. By chasing them, I fulfilled my part of the bargain. "Sorry, Eric," Travis would say. "You're just not old enough to hang out with us." Little did I know that there was no official neighborhood gang. It was a game they played, to see what crazy things I would do just to be accepted. My feelings hurt, I would yell, "I didn't really want to be part of your stupid gang anyhow," then disappear into the forest. I stayed angry just long enough to create a new game to counter the disappointment I had felt by being left out.

Emotion has a mind of its own; it surfaces when it so chooses, especially in times of distress. True emotion is the expression of the spirit. I don't remember how long I cried in Travis's arms. We eventually went to his van because people began stopping to stare. Others must have assumed that a great tragedy had taken place to bring about such emotion. In many ways, it had. The great tragedy of my life was unavoidable. No matter how far I ran or what I did to avoid it, the reality of my life revealed itself; now it had crashed into a part of me that I had long forgotten, a brother who could not save me from myself. It was impossible for me to avoid the reality of who I had become when looking into the eyes of someone who had known me before. Along with the disgrace, I understood that I could be hugging my brother for the last time.

We separated and few words were exchanged. Although I asked for a ride west, we both agreed it would be best for me to find my own way. I felt relieved by this. I told him that I loved him then disappeared into the crowd, feeling the weight of amassed emotion lifted from me. Leaf sat silently through the exchange. He never left as many would have done. In the glances he passed in my direction, he showed sympathy and compassion. He also had a family whom he loved and a life from which he had run. We wore the same scars and shared more than a common habit. We shared compassion as tortured and tested souls who had lost their way home.

We were protectors, comrades, brothers in battle, and bearers of a dim hope to light the path when the other felt lost. Partners of those who use should be thanked by loved ones. In many cases, Leaf and I kept each other alive. He understood when my desire to live began to dissipate. He could hear it in the way that I spoke and in the escalation of my use. With every shot I doubled my regular dose, entering a place of extremes, sinking far beyond what was usual. In his own way, he tried to temper me. Four eyes plus double the street savvy meant better protection. As Leaf partook in my scores, I didn't have as much to use myself. If Leaf hadn't found a way to get me to Seattle, I might have wandered into the anonymity of the Montana wilderness, seeking the crook of a tree in which to shoot up and abandon myself to the scavengers who awaited my souls departure.

The spiritual world did not disappear when I chose to pursue darker paths. Instead, it intensified and took on darker forms to intercede. The spiritual world of purity and abstinence is far different from that of substance, selfishness, and death. Much like in Seattle, I invited the demons of torment into my life, and from them I learned that I had one of two choices. I could continue on until death found me, or I could embrace life through the hard work required to make amends, to accept responsibility, and to pursue personal change and spiritual transformation. I had to choose sides and stop living in perpetual midnight.

Leaf and I decided to begin hitchhiking before everyone left the gathering so we could catch a ride with fellow festival-goers. We had become severely handicapped as a result of brining a pregnant dog named Sativa. Just before we agreed to split up, a Winnebago pulled up and the driver offered a ride for all of us as far as Spokane. We loaded up our belongings, thankful to be riding in something large enough to sleep in shifts and keep our new host busy with conversation. Mac told me he had picked us up because I had a powder scale strapped to my backpack. I neither realized nor cared what people would think. I either made my own bullets or weighed out other, less acceptable powders.

Leaf and I had entered junkie heaven. Although I spent the majority of the ride nodding in and out of consciousness, I woke several times to Mac swerving in and out of the lanes of traffic. He was quite loaded and eventually asked a woman in the back to take the wheel. Her driving wasn't much better, but she didn't have an arm full of heroin to blame. She preferred speed. Leaf found the opposite side of the chemical spectrum behind a curtain in back. Before long, he took the wheel and I nodded off into oblivion unconcerned.

I am not sure how long we were in Spokane. Leaf and I both tried to figure it out, but ended up laughing at the ridiculousness of our lives. Mac had been fronted heroine by someone. It was obvious by his demeanor that he had offended someone he hadn't wished to cross. He had bitten off more than he could chew, and in his desperation, Mac had fallen behind on paying back his debt. Adding to this, we discovered that Mac was also on the run. If and when the law caught up with him, he said he'd be doing ten years for distribution. When he was arrested, someone had posted his bail though he'd never found out who.

That tended to be a bad sign. On several occasions while staying in an RV park, Leaf and I saw a red truck and two older Mexicans inside. When we looked a second time, they didn't drive off. They sat, stared, and then finally decided to move on. There was no reason for them to be there other than to watch, create panic, and to remind someone of their debt.

Leaf and I began to realize that we had been brought on board as witnesses, to provide protection and two more sets of eyes. We spent our days weighing out black tar, traveling around the city, and standing by Mac as he made sales. We were in a precarious position because we loved being able to stay high, but we knew that doing so put us in harm's way. Eventually, we learned that Mac had taken a front from the Mexican Mafia. When he was arrested, the Mafia bailed him out to keep him under wraps. Given the way Mac responded, we were suspicious that he may have talked. The incriminating comments he made under the poppies' control only added to the suspense. He'd mumble, "Why did I do this to myself? Why?"

Ounces of heroin were stashed all over the motor home. Over the course of a few weeks, Leaf and I were able to whittle away an ounce that Mac would never miss. We weren't sure he knew where every ounce was hidden anyhow. We counted nearly a half-pound over the time we stayed there. Mac kept us fed and provided smokes, alcohol, pot, meth, heroin, and just about anything else we wanted—just as long as we stayed by his side. On runs, he carried an ounce in his underwear so that if he got caught, he could insert it into his rectum. Mac became extreme and eventually Leaf began to talk about leaving. I felt an obligation to Leaf and had committed to our journey to Seattle. I also began to feel paranoid. We knew that at any moment our world could come crashing down around us. In the eyes of the law, we were complicit in what Mac was doing. Although we weren't selling for him, we were running it with him; that made us legally culpable.

Mac wasn't pleased, but he didn't try to stop us from leaving. Instead, the night before we left, he cooked us roast beef for the most awkward meal I have ever experienced. He insisted that we sit down for a formal dinner. I could tell that, at some time in his past, he could pull off a meal for four. It was as if a part of his past life shined through the depths of addiction. Mac sought some normalcy. His disregard for the current state of his life made me feel extremely uncomfortable. I felt like his past should remain where it was, as a form of reverence. We ate the roast, collected his gifts of meth and heroin, and then rode to the outskirts of Spokane. Parting was brief, and as he drove off in the Winnebago, Leaf and I laughed in hysterics at what we had just experienced.

In our best efforts to avoid attention, we failed miserably. We stayed high on the drugs we carried on the dog and ourselves. Sativa wore a bamboo and hemp collar. Drugs could be stashed in the hollow parts of the bamboo. Although much of the tar and meth could fit, we didn't want to take any chances. The irony was that we stood out like a sore thumb wherever we went. Two guys and a dog, dressed like clowns, and carrying walking sticks. Leaf had red dreadlocks. I wasn't far from dreadlocks myself. No one in the first rest area we reached offered us a ride, so we stayed the night in the shadows shooting heroin and listening to the trucks as they rumbled down the highway.

The last leg of our trip, an uneventful ride from a kind traveler, brought us within walking distance of the University District. Our first stop was a shooting gallery. We needed to sell some of the tar for spending money.

Because many believed that Emilio and I were brothers, the two men who lived above the three-story beehive of addiction pulled me aside. Curiously, the older of the two men had his arm around Emilio's girlfriend. They had recent dealings with Emilio and wanted to know if I had talked with him in the last several weeks. Apparently, he had gone underground since their last transaction. I assured the men that Emilio and I had stopped talking several weeks before. "That fucker owes me some Benjies, too," I told them. "The last time I saw him he was living in Federal Way with a guy named Shark." In their appreciation, I was given a gram of ice from one of their backpacks. They made sure I saw the other contents: a nickel-plated, medium-sized handgun. I thanked them and said I would be in touch with any news of Emilio's whereabouts.

Leaf and I made our way up to Capitol Hill, where Emilio told me he was staying before I left Montana. When we arrived, I sensed things had changed since I had last seen him. The same guy who had been adamantly against my use of needles had fallen into their grips. Emilio's spirits had diminished, which made me feel a great sadness. His prodding had convinced me, in part, to leave the city for a while. He recognized that I had changed, too. Almost instantaneously, the sentimental exchange of glances ended as I placed a pile of crystal in the center of the coffee table. A feeding frenzy ensued.

"Have you seen Shark?" Emilio and I laughed. We'd pulled a fast one on the guys who were looking for Emilio. We enjoyed a temporary victory in the battle on the streets. Neither of us were amateurs any longer. Our appetites ensured that our demise would come at the end of a needle, pistol, or prison sentence. We shared in the hopelessness of a sickness that had been eating us from the inside out for years.

A spiritual realm opens to those who choose wittingly, or unwittingly, to participate. In this realm, demons play and the shadow walkers take on another form. In this place, the tormented pay the price for their transgressions. Many people do not believe in the demonic realm. In my experience, it does exist. I am still conflicted in my understanding of what I saw over many sleepless nights of chemical fasting. It began as a subtle paranoia and the hallucination that came with sleep deprivation, lack of food, and pumping chemicals into the system. As the shadows transformed, they morphed into people who followed me, creating a sense of impending doom that haunted my every waking hour. As time passed, my fear of the shadow diminished and the paranoia took on a different form; it became a demonic presence that gave the world a new hue. I experienced this on meth as well as psychedelics, cocaine, heroin, and even marijuana. This demonic presence ceased to be an occasional, subtle visitor; it now appeared the instant I put any substance into my system and would follow me months after I discontinued use.

I am sure that the medical world can argue this away as some sort of chemical-induced psychosis or undiagnosed schizophrenia. For me, it was neither. It was real. People I've known over the years have shared similar experiences, being attacked by these unclean spirits of the shadow world. If what I saw was a manifestation of my mind working against itself, does that make it less real? Does that make it less real for the children who've been murdered by their mothers? Is it any less real for the police who put their lives at risk every day dealing with its aftermath? Is it any less real for the person who experiences reality through the picture that their mind creates for them? It does not. It makes no difference. A demonic presence in the world of the addict is devastating, whether it's real or imagined. They appear in the same manner, and the outcome is always the same.

I was attacked repeatedly, and the more I asked for the Creator's help, the worse it got. Strangely, the same applied to my desire to end my life. Once I had finally come to terms with the fact that I would be leaving the earth, a kind of torment ensued that drove me to seek relief through chemicals, not death. I found that my only reprieve came through perpetual feeding of the shadow through IV drug use. As a result of my use, these dark entities gained strength; through abstinence they lost their power. The demons did not push me toward the edge; they kept me on it. It was a merciless search for the answer to a question that did not exist. It was a mirage of lies, division, and agony. These demons turned everyone against me, and in the final days of my use, I could feel my back turn to the only place I had ever experienced true relief—the Creator. Hopelessness and a lack of faith appeared to be moving in on me. I heard a clock ticking somewhere in the distance, yet I could not tell where it came from or why it had it been wound rather than allowed to expire.

20

LEAF AND I HAD SPENT THE BETTER PART of two weeks recovering from a multi-month shooting spree, which had brought us to Devina's doorstep. Devina was Leaf's lover and the reason he had decided to travel to Seattle to begin with. I had sores all over my face and arms from a skin condition called impetigo, which always seemed to cause infection at the end of my sprees. Filth was a matter of course when living in the gutters. I had very little concern for how or what I used. It didn't matter if I used my own needles or the group needle at a drug house. When I returned to semi-consciousness, Leaf told me we'd been at Devina's for thirteen days. He planned to remain in Seattle long enough for Sativa to have her puppies, and then he would return to Montana, Devina and puppies in tow. I intended to end my own life when the circumstances provided a way for me to do so.

Withdrawal is the closest thing that I can imagine to torture. My muscles cramp up and the hallucinations keep me from restful sleep. As the chemicals exit my system and my mind tries to reset, my compulsion to use returns making a time of healing one of great mental anguish. Devina took very good care of us, providing the food and fluids that our bodies so desperately needed. Regardless of the quality of care, my depression would not go away. No matter how much wine I drank or marijuana I smoked, the call of the needle prick beckoned.

I said my goodbyes to Leaf and to Devina, giving away necklaces and various other possessions I knew I wouldn't need where I was going. The journey toward my own death was a surreal experience with moments of reflection and melancholy. This reflection worsened the wounds that drove my demise. Memories of love and family union didn't pull me from the darkness; instead, they pushed me closer to it. Hope, now unattainable, became a place of great torment.

In a matter of hours, the rush of speed and heroin returned, coursing through my veins. I understood that I would not be able to end my life quickly using meth. Death from speed was miserable and would drag out for many weeks riddled with psychosis and insanity. Speed-balls offered the greatest opportunity for finding a quick end.

I was at a turning point. I could either face the devastation I had created or run from it by killing myself. I didn't see any other option. I had forced my life to a place of extremes; there was no grey area. My days and nights consisted of bouncing from one shooting gallery to the next, using up all available resources, and making promises that I had no intention of fulfilling. I wasn't taking fronts of huge amounts of drugs; I was nickel-and-diming them in a way that would not raise suspicion. In increments of a couple hundred dollars, I could fuel my use until I had the courage to drop several grams of tar into the spoon at once. I slowly increased the dosage, knowing that at some point I would cross over to the other side. This seemed like the easiest way to go.

For weeks, I became sicker and sicker. The paranoia and demonic presence haunted me, so I began to move around the city, trying to outdistance myself from them. The shadow people had teamed up to get me. Usually, a shot of heroin would calm my nerves, yet nothing seemed to keep my mind from wandering back to the shadows that awaited me if I stopped.

Another junkie's basement became my tomb. I believed that the world conspired against me, so I began to use a knife to peel away the rotting flesh I saw on my fingers and to dig the microphones from beneath my fingernails. I dug at both my hands and feet until I could use neither. The agents of evil were waiting, laughing just outside the basement door, and I could hear the rattling of their chains coming closer.

The sounds drove me from the basement with swollen feet and bloodied hands. Sores covered my face. Death would not find me, only its agents. I sought the one person I still trusted. When I finally made it back to where Emilio was staying, he told me that I couldn't stay with him. "I will not watch you die in front of me." He said that he loved me like a brother, and in that love, he turned his back to me. If I had known this would be the last time I would ever see him I may have embraced him. Instead, I walked away alone into the cover of night.

Emilio had a difficult life ahead of him, one that eventually landed him in a Washington State Penitentiary. The countless miseries he endured as a result of his own depression and drug use eventually caught up with him after he was released. Instead of facing the very difficult prospect of therapy and treatment, he chose to shoot himself in the head, leaving a wife, two small children, and many others who loved him, to pick up the pieces. Mons took Emilio's death especially hard. She was very close to him and had a heart meant for spreading joy, not the endurance of such pain.

The streets bring suffering people together. Our friendship meshed in the unspoken understanding that we had endured many of the same life experiences. Who can judge what another has endured up to the point of taking their own life? Who knows the soul's torment that brings a person to their knees with a barrel in their mouth? To give one's life to the uncertainty of death is a form of surrender. Emilio endured great pain and suffered agonies that most will never experience.

How can Emilio be blamed for his choice to surrender? Yes, it is a tragedy that his children and loved ones are left behind. Could it be that through his departure, he saved them from years of torment at the hands of his depression and addiction? In the act of taking his life, was he not showing more compassion for those he loved than he might have through countless apologies? I don't pretend to have the answers. It is not my riddle to solve. I defer to the Creator and thank him or her for making me a part of Emilio's life. I choose to remember the smiling Emilio, the jokester who brought levity and kindness into my life. In memory, I can select what I like and place that image in the forefront. Doing so does not take away the other aspects of his existence; it simply highlights the parts that honor his spirit the most. He will forever live as a hero of endurance. He was a loving brother, a kind friend, and a father who made sacrifices. He was also an addict who died from an untreated disease of mind, body and spirit.

Weeks later, I found myself at the steps of the ferry terminal, moneyless, paranoid, and seeking anything that could bring me back to some semblance of sanity. I had experienced death while living. I hadn't been able to end my physical life, but my hope and faith had diminished such that I had to make a decision. My contract had not expired, no matter how hard I pursued the end. I was required to continue suffering, the end to some cruel joke from the other side. I had loaded the spoon with copious amounts of heroin, enough to kill most full-grown men, yet I was still here. I had taunted those who had used weapons for less and they only laughed as though, in my pitiful state, their violence would be even more pitiful than the fool before them.

Unknown to me at that moment, I had made an agreement on the spiritual plane prior to birth that disallowed my early exit from the physical. I had chosen this very difficult path as my part in the evolution of humankind. In my suffering came enlightenment, if not for me then for others. Whether I understood at the time or not, I remained in my darkest hour, fulfilling a greater good. In my pitiful condition, I was as much a spiritual entity as the greatest yogi; my desire to make it back to my island home punctuated this fact. By returning home, I was dragging myself out of the darkness and back into the light. I would be forced to face my obligations, and in doing so, I would learn from them.

Barrette was an angel from the other side. She was a lifelong family friend from the Island and just so happened to be heading home. She and her boyfriend happened upon me on the steps leading to the second floor of the ferry terminal. As I fumbled for the change in my pockets, she gently touched my hand. "We have a ticket if you're trying to get back across." The deep shame returned as I saw the sadness that my presence brought to the eyes of island people who ran into me in Seattle. As she spoke, I saw the demons circling behind, unable to get at me. Barrette's kindness shone like a beam of light through the darkness. Her familiarity made me feel like a child being reassured that nothing could be in the closet. She paid the ferryman and thus I reentered the land of the living. I don't remember our conversation as we crossed. I do remember that she offered me a place to stay for the night, and when I refused, she gave me a kiss on the cheek. Then Barrette and her boyfriend disappeared into the crowd of passengers getting off the boat.

As I walked up the main street, I would not turn around. I feared that I would see the demons following me. Sitting on a bench outside the local grocery store, I could see a night stockman working. When he came out to smoke, I realized that it was Alfred, a man I had spent time with in recovery meetings. His eyes reflected the same sadness that Barrette's eyes had. He asked, "Will you stay here for a couple of hours until I get off work?" He offered me a pack of smokes plus a shower and a meal after he finished up at work. For four hours, I listened to people drill under the local bank then saw them walk across the store rooftops. When I explained this to Alfred, he only sighed and assured me that it had been just a figment of my imagination. He spoke in a language that seemed foreign and out of reach. Recovery seemed unattainable. I was not as unique as I had believed. In thinking myself to be different from the others, I had further distanced myself from the help that I so desperately needed.

Calling my mother was the most difficult. Paranoia told me that she and Mick were involved in a plot against me. I believed that all the shadow people worked in unison with those who had been closest to me. As I entered the van, I forced off tears with a practiced toughness. At the house, I retired to the bathtub to soak my achy bones, deep sores, and malnourished body. I am not sure how long I slept, but when I woke, I lay in cold water. In a bedroom on the second floor, I went through withdrawals, placing a knife beneath the mattress so I could slash at anyone who came through the door. If my mother had entered the room in the hours that followed, I might have cut her into many pieces.

Thank the Creator I was left alone for the first several days of my withdrawals, allowing the demons to diminish. After the worst had passed, I made my way downstairs. My parents informed me that my stay would be brief as they were unwilling to have a fugitive from justice in their home. The prospect of jail is never a decision made lightly. I don't believe I would have returned had I thought I could follow through with death. Instead, I felt convinced that I remained alive as punishment for the things I had done in addiction. My soul's purpose was to suffer at the hands of others as I had brought suffering to the lives of so many.

My parents were not devoid of compassion; they were as concerned as any parent seeing their child at the edge of death. They were very clear that breaking the rules brought consequences. They understood that because I was on the run from the police, the only thing I could do was turn myself in. They had a responsibility to tell the law that I had returned home and made an airline reservation to send me back to face my consequences. They believed that the judicial system would treat me fairly and that being locked up would buy me some clean time, time that would give me another shot at a clean and sober life. I was unable to make the decision myself and had to trust them in their guidance to do the right thing.

Being home affected me in a way that nothing else could. In familiar surroundings, I yearned for the relationships and experiences I had had before my departure. It awakened a part of me that had not existed in many years, giving me a brief hope in the potential to return to who I had once been. I had not degraded so far that I couldn't remember that I was fundamentally a compassionate man. Drugs could not keep me from myself no matter how hard the disease of addiction tried. The potential of a full recovery still existed, and in that revelation, I charted a new course, one that began on my knees. I kneeled not in humiliation, but in the humility of a man seeking guidance from a power greater than anything I could fit in a spoon.

The journey from Montana back to Seattle was meant to be my end. Although I didn't realize it at the time, facing the things that terrified me began the hard work that would bring me out of darkness. Coming home had sparked a desire to make things right so that I could continue the relationships that had made my earthly existence bearable. The most difficult part of the journey was about to begin. It would take every bit of courage I could muster to face the judicial system and those I had victimized in my use.

Mick volunteered to take me to the airport. The ride across the ferry renewed the paranoia that had pushed me back home. Several days of clean time didn't mean I had made a full transition back to the land of the living. Our ride was silent for the most part. His words came just before our parting. "Good luck, Eric," he said quietly. "We will never give up on you." With that, I turned from him.

I arrived at Glacier Park International Airport where a member of Bill and Patty's church picked me up and delivered me directly to the Flathead County Jail. Pricilla had proven to be one of the least judgmental people I had ever met. Her lack of judgment had been born of a life lived with a child with experiences similar to my own. She had the compassion of a woman whose hope had been fractured many times. This allowed her to turn to God in an effort to heal on an emotional and spiritual level. She told me that she saw a reflection of God in us all, and in that reflection, hope remained. This allowed her heart to remain open for those whose hearts had become calloused. I loved Pricilla for not judging me, and as I walked with her into the jail, I held her hand.

The Creator has a way of working lessons into my life, teachings that go beyond logic and understanding. With impeccable timing, the Creator chose that day to impart wisdom with optimal impact on my learning process. Speaking to the officer behind the glass stood Steve and his roommate. They *just happened* to be at the jail at the exact moment that I returned—months after I had robbed them and fled the state. They remained silent, slow to realize that the sunken-faced man before them was their former friend. I could not meet their eyes and lowered myself to the ground against the wall, trying to appear as small as I felt. This chance encounter had a great affect, forcing me to face the damage my behaviors had caused two people who had trusted and believed in me. Walking over, they looked at me with compassion. I listened as they told me how my actions had led them to lose faith in humanity, to the point that they now suspected everyone in their lives of potentially causing harm. I had altered their psyches in a way that no apology could mend.

The guard who brought me in witnessed the spectacle in silence. When I approached him, he looked at Steve and asked, "Are you done with him?" Steve put up his finger, asking for a moment. He helped me to my feet, gave me a hug, and then patted my back. The way in which he handled the confrontation and then showed forgiveness seared me to the bone, branding a lesson into my innermost being. Steve told me that he wasn't going to press charges because it was apparent that I had already paid the price. He didn't wish to complicate my legal problems further.

As I watched them leave, I realized that what Steve had done was not for me. He was freeing himself from the poison of resentment I had inflicted on him. With compassion and forgiveness, he showed great depth of humility. I had witnessed similar behavior from my parents and others who practiced a spiritual way of life. The Creator had just served me a slice of humble pie, the very thing that might help me through the very difficult days ahead. The doors slammed behind me, the sounds reverberating through the steel and concrete warehouse before me.

Jails and prisons are created to make every moment of an inmate's life uncomfortable. The sterile environment is intended to take away the organic qualities of the outside world, leaving those within devoid of such things. I thrived in the outdoors. Cement and steel sucked the spirit from me and in its place, callousness settled. Months spent in captivity inevitably harden a person. The lessons I had learned in recovery could not be applied in jail. A mindset of every man for himself replaced any semblance of nurturing or compassionate behavior.

I was introduced to the felony pod through a barrage of profanities directed at me from the correctional officer who escorted me there. He'd begun making personal threats when we were alone in the elevator and continued until we were standing in front of the Plexiglas doors of the cell-block. He had a reputation for being a hard ass to most of the inmates, and I had apparently just taken his bait. "Fuck you pig." I said in response to his insults. When I entered the cell-block, all correction officers were called to converge on A-block to suppress my assaultive behavior. It had begun a wave of similar insults from the three pods that faced each other. When the guards rallied, I was forced to lock down. The instigating guard turned, smiled, and mouthed, "No, fuck you," then followed the other guards out. I had entered a world of us against them, and what I experienced on the streets had done little to prepare me for the close quarter combat of jails and prisons. In reality, the guards always won. This small incident showed me that I would have to find a way to deal with that reality.

My entrance into the cell-block had raised the attention of the other inmates, and as the guards left, rowdy applause ensued. Little did I know that they were cheering for me. One after another approached my cell door yelling, "Way to go" and "Keep it up." I had not said anything they'd not wanted to say themselves–or hadn't said already. Behind bars, those who stood up for themselves received respect for doing so—many times over.

I sized up each individual as they passed, deciding who to keep a close eye on, who to avoid altogether, and who to befriend. The white inmates outnumbered the others by nearly ten to one. What mattered more than ethnicity was who would stand their ground in an assault despite the risk of more time or potential injury. On the plane ride back to Montana, I decided that I would try to do my own time. I also decided that if I had to defend myself or to prove my worth, I would have no trouble hurting the first person to give me a gut check. In time, I would have plenty of opportunities to prove myself to others. For the time being, I just wanted to get some sleep. I was still detoxifying, so I felt weak and paranoid.

Jim was one of the men who I decided would make a better ally than an enemy. His tattoos showed that he wasn't a stranger to doing time and he grinned like the Cheshire cat. I liked Jim immediately and understood how dangerous befriending him could be. All new inmates are put through a sort of test when first entering jail. You check paperwork for crimes, find out what you have in common with people on the inside and out, and assess ideologies. If your paperwork shows a sexual offense towards women or children you can expect to have a very rough time.

Jim had done a ten-year bit prior to his latest arrest for gun possession and absconding from parole. He believed that he'd more than likely spend the rest of his life behind bars. He said he felt more comfortable there than on the outside. Jim's family had disowned him years before. He had a daughter but they'd lost contact as a result of his lawlessness. Jim had been clean in prison before his last parole and had worked for one of the prison treatment counselors. We hit it off immediately, as our struggles with recovery were nearly identical. Jim understood that I was green when it came to the inside, and we spent hours discussing prison politics and issues of respect. We sparred at night and it quickly became apparent that I had some work to do if I intended to protect myself against others like him.

The other inmates saw me differently than I saw myself, and as a result, they rarely challenged me. I tended to take a more passive approach, which left most feeling unthreatened. The fact that Jim and I had become close helped, and through him I got to know others who were headed to prison from jail. It was good to know as many people as possible, not necessarily as friends but as sympathizers. I began to work out with others, attempting to strengthen my body. I had several things going for me: I was facing a long sentence, my charges earned me some respect, and I was not a "fish" in the drug world that led me to jail.

Most both loved and hated news from the outside. Those who didn't receive letters at mail call generally wished they had. Those who did get letters often times wished that they had not. Reminders of the outside world can make life on the inside more difficult. Each letter represents hope. Hope is a dangerous thing in prison, especially for those who must act hopeless to survive.

November 9, 1997
Dear Eric,

First things first. Has anyone told you today that they love you? If not, I do, as do many other people. Never forget that! At 1700 hours EST, I called your mother and she brought me up to date on what's going on. We had a long conversation.

I am exceedingly pleased that you elected to go back to Montana to turn yourself in. I've had a number of phone conversations with a detective named Roger Krauss. I told him that I thought you'd do the next right thing, and you did. Good for you! I am proud of you for taking that step, however, I am disappointed at your actions that caused the authorities to begin hunting you down. So much for that. What has been done is done. Now be a man. You told me yourself that at twenty-one you would be. Stand up and take responsibility for your misadventures.

I firmly believe that when one door closes, another opens. The new door often leads us to the potential for wonderful things, but you have to be willing to do the next right thing as well as the work required. There is no such thing as a free ride in life. It's time for you to get your act together. Get out there and earn a life that is worthwhile, productive, satisfying, and always be of service to those less fortunate than you.

I recall a Thursday night recovery meeting at a church at Ninth Avenue and Twelfth Street when I first met you. You had a darn baseball cap on in a church hall. You weren't more than fifteen years old. You looked a bit confused and unsettled. I asked you a few questions and learned that you'd just recently arrived from the West Coast, and that you were living with your grandmother because of some trouble you'd gotten yourself into. I recall asking if you had a local sponsor. You told me no, so I said something to the effect of, "No sweat! You do now—me!" Little did I know what a task that would be. Little did I realize the great affection I would come to have for you.

There were indeed times when I believed you needed your backside reddened by my hand. Now I regret never having done so. There's still time.

I also recall with great fondness our midnight beach meetings on Siesta Beach. Eric, you are not a dumbbell. You have brains, natural talent, and a most pleasing personality. Damn it! Put all of those things together and make something of your life. Education, education, education!!! Of course, I expect you to be free of drugs and alcohol for starters. You're a bit of a con artist. Actually, you're a LOT of a con artist. That's going to have to change and you're the only one who can bring about such change. Not because you have to, but because you want to. Ask the guy upstairs for some help. Try it on your knees.

Should you have to do jail time for your misadventures, try and turn that time into something positive. There may be educational opportunities or you may even get help to address your learning disability.

Look for open doors. There's still a chance you may get probation with restrictions, though I am certain you'll have to make full restitution for the checks you floated. Your mom advised me that the people you burglarized may not press charges. Still, you must pay them back, not because you have to but because you really deep down in your heart want to make things right. Those acts are up to you. Always try to do the next right thing.

Life has not been a bowl of cherries in the last year or so. A year ago, the doctor took the remaining half of my left lung out. Agent Orange plus years of smoking have finally done me in. The VA has classified me as one hundred percent disabled. I am no longer allowed to work. Not working has been very difficult for me. I have no stamina whatsoever. I try to do chores outside but find that after ten minutes of work, I have to sit and rest for thirty. I play bridge with other recovery members and at the age of sixty-five, I am the youngest member. I enjoy the game and the people I play with very much!

I want to make a point. At my age, with a BS degree and masters, I still want to better educate myself by going back to college. I might also add that I, too, suffer from a learning disability called dyslexia. My son also suffers from dyslexia, and he has a BS and an MS in computer science plus an MBA. The point I am making is that you can get beyond your learning disability and you can succeed at higher levels of education, but only if you want to.

Eric, I am willing and want to learn. Although the VA doesn't want me to work in a stressful environment, with a degree in accounting I could at least find a part time job to keep myself productive. I don't really need an income. What I do need is a purpose in life, much like you. I also need a young man like you who I can help in one way or another. I guess it's the commanding officer part of me, wanting to take care of my troops.

Please write me and let me know what's going on in your life. Where is your head? What are your feelings about yourself and life in general? What are your aspirations and your dreams in life? (Unlimited, from my perspective.) Some may think that I put too much faith in what you can do, and more importantly, in what you are willing to do to reclaim your life. I can't answer these questions for you. You must struggle with them on your own. I still firmly believe that you have a great future ahead; however, you alone must make that decision. You must make a commitment to yourself and to others to take action then to see it through. There's not much more I can do for you other than share my thoughts, which are based largely on my own life experiences.

Eric, I love you as much as I love my own son. Hardly a day passes without you in my thoughts. I wonder where you are, what you are up to, what new adventures you may have been involved in, your educational progress, and a host of other things. So write and bring me up to speed.

Don't forget to thank God every morning and every evening. He is in your corner if you let him into your life.

Time to close,
Laire

At the end of his note, Laire attached a sticky note on which he'd written a reflection from a daily devotional. He said that it reflected the great love he had for me and that I should picture him reading the words to me.

"I will always stand by you, my beloved child.

You are my beloved child. Know that I will never forsake you. I will stand beside you even when people have forsaken you. I will stand by you even when others have turned their backs on you. I love you unconditionally. I know what you have been through and that you did the best you knew how at the time.

I know your deepest thoughts and desires, and love you. Sometimes you are too distracted to listen, to know that I am there with you, but I will never leave you or give up on you.

You are my child-creation of life and love. There is no one else like you. I will know this is the truth about you even when you refuse to know it yourself. I love you with a love that knows no boundaries. I will always stand by you."

Pillows muffle emotion well, and when Jim entered, he could tell by the letter in my hand that I needed privacy. He silently closed the cell door, giving me what little privacy jail provided. I had always loved Laire for the tenderness and firmness of his words. I never once felt abandoned by him. He always made me feel as though I was one of the most important people in his life. His letters provided me with a sense of stability, consistency, and accountability—things that I desperately needed. He and my grandmother had shared the burden of helping to raise an unstable, fearful, addicted teenager, and they did so with great tact and dignity.

Laire's words were a reflection of what I feared most about myself, yet he assured me that even though I felt alone and forsaken, he loved me unconditionally. He expressed an understanding of what had taken place in my life, and despite everything, he still loved me as a father. Laire had always tracked me down and he had always shared his love for me. He pushed me to greater heights and nudged me to go further. Were it not for Laire, I never would have completed my GED—a minuscule accomplishment for some. For me, to do so required overcoming a debilitating fear of failure. It meant getting beyond my learning disability and putting in the effort necessary to be successful even when my whole being revolted at having to be still.

Although only weeks had passed since my last use, I felt a renewed, sincere desire for change. My circumstances may have added to my willingness, although I could have chosen to continue the behaviors that had led to doing time. Drugs were accessible regardless of the walls meant to keep them out. Some guards were willing to take advantage of their position of power, and pumped drugs and tobacco into the system. Others turned their heads to what was going on. Drugs were lucrative items for trade; they had the potential to turn beans into steak for those willing to place greed before principles.

A short time after turning myself in, I was served two new felony charges. The first charge was issuing a bad check as part of a common scheme, which was a result of the four hundred dollars in bad checks I had written during my flight from justice. The second felony charge was bail jumping, which I had gotten as a result of not returning to court after I had been granted a court-ordered bail. A possible third charge of burglary had not been issued. Either Steve had not filed charges or the prosecutor was still building his case against me.

Public defenders are overworked and constrained by the politics of the justice system. To be represented fairly, experience taught me that I needed to have the money to hire an attorney who would live up to the standards that our country envisioned. The fact that my attorney did not know my name or return my phone calls was an issue that went unaddressed; given my lack of familiarity with the system, I simply accepted this as a matter of course. Justice may exist for some, but like anything else, the courts abide by a "pay to play" system: those with money fare far better than those who do not. This is not an attempt to justify or excuse the choices I made and the crimes I committed; it is merely a discussion based on my observations about a system that caters to some and aggressively pursues others. A great disproportion exists with respect to the level of "justice" one receives over another. This discrepancy is often based on social status and financial access.

I pleaded guilty to all of my charges. I did not seek a prolonged trial, which would have taken even more taxpayer money in an attempt to gain leverage. When Detective Krauss questioned me about the burglary and the checks, I admitted to everything and omitted nothing, save where the drugs came from. I took full responsibility for my actions and in so doing had sealed my fate. The system does not honor honesty as such. I had slighted the system by not pointing my finger at others and absconding; consequently, I paid a considerable price.

I will never forget the prosecutor leaning over to tell me, "If you choose to fight any of the charges, I will prosecute the burglary as well and you will spend many more years in prison." Despite my anger, I took responsibility for my actions. Not because he threatened me, but because it was the right thing to do. I felt ashamed of the things I had done, but my conscience had kicked in again, forcing me to stand tall to face what I believed I deserved.

To his supporters, the prosecutor was a hero—tough on crime regardless of the circumstances. The problem with this "across the board, hard on crime" attitude is that the circumstances that lead people to crime are never taken into account. By overlooking the core of the issue, the solution is overlooked as well. An argument based on the deficiency of one's moral compass worked well when trying addicts as a means to feed a system that fills the pockets of the elite, those who profit from the warehousing of alcoholics and addicts. Yet such an argument does little to solve the very real problems that lead people to commit related crimes. A sincere desire to protect the public would lead to the establishment of more safety nets and programs designed to address the mental health issues leading to crime.

When weighing the good and the bad during pre-sentencing investigations, little balance appears to exist. Why are the positive choices that a person has made in his or her life not considered equal in importance to the negative choices? Police officers, members of Congress, and some elite players in society are afforded this balance. Justice should be applied to the full picture, not to the skewed tale of events leading up to an arrest. Humanizing a defendant creates compassion, and once compassion is involved, prosecutors are unable to do their job effectively. They must view all criminals in the same light or the weight of their judgment could force them from their profession.

Most don't believe that crime should go unpunished. Those who support statements like mine simply want to see justice served, while also addressing the many issues that lead people to make certain choices. Of course, some crimes require severe punishment, yet if those criminals were the only ones filling the prisons, the prisons would be at quarter capacity. Instead, prisons are filled with non-violent, mentally ill offenders who stand a better chance of experiencing change in a crack house than they do in a system that expects them to go without the help they need. During the time I spent incarcerated, five new private prisons sprung up in Montana. All, save one, were full within a few years. There were more prisons in the state of Montana than there were correctional inpatient treatment facilities for addiction. The most advanced program Montana had established was a boot camp program that punished felons through physical exertion while giving them "therapy".

I am aware that some of what I say may sound harsh, yet the brutal truth provides the potential for change. At times, people in positions of power don't hear the truths that could help them to move beyond themselves. By moving beyond themselves, they may be able to help those to whom they've been entrusted to serve, not to abuse. In my life, it didn't matter who advised me. I stood before the judge and plead guilty to every offense. My defender was a perfect fit. We spoke on the phone once then met fifteen minutes before the hearings to achieve such ends. I watched as people with fat pockets were defended vigorously, while the indigent slammed the cellblock phones in frustration, unable to meet with their defenders. The secretary parroted the same message with every phone call.

"I am sorry, Mr. Adreon, your attorney is in an important meeting. He will get back to you when he can."

"I understand that, but I have called five times and he will not respond to my calls. My court date is in five days. I have only met with him once, he called me by someone else's name, and he didn't have my file."

The topic of mental illness never came up, even after our discussion about multiple assessments, suicide attempts, and treatment stays. Now, some will cry foul while others will applaud my statements as fact. I have personal experience to support my opinions. I have also paid attorneys at different times in my life that answered every call, met me when they had agreed to do so, and offered sound council as requested. I was fortunate enough to have the resources that most do not. I received a level of care directly proportionate to my checkbook.

Here is the issue. Most people who end up in jail are at the poverty level. Crime and punishment statistics prove as such. Therefore, those who need the most help get the least. Poverty perpetuates crime, which makes a system that punishes lawbreakers a necessity. The existing system claims to promote justice while punishing society's real victims through the provision of subpar defense in trial. This, in fact, reflects an injustice. The cycle becomes a human rights issue, not an issue of lawfulness. In essence you should be prosecuting poverty not the victims of it.

I stood before the judge to receive my sentence.

"It is the judgment, sentence, and order that the defendant be committed to the Department of Corrections for a period of five years on count one: two years suspended with a recommendation for a placement at a pre-release center. On count two: the defendant shall be incarcerated in Montana State Prison for a period of five years to be served consecutively to sentence one and suspended. On count three: the defendant shall be incarcerated in Montana State Prison for a period of ten years, and it shall run consecutively to count one and concurrently to count two, all suspended."

In sum, I was sentenced to nearly twenty years. I received ten years for the checks, five years for the meth, and five years for jumping bail. I was remanded to the state of Montana with a direct commitment to the Montana State Prison Boot Camp, which would save me from the insides of a prison cell. I had been shown as much mercy as I could hope to be shown. The twenty years was a stark reminder of the world into which I had crossed, both in terms of my age and my actions.

As I left the courtroom in shackles, I watched the prosecutor smile with satisfaction at a job well done. I didn't fully understand the sentence I had been handed, so his grin remained a mystery until I gathered all the specifics from the others in my cell-block. I walked out of the courtroom satisfied that I had taken full responsibility for my actions, and if the twenty years had been one hundred, I would have faced every year in the same manner. It was a sentence that would allow me to make up for the crimes that had brought me shame—and then some. It's impossible to quantify the amends that I felt spiritually obligated to make. Though Montana placed a number and a price on my obligation, my conscience would not tell me the exact time it would take to balance out my debt to society. I had chosen my present course and was unwilling to deviate from it. If I stumbled, I would pick myself up and continue on until I became the type of person that my mother, Mick, Laire, my father, and the many other people in my life said I was. Although I didn't believe it myself, I felt obligated to live up to their hopes despite the odds.

As the steel doors slammed again, I felt content in the fact that I had faced a fear. I also understood that I had received a harsh sentence, yet it was smaller than what I deserved for my many years of lawlessness. In fact, I had come out ahead given the tally of poor choices I had made and my near misses. Payment of a debt I owed to myself and to the world around me had just begun. I would humbly face whatever came my way, earning my freedom through opposites. Acting against the norms of prison life in order to survive it.

21

TREASURE STATE CORRECTIONAL TRAINING Center proved to be everything that the inmates from the county jail said it would be. No amount of physical or mental preparation could have made my transition to this military-style boot camp easier. Programs of this type are designed to make the inmate pay a physical and an emotional price for crimes committed. They combined extreme physical exertion with intense cognitive and behavioral therapy; classes in anger management, parenting, and chemical dependency; studies based on the book *The Seven Habits of Highly Effective People*; as well as classes on victim impact and victimology. Though the program was archaic in some respects, it was the only alternative to prison that Montana had to offer those charged with drug or alcohol related crimes. A logging camp in the Swan Valley had been morphed into a full-fledged, multi-million-dollar, boot camp facility on the prison grounds.

The drill instructors warned that we faced some of the most brutal basic training they had seen or experienced. The stress of my sentences plus the horrors of prison combined to create a sinister element. The drill instructors and the counseling staff knew exactly how to use their leverage to bring about the desired behavioral changes. The program often drove men who were facing ten and twenty-year sentences back to prison because they could not complete the grueling ninety to one hundred and twenty day program.

My first day was a blur of screaming, sweating, crying, mixed with the smell of shitty pants and vomit. Vomit-coated garbage cans lined the barracks for the new "trainees." Changes of clothing were strewn about for those trainees who couldn't control their bowel movements under the constant stress. Groups of college students and state workers watched as if our suffering would give them insight into the minds of convicts. Some of them stared in silence while others looked away in apparent disapproval of what they witnessed. It was important that the system sell a particular brand of change to the powers that be. The administrators there held to the belief that the more severe the punishment, the greater the change, yet the recidivism rates across the country showed this view to be flawed. The fact that we have the largest prison population per capita in the world is a testament to the need for change. In many ways programs of compliance created well mannered convicts no closer to lasting change then when they arrived.

The people hired to work at the boot camp held varying views on the most effective way to bring about change in inmates. There were rules and guidelines in place, as well as committed staff that showed a genuine concern for us. There were others who approached things differently. They worked outside of the lines set up to protect us. They arrived full of frustration and bias, and they abused their power for personal gain—or for pleasure.

Though punishment is necessary, it is not the sole motivator of change for most. Speaking for myself, punishment did very little for me in the beginning. Instead of changing me, it formed a deep resentment of the system as a whole. This form of punishment does little to create lasting change, but can be very effective to generate compliance. Because I was already interested in change, I gravitated towards the straightforward, common sense lessons taught in recovery groups, drug treatment classes, and victim impact classes as opposed to the verbal brutality and physical torture I endured elsewhere.

Boot camp was not meant to be a pleasant place. In order for Montana to offer a shorter sentence to men with multiple years left on their sentences, they had to make certain that the trainees paid for it. That payment came in the form of blood, sweat, and tears. Abuse begets abuse; in this case, the abuse was state-sanctioned, permissible given our shared status as convicts. It was easier for society to look past the realities of abuse than to address them. Further, blame couldn't easily be assigned given that attendance to boot camp was one hundred percent volunteer. This meant you could either attend boot camp or go to prison.

I was at peak physical condition and could execute one of a dozen commands within milliseconds of being given the order. When the sheriff or other visitors came to visit the facilities, I was often the one asked to demonstrate various exercises and commands. It must've been quite a spectacle for those who believed that compliance and military behavior were the answer to poor behavior. If that were the case, military men in this country would never be brought up on charges of murder, rape, or other unbecoming behavior. The notion that behavior modification through extreme deprivation, breakdown, and stress form the best tools to bring about real and lasting change has been disproven. This approach may be effective for creating fighters for war, but to create citizens out of drug addicts and convicts, there must be a better way. An approach intended to build self-esteem, lower shame, and improve the skills necessary to survive as responsible citizens makes more sense. Most people enrolled in the boot camp program had little to no education, zero basic living skills, and the emotional development of an adolescent. How to do a proper push-up did little to improve these deficiencies.

When I had finally figured out how to avoid the attention of the Drill Instructors I actually began to like the strict discipline and constant release of endorphins that accompanied the exercise and training. The daily PT runs enabled me to disappear into a twenty-minute haze of endorphins and prison scenery. I found comfort in the mountains to the north and south. The frosty air caught the sun as we exhaled, veiling us in its brilliance. On most mornings, the frost could be seen coating the blades of grass. In the repetition of breathing and pounding of feet, I practiced my daily meditation. In this state of mindfulness, I found that even in the most severe circumstances, I had something to be grateful for, something that would help me make it through the next minute, even when I didn't think I could last another second. Looking back, I realize that beyond all the negatives of the program, I gained a great deal of inner strength I had never known existed. I wasn't the pitiful drug addict hiding from shadows in the city. I was a grown, powerful man; compassionate, caring, willing, and open to the lessons I needed to learn to evolve emotionally and spiritually.

The reflection of the Creator appeared atop the snow-covered mountains, their rocky composition reflective of what I needed to become in order to make it through my circumstances. In the mountains of northwestern Montana, I learned that nature had the potential to teach me lessons—if I paid attention. Some of our world's most respected teachers gained much of their wisdom from their surroundings, and in their wisdom they passed on insights as indisputable as the doctrine of newer religions. For me, nature held truth and in that truth, secrets and answers to questions that I had asked for as long as I could remember. Instead of bowing my head in prayer, I raised my head high to look upon the world in which I lived, to learn from its voiceless teachers.

I felt grateful that this could not be taken from me. Perhaps I could grow in boot camp. Perhaps if I didn't take a stance as the victim, I could take the stance of the survivor. Perhaps I could complete something in my life that would lead me to open a door as Laire had described. When I trained, I thought of Laire and the many sacrifices he'd made. When I wanted desperately to quit, I thought of the many people whose lives I had affected negatively then made every tear and every drop of sweat the price I paid for my actions. It wasn't the program that was changing me. The program had been the catalyst that enabled my desire to improve myself. Rather than allowing the system to beat me, I intended to rise above the system and to become the person I had been before substances took over my life. I could do it now. With the help of the creator and others in recovery, I would never return to jail or prison again.

After one hundred and twenty days, I completed the program. On June 3, 1998, I was released from boot camp having earned the highest level possible. Then on August 8, 1998, I returned to county jail after violating the conditions of house arrest and parole. I had left with all the pride of a healthy, twenty-three-year-old male, and returned to jail ashamed at my rapid failure. My pride was replaced with a shame that told me that I was every bit the failure I had always been. Within a week of my release, I had found marijuana and justified its use by smoking with a beautiful woman.

In spite of evidence to the contrary, I still didn't understand that women and drugs combined could sidetrack my intentions quicker than almost anything else. I returned to a state of compromise, willing to risk everything to fulfill my base needs. As usual, the confidence I lacked with women in recovery was replaced by my confidence in use. I could not blame women. The flaws of my thought processes made use acceptable despite the dire consequences. This epitomized my craving's power. Once desire set in, I was willing to do whatever it took to satisfy it. I was even willing to sacrifice all that I had worked for.

Some scientists say that sex creates a powerful biochemical process in the human body. Intense emotion and sexual relationships stimulate the production of hormones that create feelings of pleasure. Love can also produce endorphins, as humans enter a state of euphoria during orgasm. Dopamine and serotonin are considered two of the best antidepressants known to man. For some who stood on the outside looking in, my gravitation towards activities including relationships that produced such chemicals may have seemed obvious. Emotional detachment allowed me to remain distant from any potential emotional injury caused by the person with whom I fulfilled my base needs. To avoid having my heart broken, I was willing to sacrifice all the positives to avoid any negatives.

I am not alone in experiencing the emotional and sexual dependence I've just described. A good portion of the world uses substances to make socializing and sexual encounters easier. The pornography industry raises people's desires by exploiting the weak and impressionable, and then posts the abuse on the Internet. The sexual content leads people to act against children or others in ways that they may not have done previously. Acting against human beings, by placing a physical need before the simple recognition of them as spiritual and emotional beings, is exploitation. Someone always pays the price once sexual desire is prioritized over the well-being of another. This abuse ends in the same manner as chemical addiction. They are the same, encompassing different symptoms. This exploitation comes from the same spiritual cancer that eats at the souls of those who sacrifice others for their own pleasure; it is complete and total selfishness.

On August 20, 1998, I was transported from Flathead County Jail to Montana State Prison (MSP). The experience of transport is one I wouldn't wish on my worst enemy. Without warning, the guards woke me and ordered me to prepare for transfer. They didn't tell me the destination of my transfer, and though in this instance I knew I was going to MSP, in other instances that information is guarded until the transport vehicle is in motion. Most of the other facilities don't permit bringing personal belongings; at times, I could take nothing but legal papers, a few items for personal hygiene, photos, and letters. Once in the possession of the state, I wouldn't be released until I had paid every last minute of my sentence. For those who chose to disobey, that time could be quite unbearable.

The weight and chill of shackles sapped the life out of me, stealing my dignity, and making me feel helpless. I pumped up my chest and made jokes in a feeble attempt to distract myself from how I really felt. My ability to protect myself had been taken away. I was at the mercy of those around me.

During transports, the guards never stop and they always drive fast. Inside what looks like a steel bucket, small windows let in just enough light to identify the time of day. On board, it's impossible to sleep because the steel echoes and the men, all anxiety and nerves, spend the whole time talking about the prison we are speeding towards. On occasion, insults are thrown with promises of "we'll deal with this later." Once the panic settles, an eerie quiet punctuates heavy thought. Even the most seasoned are not prepared for entry into prison. It's like diving into an icy pond after sitting by a raging fire. I went from being one person to being another, always on the defensive, always vigilant. Protecting oneself against the evil that lurks around every corner is tiring and incessant work. Prison is exactly that. It's a place where humankind throws its rejects in an attempt for self-protection. The worst of the worst live within those walls, and I had become one of them, locked in with the rest and surviving the best way I knew how. Inmates generally wear a game face because any lack of composure draws attention. Attention is not good when others are incessantly looking for chinks in the armor of those around them.

Reception—or "fish row" as the inmates affectionately called it—consisted of the processing unit for all the prisons in Montana. I went through the unit to be searched, oriented, and then classed to the appropriate security level. The initial day is the most traumatic as stone-cold guards perform cavity searches, enter information into the National Crime Information Center database, and then assign a cell. Although many throw insults back and forth as a kind of ritual for those who've been through the process before, I kept my mouth shut, eyes to the floor, and answered questions with "yes, sir" and "no, sir." I was not yet confident enough in my surroundings to join in the exchange. For others, it seemed like some deranged homecoming for the men who'd been there before.

When I was finally released from intake, I retreated in gratitude to the sanctuary of my cell, finding a blanket, a pillow, and a bunk. These necessary ingredients would allow me to cocoon myself away from the reality of my circumstances and to return to the world of sleep—a well-known escape for the depressed convict. I felt relief when the bars of my cell door rattled shut. For the first time in many hours, I was able to relax. Although I had a cellmate, dealing with one person was easier than constantly assessing every angle around me. I never knew where danger might come from. Hyper vigilance is a tiring state.

August 21, 1998
Dear Mom and Mick,

Well, here I am in MSP. I experienced much the same emotion as you experienced when you drove by it on your way to pick me up at boot camp. At first, I felt as though I would vomit with fear because I've never been somewhere as severe as a state prison. As I prayed to God, I became quite calm and content despite my surroundings. I am writing you this initial letter to ease your burden and to let you know I won't be able to write again until I get more envelopes. This may be a problem, though, as I have no money to buy any. I'll check to see how indigent status works, but I believe it will be thirty days before anything happens.

You aren't obligated to send me money and I wouldn't hold it against you if you didn't. When or if I hit population, I'll be able to get a job that covers my basic necessities. I've tried to spot Jim, but I am sure this will be quite the challenge given the number of men here. I have to grow up quickly here, knowing that how I relate to the people around me affects my every-day safety. My first reaction is to sink within myself, like I do when I use. I don't really think this is healthy, nor is it how you make it through this sort of setting. Friends pay off here. Though I recognize the necessity of others, I won't compromise what's right just to be accepted. The consequences I would suffer within myself if I went against my principles would be far worse than any I could suffer at the hands of another.

By now, you're well on your way back to Arizona. I prayed for you as I passed under the viaducts. They were pretty much all I could make out in the transport van through the windows. I thought of your love and knew that I wasn't alone. From what I can gather, I'll spend several months here, seeing general population before I go to Butte pre-release. That is if they accept me. I am almost positive they will. My destiny rests in my hands and I choose not to remain stagnant.

We pass a sweat lodge and a chapel when we're taken to the chow hall. I think I'll explore them both.

Writing to loved ones in prison is difficult. The luxury of honesty doesn't exist. To share with them the reality of what exists within the walls brings them further inside, too. I wished to protect my family through half-truths. I had already brought my parents into the darkest parts of my existence simply by being born to them, and when my head cleared up through abstinence, I decided that I would protect them as much as I could. I wrote both of my parents on a regular basis, sharing things that, within the prison walls, would have been a liability. From the very beginning, I could sense the predators seeking those who showed any sign of weakness. Through years of therapy and treatment I had been taught that emotion was a sign of strength and freedom, but I wasn't about to have that debate with the men who surrounded me.

Jim had tried to prepare me for what I had face if I made it to the reception cell-blocks. His explanation did little justice to what awaited me there. There were four cell-blocks with fourteen cells per block. Each cell-block was open-faced with barred cells that faced each other. Each cell housed two men, a sink/toilet, a small desk, and metal bunks, one over the other. The cell-block was Montana's old death row. I imagined the spirits of those who had been executed slowly walking the hallways, sizing up the men who'd taken over their cells. Sounds echoed constantly and the grating of steel on steel reverberated through my body until I stopped feeling its pulse. Men shouted all day and night, bartering, playing cards, and discussing the politics of the strange new world they already called home. The men who dared—either through courage or sheer stupidity—to get the others to quiet down were met with insults and threats of violence. The constant chatter was a losing battle. I stuffed cotton from Q-tips in my ears and pulled my blanket over my head to avoid it.

Reception used a dog run to bring us between the high side and the low side. A long fence about the length of a football field skirted the low side, the high-side gym, the chapel, and the high-side chow hall. For chow, we made the walk three times a day, at 4:00 am, 10:00 am, and 3:00 pm. Men jeered at us—"fresh meat," "fish," "new guys"—from either side of the prison. I was most interested in filling my belly and checking out the sweat lodge. I tried to walk as slowly as possible because it seemed like those who did were a little less temperamental. Doing so also got me more natural light and fresh air.

September 8, 1998
Dear Mom and Mick,

I hope the trip to your new house was wonderful! I prayed for your safe journey. I often find myself praying for everyone I love now. Life can be so unpredictable and it's all I have to give. I've looked at the weather for your area, and it looks like a good-air conditioner is a must.

We just started forced labor. It was passed by the Montana legislature. Every returning inmate who comes through reception has to work a minimum of forty hours every week before they reach population. I love it because I get fresh air daily, which wouldn't happen otherwise. I also feel like I am doing something productive. It keeps my mind off my surroundings, too.

I'll be assigned to a security level this week. Here's the deal. Contrary to what I was told, I'll be classed to population for four to six months. To have any chance at pre-release, I have to have at least one hundred and twenty days of clear conduct. This means no smokes, fights, drugs, etc. When I make that happen, I'll be eligible for work release. At that point, they'll come review my file and decide if I am a good candidate for their program. Pray!!!

Here's the bad news. Because I was considered an inmate when I smoked pot in Kalispell, I was given five more custody points. I was also given five points for bail jumping. Anything over ten points gets me classified to the high security side of the prison, where most of the more serious offenders are. On the lighter side, that's where Jim is as a result of his classification. I've not been able to get a line to him. I feel like it's important I get into contact with him.

I was wondering if you'd be willing to send me some shoes. All that I have are these prison boots and they're causing some problems with my previous injuries (my left hip and back). If you're willing to do this, the best shoes would be some non-flashy ones because I would like to keep them. Keeping them really shouldn't be a problem, but I know how life saving humility is in a place like this.

I pinch myself every day to remind myself this is real. I try to soak in as much as I can so that I can add it to my list of deterrents. This place is a trip. I can see how others get so aggravated with the system. Thank God for God, recovery, and acceptance!

I love you both and know that your fears are simply that. I am safe, untouched, and doing as well as possible.

P.S. I love you, Mick, and often think about how committed you've been to my life.

I found that adjusting to prison life required finding a group of people willing to have my back in case of a riot or an assault. In many prisons, groups break off by race, background, or gang affiliation. Most of the inmates at MSP were either white or Native American—"skins," as they called them. The skins largely ran the prison; they quickly came together when something needed to be handled. Their shared hatred for the whites erased most of the tribal conflicts they may have had outside of prison.

The whites didn't have the same reasons to come together as the skins, so they didn't show a unified front. This took away the dominance that sheer numbers could have provided, and limited their ability to influence things. The whites ran in several different clicks and each click had come together for different reason. There were

Aryans, Separatists, religious affiliations, among a long list of others.

I chose an independent stance when I first arrived at the prison. I had decided to remain true to my belief that all human beings were equal and so I would avoid putting energy into the separatist ideals that seemed to rule the yard. I wasn't interested in bringing attention to myself; if I chose a side, I would draw attention. It was actually the opposite. Although fear was a major motivator in the decision to take sides, I wasn't willing to let fear dictate the direction I chose. I sat on the sidelines, intent on choosing a side as the situation dictated. I had already made a few friends and I felt comfortable enough to go to them if I needed assistance with anything. In theory, my approach was fine and it lasted for a time. In all practicality, I would have to compromise to survive.

My friendships went beyond the racial divide. They were formed largely through the honesty of my gut instincts and kindness, which I assumed would break many of the social laws that governed there. Love and compassion had to be more powerful than hate and violence. I was betting my safety on it. I believed that to break the bonds of being institutionalized, I had to separate myself from the politics and attitudes that sent men back to prison repeatedly. The so-called revolving door would not take me!

Jim was my go-to guy. He let me know that if I ever ended up at MSP, he'd tell the others that I was his brother. A similar relationship had worked well for me with Emilio in Seattle and on the road with Leaf. In many ways, Jim and I were already like brothers. We shared similar life experiences and I felt grateful that I didn't have to sink to the level of protection that came from becoming someone's "kid" or "bitch." I would fight before I allowed myself to be compromised at that level. If I stayed away from drugs and debt, I would have a pretty good chance. I was able to send a series of messages with swampers (prison janitors) to Jim. It was difficult to breach the high-security side, but not impossible. Within a week, I was told not to worry. Jim had sent word to both sides that I was to be both respected and taken care of. That gave me some reassurance, but it didn't protect me from everything. The rest would be determined by how I decided to handle myself within the walls.

Sometimes, parents and loved ones of those in prison don't know what to do for their loved ones within the walls. They wonder if sending money or care packages is the right thing to do, for instance. For many inmates, the inability to provide for themselves financially forces them into the black market of prison life. This is a dangerous avenue and can lead to harmful retaliation. This is especially true if an inmate is unable to pay back a debt as promised. Many inmates use debt to manipulate and control situations around them. Predatory inmates use debt to continue the pattern of abuse that followed them in from the outside. Under the threat of physical and sexual violence, this control enables the predator to make the person indebted to them do whatever they please. Some men do this intentionally to fulfill a demented desire for power. Among the most sadistic are the bottom feeders, who live off of the need for enforcers or simply seek to be a part of the continued abuse of others around them. This is what I feared most.

I was saved from this threat through my choice to remain largely removed from the card tables, the drug circles, and the gambling rings. I did not accept "gifts" from people I didn't know, and I worked and hustled in ways that kept me away from the power on which these men thrived. My mom and Mick understood that by providing just enough to take care of my basic necessities, I wouldn't have to find other ways to support myself in prison. I remained committed to recovery, and their help both blessed and protected me in ways that they will never know.

September 10, 1998
Dear Mom and Mick,

Well, good news or at least better news. I was classified today with only six points, which puts me on the low security side of prison rather than the high side. A ton of weight has been lifted off my shoulders and I am sure yours as well. They want me to take two aftercare programs while I am here.

From what the classification committee tells me, I am eligible for parole right now but I am better off applying for it from a pre-release center with a job and treatment plan established. As of right now, it's quite possible that I'll be released sooner than the one hundred and twenty days. It will depend on the next screening I get when I hit my unit. There was a riot in one of the other regional prisons and they moved thirty inmates back to MSP. From what we've been told, this was the rioters' original goal. As a result, the energy has been high in here today and yesterday.

We can thank God for my placement here because, by all rights, I should be on the high side. For some reason, my pot-smoking points went overlooked and weren't calculated. Call me crazy, but I didn't point out their apparent math mistake.

It's sad, the people who come through here. There's a kid here who's seventeen and looks about fifteen. The predators are already sizing him up. Despite what we think of the fear we all hold within us, it serves as a gauge for the very reality we find ourselves in. I pray that no matter what happens to this boy, his spirit is protected.

Well, it's chow call, so off we go. I think I'll walk close to him to chow.

Sometimes the bureaucracy of prison worked in my favor. For whatever reason, I was classed to the low-security side because they missed two points when tallying my total classification points. Points are assigned based on many different variables: age, crime severity, and perceived security threat. Due to my bail-jumping charge, I was classed as someone who had escaped from actual prison. In my eyes, their point miscalculation seemed like a miracle; others might have simply considered it a human error. Miracles live in faith and not reason. Reason has the ability to turn a miracle into something banal like a mathematical mistake. My faith transformed it into a miracle.

I realize that by living in the world of the spirit, something stayed alive within me that would have otherwise been drowned out by the sterility and brutality of my surroundings. Faith became a tool of survival, and I looked for ways to link anything out of the ordinary to my relationship with the Creator. While others sharpened shanks and formed alliances, I searched for ways to protect my physical and spiritual being through the gifts of a spiritual way of life. This had less to do with any virtue I may have had at the time and a great deal to do with what I had learned throughout my life. I fared best when I constantly sought the things that helped me to develop spiritually.

In prison, many viewed spiritual living as a weakness. Even though I looked within for answers, it was essential that I maintain a hard exterior. I felt like a puffer fish, swelling to different sizes depending on my circumstances. Just because I could manipulate the way in which people viewed me didn't mean that I transformed into a different person. I simply adapted to my surroundings—a shape shifter of sorts. The years I spent wearing different masks had prepared me for this. My goal was to remain true to myself and not to conform to the environment in which I found myself.

All of my hopes rested on my ability to keep a record of clear conduct. If I could follow the rules and avoid conflict, I would have the opportunity to go to a pre-release center within six months. At the pre-release center, I could live outside of prison, working and going to recovery meetings free from the harsher realities of confinement. This possibility became my light at the end of the tunnel. Anything would be better than my present circumstances. Although my goals were limited by circumstance, they were every bit as valid as the goals of an Ivy League student. I was working to improve the circumstances of my life. It didn't matter that I did so from a prison cell and not a dorm room.

22

OLLIE WAS AN EX-ARYAN BROTHERHOOD member who had denounced his old ties in search of a more reasonable view of others. His faded, blue-green prison tattoos were a testament to the years he'd been affiliated with various prison gangs around the United States. From our conversations I learned that he felt grateful to be in a prison where a man could make the decision to be independent despite his previous affiliations. He was unlike any other man I had met on the inside. He'd grown far beyond his prison ink.

Ollie had been in MSP several times before, so he understood the security standard that prevented drugs from entering the facility. He also knew the guards who overlooked the rules—for a price. With caution, he was able to get by the cavity check, which enabled nearly a full can of rolling tobacco and marijuana to move from county jail into our jail cell. The unpleasant sounds and smells of Ollie removing the canister from his rectum will never leave me.

Under my bunk, mounds of drying tobacco waited to be distributed to the rest of the cell-blocks. Ollie knew the quickest way to a con's heart was a free cigarette or a couple hits off a joint. Ollie wanted to form alliances as a kind of truce before any conflict could take place. The tobacco dried then we began to distribute, and I realized that Ollie was giving me my fair share of the credit for taking a risk and hiding it under my bunk. After the evening's last count when the lights dimmed, our cell-blocks filled with blue translucent smoke. The men took part in a kind of selflessness seldom shared with anyone outside of their circles. It became an elite smokers club.

I joined only a few smoking sessions within the walls of the prison. On one such evening, each inhale and exhale brought the all-too-familiar feeling of a marijuana buzz, and with it came the all-too-familiar understanding that I was risking my freedom. I had decided to act against my better judgment to show the others that I wasn't a threat. I believed I could help shape the opinion that others had of me by partaking. In reality, few really cared what I did. They were more concerned with themselves.

On the inside, people use drugs to gain power and status; they are therefore fiercely protected. They can also be a huge source of income. No one controlled the drug trade within the walls. Every man looked out for himself. The market was wide open. Cigarettes had been banned in the prison system just prior to my incarceration, so the prices had inflated dramatically. The cigarettes we distributed could be sold for five dollars per rolled smoke or twenty dollars for a pre-rolled smoke. A pre-rolled cigarette from a pack was referred to as a tailor-made. A tailor-made could be used to roll five or six cigarettes. Bringing tobacco into the prison held the same consequences as bringing in controlled substances. That drove the prices up. A can of rolling tobacco could make a guard a few hundred dollars; for the inmate distributing it, it could bring in over a thousand dollars.

Because smuggling and selling was such a lucrative business for the inmate's families, anyone who threatened the supply line—at any level—received severe punishment. The guards, to protect both the inmates and themselves, passed on information about other inmates who snitched to other, less corrupt guards. On one occasion, as I was walking to yard with my weight lifting partner, a guard approached us with a warning. She said that a man had sent the guard in the cage a note, which claimed that he was selling drugs on the unit. This was a very brave move as it was difficult to know exactly who was involved in the various circles. The guard was especially concerned because she was well-known for passing on key information and doing favors for the main players. "You will handle this or I will handle you!"

After returning to our cell-blocks, the inevitable happened. The man who'd sent the note was assaulted by two younger inmates and was being hauled away on a gurney to the infirmary. Several days later, he died from his injuries. Two young, native kids had used socks filled with cans of tuna to beat his midsection where the signs of trauma couldn't easily be seen. Events like this were often covered up, the reports manipulated. I am not sure what the autopsy showed, but I know what I witnessed. Brutality is swift and severe within the walls. To go against those who have the power is to put one's safety into one's own hands—an incredibly risky and sometimes deadly move.

Anything could be found and bought within hours of asking the right person and offering the right price. While I was incarcerated, I saw meth, heroin, coke, marijuana, mushrooms, acid, painkillers, fifths of whiskey, rigs, pipes, cell phones, knives, rounds of ammunition, and razor blades, just to touch the surface. Some men specialized in the manufacturing of pruno, an in-house alcoholic drink.

Like any alcohol, pruno could produce a happy drunk or it could fill a man with rage. In prison, it tended toward the latter. Just the smell made my skin crawl from its association with extreme violence.

Other men specialized in substances that fit into a spoon. It was not unheard of for ten to twenty men to use the same dull needle, over and over again. Consequently, hepatitis C ran rampant within the walls. The men weren't concerned. For many, death meant being spared years of confinement. In those circles, hope was dead.

September 14, 1998
Dear Mom and Mick,

I will continue to write you until I have the means to send my letters. I sent a letter to my dad with my last stamp. He has deserved an apology for a few years now. I've finally closed a door that has needed to be closed for quite some time.

Today, I watched a man fight himself. Like a time warp, the old look upon the young as though they're looking at themselves twenty years prior. In this case, I wasn't seeing my own reflection. My friend Ollie saw his reflection in the words and actions of the man in the cell directly across from ours.

For the last week, I've watched this strange drama unfold. Chris is a member of the Aryan Brotherhood with short, red hair and a bushy goatee. He has swastikas and other tattoos, signs of his ignorance, hatred, and lack of compassion for others. He obviously missed the class on ethnic diversity. Mind you, I tread lightly as I relate both my views and my opinions. Misplaced words can create misunderstandings, which spark and set flames roaring.

Chris had been spreading his views about white supremacy, Hitler's genius, and how Jesus was an "Okie from Muskogee," or something along those lines. Please excuse my sarcasm, as this guy's rants were getting annoying. As you know, I have a way with words. I tried to remain respectful, recognizing that everyone has a right to their own opinion. In this case, that wasn't easy. I tried to be cautious when I confronted him. I told him that I loved a man and he was in fact Jewish. We know you to be that man Mick. I said it in words far less constrained then in this letter

This tamed his tongue as he went from a roaring lion to a cautious kitten. I was aware of the quiet murmurings of the offended throughout the cell-block. My vocalization of the majority's consensus earned us a few hours of freedom from his opinions, at least on that particular subject. He's one of several thousand prisoners with plenty of opinions.

At some point between my comments and lights out, an altercation broke out between my cellmate and Chris. Disrespect begets disrespect, as both men locked eyes in some sort of battle for dominance. A fight seemed inevitable if only to maintain reputations in the eyes of the others. Torment follows anyone who could be perceived as weak anywhere they go.

I say that Ollie and Chris reflected past and present. Ollie has the same swastika tattoos, though they've faded over time. Although he is forced to wear them, he chooses not to revisit that part of his past. He gets angry any time he's reminded of his former ignorance. Ollie explained to me that through the years he's learned many things, the most important being that he was wrong at many points in his life. He understood that he'd been ignorant and had hurt many people as a result.

It seemed to me that despite the many things he'd learned, Ollie had missed one important lesson: hurting the people who hurt you doesn't stop the cancer of hatred from spreading. Instead, it makes it worse. I recognize God as the balm placed upon wounds, and both Ollie and Chris had obviously been wounded.

After a few minutes, the racial argument resumed, one person feeding the fire of the next. The exchange reached its climax then was followed by an eerie silence. You can't argue with ignorance, although you can curb it with love and respect.

Suddenly, I was yelling, shouting that there's nothing wrong with being proud of who you are. There is something wrong with using that pride to hurt others. Once opinions begin to offend the people around you, it's time to stop. I continued for quite some time. To be honest, I remember very little of what I said. All I know is that at the end, everyone fell silent and that silence lasted until the morning. Obviously, my words were catered to a different sort of crowd, not you both, but they had meaning all the same.

Based on the way that others have treated me today, I suspect they appreciated what I said. People on the block I don't know have even slapped me on the back. One guy told me, "I liked what you had to say last night." I receive this attention humbly, knowing that thanks aren't really for me. People far better than I taught me these lessons. I have many more friends now—Native American, black, white, and even a gay man who appreciated my stance.

I've learned many lessons here. One is that love multiplies and engulfs, and the consequences of which *are profound. Hatred is not nearly as powerful, though it can be twice as damaging. There are always several ways to approach a situation: silence, words, respect, love, or maybe simple avoidance.*

Ollie chose to respond with violence and is now on his way to the maximum-security unit with the knowledge that he hurt another man. He gained very little except for saving face among the others. Ignorance versus ignorance. What is the point of standing against a philosophy when the end result in how you deal with differences is the same? I sit alone in my cell now, feeling a bit sad. Although the others respect me a bit more, the greatest respect I received is the respect I have for myself. I still have faults. As I watched the attack take place, I silently rooted for Ollie.

Now I wait here for a new cellmate and hopefully a new lesson. I traded an orange for an envelope, so I am now able to send this.

Three times a week, we were allowed to leave reception to get fresh air in a fenced-off section on the low side. This was really so that the guards could search our cells, not so we could get some much-needed fresh air and natural light. Our last chance to get outside just happened to fall on the day following the exchange of insults between Ollie and Chris. Assaults are lightning fast, as the participants look to inflict as much damage as they can before the guards decide to break it up. Depending on who's involved, this may take minutes or seconds. The guards prefer not to get involved in fights, especially if they don't like one of the inmates, and certainly not if they are outnumbered by them.

Because I was Ollie's cellmate, I was obligated through friendship and the politics of prison culture to watch his back as he targeted Chris. Everyone knew what was happening and when it finally popped off, I felt the crowd pull away from the four of us. Ollie and I stood in the middle of the clearing with our backs turned to each other. Ollie faced Chris while I scanned the crowd for any source of a threat. Chris's cellmate did the same and he seemed just as unsure as I was. Although I had no interest in being a part of the violence, I got swept up in the politics and the excitement of the moment.

As quickly as it started, the fight ended as a mass of guards pushed through the wall of men looking for the perpetrators of the assault. As they made their way through, I tried to blend into the crowd, aware that standing watch made me as guilty as the men who were fighting. Ollie won if the one who started the violence can be called a winner.

Fights were generally predictable and occurred more frequently under certain circumstances: at the end of long days; after changes in schedules; as a result of an argument; after sways in personality types within the block; as a result of money exchanges; in connection with beefs from the outside; the holiday season; after letters from loved ones; or following the introduction of chemicals to the unit. Although I tried to avoid fights like the plague, their sheer brutality became inevitable. As adamantly as I opposed physical aggression, others believed it was their only solution to deal with daily life situations. Most had not been taught that there were other ways to deal with disappointment, anger, sadness, embarrassment, and being slighted or disrespected. Pride and ego ruled the roost. Anything from a sideways glance to a simple misunderstanding could lead to physical repercussions. Others sought escape through violence as I had sought escape through chemicals. Knowing this frightened me. I was swept into the current.

There was another element to the physical abuse that surrounded me, an element with a more sinister feel. Some of the men enjoyed inflicting pain and suffering on others. Those who did deserved the confinement they earned as a result. The crimes that brought them into prison—beatings, sexual assault, and the dominance of others through humiliation and degradation—followed them in from the outside. I won't describe all the things I saw during my time there; there's no reason to do so. Prison can best be described like this: consider the most despicable person imaginable and then lock yourself into a room with that person for months at a time. Prison contains the most deviant forms of behavior. I can only begin to describe the terrible things that go on inside.

October 5, 1998
Dear Mom and Mick,

I am fighting my demons now. Not drugs or alcohol, but a poor opinion of myself as a man and as a human being. I guess I could write you a letter full of false impressions and lies, but it wouldn't do any of us any good. You'd read right through it, anyway. Plus, I had know that I was lying to you. I can't continue to create situations in my life that make me feel guilty.

I do not and have not believed myself to be the good person that you and others believe me to be. I have only my choices, my decisions, my consequences, and my secrets by which to determine who I am. Even though I've struggled the last few years, trying to salvage a life in which I respect myself and maintain my dignity and honor, I now find little justification to do so. My body shows the consequences of my actions, from scars to tracks to fungus under my fingernails. Even though people say that the outside isn't a good indica-

tor of what's inside a person, I carry internal scars that match my exterior. I hate this! For so long, my outward appearance has been the camouflage behind which I hid the pain that I felt within.

Now I don't want you to think that this is only about my physical problems. It has to do with me, and how I view myself. It stings when I hear people say that they see positives in me. These comments don't make me reevaluate my own, low opinion of myself. They don't make me continue on with the process of healing and rebuilding. I don't want to let you down.

I hate this place. I hate how days blend into months, and how time seems to be in slow motion. I remember the feeling of not being clean that Shea used to talk about in recovery group. It seems to be a pretty common occurrence for me now. I am surrounded by people who remind me too much of who I've become and who I choose so desperately not to be. I take in hope like an exhausted, dehydrated man drinks water at the end of a long journey. He knows exactly what the day holds in its scorching heat and dancing mirages that never become real.

Another inmate just came out of his cell and we talked for about fifteen minutes. I am not very good at small talk. There's just no substance to it. I've spent a good portion of my life relating to others on an emotional and a spiritual level. To me, those topics are the most important, even here. For most, it's difficult to relate on that level, but given time, I generally connect that way. You can't share a piece of your heart and soul and not feel connected. That's how friendships solidify.

The man I just talked to spoke about his kids. They are being raised by other people without him. I asked *him how he deals with being here, away from them and their mother. He was unable or unwilling to open the door to the feelings that might ultimately lead to his freedom and the freedom of those who love him. I never want to be content with this life behind bars. To survive here, I've built a prison around my heart, one that's far more oppressive than the walls and razor wire I can see out the window.*

Those walls, that wire, the guard towers—none of those things can contain my heart, mind, or spirit. I hold the power of my freedom from confinement. I am grateful for this.

Writing is so wonderful for me. It saves me from myself. Words give me my wings. It is my wish to use writing to help others in my life and to help myself. We will see how God wishes to use my words. I feel much better now that I have opened the floodgates to my heart, to those who I know truly love me, to the people who know my battles. You are both loved, as I imagine holding you gently in an embrace. I love you, my parents.

Writing did save me from myself, and although I could not communicate with others within the walls, I could write to loved ones on the outside who were invested in me emotionally. I had connected with a select few on the inside, but I remained unable to make the leap of faith as I had done with my parents, stepparents, and close friends. There was anonymity in distance in the written word that allowed me to explore things about myself while living in prison that I could not express in person or over the phone.

Many times in prison, my surroundings agitated my depression. The things that I needed on a molecular level weren't available. I felt myself slipping further and further into myself, preoccupied with the idea of ending my life. I often slept for extended periods, waking only for food, water, and to use the bathroom. People who knew me best would ask if I was doing ok and I would wave them off as if I was. For the most part, though, no one bothered me. How people spent their time was nobody else's business. There were no safety nets established to assess and take care of the mentally ill. Once a major crisis ensued, the prison would explain how they'd done everything they could to ensure the mental well-being of the inmates and the prison as a whole.

There were stories of men smearing their own fecal matter all over their cell walls and then being left to live in it. The punishment of such behavior made the problem physically and mentally worse for the mentally ill, leaving them in a far worse state than when they arrived. Unfortunately, the people placed in positions to ensure the safety of the inmates often increased the occurrence of such acts due to their lack of action, understanding, or training. I feel like crying every time I hear about another suicide in a jail or prison because I understand the torment leading up to such acts. My tears turn to anger as I remember how jail officials scrambled to rationalize suicides to the community outside the walls. The inmates understood that doing a head count every hour isn't enough to keep a man from ending his own life.

Confinement exacerbates mental illness rather than helping it. Some argue that mental illness is just as excuse used to avoid taking responsibility for one's actions. Those people cite the number of people who use or try to use mental illness to their advantage in court. This argument is flawed. One of the primary safety nets established within our society to catch the mentally ill is our judicial system. Instead of acting accordingly, the courts choose to punish the symptoms of mental illness rather than addressing the problems that bring these people before a judge to begin with. Half of our society screams out to the powers that be to treat those who are afflicted. Doing so will empty our prison systems of those who are mentally incapacitated and addicted while saving money in the long run. The other half screams for harsher punishment, yet they complain about the money spent to do so. Their shortsighted solution fails to acknowledge that by trying to put out a fire with gasoline, the problem just gets bigger and bigger.

The one thing that saved me from following in the footsteps of so many depressive inmates was a spark of hope in the knowledge that my circumstances were temporary. Although my stay felt overwhelming and intolerable, I had loved ones who reminded me that, in due time, it would all be over. If I had been sentenced to life, and if I had not had positive influences speaking out against the thoughts in my head, I would have been the next fatality. The system would have covered up my sickness by cleaning the feces off the wall after the fact, claiming to have done everything that they could while, in fact, doing nothing at all.

October 6th, 1998
Dear Dad,

Thank you for the letter. I received it yesterday while I was playing a game of cribbage for push-ups. When you play for pushups, it's a win-win situation. You get in shape and you don't get into debt with the card sharks.

I've managed to stay as busy as possible working nights swamping the unit. I work from 10 pm to 3 am.

I work these hours to avoid most of the daily politics. I sleep during the day when most of the population here is on the move. This is good because the games tend to bring out those who wouldn't normally get involved. The games here are best left to those who want to pay the price for playing. I choose to avoid them. I also enjoy the evenings because they've become my time for prayer and meditation—sanity-saving rituals. It doesn't matter who you are or where you come from, this place is horrible in every sense of the word.

I don't attend church on a regular basis. I don't want to be religious; I just want to know God better. I also attend Buddhist meditation groups and pretty much any other spiritual activity I can find. I read books on all beliefs so that I can better educate myself and, in the process, better understand myself. I like the Buddhist meditation group the most because they burn incense, a smell that's foreign to the rest of the prison.

I find blessings in the little things here. I am lucky to have the ability to learn more about others and myself. Through the emotional upheaval I've been able to take a better look at myself, and the things I've done to others. My hope is to learn to avoid doing more of the same. I am beginning to see that I am a wonderful person as you have said in previous letters. I, too, believe that you're a wonderful man. You're also a wonderful father. You've remained true to me despite my rebellion.

At the end of September, I was moved into population on the low-security side of the prison. C unit was the medium custody unit. I felt grateful to be moved to a less restricted area. I was now free to go to the library once a day, as well as to the yard two times a day. Although this opened up a whole new set of issues, I needed the change for my own well-being.

The chapel gave me an opportunity to get away and to focus on something bigger than my circumstances. Although many of the men who attended church were rapists and child molesters, I didn't allow that to stop me from going occasionally and learning what I could from the sermons. I sought wisdom from others and something besides the day-to-day banter of other inmates. They were far more concerned about the physical than the spiritual. I recalled my previous spiritual experiences and the understanding that my very survival depended upon a relationship with my Creator.

Many of the treatment facilitates I had attended had diagnosed my medical condition as one that was three-fold. If that was true, then it seemed reasonable that part of the solution could be spiritual. I began to focus on my mental, physical, and spiritual well-being. The physical aspects could be addressed through not using. The mental issues could be addressed through input from a mental health professional, recovery groups, and a counselor. The spiritual side, which seemed to me to be one of the more critical aspects, wasn't restricted to the confines of a chapel. Instead, my spiritual issues could be addressed by what I did in the present. As most church-goers defined their God in name, I generalized the concept so that I would remain unbiased and free from a belief system to which I could not bind myself.

This worked for me, opening up many doors to learn from those with whom I didn't share the same religion. I practiced with Christians and participated in Buddhist meditation groups. I never turned my back on the compassionate teachings of Jesus; I did turn from man's interpretation of the Bible and spent more time exploring the philosophy of Buddhism. I felt freedom in all spiritual avenues offered at the prison, and I put to use an idea that had been passed on many years before when I found myself picking at the flaws of a group or individuals. The suggestion was, "Take what you like and leave the rest." I applied this approach and found it to be wonderful. It enabled me to embrace the idea of a Creator I didn't fully understand. For me, that was far better than pretending.

Along with my spiritual pursuits, I was given a job as the night unit swamper, or janitor, which allowed me to leave my cell in the evening and early morning to clean the open inmate areas, staff offices, and the guard cage. The new job also gave me a secondary income. This allowed me to provide something out of the ordinary for others within my click. Access to the laundry room meant clean clothing daily for those on my block, my friends, and those who were willing to pay me for the services. Hustles don't always come in the form of something illegal. They can also conform to the rules, or they may fall just a hair outside of them. The guards generally didn't get involved in hustles unless they wanted to give someone a hard time or sought something in return for a turned head. Luckily, my hustle had been well established, so I was given free reign to do what I wanted—for the most part.

The second job required a change in my schedule. I would swamp until the early mornings and then enjoy time alone in the day room. This was the best part of the job. For a couple of hours, I had the entire place to myself. I didn't have to worry about survival; I could rest quietly reading, drinking my tea, and writing letters to those on the outside. For the first time in many months, I felt like a human being again—finding a nook in a tree where no trees had grown before. I embraced my surroundings and made the best of what I had. This was a new side of me, one I wasn't aware of at the time: the ability to acceptance circumstances and to make the best of things. I challenged my own beliefs rather than retreating into chemicals.

October 23, 1998
Dear Mom and Mick,

Hello to my two favorite people! I love and miss you very much. It's 4 am and I just finished a meditation focused on the four seasons of the year. I've been reading a book about modern Celtic Shamanism. It's interesting. I decided to follow through with several of their meditations and I've really benefitted from them. When I get done with work in the morning, it's the perfect time to meditate. I finished the last meditation literally buzzing. What I've learned from this book is that, in religion, we're often programmed in a way that doesn't allow us to explore the truths of other religious and spiritual beliefs.

A major part of the meditation involves imagining the act of casting stones into a calm pool of water. It signifies casting worries, fears, and past beliefs away to remain open. It also focuses on cocooning oneself in white light—God. I am so grateful that I was raised with an open mind and that everything doesn't have to be set in stone.

At Bill and Patty's house, I recognized what I read in your eyes. It was fear, the fear of my concrete-like thoughts keeping me from spiritual growth. This is a life and death issue when dealing with addiction. Now, I am hungry to learn as much as I can about anything and everything. I have plenty of time. I may seem gungho right now, but really I am not. I feel centered now that I've come out of my depression.

I am still safe. I continue to follow the rules that govern here in an attempt to get out.

Meditation began to play an intense role in my life. Although I was new to the idea, I could see results immediately. In the quieting of my mind, I found a relief I had seldom found outside of chemicals. In this state of being, nothing mattered besides being present in the moment. By being in the moment, I could ultimately escape my present circumstances, which seemed like a paradox. I could feel my mental state begin to balance out. I could sense my thought process, which was typically in constant motion, begin to slow. This relief, for even a short period, did more for me than anything else. Previously, I had missed something in the ancient use of ritual and meditation. Meditation slowed my mind long enough for me to realize how much I had missed as a result of being in constant movement, both internally and externally.

Along with my spiritual exploration came a desire to learn as much about every belief system I could. I didn't allow any preconceived notions to keep me from at least opening a book to see what information I could find and apply to my life. The more I read, the more I recognized commonalities between all the belief systems. Just because one group purported to have the market on a particular spiritual principle, that didn't mean it was so. Spiritual principles appeared to be universal and common threads that ran through most belief systems, weaving an amazing tapestry for those who were willing to look. Things like hope, faith, love, purity, forgiveness, compassion, and selflessness were taught in so many differing ways. This allows many different people to understand the same concepts at different levels of spiritual growth.

I understood why different religions claimed certain concepts as their own. They wanted to share the many gifts of their experience with those they loved so that they, too, would experience what they'd found. As

I stepped back and considered the problems of the ages, I could see that when humankind tried to bend spiritual truths to meet their own selfish ends, power was lost and only a shell of what had once existed remained. There is no point in trying to manipulate that which was perfect from the beginning. Divinity is best left for the divine, not those who would use it to benefit themselves. I could see residuals of this in most religions, especially when individual experience replaced group experience and was led by those who claimed to speak for the Creator.

23

November 9, 1998
Dear Mom and Mick,

Thank you so much for the birthday wishes as well as the pictures of your latest adventures. What a beautiful place you have to call home! My birthday was just another day. I thanked God for my life and the lessons that I've learned thus far in my journey. God and I spent this birthday, like numerous others, together in reflection and prayer. I believe this has been the most important part of my day today.

Despite what I say, it is always difficult to spend birthdays and holidays away from family. Having God to celebrate them with eases the burden, though I will never quite get used to it. You deserve credit, too. You put forth all the effort by bringing me into this world. Life is very precious and is easily taken for granted. I pray for the knowledge to live far from places like these.

I ordered some pictures. As soon as I get them, I'll send them to you. I am tired and don't feel so hot, so I'll cut this short. I love you both and miss you deeply.

P.S. I am safe, untouched, and living separate from prison drama. It is a choice like all things. Most everything can be avoided. What can't I learn from?

At this point in my life, birthdays held little importance. My last birthday celebration was with my grandmother, six years prior in Florida. It was my sixteenth birthday. Now, at twenty-two years old, it seemed natural to receive good wishes for holidays over the phone and without loved ones present. The ordinary began to feel strange. All holidays lacked luster

November 17, 2012
Dear Mom and Mick,

Winter has descended on MSP. It brings the sparkle of freshly fallen snow and silence from the shroud of white falling all around. Winter creeps in like a fine stroke of a paintbrush, along the mountainside, slowly moving downward as if in subtle warning. The wind whistles through the razor wire making it leap to life, the eeriest of wind chimes. Howls and low whispers come through the cracks in the doors and hidden hollows. I watch as flocks of black birds fly in panic, prodded by gusts of cold wind. They travel in slow arcs to the east, then fast sweeps to the west, always in unison as if any deviation would destroy the whole.

I just got off work and thought I would write you a letter over beans, rice, and chamomile tea. I've decided to try becoming a vegetarian. The meat here makes the transition much easier. The chow line offers an alternative to meat, but the alternative looks even worse. The tea I am enjoying costs a day's work, so I cherish every sip. It's a treat I enjoy very much.

Everything else remains the same, including my safety and well-being. I seem to be respected by those who know me. The others size everyone else up. I carry myself in a non-threatening manner, usually with my nose in a book, doing exercise, or playing the guitar. I think some people are a little curious about me because I avoid compromising situations. I am not naive or unseasoned, so they respect my lifestyle as a choice made rather than a course I've always taken. I am also not easily taken advantage of, and around here, that earns one respect.

I am lucky to have so much love and support from friends and family. I believe my choice of a mother could not have been better. You are truly wonderful and have always been a source of strength when I find myself on reserve.

I am a month away from applying for pre-release. Thank God, as I am sick of this place! Well, good night. My latest studies have been on Buddha and Native American religious beliefs. I've also been reading about Jim Morrison. He was a musician, a poet, a philosopher, and a drunk. Who would have thought?

I believe I was an oddity to those around me. I didn't fit any of the typical inmate categories. By separating myself from the everyday goings-on of the prison, I believed I could somehow bypass the worst of what it had to offer. I was selective in terms of choosing who to associate with, sidestepping the clicks that many joined out of fear of being alone. The old-timers spent more time talking to me than they did to many of the other, younger inmates. In my solitude, I practiced a "do your own time" philosophy that had been in place for centuries.

The lifers complained a great deal about how the new generation had no respect for their elders or for systems that had been in place longer than their oldest relatives had been alive. For years, the only people who were sent to prison were those who had committed very serious crimes like murder, rape, robbery, and assault. During that time, prison populations were much smaller and the inmates faced substantial sentences. The reality of a twenty-year stint generally made men find a way to get along with each other, especially since most spent the majority of their lives within those walls.

The relatively new concept of warehousing inmates plus an influx of young short-timers produced a certain level of disrespect. The youngsters had no deference to the hierarchy that had been established. They would finish a five-year sentence and then return to the free world, forgetting, for a time, the place they had just been. Those who would call it home forever were left fighting a battle to keep things as they once had been. The idea that a temporary visitor didn't have to treat another's home like their own didn't sit well with the old cons. As a result, a power struggle left the penitentiary of old a thing of the past. The battles and power plays that ensued took on a new level of brutality as each generation fought for their own ideals.

The disrespect carried in by the new generation created a prison system that further punished those within. The sentence itself was no longer the primary form of punishment. Other inmates—not the judicial system—caused a greater threat. At some point, my ability to "do my own time" disappeared. My books, calming walks around the yard, and meditations were no longer enough to ensure that I could avoid the conflicts in which I played no part. Many who tried to avoid the damaging currents of the youth, found themselves swept up and away by them.

November 27, 1998
Dear Mom and Mick,

Well, no news yet. I just called you and you were out, so I thought I would write a letter to let you know that all is well. I have heard that Mexico is in a civil war of sorts. How safe is it for you there? I've heard some horror stories, but they're generally from the types who create the horror themselves, not those who have to endure it.

Thanksgiving was just another day, except we got more food at chow and football is on all day. In time, the holidays will have more substance for me. I wrote a list of things for which I am grateful, looking at the mountains as I wrote. It's always hard to keep things in perspective here, especially during the holiday season.

I don't feel too inspired, so I'll cut this short. Oh—I read The Catcher in the Rye *and* Of Mice and Men. *Now I am reading* To Kill a Mockingbird, *which I love. I remember starting it in ninth-grade English, but I never finished it for reasons we both know. I guess I've come full circle.*

When I look out onto the hills that surround this place, I can almost see the boundaries expanding. I can feel in my bones the rhythm of the life I am privileged to be a part of. My heart bulges with joy, and in a way, I fear that it may shatter from being frozen for so long. Yearning for something better is not the best of pastimes when you're confined as I am, but this discomfort is also the key to my freedom. At times, I feel as though my emotions are a vessel on the high seas, rising and sinking with each wave.

My birthday and holidays tended to fall one after the other, starting in early November and ending with the New Year's celebration. In prison, these months began a slow emotional regression for those separated from loved ones. It seemed to me that the guys who had just come in from the streets struggled with this most, and those who'd become desensitized by years of separation fared better. The latter found ways to get through the holidays, knowing that the season took on the role of an instigator or an antagonist, rather than that of a celebrator.

Around this time, fights broke out more regularly, causing a feeling of constant irritation to settle over the cellblocks, adding to the miserable existence we all shared. Anyone who touted their return to the real world in the months leading up to the holidays was looked upon with bitterness; such disrespect would not be tolerated. I communicated with my family, trying to find reasons to be grateful, and although I spoke positively, I fell into a mind-set that left me hoping the days would rush by. I tried to disregard all that I had missed as a result of the actions from my past.

The demons of my past had a way of reaching into the present, forcing me to separate myself from any lighter side of life and creating fear of the future. The consequences of my actions felt especially painful years after I had made the initial mistake. The hard work and change seem to lose their significance when the greater consequence remains.

Separation during the holiday season produced a pain and isolation that registered deep in my consciousness. Sadly, pain remained one of my greatest motivators and the holiday season gave me plenty of it. I created my list of things for which I felt gratitude in an effort to show that, beyond my surroundings and even in the bleakest times, I possessed something of spiritual value. Being spiritually minded became my salvation. I still worked to achieve different circumstances even when I hardly had the will to do so.

December 22, 1998
Dear Mom and Mick,

Well, my writing may be a little messy until my hands thaw out. A walk from the unit cage to my housing unit, which is about thirty yards, has left my hands numb to the bone. I don't think I've ever experienced the type of cold we have here. It's incredible. Ice surrounds the windows and forms on the walls and ceiling of our housing unit and cells. It's like some horror flick where the ice inches its way towards you until it consumes you. It's probably not that dramatic, but you get the point. One of the main reasons for this icy invasion is that they came in and sawed out our windows, but they didn't seal them after the windows were replaced. Mother Nature is now our thermostat, and she isn't all that comforting this winter. It may be minus twenty by next Tuesday.

We had a bare Christmas tree in the unit for about a week and a half. The bare limbs were a reminder of where we are. I pestered the guards to let me decorate it when I swamp at night. I thought it'd be nice to bring some life to this sterile environment.

Out of our whole unit, only one other person asked about decorating the tree. He happens to be a guy I had a confrontation with several weeks back. God works in mysterious yet wonderful ways. We were both allowed to decorate it, leaving the past where it belongs. We stayed engaged in the moment, and that was the most important thing. What a wonderful gift to feel lifted out of this place, if only for a moment. I guess you can call that freedom.

I am now looking down into the lobby of the unit staring at a decorated tree that greets people as they go to and fro. Some stop and stare, while others pass by oblivious to the tree's presence. Those who simply pass are most likely trying to avoid unwanted thoughts or emotions that may be provoked by seeing the tree.

Now isn't that a part of the season? Reflection and inventory the outcome a gauge for the days to come. I look upon the tree with mixed emotion. It reflects back to me memories that touch my very soul. Some good, others not so good come to mind in the lights and tinsel. The presents underneath are empty; they're just for show. There is no star, but a piece of tumbleweed has mysteriously made its way to the top to await an absent angel. Hope is something you must create for yourself and, if you are so privileged, for others. It is the mountain meadow, scented with spring's bloom just over the next rise. It is your mother's loving words or a warm embrace on the days that seem just a little harder. It is the compassion of a father when none is due.

You are both Creators of hope in my life. I have been blessed with many in my journey, yet none have touched me as much as you both have. When I decorated that tree, I felt a sense of the home that you helped me reclaim, even though I didn't recognize it at the time. Through your attempt to recreate what was once shattered, wounds that I avoided and allowed to fester have begun to heal.

So now I understand those who sit and stare, and those who simply walk by. I also understand why there were only two who took the time and care to decorate its branches.

Christmas felt like a continuation of Thanksgiving and my birthday. Men simply went through the motions just trying to survive the season. As the deputy warden passed out candy and cookies at the chow line, more men walked by empty-handed than with bags. In many ways, it was an insult to be handed something by a man who symbolized a system that took so much away. It was like a huge "fuck you" from the warden. The real eggs and gristly steak that the chow hall offered eased the spite that followed. That was what we looked forward to: a real, unprocessed meal, not the holiday itself, and certainly not a bag of cookies. Others enjoyed the football and other sports as they promised a win. For some, they also promised a payoff.

For me, the holidays were a time of reflection. Decorating the Christmas tree had been a way for me to practice some of the principles I had learned in the various spiritual and religious books I had been reading. Forgiveness of my father, for whom I had felt resentment for many years, still lingered. I vowed to face the remaining "soul poison" I felt by making myself a promise not to return to a time when I considered my father one of the architects of my failure. I was working to take my foot off of his throat and off of mine as a result.

Several weeks before, I had had a physical altercation with a man on the basketball court. It came to blows, but it ended as quickly as it began. Since the event, I had been vigilant whenever I was around the people with whom he associated, uncertain as to whether the incident would go beyond the game as was often the case. As we both decorated the Christmas tree—two men out of hundreds—we began a discussion that ended our disagreement. In compassion and forgiveness, we were able to come together and do something that symbolized a new beginning for us both. This experience also gave me an opportunity to rewrite my holiday. We shared silence more than conversation, which was fine with me. My mind wandered, remembering the many times I had spent with my family decorating our Christmas trees.

There were far less positive experiences during the holidays than negative ones. One positive experience overpowered more than a hundred negative ones though. Love always triumphs over sorrow, and no matter how hard the bad habits of my past tried to resurface, the memories of my loving family prevailed. I had been preparing for this time in my life. All of the love, spiritual focus, and direction I had been given by those around me throughout the years came together, allowing me to choose light over darkness, joy over sadness, and decorating a Christmas tree with a one-time adversary over escalating the altercation.

January 19, 1999
Dear Mom and Mick,

I do love you. Love truly has the power to embrace the spirit and protect the one who happens to be the soul's carrier. Love enables those who choose life's bumpier paths to remain sensitive to others and to their feelings, taking into account their rights as human beings and children of the Creator.

I've read about newborn babies who exit this world prematurely because they lack love through touch and gesture. I believe, based on my personal experience that even adults can die from a lack of love. Their spirit fades, and with it, their will to carry on.

As one who has experienced the love of others, it is my responsibility to tap that source and to teach others who have lived without love. I must show others how to love themselves and, as a natural consequence, how to love others around them. We should embrace those lacking in affection, knowing and trusting love and the Creator to be our protector.

I am blessed with an understanding of love learned from those I believe to be great teachers. I am capable of feeding a flame that burns within, guiding my conscience. I have experienced that which extinguishes such flames, yet was spared because I found an ember in the darkness. That ember was my potential as a child of God. In this, I have learned to seek out the Creator.

Even in the confines of prison, one can use love to extinguish the aggression that exists around them. I focused a great deal on this while I was at MSP, believing that through love, I would emerge on the other side, protected from the things that scared me most. I am by no means an expert on love, and when I was in MSP, I had to learn about love through others in my life, through readings, teachings, and its opposite—hate.

My sole purpose consisted of showing compassion to those around me. This was something I had not experienced before. Every day I was challenged to find ways to bring light into the darkness. I found that the best way to express love was to show genuine concern about the lives of those around me. Whenever I felt intimidated by a person, I searched for ways to make a connection that allowed us to transcend our conflict.

In so doing, I felt empathy for others in a way I had not previously. The men I approached were those who'd been rejected by the mainstream population or who seemed to be burdened by their lives. Most people like to talk about themselves and appreciate the opportunity to do so. Once I was able to assure these men that their confidence would not be compromised, they became willing to open up. We were then able to enjoy a growing friendship built upon the very things that healed our wounds.

Men naturally tend to live within themselves, portraying an image of strength in order to live up to society's expectations. This is even more apparent in prison. Because emotion is considered a weakness, the other inmates tended to shy away from the type of interaction that I sought. My theory about love was tested on several occasions as I tried to relate to those who didn't want to make a connection. These men had reached a certain point within themselves as a result of which love and compassion became threats. They'd done things in their lives that they believed were unforgivable; for that reason, they rebelled against anyone who tried to show them compassion.

Although I tried, I understood that pushing too hard would provoke an even harsher response than that which I had already received. I didn't want to preach at anyone. I simply wanted to create something that went against the spirit of a place that sought to break men's will. Some of the inmates were beyond reach, and in them I felt the void I had known in the darkest days of my addiction; like a cancer, it consumed the marrow from their bones. I knew that, short of a miracle, they would remain in a place of torment until their dying days. I felt for them in their condition. I prayed that they would get a reprieve from their sorrow as I prayed that I would get a reprieve from my own addiction and depression for one more day.

January 16, 1999
Dear Dad and Cathy,
*   Thank you for your latest letter. It was nice to hear from you. I am watching the snow fall in brilliant white*

against the midnight sky. The prison lights drown out my ability to see stars, leaving a bright halo as far as the eye can see in all directions.

I've been listening to geese squawking as they've become disoriented by the prison lights. They fly all night and then reorient themselves as the sun rises. I watched them fly to the northeast and shared in their freedom. I am always happy to see anyone—or anything, for that matter—free themselves from the grip of this world I am in.

It looks like we're going to get a pretty good storm. The wind has begun to blow the snow parallel to the ground, a good indication that a front is moving in. It looks as though the flakes may never find a home, constantly moving sideways. It's quite a sight to see. The razor wire dances in step with the wind, which makes a whistling sound as it blows through the cracks in the walls. That shrill sound seems to match the bleak nature of my surroundings.

My screening went well. The parole board has recommended pre-release and I should know for sure within three weeks. It was very awkward standing before eight people who would decide my fate based on pieces of paper. It seemed as though they were trying to provoke me through sarcasm and direct attacks on my character. I kept my cool despite myself, avoiding any reactions that might complicate my release. I might've danced a jig if I thought it would improve my changes for an early release from here. Thankfully, that wasn't necessary. I am a terrible dancer!

I pray that I am never again put in a position like I was today. I understand that life isn't always about being comfortable and that humility often comes at a price. Sadly, the prices I pay in here tend to border on *humiliation, and every time I am subjected to a cavity search, shakedown, or urinalysis, I remember that I put myself in this position to begin with. In many ways, I've learned to tune out the negativity, yet deep down, it will always remain, producing deep emotion, strengthening my will to change, or creating lasting torment.*

The parole board had a way of getting under the skin of even the most seasoned men. The hopes of every inmate rested in their hands and in their willingness to offer a second chance. Every question they asked led me to believe that they would act against my wishes. They seemed to see me as the worst sort of human being. I believed that I had earned the right to come before them. The shame of the life I had lived stood beside me like a sulking twin. Everything about the system forced me to look at myself as a monster. Their questions about whether or not I would be a threat to the community if they agreed to release me cut straight to the bone. I had never thought about it in that way. I had never viewed myself as a threat. I left that label for those who raped, murdered, assaulted, and robbed. Had I not fit at least one of those categories in my life? Had I not victimized men and women who had taken me in and trusted me as a friend? Every seemingly offensive question could be asked of me just as they could be asked of those who'd committed crimes considered more heinous than my own.

In their gaze, I imagined every person I had victimized staring at me—and in a way, they were. The men and women on the parole board were representatives for the people of Montana. It was their job to find a balance between protecting people from further abuses and emptying the prisons to make room for new offenders. They made their decisions based on compassion for their community rather than animosity toward the inmates. I misinterpreted this at the time. I was just another face coming through the door. What they knew about me came from the sheets of paper in front of them and not me as a person. This took away the personal affront and replaced it with a bureaucratic efficiency limited to classification, the nature of crimes, and clear conduct. Much is lost as a result of this type of system; the individual is not always fully and clearly represented. That process differed little from the courts that had sent me to prison.

I had no other option but to remain humble and honest. Doing so, I answered their questions to the best of my ability. The outcome could go only one of two ways and their decision had ultimately been made prior to my entrance. Worrying wouldn't change a thing. My best option was to turn the outcome over to the Creator and have faith. Even if doing so didn't produce the results I desired, it calmed me and put me in a place where I was better able to handle whatever decision was made.

March 3, 1999
Dear Dad and Cathy,

Thank you for your latest letter. As you know, I am now at the Butte Pre-Release Center. Butte is a run-down mining town with a small college, a bar, and a church on every corner. In the early 1900s, the underground mining industry there was booming. Copper was their great moneymaker. Around one hundred thousand people lived here at that point. Now it's but a shell of what it was back then.

Many of the inhabitants were Chinese Americans brought here as cheap labor. They experienced severe discrimination. There are supposedly hundreds of tunnels underneath Uptown Butte that used to house opium dens. Hundreds of miles of mines are located directly beneath where I am writing this letter.

Work is hard to find here. I guess it will become easier to find the closer we get to spring. Construction is always a possibility. I am not picky. If they ask me to refill every mineshaft in Butte with a shovel, I will.

I can't even begin to describe the emotions I felt watching the gates close behind me when I was released from prison. It was as though the weight of a thousand worries dispersed into the air and a thousand promises took their place. I promised myself that I would never do the things I had done to send me there in the first place. I was at a crossroads and the realization that I held the key to my future was a bit intimidating. For the first several weeks, as I adjusted to reentering society, I wasn't allowed to leave the pre-release center. No matter how I tried to avoid prison mentality, I could not avoid the changes I had made to conform in order to survive there. I had adapted my mannerisms, language, and social skills to the prison environment, leaving me feeling as exposed as a toddler lost in a crowd. It took me a while to get used to the sounds and smells on the outside even though I had only spent a few months locked up. My adjustment progressed slowly.

After a while, I was allowed to attend recovery meetings and began to form friendships with those who took me under their wing. Life took on a new meaning and the things I had once taken for granted I now treasured more than anything. Although the pre-release staff monitored my every move, I could walk down a street and smile at a stranger. That simple act made me feel like I might have finally reached the other side. Prison and pre-release applied many of the same codes of conduct, though it was easier in pre-release to separate oneself from those who lived by the immoral codes of captivity.

People were friendly enough in Butte even when they found out that I lived at the pre-release center. They were gracious and I felt grateful for the respect they showed me having been recently released from prison. The animosity, that some felt towards the pre-releasers was a result of job competition. Though some didn't realize that every job given to a pre-releaser created at least two jobs through the supporting businesses. A compromise came with allowing several hundred inmates to enter their community. The community had seen its own share of hardships as a once-thriving mining community deteriorated over time. In this they were also able to show great integrity for others who struggled.

Butte and the people who lived there were a perfect fit for me. I could relate to their resilience. With my harsh exterior and softer interior, I found a place among them and within the recovering community. I was one of few inmates who chose to go to meetings. As a result, I enjoyed separation from the others in pre-release several times each week. I could be myself and discuss the things that were difficult for me to discuss around other convicts. Through this honesty, I discovered that I had very little faith in myself. Hope and faith don't always exist together, and although I had hope, I did not have faith that I could get beyond my depression. Depression always seemed to attack when things in my life began to improve. Like a vicious dog, it circled then attacked from an angle for which I wasn't prepared.

March 8, 1999
Dear Mom and Mick,

It's mid-morning and I am taking a break from my job search. I've been given several leads for places that are hiring, so I am going to check those out as soon as possible. I have to take whatever comes my way based on the lack of jobs this time of year.

I am excited to begin school. It's been so long since I've gone. I have very little confidence that I can do what's required despite my desire to do so. Even with doubts, it feels good to finally have some healthy goals in my life.

It's so pleasant to be able to talk with you about things that are not prison related when I call. I am so ready for that type of relationship. I can't even remember the last time we were able to have a conversation that didn't somehow relate to the consequences of my past. Thank you for remaining in my life long enough for this to happen.

A man with whom I spent time in prison gave me a lead on a job. Typically, as soon as someone mentions a job opening in Butte, several people from the center were already there, résumés in hand. In this case, I kept the lead quiet until I had an opportunity to talk with the manager. The man who'd given me the lead was someone I had approached while walking alone on the low-side yard in prison. He seemed like he could use a friend, someone to talk to. As a result, I gained a friend, too. Compassion brings many things. In this case, it brought me a job. I wasn't given the lead as some sort of repayment, par for the course in institutions. It was passed on because we shared a genuine friendship, one that wasn't contingent on what we could get from each other.

The restaurant manager took my application but he didn't read it. His decision would be made on how I presented myself; that gave me a pretty good advantage. Had the manager looked at my application and seen my felony convictions, he might not have given me a chance. The many other applications I had submitted around town hadn't produced a single response.

The one group of people I can relate to with respect to discrimination is the African American community. I understand very clearly that they were discriminated against through no fault of their own. I also mean no disrespect by comparing my experience as a convicted felon to theirs. However, I relate to descriptions of the shame, deprivation, abuse, and dehumanization that they endured at the hands of others. Every time I was turned away when applying for housing, college, jobs, or even trying to date someone's daughter, I felt as though discrimination still lived as strong as it ever had.

Repeatedly, I threw my hands in the air out of frustration. I began to think that a run to Seattle to return to addiction would benefit me more than the constant humiliation of being judged by my past with no chance at a new life. I came to understand why a good portion of those released from prison returned a short time later. Restrictions placed on them by society added to the already difficult circumstances of their lives. Legal discrimination, lack of education, mental disorders, learning disabilities, lack of personal resources, no job skills, and addiction resulted in continuous failure. The system in place for dealing with the challenges convicted felons face after paying their debt to society is extremely poor. It sets them up to fail rather than giving them the opportunities they need to succeed.

I felt like a marked man and it seemed as though every person who looked at me knew that I was damaged goods, a no-good convict unworthy of becoming a part of the community. Every time I had to list my previous crimes on an application, I was reminded of my subhuman status in society. The person accepting the application would look uncomfortable and shift in their seat. The interview always began with an optimistic, upbeat tone, and then ended with an awkward silence and a promise to call. Those calls never came, a reminder of what my choices had done to my credibility with others.

Punishment is meant to end when the sentence expires, yet for many it continues for a lifetime. Constantly being judged makes it very easy for a person to become disheartened by and resentful of anyone who symbolizes their difficulties.

Given my circumstances, I was quite excited to be offered a job as a dishwasher. To many, such a position could be humbling; to me, it marked the beginning of an opportunity to show the world that it could not beat me. Despite the odds I had created for myself, I was capable of achieving great things. It didn't matter that I had friends from high school who were completing masters programs. I held my dishwasher's uniform with as much pride as they carried their diplomas. I was grateful to have been given an opportunity to show my worth. My life had begun again. I would not allow it to slip away as I had so many times before.

May 13, 1999
Dear Mick and Mom,

Here is your first payment for the bike you helped me buy. I want you to know how much I appreciate your help. You have no reason to support me in the way that you have, and I am humbled once again by your kindness. Tonight was my first night serving. I love it! When you talked about jobs that might be good fits for me, this in one of those jobs. I love interacting with the public and the constant motion.

I applied for parole this week and I'll find out next month if they're willing to see me. I'll more than likely be released to ARC, a home supervision program through which I can live in my own apartment as long as I check in at the pre-release center every day. As soon as I see the parole board, I'll have about two weeks to find a place and get ready to transition out. This is my first step towards relative freedom. I am very excited.

Within two months, I was offered a job as either a cook or a waiter. After some discussion, I decided that serving would be a better fit with my personality. I enjoyed the fruits of my labor and the hard work and fast pace of the restaurant business. I also got along well with the other servers and the fact that they were mostly women added to my enjoyment.

I never knew if the people who entered my life would be there for a short time or if they would stay and change my life forever. I had no idea when I met Jenny that she would be a catalyst for some of the most poignant spiritual experiences I would have in my life. Had I known, I might have slowed down enough to hear the voice deep within telling me that she would become very significant on my journey.

Jenny was nineteen and beautiful. When I was with her, I acknowledged the loneliness that comes of the absence of female influence in my life. Our relationship began as flirtation at work and evolved into spending more of our days off getting to know each other. She shared with me that her father worked at the prison from which I had just been released, which gave me second thoughts about taking the relationship to another level. Fortunately, my personality wouldn't allow second thoughts to get in the way of my immediate desire. In time, our relationship became more serious.

Jenny's feisty nature and sense of humor brought out those same attributes in me—traits I thought I had lost. I respected that as a young, teenage mother, she had stepped up to care for her son and was fortunate enough to have the help of a very supportive family. I had no idea what it meant to be a parent, nor did I want to know, but I understood that it took a great deal of courage to do what she had done.

> *June 28, 1999*
> *Dear Mom and Mick,*
>
> *Here is my final payment for the bike. I am very pleased to be able to say that I followed through with a promise I made to you. To have paid you back shows the progress I've made in my life. Thank you for giving me the opportunity to do this. It means a great deal. Although things are going well, I've been fighting depression and the feelings of impending doom. I have no reason to feel the way that I do, I just do. I am telling you so at least someone knows where I am emotionally.*

For the first time in my life, I was able to pay back my mother and stepfather for a bicycle they'd purchased so that I could commute to work and to school. I had never in my life been able to follow through with such a promise because my recovery usually terminated before that was possible. I had reached a point where I could budget for a bike, pay back the loan, and still pay my other bills. I had grown exponentially since my initial incarceration.

My progress enabled me to leave pre-release and to move into a small apartment. Although I lived on my own, I would still be considered an inmate for several more weeks until I completed the ARC program (Alternative Living Component), which helped inmates' transition into homes within the community. My life had never looked better. I had a good job, a girlfriend, I lived on my own, and I participated in meetings where I had found a mentor who was helping to guide me in my recovery. I had even completed my first semester at the local community college earning B's. Despite all of those positives, a depression began to loom in the distance bringing great uncertainty.

July 9, 1999
Dear Mom and Mick,
    Thank you so much for your continued support. I am so grateful for all that you've done for me despite my mistakes. You are a large part of why I am a success today rather than a failure.

24

I N THE DAYS FOLLOWING THE MOVE into my new apartment, I began to smoke pot again with some of my coworkers. Although they knew I was in pre-release for drug use and related crimes, they didn't try to talk me out of smoking. Ultimately, when I decide I want to use, there is no human power capable of keeping me from doing so—not my mother, my father, a girlfriend, or the judicial system. I bypass rational thought and focus solely on my desire to use. This time, my relapse would cause me to lose everything I had gained, bringing back heartbreak to those who had supported me.

From the moment I chose to inhale, it took exactly six days for me to pack up my valuables, abandon the rest of my belongings in the apartment, and head back to Kalispell where my old running partner Leaf and his girlfriend lived. Leaf always gave me a place to stay even when it meant aiding and abetting a fugitive.

On August 2, 1999, I was charged as an escaped convict because I didn't report to the pre-release center by evening count. By 6:30 pm, my name was all over the news, and by 7:30 pm, I was injecting methamphetamines into my arm. The promise of a bright future diminished into the shadows as I had given up on hope and replaced it with the hopelessness of use.

To my friends, I kept up appearances even though my heart and my spirit cried out in protest. My use had once again turned me against myself; I was wanted for the crime of escape. In the eyes of the law, I was no different from a man who had scaled the walls of a penitentiary. At this level of crime, they played for keeps. At one point I just about turned around, but as my addicted mind mulled it over, the chemicals made the decision for me. I had a needle in my arm again and there was no telling where it might lead me.

There really is no reason to go into detail about what happened while I was on the run. This escape was similar to the last. I binged, I sold all of my belongings, and then I began to make runs to Seattle and back, as there was little else I could do to support myself. If I gave my ID or Social Security number to any employer, it would be only a matter of time before I was brought back to face my new charges.

Jenny had proven to be a solid woman with regard to helping me while on the run. She was a bit naive to the reality of the position that she put herself in, and out of my absolute selfishness, I did not tell her. She drove me all over the state. At that point, our relationship had moved beyond the physical and become a genuine love affair.

Within a few weeks, I was back in Butte, hiding out with the intention of turning myself in once the bag was finally empty. The problem was the bag never became empty because I had a woman who knew how to satisfy her man's voracious appetite for her flesh and need for the tip of a syringe, which only push tomorrow into the day after. As always, I reached a point where I was willing to reach out to someone. I called Laire. I had memorized his number and every time I used it, I heard his raspy, east-coast accent and felt loved and supported.

This time, Laire's wife Diane answered and when she heard my voice, she went silent. When she finally regained her composure, she spoke gently and her words left me feeling overwhelmed and full of grief. "Laire passed on several months ago, sweetie. I am so sorry you had to find out this way. I tried to find you to tell you before his funeral, but I couldn't locate you." In disbelief, I gave my condolences and hung up the phone. I couldn't fathom that a man of his makeup could have passed from this world into the next. I was at a loss because I had relied on him so many times before. No longer would I receive his kind words, his gruff rebukes, and his not-so-gentle prodding intended to improve my life.

I thought of the line he always said to me. "If no one has told you today that they love you, know that I do." I lost all composure and descended into the depths of sorrow I had not known since the passing of my grandmother. I regretted that I would never be able to give Laire the gift of my improved life and education. I wouldn't be able to honor him by living up to the potential that he believed I possessed. In his death came a deep despair. I had never told Laire how grateful I was to have him in my life. I didn't get to say goodbye.

When I finally came to, I recalled what he'd written in his previous letters. I decided to call my old mentor, Tom, who'd been all over the state looking for me, hoping to bring me in before it was too late for some leniency. It seemed only natural to take the trust I had had in Laire and to pass that trust to Tom. He'd never let me down and his words were sincere and full of understanding. Tom had lived in the shadow as I had, and he'd come out the other side. As I hung up the phone with Tom, I decided to face my fears and reenter the system.

On October 14, 1999, I reentered the Montana Department of Corrections through the doors of the pre-release center. They were the same doors that I had walked out of as a free man only three months prior. The staff greeted me and more than one asked the same question: "How could you go through eight months of pre-release without so much as a sideways glance from the staff, only to throw it all away within weeks of being released?" To them, my choices seemed insane. They were insane. "I don't know," I replied. The choice to use drugs in light of years of devastation is complete insanity. If I had known how to avoid the mindset that led me to use again, I would be a millionaire. Sadly, there is no cure for addiction. Anyone who says otherwise has been misinformed.

I hadn't intended to get high. In a moment of insanity, I set aside good judgment, ignored consequence, and partook without even a second thought. In that moment, I experienced a relief, one that only comes through dopamine release.

October 23, 1999
Dear Mom and Mick,

Bear with me as I sort through my thoughts and feelings. I am at the end of another emotional tornado. I am confused and angry with myself and with the disease of addiction. I think I am most frustrated by the fact that, once again, I have cashed in my success and hard work for pain and misery. This is the same mistake I've made repeatedly for many years now. It has become a pattern that seems almost impossible to break. Sadly, I must return to prison where I once experienced a measure of freedom through abstinence.

At the moment, I am upset that I turned myself in even though I know I have to face my mistakes. I am not eager to face the days to come. I am scared! I don't know if you and Tom were misinformed or if you intentionally painted a false picture. As of today, I am classed to the high security side of MSP. Because of my prior charge, I'll be sent to either close I, or maximum security, for at least six months. They place people there who are considered to be a threat to the security of the prison. On paper, I fit that description. As a result, I'll be placed among the most violent offenders in the state. I am pretty sure this will be more difficult for you than for me, and I am sorry that I've decided to be honest rather than shield you from the realities of my life, as I've done so many times in the past.

I am so very, very sorry for placing you in this position, for making you a mother with so very little control over the safety of your own child. I must return to God and I ask that you continue to wrap me in angel's wings. I find peace in the understanding that no matter what happens, my spirit will be protected by my Creator. Fire begins with an ember, and if I can manage to come out of here with only that, then I can be rekindled in time.

I hope that they choose to put me in maximum security because it's solitary. I would pursue books, meditation, and prayer in the hope of understanding what brings me back time and time again. I have been warned about how solitude can affect a man's mind. I don't know if solitude is worse than the brutality of this environment. I would much rather fight my own demons than the demons of others.

I've not yet decided if I am going to send this to you. The act of writing brings me some comfort. I love you and I wish there was some way to cushion you from my reality. I understand that my pain is yours *to experience as well. I wish this could be different for us both. I'll write you again in a few days, though I am not sure when this will reach you because I lost your address.*

I will continue to fight for my health and my freedom. I will ask God to continue to protect me as he or she has throughout my journey.

I felt resigned to the fact that I would be sent to the high side of the prison this time. Although I was better prepared, I don't think anyone is ever ready to enter the belly of the beast. As always, my mother, Tom, and I had been lied to. Despite my experience, I believed that I would not see the high side if I surrendered. The laws existed for a reason and those meant to enforce them had a job to do. They often went against their word to keep criminals like myself behind bars. Based on my behavior, prison was exactly where I needed to be. Previous incidents had proven I required extreme intervention in order to stop my drug use.

October 26, 1999
Dear Mom and Mick,

Within the week, I will be going to close two. Shortly afterwards, I'll be going to the hole for a while. I considered going to see a prison psychiatrist about my depression and ADD. Could you send some past assessments for them to look over? Maybe it will help the people here to better understand me. Heck—maybe it will help me to better understand myself.

I began to believe that I had become someone incapable of doing the things necessary for long-term recovery. As I inventoried all I had done while in prison the last time, I couldn't think of one thing I had not done that had been suggested as a means of recovery. I had been relying on a higher power, working with a recovery mentor, going to groups, exercising, helping other addicts, sharing honestly, relating to others, and so on. The only things I hadn't done were give Jenny an accurate account of my addiction and address my issues with depression. Rather than minimize my recovery, my depression, and all of the associated symptoms, I began to get worse. This is often the case with mental health issues left untreated.

The things that work for addicts in recovery who don't have such imbalances didn't begin to scratch the surface for me unless I also addressed chemical imbalance. That is why, despite my efforts, I was still unable to stop my regression back to self-medication with marijuana and speed. The sad reality is that the very things that destroyed my life were the same things that relieved me of my mental and emotional anguish. They worked even better than the spiritual remedies suggested by those who'd experienced long-term recovery.

This is my point. Those with a dual diagnosis must address each issue both independently and together in order to recover. This may seem strange and impossible, but it's not. While addressing my addiction through abstinence and other spiritual means, I created a window of opportunity to also address the issues surrounding my chemical imbalances. While the substance issues can be dealt with through treatment or recovery groups, the psychiatric issues must be addressed by those licensed and educated to do so. By addressing one, the ability to address the other becomes possible. Though there is much debate about which should come first, I can speak only to my personal experience.

Why would I ever choose the painful route of recovery to address the equally painful route of trying to find the solution to my clinical depression issues when neither one is a guaranteed success? I know that within seconds of a blast of meth, I experience relief from both, but I must remain loaded at all times and avoid the consequences associated with withdrawal from chronic use. If I knew how to do so, this argument would be moot. I could not be convinced to address my depression while loaded. Only in desperation and without chemicals could I have the mindset to address both. Recovery groups and proper psychological treatment are the yin and the yang of dual diagnosis. In each lies the strength of the other, creating the balance needed for the unstable to find their center with respect to both issues.

The fact that I felt willing to address this issue meant that I had run out of answers. For me, that was the best possible position to be in. Without answers and while in emotional pain, solutions become easier to digest. An empty cup can be filled with fresh water, while a full cup that sits becomes tepid.

November 3, 1999
Dear Mom and Mick,

It's day seven here in the hole. It's not all steel grates and dripping water, though the solitude still wears on a person. There's no fresh air or sunshine. I do, however, have a window that's six inches high and runs the length of the northern wall. It's been sand blasted so I can't look out, but at least natural light makes its way through during the day.

I didn't get your letter until today. I think it takes longer to get through because I am on the high-security side. In a few more days, I should be back in popula-

tion. It'll be three years before I can be considered for the low side. At least that gives me something to be hopeful for. I've seen several people from before as well as Christopher from the island.

I've already written you several letters, but I decided not to send them. Your letter evoked some pretty intense emotion and I didn't want to react. I accept the fact that I'll be doing a good chunk of time for escape, a choice I've been beating myself up over for the last several months. I need you to understand that I stayed clean for myself, and as a result, I respected those who had the same wish for me. I put forth tremendous effort to build a life for myself again. I was quite proud of what I had accomplished in such a short time.

When I escaped, I was missing some key ingredients to my potential for continued success. Help with depression should have been of paramount importance. Because it was not, here I am again. I am very sorry this hurt you. It hurts me to know that my choices hurt you again. I would like you to understand that nobody is suffering for my choices more than I am. For the first time in many years, I was a responsible part of a community. Because of the changes I had been making, I was loved and respected by those who knew me.

Sadly, my choice to use won out again. As a result, here I sit. Fear drove my use and now here I am, humbled, beaten, dizzy, and suffering from the poorest opinion I have ever had of myself. I am in a place where these emotions are detrimental. My time in the hole has been painful. I fight my inner demons and they are powerful. I realize now that they began to resurface in Butte, and because of my busy schedule,

I avoided dealing with them. I never stopped running. Although chemicals were not the cause for this avoidance, my drive for success was. I wanted so desperately to catch up with the world and so I quit doing the very things that brought me back to it. This system is so unforgiving. The positive things that I've done over the past couple of years don't seem to factor into the scale of justice. One poor choice and the dominos fall.

A man is losing his mind in the cell next to mine. He's been in the hole for forty-seven days as part of a peaceful protest. It's heartbreaking to hear a human being lose their sanity with no means to stop it. If I could reach through the walls and embrace him, I would.

I need help. I need more mental help than this place can offer. I have problems that I've avoided, hidden behind a clean-cut face and well-chosen words. Impulse, paranoia, and depression—they all torture me at different times. The man in the cell next to mine sounds like I feel inside.

I am aware that I am not capable of using like others. For years, I've not wanted to admit as such. Doesn't that show in how I use? When I use, I want to do so unlike other people. That is the problem. When I decide to put a needle in my arm, I've given up on the idea that I can use like the rest of the world. I am unstable when I am clean and even more so when I use.

I would trade anything to travel back three months to say no instead of yes. I wish I would have picked up a phone instead of a bag.

PS. Tom told me I would likely see two to three years before I am released. I have accepted as much. I have learned to never trust a prosecutor. They lie more than any street hustler I've ever met.

I was able to find a mental health group within the prison walls and was prescribed medication for bipolar disorder. Strangely enough, I don't recall receiving any mental assessment. To start the process, I had a conversation with a mental health professional, received a prescription from the infirmary doctor, and then was placed in one of the outpatient mental health classes.

My problem was, and always had been, my ability to cover up my symptoms with a smile and a clean shirt. In the midst of an antisocial, depressed episode, the last thing I want to do is let someone in. I build up those walls in an attempt to isolate myself from the world. Over time, this happy persona fades and what's left is a grizzly human being who has been put through the emotional ringer once more. At that stage, I am unwilling to ask for what I need.

With my depression comes a long list of symptoms: paranoia, self-loathing, antisocial tendencies, erratic behavior, extreme changes in appetite, dramatic shifts in sleep patterns, anxiety, severe mood swings, agitation, and a physical intensity that, on more than one occasion, led me to seek medical attention for high blood pressure. With every one of these symptoms comes a range of secondary symptoms; if I am not fighting one set of issues, then I am fighting the others. This goes on incessantly without help. In the letter to my mother, I wrote in part to convince myself that the approach I described would work for me. I hoped that it would. My greatest reprieve always came through hope, faith, gratitude, and love, yet even those things didn't have the staying power that I so desperately needed. Despite my undying belief that the Creator could cure my condition, I still suffered from it. In that unwanted truth, faith began to recede from my life.

December 6, 1999
Dear Dad and Cathy,

I hope all is well with you. May this season fill you both with joy. As you have probably already figured out, I am back at MSP. I've avoided writing out of shame. The lack of contact with you both has made me set aside my pride in order to correspond.

I go to court on escape charges next month. I should have a good case. A lawyer from Butte has taken my case pro bono because of the successes I had while in pre-release. I am truly grateful! I'll write you more in the days ahead. Know that I love you as only a son can.

Whether my faith remained or not, a higher power continued to work on my behalf. Without asking for help, help came through the relationships I had started in Butte. The people I had met there were both solid and compassionate. Paul, a local doctor, and two other lawyers in a recovery program had come together to defend my character and to contribute what they could to my case. With them, others in the community, including my manager from the restaurant as well as Jenny, stepped forward to help.

I had never in my life been supported by so many. The hard work I had put into rebuilding my life and the friendships I had acquired as a result paid off when I least expected it. This gave me new hope, which was critical as I had slowly begun to devolve back into the person who focused only on survival within the penitentiary. This time, an anger within fought to be released. The only thing that kept it at bay was my hope for a successful outcome in court. The woman who sat in the back of the courtroom every time they brought me in for a hearing had proven herself loyal in flight, but also in captivity. This was a rarity, and I wondered what I had done to deserve such a thing.

December 20, 1999
Dear Mom and Mick,

Well, it's about time I wrote you a letter. We just locked down and my cellmate, Chollo, is giving me a hard time for drinking herbal tea. I am pretty sure he thinks I am strange. I don't participate in smoke sessions and I eat only one meal a day at the MSP café. I don't hustle like the rest of the block and I am comfortable with just the basic necessities. When they release me again, I am really going to focus on bringing this habit out with me. I am positive I will be content just drinking warm tea and bouncing my prayers off the midnight moon.

I've received many letters from supportive and forgiving friends. They give me the strength I need to avoid conforming to my surroundings. I am working for my freedom through opposites. Every day I see what not to do; I try to do the opposite, to learn from the mistakes of others.

Some may believe that I won't make it on the outside. I understand why they feel that way and I don't blame them because they have very little evidence to the contrary. I've thought about using anger towards these people, as a way to motivate myself to succeed, but I've decided to do away with this philosophy. It's not the right motivation. Instead, I will draw upon my successes in Butte and try to build upon those. I know how to accomplish the things necessary to be successful. The key to my success is to ask for help and to remain willing to follow the direction of others who have walked this path before me. With the help and support of those who do believe in me, I can succeed.

I am learning not to fear being myself here. For a while, I also perceived compassion as a weakness. Now

I know that compassion is a strength. I think that it amuses people here and draws attention because its so foreign. I now realize that people here respect those who are themselves more than those who try to fill a role out of fear.

At chow, I sat at my table. We all have our own, as it's quite territorial in here. The races separate and it's dangerous to sit in another's area. Liam asked if I was religious. I told him no, although I love God and try to be the best person that I can be. I acknowledged that my attempts didn't always work out as planned. This gave him a chuckle. He'd been eyeballing my corn dog and looked ready to go for it. I told him, "Like I said, sometimes I fall short of being the good guy," then I took a territorial bite. We all laughed hysterically.

I have a difficult time with Liam because he killed his mother for her social security check. It's very sad and equally confusing to try and understand how a person can make that type of decision. I try to accept him regardless and to show him love and compassion in any way that I can. As a result, I've seen a marked difference in how he treats me as opposed to how he treats others. Mostly I just try to tell the truth. Speaking truthfully doesn't mean I plan to have him over for teatime on the outside. It just means that I show him the respect that all people deserve despite their past.

You may be thinking I should change tables at this point. If I switched tables to sit with someone who has no regret for any of his actions, then I would never get to eat. There aren't a whole lot of people around me who are here for less appalling charges. I am in the minority on the high side with no violent or heinous convictions. I like my table because Liam doesn't usually come to chow and because there's a nice, quiet

Mexican kid who I can talk to about politics, books, and God. He is thin, pale, wears glasses with wire rims, and used to have a long, black goatee. He's interesting to look at. His smile is warm and takes me away from here for a moment. He watches Discovery Channel every night and we quiz each other on the previous night's show. He's here because he smoked pot and took the police on a low-speed chase so he could finish his six-pack of beer. Although I laugh, it's sad that people like him make it to the high security side of a penitentiary for such things.

I hope you have a wonderful holiday. I will be thinking about you and praying for the family. That's what makes my holiday bearable. I love you!

January 25, 2000
Dear Mom and Mick,

Is life a constant battle between good and bad? It seems as though I am constantly trying to tweak my personality to comply with a God I don't fully understand. I seem to be both blessed and burdened by a conscience that cuts me to the bone when I do wrong. Why can't I listen to my conscience before I make a poor choice? Why do I wait until I am suffering the consequences of my mistakes and the resulting shame?

I know that payoff comes with choosing a sober life over a lawless one. Even here, I experience rewards for choosing to do the opposite of what the prison culture tells me to do. There is a power in the spirit of compassion that is far more powerful than the oppressive spirit that haunts me in use. The latter is forever doomed to lurk in the shadow of God's brilliance.

In the distance, I hear a wolf pack howling as if in recognition of my solitude. I think they share my distaste for the surrounding walls. We have a common past, the wolf and I, and it's as if our spirits merge. For thousands of years, wolves have had the freedom to roam these hills, to drink from the streams, and to bask in the warmth of a sunlit day. For years they have existed in harmony with the cycles of life.

Listening closer, I hear a tone of sadness like a yearning for days passed and a bitterness at the encroachment of those who view them as unwanted beasts of the night. The seasons change despite those who wish the world would remain in perpetual spring. I close my eyes and run with the wolves in the darkness. Under a veil of darkness, we avoid the gaze of our enemies and enjoy a freedom that will end with the rising of the sun.

February 4, 2000
Sweet Mother,

I love you dearly. I was touched to the point of tears when you explained your relationship with Eileen. I've added you both to my prayers, asking for God's will as always. I, too, have had men in my life that filled gaps. This woman is a gift in your life.

When I learned of Laire's death, I was shaken. I had wanted to show him success in my lifetime and felt deeply saddened that I wouldn't be able to do so. I felt so blessed to have had him as a loving participant in my life. He used to say, "Has anyone told you today that they love you? Well, I do." I hear his words even now. It's as if they bounce off of the cement and steel in protest of my confinement.

Tell me that God is not the author of all that is good as well as all that is evil. Even that which we label as bad can, with time and faith, turn to good in ways that one might never have imagined. It's important for us to have the Laires, Micks, moms, Cathys, dads, and Eileens in our lives because they are the threads that help us repair the holes we created in our tapestries of life. They help to repair the tears left by heartache and suffering.

I am so lucky to have you as an example in my life. I am inspired by your strength despite all that has happened in your life. I have tried to mirror your faith in my own life, even when I've faced difficulties that seemed impossible to overcome. We are so blessed to have a God who holds us so tenderly and guides us through the quagmire of life, not avoiding it, but navigating through it.

God lets us know that those we've lost in our lives will always remain in our thoughts, spirit, and in the ripples that they send to us from the other side.

February 7, 2000
Dear Father,

Thank you for your letter. I am hanging in there. My attitude fluctuates between good and not so good. I must try to stay on top of this at all times. In this environment, poor attitudes attract the most attention. It's a hard place and I do all that I can to protect what I believe to be most important: the spirit and the heart.

I've been sentenced to two more years to run consecutive with my current sentences. A partner in a well-known law firm, my lawyer, a doctor of medicine, my manager from work, and my sponsor, Tom, all testified to my good nature and value on the outside. The prosecutor, who had made some promises during pre-trial discussions, changed his tune when he saw all of my support. He seemed to go on the same sort of power trip that the prosecutor in Kalispell went on when he realized I had the support of a pastor. To justify their decision to send me back to prison, they had to say that I am a threat to society. It's a little frustrating given the nature of my crimes.

This state has an insane notion of justice. Although I don't argue with punishment, I do argue against the punishment that they think the multitude of cons doing time in penitentiaries for drug-related offenses deserve. They don't understand that such punishment creates an army of criminals who come out in worse shape than when they went in. They make the problem worse as a result of their misguided solution. In the future, they'll be forced to look at their failings as their system bleeds the state dry. They must realize that treatment, therapy, and community-based corrections are their best bet in terms of real, lasting change. As always, compassion will win out over hatred. They will learn from their mistakes as I am learning from my own. For now, I am returning to my cell in close II, waiting for another opportunity.

The good news is that someone on the parole board has decided to parole me from one sentence to another while still in prison, which is unheard of. This very act will potentially save me from having to serve nearly three years before even the possibility of a parole hearing.

Even when my faith is being tested, miracles continue to occur in my life whether I acknowledge them or not. The parole board's decision nullified the sentence given to me for escape. This meant that I would be allowed to see the parole board within a year instead of in three years. As a result, the judge's recommendation to return to boot camp could get me out of the penitentiary and moving on with my life in a matter of months. I had no idea who it was I knew or why I had been given yet another chance. Instead of trying to figure it out, I began the process of acting against the social norms within the walls so that I could find a way to stay away in the future.

March 13, 2000
Dear Mom and Mick,

Wow, TV gets old! I thought I would write you a letter to break up the monotony of the day. I have a new cellmate who was raised on a cattle ranch. He's also a Harley-riding, right-wing fundamentalist, which keeps things very exciting at night. I like him because he forces me to test my own beliefs when we discuss his.

I tricked him the other night. I read him a Maoist movement newsletter intended for people who are incarcerated, attempting to bring them over to the Maoist side. He was really getting into their slant on social issues as I read them aloud. The best part was when I revealed that I had been reading from a newspaper written by the Communist Party. He immediately tried to rescind his statement, claiming they'd come from the "enemy."

I am grateful for him and his religious beliefs because they are showing me just how far apart our beliefs really are. Although I love many of the Bible's teachings, I am unable, without being dishonest, to say that I am a Christian. What a relief this is for me! Although I respect his teachings, I have never been able to digest much of the other dogmatic ideas associated with Christian beliefs.

This had been a very uncomfortable process for me because for years I have associated God with Christ. The realization that I don't have to associate any reli-

gious ideology to God in order to have a relationship with God has been a sort of spiritual liberation. God has never lied to me and for years I've prayed for revelation concerning my belief system. It's not important that I know who or what God is; I must only understand that God exists in some capacity. My future is contingent upon my spiritual growth. An unchanging or concrete belief seems stagnant. This doesn't mean that I am against anyone else's beliefs. It simply means that some belief systems don't work for me. Much rests on my ability to develop as a spiritual being.

I am grateful for religion and religious followers because they have taught me about unbreakable faith. Religion has helped me through some very difficult times in my life.

I've been attending my mental health group and I like it. Groups provide me with a certain level of comfort. I respect group the dynamics and the healing that can take place there even while in prison. I also sense a change within myself as a result of the work I am doing.

May 2, 2000
Dear Mom and Mick,

I am being transferred to a regional prison in the morning. I am scared! My goal is to keep that fear from showing. Confidence is the key. I believe that kindness, when applied in the right circumstances, can melt barriers and create an understanding between those who would otherwise not mix. I am making this letter short as they're gathering our belongings and I want someone to send this letter in the morning. I don't know when I'll speak with you next.

In a state where the constant need to fill up private prisons outweighed the requirement to keep the inmates comfortable, I was told to pack my belongings. Although rumors had been spreading through the cell-blocks, I had assumed that I would not be selected, as had been the case many times before. This was not my lucky day. Each prison follows its own set of policies concerning personal belongings. As such, being transferred meant that every personal item I had collected to make my life a little easier had to be either destroyed or sent home. This made the inmates resentful, especially those who had no resources; each move meant they would have to buy new things.

My greatest concern was not about losing my physical possessions. I was concerned about the rumors I had heard; some referred to the regional prisons as "gladiator schools." Worse, sexual assaults had become a plague there. The regional prisons had no outside yard, so I would be stripped of the beauty of the surrounding mountains, a view that had become my escape. I also feared the aggression of those who had already established a pecking order in the blocks where we would be living.

When my cellmate was sound asleep, I dropped to my knees to pray for protection and guidance. Although my Creator had not yet let me down, I felt fairly certain that my protection would fall into my own hands. I had the creators' protection as well as my own ability to maneuver around tight spots. I was also willing to break my code of nonviolence if needed. I would never allow myself to be victimized again, and if that meant hurting a victimizer, then so be it. I prepared myself to survive and felt the change begin.

25

May 20, 2000
Dear Mom and Mick,

On a daily basis, I battle with reflecting on my childhood memories versus avoiding the past through the numbing isolation of my cell.

As a child, a walk on the beach felt like a magical journey filled with the sound of waves crashing against feet. A new adventure waited around every corner adding to the day's mystery like treasures held closest to the heart.

At times, I seemed to glow in proximity to the Creator. As my hands cupped a tiny flower, I maneuvered it delicately to glimpse the delicate folds, silky to the touch. How could something so small envelop all of the senses? Even my sixth sense seemed heightened by the flower's brilliance.

In a single childhood memory, I could see and feel God's presence. What amazes me now is that, as a child, those experiences occurred daily. This had nothing to do with religious ideology or spiritual principles. Preaching and teachings held little weight in comparison to the pureness of heart. If there is a living God, I suspect that he or she exists in the folds of flowers, in dewdrops upon the forest floor, and under barnacle-covered rocks on the beach.

As I've grown older, my innocence has been replaced by knowledge and experience. As a result, God's presence in my life has diminished. What my senses once gathered has been pushed aside to make room for theory and data collected by my intellect. My decisions led me to this cement fortress of steel and razor wire. Inside, I have begun to see the near-death of that which has fed my spirit for so long, the natural world.

Seasons do not change in this environment. If by chance I were to find a place to plant a purple flower, I am sure that someone would find pleasure in stomping on it. If by some miracle I could hear the birds singing in praise to the rising sun, someone's uncaring voice would surely destroy the birds' splendor.

Do I sound beaten? Do my words reflect bitterness towards my surroundings and the so-called lay of the land? I guess you could say I lack compassion for those who see no need for the touch of the almighty. I ache for the basic freedoms of life. Yes, I appreciate having food, clothing, and shelter. I am aware that some lack even those things. I believe the natural world to be a necessary. The spirit must be fed like the body or it grows weak and bitter. This need can be quenched by the sun on one's face, or the wind through one's hair—if only for a moment.

Although I am a grown man, I still feel uncomfortable in new settings. I am experiencing fear and apprehension now. A group of men on my block have begun raping people as a means of retribution. I am afraid of how I might react if I have to experience this firsthand.

Great Falls Regional Prison proved every rumor true. The constant brutality and abuses that transpired there left me with no alternative but to join with others from my own race in search of peace of mind—if that was even possible. There was no initiation into the ranks, but simply blended experiences and the requirement to prove affiliations with other men known both inside and outside. To do so, they looked at my court paperwork and checked on my past associations.

Although I lifted weights, ate chow, and went to the outside cage for fresh air with my group, I still mixed with other racial groups. To my surprise, Jose, the Hispanic kid from my table at MSP, had also been transferred that morning. I didn't care about racial divides. I did care about protection if and when a riot went down. Entering the regional prison, I entered the world of the penitentiary known to most other states. Being locked in county jail-style facilities led to degradation and animalistic behaviors.

At the weight pile, we discussed politics and any other issue that might affect any member of the group. Although I didn't like many of the members, I showed proper respect. Our strength relied on presenting a unified front. Any internal bickering would only weaken what we had as a group.

The rapes continued, but I didn't find out about them until they'd already taken place. My rage built in anticipation of an attack on the two men leading the brutality. I felt torn between the anger I felt seeing the abuse through the eyes of an abused child and compassion, which I believed to be the answer to all problems. Under these circumstances, I couldn't decide if compassion might come as a result of the inevitable physical confrontation. I felt ready to hunt down the abusers.

Thankfully, the situation resolved itself before more people got hurt. Those who had initiated the assault were sent to Administrative Segregation for intimidating other inmates and extorting money from their families in exchange for protection. Although this did not stop all sexual assaults, it did stop the majority; for me, that was a welcome relief. I was able to stop reliving my own abuses every time I heard of a new assault.

Physical assaults were just par for the course there. In many ways, though, I had become impervious to them— at least on the outside. Within, I cringed every time I saw a conversation explode into blows. There was no way to avoid feeling affected on some level, but I was adapting to my new surroundings. In so doing, I sacrificed some of my nonconformist values to survive. I continued to fight against hatred in my own way. In others ways, I had gone astray.

To stay true to myself, I meditated, prayed, wrote, and took up weaving horsehair. Hitching, a craft brought into the Americas by the Spaniards, is practiced by various southwestern tribes. I used this time-consuming and beautiful craft as a creative means to escape the realities of my existence. In the early morning hours, I disappeared into the hum of the hitching string, meticulously knotting each length of horsehair around the dowel. In so doing, I escaped to the places I had been, to the places I longed for and hoped to explore again. Once my creative force united with my mind, body, and spirit in the rhythm of the hitch, the sky was the limit.

Creativity returned the natural world to me; it brought the outside inside the walls of my cell like my very own silent protest. Creative pursuits transported me back to when I was a child, staring at the tiny folds of a purple flower. I ceased to be a weathered inmate, but instead transformed into an ageless being unhindered by the world that hovered like a hazy halo just beyond my consciousness. This type of meditation lifted my spirit away from the jail cell and allowed me to travel to places previously unknown.

Free from the anchor of the physical realm, I could explore the boundaries between this world and the next. It was like peering through the surface of a mountain lake, watching the movements, color, and patterns of a world that lies just beyond. I watched the realm of the spirit through the filter of my human consciousness. The physical world blinded me to the limitless world just out of reach.

The sexual and emotional relationships that I had once placed before all else became blinders to what existed all around me. It became apparent that the use of anything that bound me to the physical realm limited my spiritual awareness. The prison I had despised for so long became the vessel through which I found my freedom; this went entirely against the beliefs of so many who lived there. I was able to explore the spiritual realm because prison's isolation forced me to set aside my hunger for the very things that distracted me from the truths I now embraced.

The Department of Corrections was just the physical manifestation of the spiritual prison I had inhabited since I placed the desire to get high ahead of abstinence. The many possibilities of my existence had remained dormant until this moment. The reality was life was only the shadow of what truly existed. The doorway to this spiritual realm opened through the innocence of the spirit and as a result of a willingness to work through the lessons I had chosen before my birth. I surrendered to all that I had fought against in my life. I had not forgotten the keys to the kingdom; they were written within me prior to my birth. They had been etched into my very being and remained hidden due to my selfish intention and my desire to remain altered. They were time-released, dispensing only when they were needed most.

I began to understand that not just addicts suffered from the anchors and lies of this world. Through ego and other physical manifestations, every man, woman, and child struggled, each working to reach states of being that allowed the transition I now experienced. Drugs, sex, work, sports, school, food, pride, ego, selfishness— these all held the potential, through imbalance, to bind. I had been so wrapped up in myself that I had missed the subtleties of the spirit. I had missed out on my reasons for being.

September 7, 2000
Dad,

I hope you're well. I am sitting on my bed, enjoying the sun shining through my cell window. I have a window that is six inches wide and four feet tall that gives me direct sunlight between 1:30 pm and 4 pm every day. I take advantage of this time by mediating. This separation from the outside is probably the most difficult part of being incarcerated. I find that it disorients me and limits me to my immediate surroundings.

Of course, prison tends to be tense and dangerous. For the most part, I know how to survive here. I understand your concern, but be assured that I am well taken care of and I am quite capable of taking care of myself. My head is my first defense. I stay out of prison politics and associated games. The brutality that people hear about on the outside is generally linked to debt, drugs, and disrespect. If I haven't told you enough, please know that I am safe and I've befriended some guys who watch each other's backs. I know that, as a parent, you'll always feel a certain amount of anxiety around my being here. That's understandable. I am truly sorry that I've put you through this. With some help, I hope to be out of here soon.

Dad, I miss you, too. Doing time weighs upon me, especially when I am not present for the miracles of life, like the births of my nephews and cousins. Maybe my separation from the blessings of the outside world is actually a blessing in disguise. I will never again take such things for granted. I am also learning to embrace life, a lesson I am practicing here so I will be prepared when I leave. I've been very selfish in the past. I hope that with age, I can make the transition from selfish youth to selfless adult. We will see how this plays out.

On December 12, 2000, I was transferred back to MSP's boot camp after the parole board decided they would not release me otherwise. After several months going back and forth with the idea, I finally decided that it was once again time to move on with my life. I had adapted to prison life such that I would have been able to complete the remaining years of my sentence. I was afraid that if I stayed, prison might never let go of its hold on me.

The state had reevaluated the boot camp program since my last visit. They reduced the physical requirements and increased the intensity of the mental and emotional work required. In the many treatment groups I attended, I was pushed to look deeper, reaching new levels of personal understanding. Although the program was still unbearable in some respects, it had incorporated balance in a way that it had not done previously. Montana had made a shift. Someone at the top had finally realized that punishment needed to be tempered with the compassion that came of providing people with the opportunity to address the psychological issues that brought them there. Montana had moved from warehousing inmates to providing the treatment necessary to produce long-term change.

They weren't easy on anyone who entered the program for a second time. I had insulted them by graduating at the highest rank last time only to have my parole revoked three weeks after release. The PT sessions were grueling as they again tried to break me emotionally through physical pain. Two weeks before my release, I damaged my lower spine so severely that I couldn't complete the physical requirements of the program.

Despite my injury, I was allowed to complete the boot camp program. Their decision not to send me back to the prison gave me a new perception of the system. The injury, which took away my ability to thrive physically, forced me to slow down and to address my characteristics that had blocked permanent change.

Part of this change involved eliminating my belief that I had to hold my father accountable. I felt that he'd not met my expectations as a father. At last, that feeling began to wane as I realized that I had used it as an excuse for my own self-destruction. My poor behavior had surpassed his tenfold. The father that he'd been when I was a teenager was a far greater man than I had become in my own life.

As I considered his strengths and his weaknesses, as I had at many other times in my life, I realized that he'd been a saint compared to the men who now surrounded me. He was a saint compared to me, too. This was not an easy pill to swallow. The great villain of my teenage years was more of a hero. Sadly, I had wasted many years avoiding him instead of embracing him. I could no longer use him as an excuse for my continued self-destruction. I had years of experience now to fuel my own resentment and shame. I could no longer consider him in terms of abuse, neglect, or abandonment. What he'd done in my mind did not match up to who he was.

Was I not the man now sitting in a cell, a convicted felon, thrown away by society to pay for my crimes? Had my father not worked, participated, and done his best to be a member of the society I had turned my back on many years before? I could no longer believe the stories I had fabricated as a teenager looking for sympathy. Beliefs can be changed; in boot camp, they can be shattered. Although my father's participation in my life hinged upon my own willingness to let him in, he had made himself available in many of the same ways that my mother had. He simply offered his participation in different ways.

I finally realized that I had treated my father in ways that were cruel, unkind, and much more severe than I had treated anyone else in my life—including myself. I had measured him against the perfect father of my youthful imagination, an image that he could not have lived up to; no one could.

Despite my constant assault upon his character, he had never blamed, shamed, or belittled me. He remained a loving father. He stood back, allowing me to work through my defiance and bitterness, never adding fuel to the fire. I am not sure I know others who would have remained as compassionate and as willing to continue a relationship given those circumstances. In the love he had for his child, he was able to look beyond the abuse I had forced him to endure.

In my defiance, I had gotten to know Cathy, his wife. I attended their wedding but spent little time with them in the previous years. I did not want to know her. Accepting her would have meant letting go of my illusion that my parents would reunite and we would be a happy family again. After ten years, I remained the little boy staring into an empty closet, wishing for my father to return.

In Cathy's love for my father, she too took on the role of mother, waiting for a child to return from a long journey. In the several exchanges I had had with her over the years, she'd been both cordial and defensive, showing her tenacity in defending their honor. She refused to back down even when I was disrespectful. When I was verbally abusive, opening old wounds, she met my charge head on. This forced me to understand that she would remain in my life, beside my father, willing to be a part of my life if ever I allowed her to do so.

March 27, 2001
Dear Mom and Mick,

I don't know if I've ever felt as accepted in recovery as I do here in Bozeman. I think I am going to make the meeting I went to tonight my regular meeting. I like the people and the spirit there.

Tonight, I made my own dinner for the first time in quite a while. It was amazing. I am drinking tea now, reflecting on the many times I drank tea in prison, wishing for this very moment. I can't even express what it feels like to be sitting in my own home writing you a note. My gratitude for you and for Mick goes beyond words. If it were not for you, I would still be trying to find a place to stay. I could be on crates in a sleeping bag and still feel grateful for the life I am living!

In two hours, it will be your birthday as well as my personal record for staying clean and free from trouble on supervision. I would say this is a pretty good birthday present.

I had once again been released by MSP boot camp to intensive supervision, this time in Bozeman, Montana. Because of my hard work and promises to remain abstinent, my mother and Mick offered to help me get an apartment, which led to my release. I settled in well and was rehired by my old boss, who owned both the Butte and Bozeman restaurants. I quickly began to adjust to the outside world again; making friends at work and in the recovery meetings I attended. I took full advantage of my freedom in every way that I could, believing that if I was an active participant in my life, I could avoid returning to use.

I braved taking several college classes, bought a bike to ride in the surrounding mountains, and began to blend in with the community around me. I almost felt normal, though the weight of my past and the memories of prison still lingered. Even so, I made a couple of very good friends as a result of my new lifestyle and I was able to let go of a part of my burden by being honest—a show of solidarity I had forgotten existed beyond watching each other's backs on the prison yard.

Inevitably the thunderclouds began to form in the distance. Emotionally, I could not remain balanced despite all of my efforts to do so. If I were to mimic another healthy person's life exactly—from school, to work, to exercise, to eating habits, to recovery groups, to following the directives of parole—my mental and emotional capacity would still diminish as a result of my mental health issues.

Despite all that I did in an attempt to avoid my past regressions, I still regressed. As always it occurred after a depressive episode, I returned to use in an attempt to relieve the symptoms. My one mistake had been to neglect establishing a safety net through mental health counseling. Although the prison had given me medication before I left, the meds began to make my symptoms worse and not better. Even though I had gone to groups in prison, my parole officer on the outside had not been given adequate information concerning my condition and therefore what he was dealing with.

This type of communication breakdown occurred not due to a lack of concern, but because I was in a system in transition. Further, I didn't know what I needed. Previously, I had avoided addressing my mental health issues, so I was still in a great deal of denial. I was like a child, believing that if I covered my eyes, the monster couldn't see me. I felt like admission of mental illness made me less of a person.

I found relief through marijuana and injecting Ritalin, a new and potent mixture. All that I had been doing slowly diminished until those I had brought into my life exited. I pushed anyone who questioned my actions out of my life. It had always been easier to face the inevitable destruction without the reminder of those that I loved. I ceased to communicate with my parents, friendships went cold, and I began to set the stage for my eventual sprint away from my life back to the shadows.

Jenny could not have chosen a worse moment to cross paths with me again. In her embrace, I found a familiar escape. The release of dopamine that comes of such a powerful emotional and physical relationship triggered euphoria and filled my needs. It didn't matter if the chemicals my body craved originated from my own brain or were provided by some back-alley pharmacist.

As we lay in each other's arms, exhausted as a result of one of nature's greatest gifts, another of nature's gifts began to form. I became a father. When she knocked on my front door a month later, I was so far into a binge that I was incapable of making the decision that a better man might have made. Jenny had already made her decision, and before she returned to Butte, we were engaged.

Along the Gallatin River, I proposed to her formally encouraged by the cheers of those floating by on rafts and in kayaks. I was caught in a whirlwind and let it carry me into the unknown. She might have run had she been aware of the ticking clock inside me, counting down the minutes until I no longer had the power to choose whether I stayed or fled. Something inside me seemed to sacrifice all that was good in favor of all that was not good. I've wished I could reach back in time to change the course of history. Not from the point of splitting cells, but from the point when I split from taking on the responsibilities of being a father, a husband, a son, and a brother. My obligations as a father began the moment I asked her into my room and chose not to use birth control. I didn't understanding that my choice in that instant was the single most important moment of my life, the moment when destiny brought three souls together for better or for worse.

26

ON OCTOBER 1, 2001, I ABSCONDED FROM the law for my third and final time. There were no goodbyes as I packed my life into a bag and abandoned the rest, a routine I had repeated many times before. Chemicals quelled the feelings of shame, anger, sadness, and remorse. I knew that my probation officer was on to me when he asked me to do a random urinalysis. I had spent a weekend in jail several weeks earlier for a positive result and was told that any further use would send me back to prison. I knew he wasn't bluffing, as he'd been upfront from the beginning—a trait that I respected.

I was past the point of no return, or so it seemed, and once the avalanche of craving started, my worst fear was not using. The survival impulse kicked in and my brain told me, as it had many times before, that not using would kill me. This instinctual drive, a false reality created by my addicted mind, felt as real as the need to drink water or eat food. I also believed that by leaving I would be giving my child a better life than if I stayed. My shame and poor opinion of myself had returned in full force with the first use. The belief that I was tainted and flawed beyond repair forced me into the shadows once more.

These feelings did not all come at once. They crept in over time, then fueled my continued use and justified my destruction. I no longer used for enjoyment—that idea had been abandoned years before. Instead, I sought relief and self-destruction. My hope was that through inebriation, I would find accidental death. In the past, my choice to leave had been an impulsive one, which was followed by feelings of remorse for having done so. This time, the idea of turning around seemed an impossibility. The road beckoned, awakening something inside that erased all reason. The weight of the world lost its hold on me, and I was able to avoid everything that scared and intimidated me. I worked my way west needing only chemicals and the shelter of an underpass. I would follow my regular migration route, stopping in familiar places where I could find the resources I needed to survive out of sight from the law and my conscience.

I had stopped taking my medication, prescribed for manic depression, and entered full-blown relapse. The shame brought on by my failure and my fear of the responsibilities of being a father and a husband propelled me forward. I moved away from everything that could restore joy to my life. Before I left, Jenny had made it clear, in no uncertain terms, that we would be together to have the child. Rather than embrace this opportunity as a blessing, I felt claustrophobic and trapped.

Like a leaf in the wind, I traveled wherever circumstances carried me. In Flathead Valley, I knew a group of men from the prison who I could call upon if needed. I stayed on a couch much more comfortable than an underpass and within walking distance of the Canadian border. I felt comfortable knowing that with a pack and some rations, I could slip into Canada by one of the many routes used by smugglers. Unbeknownst to me, the law followed close behind. I was nearly caught when the owner of a laundromat found an ounce of marijuana in the jeans I had paid him to wash. Despite this near miss, I continued my escape into the Yaak, an area of wilderness in the northwestern corner of Montana, which welcomed those who preferred anonymity.

Although my life has been characterized by much selfishness, at times I acted in compassion, even while using. These glimmers of hope reminded me that I was still a compassionate being. During my time on the run, I migrated to a small town perched on the edge of the Columbia River east of Portland, Oregon. There I met a woman from the drug circles who offered me a job caring for her bedridden father. Sheena had gone through several nurses in the months leading up to my arrival. When her father's check from Social Security began to go into her arm rather than his care, she asked me to take care of him. Given my circumstances, I jumped on the opportunity and agreed to take half of what she paid others.

When I began caring for Joe, he had a urinary tract infection, infected bed sores, and was horribly emaciated. I had walked into a horrible case of elderly abuse but due to my status as a fugitive, I couldn't alert the authorities for fear that they would nab me in the process. As an alternative, I did all that I could to give him the best care that my limited knowledge could provide.

Joe was blind, though he said he could see me better than I could see myself. He always thanked me profusely, telling me he felt like less of a man having a woman bathe him and change his catheter. He was embarrassed by his dependency. Though he liked women and had been quite the ladies' man in his earlier years, he lost all sense of pride being seen in such a broken state.

My duties consisted of washing him, changing his sheets, feeding him, and giving him his medications. His sores began to disappear, his weight increased, and his sense of humor returned. I enjoyed Joe's company as much as he enjoyed mine. I spent many days at his bedside, taking care of his needs, and many nights falling asleep to his wonderful stories. He had also lived a difficult life, and although I was guarded about my own, Joe shared his experiences with me much like a man might with his grandchildren in preparation for death. I was both honored and relieved to live in the anonymity of our friendship, and for the first time in a long while, I felt like a part of the human race, bringing some good into a world from which I had taken so much.

It didn't matter how far I traveled or how I spent my time while away; the thought of my child in its mother's womb beckoned to me in a way that the road never could. I felt pulled in two directions. The more miles that I put between Oregon and myself, the more weight I carried on my shoulders—something that had never happened before. I felt discontent everywhere I went and the use of chemicals no longer provided relief. I felt driven to return to my unborn child or to end my life. Death beckoned.

I returned to the Yaak where the deep, blue water brought a finality I could not find otherwise. Below the Koocanusa Bridge lay the promise for an end to my suffering. The only problem was the list of questions I would leave behind for a small being who was not yet fully formed. I was not even sure when my child would be born; only that it might enter this world as I was leaving it. I wasn't sure I could cause emptiness in someone's life just as they entered the world.

In that moment, I heard a voice. It was not the first time I had heard one and it would not be the last. The voice held no judgment. I sensed compassion and tears formed quickly, disappearing into the blue void below. Taking my life was no longer an option; all of my desire to do so vanished in that moment. The voice spoke two words and then fell silent: "Go home." They weren't the words of a stranger. Instead, the voice seemed to know me and therefore knew what I must do. I heard cars racing along on Highway 37 as the words of the voice reverberated within. Slowly, I leaned back against the railing, not away from it. I had experienced a spiritual shift, and with it, the direction of my life changed. There was no longer room for doubt.

I spent the weeks that followed walking in the woods and exploring the reservoir in search of arrowheads and other natural treasures. I experienced freedom and found a compromise between oblivion and awareness. Even though I continued to use, something within me was changing. It was as though I was connected to the baby forming in Jenny's body. Had the voice been my child reaching out to me before she crossed over from the spirit world, or was it some other being beyond my limited understanding?

Everywhere I looked, I saw animals with their young showing me my place. Bears, wolves, doe, and other small mammals made themselves known in my hikes, disappearing as quickly as they appeared. In glimpses, I recognized the instinct with which we are all born: to protect our young. The gift of this knowledge remained within me. How could it not? I had never experienced animals in this way. Whether it was I who looked for answers in the wild, or the wild that came to me with lessons, the outcome remained the same. I would never be a lone wolf again. I was responsible for a child, a sacred gift that I could no longer deny.

I don't remember the exact day that the voice talked me down from the bridge and pushed me back to the world of the living. I don't know exactly when my very being began to change—but change, it did. From that moment, I found no relief through chemicals. They could no longer make me feel numb to reality, regardless of the substance. I could feel the chemicals lessen their hold on me. In their place, a desire to go home grew strong.

I traveled back to Oregon one last time before turning myself over to the law. On this last trip, I visited Joe. He was very happy to see me and shared with me a vision he'd had. He described being in a realm between life and death, a place he'd visited often in the days before my return. Joe said that the vision took place at night, though a bright light shone in his room. I stood on the edge of a great precipice next to a grandfather clock. Joe yelled out, unsure of whether I could hear him. He had no knowledge of my life's circumstances and was unaware that I had indeed been standing on a bridge railing only weeks before. He had no idea that Jenny was pregnant or that I was supposed to be doing time in prison. Joe told me that the clock in his vision was losing speed and that time was running out for me. He screamed out, "Go home!" as his vision required him to do. Joe said he hoped that I had returned because I heard him calling out in the distance. I didn't respond. I simply kissed his forehead, and then asked if anyone had told him they love him that day. He shook his head and I assured him that I loved him and always would.

The world of the spirit is constantly working through the lives of those around us. In my life, it continued to manifest itself through nature, prayer, and the Creator's handy men and women, like Joe. Joe was a conduit of sorts who worked in the world of the spirit while enduring his final days in the physical realm. He would be moving on soon based on his description of the world beyond the living, the place in which he had seen me.

With that recognition, I understood that if Joe could reach me in the world of the spirit, in a place between life and death, then I had been there as well the night that he called to me. I realized that I had begun to deteriorate spiritually before I went to jump. In some instances, the physical is the last to go; it is in those times that the spirit meets with the soul in preparation. The spirit, the mind, and the emotions work together, a perfect dance with the laws that bind us to this existence.

I had always known that I danced with the shadows when I used. I just hadn't known that my internal spirit was dimming in protest to my destruction. Knowing this, I hoped that Joe would return to the light sooner rather than later. He deserved peace and a break from the physical realm. I walked away knowing that he felt loved.

Taylor was born on April 10, 2002. Several months later, I boarded a Greyhound bus and headed eastward. I considered what would happen once I returned to Butte. The ticket I was traveling on had a final destination of Colorado. Although my mind was made up, I always had another plan just in case. I had little money and the job I had been promised in Colorado was the best thing I had going. I traveled with a bag of marijuana, some clothes, a little money, and an alert conscience, one that had been awakened many months before. With the boarding pass in my pocket, I called Jenny and asked to see my daughter.

When I heard the knock on the hotel door, I felt anxious and frightened by what was on the other side. In my mind, it would have been easier to face Jenny's wrath than the little bundle I imagined her carrying. Children had always intimidated me and the fact that this one was mine made it worse. I was scared, as I always had been, that I would somehow negatively affect this child. Although the only home I could imagine was near Taylor and her mother, I wasn't certain that I would not stay around long enough to grow attached to them.

When the door opened, it felt like home entered the room. The sun reflected off of her rosy cheeks creating a golden aura. It was impossible for me to hold back my emotions. In her, I saw the miracle of creation and the reason for my existence. The message from the bridge returned to me, but this time in a smile. I had never seen something so beautiful. The sight of her provoked an instinct far stronger than any I had every known—I was a father. At that moment, my recovery began anew. In that moment, I found my reason. In that moment, I understood that I was responsible for not just my own life but also the life of another.

Jenny told me I had two choices. I could turn myself in and get clean, or I could continue on my current path, removed from my daughter's life. Taylor could decide at eighteen whether or not she wanted to see her deadbeat dad. In Jenny's eyes, I saw the pain and anger of a woman that had been betrayed; forced to go through her pregnancy alone. Although I could never fully understand her experience, my heart began to ache for the very real pain and suffering that my absence had created. I knew that I had only one choice, the choice of a man trying to reclaim the right to be a father and husband. Jenny had no reason to treat me with kindness, and yet she did. I did not get what I deserved; instead, I was given what Taylor deserved—a chance to be a father. Taylor Breanne had chosen me to be her father, and what a brave little girl she was for that.

In August of 2002, I turned myself back in to the state of Montana at the Gallatin County Sheriff's office in Bozeman, Montana. Although I entered without fear of prison itself, I did fear failure because the stakes had become much higher. Although I did not believe in the value of myself, there was a young girl who had value. I would never be able to live with myself if I failed as a father. With that, I entered the bowels of the Montana Department of Corrections for the last time, prepared to do whatever time was required to earn my right to be with Taylor. I had never been caught running from the law because I always turned myself in. What always caught up with me first was my conscience, not the badge.

July 2, 2002
Dear Mom and Mick,

It is not your responsibility that I am in this position. The learning process would have been the same regardless of whether you had paid for an attorney early on. I had to make every mistake on my own. I stole, ran, carried meth, and wrote bad checks. These are my mistakes and I will pay the consequences.

I have a responsibility to my precious Taylor as well as Jenny. I know that recovery programs say that addicts must be selfish in their pursuit of recovery, but I have been selfish my whole life. They say that you must do it for yourself, but what if you can't stand yourself? If I focus on Taylor, I have a starting point at minimum. I've lost the will to continue on my own. If it were just about me, I would still be on the run, living in the misery of selfishness and addiction, a slave to my fears.

Taylor is a gift from God. I never thought that I would be a father. I never thought I would one day be responsible for another human being. I never thought

*that I would be needed. I am both proud and ashamed.
I am present and willing, yet I am very scared and have
been since I was told that I was going to be a father.
I don't want to fail. I don't want to let anyone down
again.*

*Your emotional response on the phone was exactly
what needed to happen. You don't always have to be
the strong one. Although it was difficult to hear your
pain, I needed to hear it all the same.*

*I am glad you'll be coming to Montana to see Taylor and Jenny. I understand your hesitation. I have built
up then destroyed my life so many times and you don't
want to see me do it again, especially when others are
involved. I understand that love is more than just a
ring and saying, "I do." I am willing to learn the rest.*

After my last period of use and the subsequent birth
of my daughter, my world ceased to be "The Eric Show."
My mother's stance shifted and protecting her granddaughter became her number one priority. Every conversation we ended in a related discussion. I could tell
that she was angry. She was not only angry with me, she
was angry at the disease of addiction and depression. She
understood that through my use, I possessed the ability
to tear holes in the soul of a child. She stopped showing
compassion the way that she had before. Instead, our
conversations took on an air of desperation. It was easy to
accept that her desire to help me remain clean had more
to do with the infant that we both loved than the father
who had been given so many chances.

Hope had almost been lost in those final months.
It appeared to all who watched my decline that I might
just be one of those people who, despite their desire,
could not remain clean for any lasting period of time.

I had been in institutions since the age of thirteen and might remain there for the remainder of my life. This was not an easy prospect for me, nor was it easy for those who had been fighting for me for so long. In my struggle rested wagers from many years before. Hope, faith, and support were the chips in the center of the table, and the bony hands of death moved ever so slowly towards them. Now, an extension of me existed in my daughter and the hope rested in her. Protecting her took precedence over all else, and if that meant a shift in peoples' focus, then so be it. It was sobering to realize that people were positioning themselves to protect my daughter from me.

July 4, 2002
Dear Mom and Mick,

I am content in these walls that surround me, creating a womb of sorts. I am developing through prayer, pain, faith, hope, and self-searching. I think back to when I walked away from parole, and while I thought I was taking back my freedom, I was attempting to steal it rather than earning it.

I can't see any fireworks this year. My cell has a view of fog lights and a brick wall. I can hear them, though, and their sounds remind me of what I am not allowed to experience. If I close my eyes, I can recreate what it was like to experience the 4th of July from past years. Although I am alone right now, I am content knowing that by paying the price for freedom it will make me respect it more in the end.

Every time I experience a change in perspective, I am embarrassed by how I've acted. My daughter is so precious. I stare at her picture for hours, taking in every little curve, bump, and dimple. I try to match them up when I see her. I have such little time with her. It's bitter sweet.

I am grateful, though, and happy to have been able to experience any time with her. Jenny is very kind. In every letter, she includes a new picture. Mom, I truly understand now. They are so perfect at this age, so fragile, so beautiful. Missing her early development has been difficult and I struggle with the choices I made that placed me in a position to be absent from the pregnancy and birth.

It is my great hope that I will be present for my little family. I am aware that my focus must be on myself in order for this to happen. I am aware that I have some very rough corners that need to be worked smooth. Jenny has been a teacher to me in her forgiveness. It cannot be easy for her to allow me back in after what I've done. I wish I were better at learning my lessons the first time and not repeating them over and over.

July 12, 2002
Dear Mom and Mick,

Do you know why it took so long for me to turn myself in? I couldn't do it unless I knew that I meant to remain on the right side of the law. This may also be why I left Bozeman in the first place. Many people see my actions as selfish. In many ways they were, but in other ways, they were not. Strangely, both can be true. If I didn't believe that I could honor my daughter's life, then I would not be here. I am not a monster.

There was a man in here that went to court and then came back an hour later smiling. It didn't matter that he'd been sentenced to multiple years in prison. He was just happy to have seen his son. Twenty minutes later, he took his own life. He hung himself from a light socket in his cell. I've always thought of suicide as a selfish act. Today, I believe it can also be called selfless. It's a miserable place to be when you judge your own life as a burden to those who love you, and you wonder if it would be better to end it for them and for yourself. These thoughts go through my mind, too, as I weigh all the options before me. Had I made my decisions based on fear, I wouldn't be here today.

This man's death was a wake-up call for many here in the jail. He acted on what many of us have thought about. I always wondered what would be worse on Taylor: taking my own life and the pain associated with that one event, or a series of painful episodes like the ones that have led me to this point. I won't give up now that I have others to think about. I must be selfless for my family. I must offer my life as a sacrifice to be of service to them. This will come through recovery. Time will reveal if what I say has substance.

July 30, 2002
Dear Mom and Mick,

When I look at myself, I can see the changes I've made to survive in prison. I am constantly fighting off negative thoughts, thoughts that go against who I am as a person. I am bitter in many ways and if I don't keep myself in check through writing and prayer, I could very well react in ways I don't want to.

Honesty means different things to different people. Some use the expression, "What they don't know won't hurt them." Others say, "Honesty is the best policy." I've learned that honesty doesn't serve you in this system. In this system, honesty is punished.

It is not easy being Eric at times. It really sucks. I can't fully explain how when I use, I change completely. It's as if the life I lived before using becomes a burden. What kind of man would miss his own daughter's birth? Do I really deserve to be in my daughter's life? How do I know that I won't hurt her even more just by being in her life? I am watching my daughter grow up through photos and through glass. This hurts me desperately. How do I justify feeling like a victim to a disease in the face of someone who is a real victim? How can I justify this pain when my daughter's mother sacrificed so much because I made promises that I didn't keep?

How can I ask anyone to have faith in me when I don't have faith in myself? How ugly can a human being be? Of course, my mother will say that I am a good person and I will counter her argument. Is my cell a tomb? Am I the walking dead or am I man in transition? Should I have remained away carrying the burden of abandonment? In the eyes of others, it may have seemed heartless. To a man who carried the darkness of death, it seemed heroic when I walked away. No memories of a degenerate father seemed better than knowledge of a failure of a father.

August 8, 2002
Dear Mom and Mick,

I am not feeling very positive right now, so bear with me. I realize that I can still run in here. I can quit writing, quit calling, quit taking mail, and quit fighting against the evils of incarceration. I've decided to be real this time instead of painting a rosy picture. My actions may have caused me to lose my opportunity at having a family. I am not a murderer or a rapist, but I am a drug addict. Because of that, I bring a lot of baggage. I am doomed to fight my addiction over and over again. Why can't I just burn out young like the rest of my junkie heroes? I am so fucking tired.

I think that you do me harm by pointing out my positive traits over my negative ones. This is the hardest time I've ever done. Is God punishing me by putting someone in my life for which I must be responsible? This is emotional torture. I really don't think I can do another round.

I am back to sleeping fourteen hours a day. I wake up tired and am soon asleep again. I despise this place, yet the longer I am here, the more comfortable I become in the discomfort...

27

HAVING A THOROUGH DIAGNOSIS IS BOTH a freeing experience and sobering one. To some, the idea of being diagnosed with a mental disorder might seem like more of a curse than a blessing. To me, it came as a relief. I had known for years that I suffered from depression and possibly other disorders, so to have a well-respected professional tell me what I already knew reinforced that I was not simply a hopeless drug addict. I am a human being with a set of issues more complex than one simple label. Obviously, this diagnosis doesn't let me off the hook. Instead, it makes me even more responsible for my actions.

The diagnosis came at the urging of my attorney, who believed that my psychological issues played a significant role in my continued relapse and flight. He believed that a clear understanding of my emotional and physical state would pay dividends in the days to come. Even if it didn't help my case, it would help me to understand that I needed more help than I had allowed myself. My parole officer told my mother that if he'd known I was suffering from mental illness, he could have done more to help me. The breakdown in communication between institutions was frustrating for all involved; it often meant that people like me weren't given the help that they needed. My choice to use generally came before my desire to seek help. The mentally ill often have more faith in finding relief through chemical use than in a system that shows little concern.

My evaluation lasted for the better part of a week. Dr. Schaffer, a well-respected psychologist in Bozeman, was the first choice of most lawyers and courts when assessing patients as he made fair and comprehensive assessments. After many hours of questions, tests, interviews with my mother, and review of my medical records, a diagnosis was made. Dr. Schaffer diagnosed me as depressed but also identified several other disorders that had gone overlooked in previous assessments. He was particularly interested in the three, severe head injuries I had suffered while growing up, as well as the physical, emotional, and sexual trauma I had endured throughout the years of homelessness, addiction, and incarceration.

The diagnosis of bipolar came as no surprise. I had been told several times before that I suffered from acute depression. What was a surprise was the mania associated with bipolar disorder. He suggested that my mania surfaced as irritability and in the manic sexual episodes and impulse control issues that I had experienced throughout my life. He also suggested that my drug use showed a pattern of medicating both sides of the emotional pendulum—the highs and the lows—with, meth, marijuana, and heroin. Further, he diagnosed me with poly substance abuse disorder as well as attention deficit disorder. I had been under the impression that hyperactivity had to be present in order to be diagnosed with attention deficit disorder. Dr. Schaffer informed me that my symptoms included an overactive brain, difficulty concentrating, and hyperconsciousness.

The diagnosis that came as the greatest shock was PTSD, a disorder about which I knew little. When he read the symptoms back to me, I saw a picture of my life. For years, I had suffered from numerous symptoms that were a result of the trauma I had experienced; from early molestation, to rape, to the brothers in Idaho, to the extremes of prison life, and everything else in-between. When I tallied the experiences and matched up the symptoms, I felt relief knowing that what I had endured for so long had a name. The survivor's guilt, reoccurring dreams, emotional disassociation from the world around me, and a kind of fantasy world that I had created to avoid reality mirrored what had been described in the assessment.

At no point did I ask for help with my court case, yet a letter was included in the short summary. Dr. Schaffer pleaded with the judicial system not to send me back into prison, citing that continued incarceration would only exacerbate my condition. He believed that a community program combined with mental health support would allow me to remain clean and to become an active member of society. Without intense mental-health counseling and proper medication, I would continue my former pattern of continued use and recidivism. A list of medications was submitted to the jail, to the probation office, and to the parole staff. One of Dr. Shaffer's chief complaints was that the medication I had been given while incarcerated several years prior had made my PTSD and bipolar symptoms worse rather than better.

In the weeks that followed, I was given several different medications. After experiencing the side effects of each, I discontinued their use, believing the symptoms of the disorder to be better than the medications used to treat them. The doctor had a list of the medications that they were willing to give inmates. That list was short; sadly, the expense of other drugs outweighed the potential benefits of their administration to inmates.

August 13, 2002
Dear Mom and Mick,

My new cellmate is in here for spousal abuse and juvenile assault on his ten-year-old stepson. He is an angry man, and a power and control freak. He knows not to cross me, though. He's already tried and I put him in his place. He also tried with another guy last night. He waited until lock-down to fluff up his feathers, so that no one could get to him. He's that type of guy: tough enough to beat up a woman and a child when he's drunk, but not tough enough to fight men who will fight back when he's sober. More bark than bite. I am glad his wife bit off his nipple and scratched up his sides. I only wonder what she looked like after he got at her.

Maybe it's my job to show this man some compassion. Maybe I am meant to learn from him, to keep from repeating his mistakes. I have never struck a woman, although I have been aggressive towards other men. I try not to judge, yet I wonder why men like us do the things that we do? Is it a continuation of lessons that we must learn before we can move on? Many of my experiences have felt as though they were written into the cosmos. Is it my destiny to sink into humiliation and despair in order to climb back out to learn more about myself? Is this how I will come to be of service to others and to the world around me? If I don't learn my lesson in this life, will I be a child beater, the next Hitler, a rapist in my next life? Is someone using me as an example of what not to be in this world? I am quite sure there is.

I believe that despite my surroundings I could have chosen to be a far worse human being in this world. Yes, I have acted poorly, yet there are times when I acted selflessly and kind. Who holds the scales? Who decides what good cancels out bad? How can I shift my karma? How can I go against my nature to move on from this painful physical realm to the next? I wish that I knew the answers. Those who tell me that concise answers exist may be worse off than me.

August 23, 2002
Dear Mom and Mick,

I struggle with being human. I believe this struggle is what life is all about. At times, I despise it; other times, I want to embrace it. Prison is very difficult because survival here requires fitting certain roles. It's crucial to avoid becoming a target. This requires a certain duality, like laughing at something you don't find funny or disagree with altogether. You have to decide if it's worth a fight or if temporarily compromising on morals is a more sensible approach considering the situation.

Thank you for saying that you don't believe my surroundings reflect who I am as a person. Many spiritual leaders have withstood similar experiences. I am not a spiritual leader. The actions that led me here were based on selfishness not selflessness. I appreciate what you are saying, though. I struggle with what I've done on a daily basis. My past brings me pain. I wonder how I could be capable of such destructive behavior. There's nothing I want more than to be deserving of my mother's biased views.

Did any of these spiritual leaders shoot drugs, live promiscuously, walk away from their pregnant fiancé, promise hundreds of times to change without doing so, make numerous ignorant choices, hurt family, disrespect themselves and their communities? I know—I should quit beating myself up. I don't believe that everything will be forgiven once I repent. I believe that a heartfelt desire to change followed by action will be the beginning to coming back into the graces of the Creator. Yes, at times I had sincere desire, good intentions, and performed selfless acts. Yet where am I now? Prison. I am in prison with a woman on the outside who is raising our daughter alone.

In my eyes, those who remain by my side despite my many failures are the spiritual teachers; they are the ones deserving of the best that this world has to offer. A man of character acts more then he speaks, not the reverse. These are my demons. My humanness. Strangely, I must embrace the dark side to evolve as a human being. I must look into the shadows, face my fears, and then continue to monitor myself so that I don't slip back into the pit that I have dug myself into.

When I really see what my life has been about, I feel repulsed. You know why I don't use here? I am constantly aware of the harsh consequences. The consequences here are far worse than most on the outside can understand. A yet worse set of consequences exists: a mother's tears and the sound of one's daughter from behind a Plexiglas shield.

People of the shadows no longer have influence over me because light is more powerful than darkness. The human spirit is about light, not darkness. It is only when we face the light that we keep our shadow behind us. If we decide to turn our backs on this light, then we will be led by our shadow back into fear and the darkness.

September 3, 2002
Dear Mom and Mick,

My life wasn't so bad until I started calling the shots. Sometimes I believe in destiny. Other times I believe in a destiny created through personal choice and the influence that each choice has on the next. Now I believe in a combination. Maybe we're placed in certain family lines or soul groups in order to prepare us or impair us for our journeys ahead. Maybe that's why the greatest figures in history experienced challenges early on in their lives. Maybe through these challenges, they were catapulted into the spiritual realm, to a higher level of consciousness and enlightenment. I wonder what kind of social change Hitler might have created had he chosen to use his gift of charisma for compassion instead of great hatred. Why is it that so much attention has been paid to his life when so little has been paid to Gandhi's or to others who perpetuated love?

I believe that humanity has an on/off switch for God's grace, supreme love, and infinite wisdom. When it's off, selfishness, bitterness, and hatred towards oneself and others take over. When the switch is on, spirituality takes over and compassion, honesty, love, forgiveness, and creativity take root in the human condition.

Let me tell you a story about a stamp. Men in prison are always trying to get something for nothing. Though I hate to generalize this, it seems to be true. So many of us feel that we're barely getting what we need in here. Commissary has been cancelled for two weeks now and everyone is running low on basics. From deprivation instinctually you begin to act as you might never have given your basic necessities are pro-

vided. Food, shelter, and clothing are just three. Teeth brushing, writing letters to loved ones are examples of others.

I've wanted to mail letters for some time now. After staring at my envelope for a few hours, a thought hit me: I wonder if my cellmate's alcohol pads would wipe the time stamp off of an old stamp. It worked! Now phase two: Can I peel off the old stamp without damaging it? A stamp costs a half-day's worth of wages. I figured I was on to something big. Once the stamp is off, how do I get it to stick to the new envelope? Working my way through the process, men in the cells across from me are watching. This could mean payoff for anyone who wanted in on it. In addition to the thirty-seven cents, it was a screw you to the system at large. From across the cell-block, Lew yelled, "Lick your envelope then rub your stamp on it." He said other guys had been doing it since he'd been in prison. Lew looks like they may have actually built this prison around him. My stamp was a Picasso. It was the oldest convict hustle. I guess I just made it a new one, because in every cell, I saw a variation of what I had just done. I was the only one with the alcohol pad, a gift from my diabetic cellmate. Those who weren't watching before now pleaded to know my trick. Suddenly, from across the cell-block came the voice of a true businessman. He said he would teach anyone who wanted to know for one stamp. The whole block started to laugh. Laughter was in even shorter supply than stamps.

The moment that everyone else felt grateful for a new tool in their prison arsenal, I began to feel guilty about the stamp. My cellmate, who seemed to have heard my thoughts, said, "You feel guilty over washing a thirty-seven-cent stamp, yet you have no remorse for leaving your pregnant fiancé to fend for herself for nine months while you ran?" That was the lesson I learned from the stamp. It went back to the on/off switch. I could choose to live conscientiously through faith, or I could choose to live without faith using drugs and alcohol. When I turn the switch off, I delay my conscience and become capable of making rash choices with no moral compass. My disease of selfishness sets aside my spiritual center. Then, when I am forced to stop or choose to stop, my poor choices catch up with me and I overcompensate.

Another reality exists as well. One thirty-seven-cent stamp leads to another stamp, which leads to a lie, which leads to a crime, which leads to bigger and more detrimental decisions. I had done the same with pot, which led to alcohol, which led to the needle. Each choice adds to either the good or the bad, flipping the on/off switch. The same occurs with love. One good choice leads to more good choices, which leads to bigger choices, which ultimately lead to a greater good.

My inability to use the stamp despite its relative insignificance was a good sign. I have turned on the switch once more and my conscience is working again.

At some point, I began to understand the power of intention. I understood that whatever we choose to put energy into grows that much stronger. Negative choices no matter how seemingly inconsequential, tip the scale away from all that is good. One lie leads to another. Guilt festers then turns to shame; shame fuels further poor decision-making, creating its own momentum. This momentum becomes so powerful that even the best intentions cannot stop it. Only a massive moral shift created as a result of spiritual experiences or bottoming out followed by restructured belief systems and moral codes can slow the force. Ultimately, prison is meant to bring such a shift, although the walls built to keep the prisoners in could not keep out the minds that followed. Circumstances do not affect one's ability to make positive and negative choices. Thought processes exist within the individual. The mind may be our greatest enemy or greatest ally. The difference exists in choice.

My choice not to use the stamp constituted a small victory over selfishness. As a result, one good choice snowballed to create an avalanche of good intent, positive choices, and positive positioning for the future. I understood that these behaviors needed to begin where I would be tested the most, in a place where it was acceptable to choose the low road over the high road. If I could begin a pattern of positive choices to set the direction in which I wished to take my life, it would be that much easier to do so when the constant reminder of consequence was removed and I returned to the world beyond the prison walls.

In the balance of the spirit world, selfishness is selfishness; the spiritual world does not categorize one bad choice differently from the next. The repercussions of both are like the ripples on a glassy pond, each ripple eventually touching the shoreline. The same is true of positive choice and selflessness. The pebble's size has no bearing; one must simply touch the pool's surface to affect all that surrounds it.

September 6, 2002
Dear Mom and Mick,
I've been classed back to the low security side of MSP. I am so glad that I can return to the Buddhist mediation groups at the chapel. The other side is also

less physically aggressive and I'll have a chance to breathe some fresh air.

The fear of prison has lost its effects on me for the most part. I realize that's dangerous in some ways, though it can also be positive. When I felt afraid of prison, I followed specific guidelines motivated by the consequences of not doing so. Now I follow the rules because I see that by doing so, I can transition back into society that much easier.

You know what I fear even more than prison? A five-month-old little girl named Taylor. I fear her more than I fear the killers and the rapists that surrounded me here. With Taylor, I understand the consequences of not following the rules. I guess what I fear the most is her having to pay the consequences when and if I relapse again. If I let that happen, I would be allow-ing my greatest blessing to slip through my fingers as a result of my own poor choices. I understand that through abstinence, I can avoid this, although I've said that I was serious many times before.

I saw Jim today. He was disappointed that I was sent to the low side. He asked what I needed and I told him a couple of stamps. He sent me some cookies, lemonade, a magazine, and twenty stamps. I guess you get what you ask for and then some. Jim sent a "bull" to bring me my things. We're not supposed to have any contact with general population, but there are ways around it. On fish row, we're cut off from just about everything, so cookies and a magazine are considered luxuries. People say shit rolls downhill, but so can kind-ness. Because the people here are so poor and deprived of what the rest of the world takes for granted, the inmates hoard their possessions. This just makes the deprivation worse. One of the guys asked if I would sell him the cookies. He's an entrepreneur, so I am sure he was looking to double his investment. Instead of selling them, I told the cell-block to send me a line so that I could hook them up with a cookie. Within two minutes, I had twelve lines at my cell door. I was able to get all twenty-four men in the block two cookies each plus lemonade. I kept the magazine for myself then passed it on when I finished reading it. Most of the men thanked me. Others nodded in appreciation. I didn't plan this event; it just happened.

I used the opportunity to share my two cents about taking care of each other. Some agreed; others nodded more. I noticed a skin in the other cell. His name is Labo. I used to push him up the hills during our morning PT at boot camp. He couldn't run very well. After I tossed him a cookie and reintroduced myself, he turned to his cellmate and said, "I like that guy." It's not bad to have a couple of natives on your side in here.

What started as Jim showing kindness, continued through me, and then on to the others in the cell-block. One act of kindness put the whole cell in a good mood and for the first time in days, I heard laughter.

September 7, 2002
Mom and Mick,

I would like to say that every day here is like the day I got the men cookies. Of course, it's not. I believe that what separates humans from animals is our ability to reason, our ability to choose not to act on instincts. When men are locked down together for more than twenty-three hours a day, the odds are not in their favor. I've found that I can sense violence before it happens. I heard something go down last night between two youngsters. One was eighteen years old, six feet two inches, and about two hundred and thirty pounds. The other kid was eighteen, five feet eight inches, and about one hundred and thirty-five pounds. You can guess how it ended. The skinny kid came out of the cell with swollen, bloodied eyes, a bruised forehead, and a severely bruised ego, which seemed to be the worst of his injuries. It's usually over as quickly as it begins. The bigger of the two looked remorseful when he exited his cell, looking at me as if for answers. I am not a youngster anymore in terms of my experience—and I guess in terms of my age as well. At times, people look to me for answers. I think they know that I am not a threat. I hate violence. I hate it. I told the bigger guy he'd probably take a trip to the hole if the guards saw the kid's injuries. I figured the little fella would go, too, after several days in the infirmary.

It doesn't have to be this way. In the old days, they put cons in cells with like-minded people because the guards knew what would happen if they put two guys together that did not mix. Conflicting personalities generally result in a violent clash, particularly when one decides to assert their will over the other. In this case, it appears that the little man hit the big man first. The nurse just came through and asked what happened to him. The little guy said it was self-mutilation and refused to go to the infirmary. They cuffed him and took him in anyway. The big guy walks and the little guy is led off. It takes everything in me not to break down. I keep silent out of self-preservation.

Prison is the purest form of insanity. After two hours, the little guy returned to the same cell because he refused to tell the guards what they already knew. When the lights went out, I heard threats from one guy to another about his "rape-o jacket" and what'll happen when the doors crack tomorrow. Moments later, I heard the sounds of fighting. The kids were at it again. For minutes, all I heard was grunting and hitting. Someone passed me a mirror so I could look in. I yelled for them to quit out of fear that the little guy might get killed. The guards are idiots for putting them back in the same cell together. The code of silence just leads to further violence.

Thankfully, I was able to get them to break it up. One of the kids promised it was over. I hope that's the case, because what comes next in a conflict like this isn't pretty. At night, I pray that no one dies in the night. The next morning, I was surprised to see both the small kid and the large kid with matching coon eyes. The little guy won the last battle. He assaulted his cellmate during the night and came out on top—or so it appears.

Why is it that others accept this as par for the course? Violence is unacceptable anywhere else but here. The guards are no dummies. They're probably sitting in the cage with their backs turned, drinking coffee and betting on who will win the next one.

Jim sent me a letter today. I am sending it to you with this letter. Please hold it for me.

Dear Eric,

It's been good to see and talk to you again, although I wish it were under different circumstances. I would gladly do your time for you if it would put you back out there with your daughter. A lot seems to have happened since we last spoke. You're now a daddy. Congratulations, bro! She's a beautiful child and I know it must be ripping your heart out to be *in here without her and Jenny. If it's any consolation, she's only five months old, and by the time you get out, she'll still be young enough that she won't remember that you weren't around. Make the best of it! This state will not keep giving you chances like they have been. One of these times, they'll slam you hard. They don't care whether you have a family. You're in the belly of the beast. It's all about warehousing bodies for money now. Get out, Eric. The dope and shit just isn't worth it. Of course you know that. You're a smart man and you now get the bigger picture. God gave you a very special gift. Protect that little one against the corrupting influences of this world. Use the time you have to get right with God. Get your head on right. All this is an education; learn, adapt, overcome, and succeed.*

I am sorry. I don't mean to sound like I have all the answers or that I am better than you. It's just that you have the opportunities I once had and blew off. I was a fool, Eric! Every day and night my heart aches to regain all that I've lost. I dropped my dreams while high on self-centeredness and life's illusions. Now I am a pitiful man, scrambling around on my hands and knees, my sight blurred by the realization of my failures. Look around you, Eric. Do you feel the chill of the concrete and steel around you? Do you feel the hopelessness that clings to the walls from the thousands who have passed through before you? It's a slow death, Eric.

You said that you now have two more reason to change. Brother, you can't change for other people. It just won't work. You've got to change because you want to. Give it a chance. I sit here and dream about the opportunities that you have. You said you have faith in God. Well, let faith work for you. Anyway, thank you for the picture. It's next to the one of you and your mother sitting on the steps.

I've thought about both of you, hoping that life is treating you well. Whatever the board does to you on the 30th, let that be a beginning. You can still turn this around. I was selfishly hoping you would come to my side, but you're better off on the low side. It's getting crazy over here and it will only get worse. I have a hard time on the outside. I've probably sabotaged every chance I had to get out of here. On the outside, I am nobody I have nothing. In here, I am Jim. Most everybody likes me and I am someone.

I don't know what it is about you, but when you came into my cell in Flathead, I was going to kill myself. For some reason, though, I felt comfortable talking to you. You never judged me. You didn't think me weak or anything. You listened and you genuinely cared. For that, I will always be grateful. For saving my life, I will always love you and consider you my brother. You know that your mother is my dream mother. To sit and write a man she doesn't even know at a coffee shop early in the morning...To think about me or to even acknowledge my existence...You two save lives simply by being a part of them.

September 11, 2002
Dear Mom and Mick,

For some reason, I thought I could come here, turn myself in, and that everything would be pixie dust and giant pumpkin carriages. I've always thought about life in that way, and drugs just continued the myth. The only things that I've ever stuck to in my life are worth nothing. I am inconsistent to say the least. I've always run back to drugs or prison. In prison, I am a success. I am a successful saboteur. I show up after throwing away my life and do what I do—horsehair, read, workout, and write letters. On the outsider, I am good at being the bad guy. On the inside, I survive by being the good guy. I am no-waves Adreon, then back again as pot again Adreon. In here, I am neither the worst nor the best. In here, I am no longer the black sheep. I am tired of who I am on the outside, and in many ways, I would rather stay here than return to build another life just to destroy it all over again. I am not saying that I like it here. I am saying that it's become comfortable. In here, there is no success and no failure.

Personally, I doubt that I'll be able to make it on the outside. I doubt my abilities outside of prison. My hopes mix with thoughts of failure and I become despondent. How can I grow closer to my loved ones when I know that my success won't last? I can't go to school because I know I won't make it. I am scared, Mom. I am a father. Taylor is a real, breathing human being.

When I turned myself in, I made the decision that I would never return to prison. I believed that I could disappear into the world of the gypsy, never again to have to face the harsher realities of life. I thought that I could become self-sufficient and could get by on my own. That was all a lie. There's no secret world of the constant traveler—at least not in my reality. Life takes work. Relationships take work. Healing takes work.

I have a new cellmate who's been tormented by everyone for the sexual crimes he committed. The guards have started putting guys in my cell that can't make it with other people. I think they understand that I won't torment them. I find comfort in not judging and allowing others to feel safe. I don't care what they're here for, though that doesn't mean that I agree with their actions. I am simply not here to be their punishment.

September 27, 2002

Dear Taylor, my sweet daughter,

I've tried to write this letter several times tonight, but I've been struggling. I feel hurt and confused. I fear that my instincts are correct and that your mother has decided against our future together. I understand what it is to hold onto bitterness until it becomes a cancer that eats away any chance for amends. I don't blame her. Few people have the ability to place spiritual principle before pain and fear, and that is why we find ourselves here. I was too scared to stay in her life when she needed me most. I've spent a good portion of my life trying to learn to forgive others for what they've done to me. How could I expect your mother to do so in just a few short months?

You are six months old. Your very existence motivates me. I hope that at some point in our lives, I will be able to be a father to you. There are times when I want to throw in the towel, though. I will not lie. My life has not been easy as a result of the choices I've made as well as some things over which I have no control. I suffer from bipolar disorder, which has been bothering me as of late. Sure, I have plenty to be depressed about, yet it goes beyond that. Bipolar disorder is crippling and it distorts how I view the world around me. Even with an understanding of my illness, it's still very difficult to stay on top of. In here, it's easier to stay in my cell and not face the world than to get out and try to participate. I appreciate the sunset and a fresh breeze, though. The thought of them pulls me from my cocoon for a short while.

My depression and addiction are not excuses to give up, though. As a spiritual being, I am responsible for walking through every lesson that is placed before me by expressing compassion and gratitude for the *opportunity to grow. If I were to give up now, I would disrespect everyone who has come through before me, many who have dealt with a great deal more than I, and yet they still found the courage to overcome.*

Your mother is a good example of this. She has a great deal on her plate, and yet she still moves forward, succeeding for herself and for you regardless of her extreme difficulties.

I write to you today because I love you. Writing to you seemed like the best thing I could do considering my circumstances. Your very being centers me. You are purity, a great gift to a man who has lost his own purity through life's struggles. My reaction to fear is to run and never look back. You have drawn my gaze back. I am committed to you and to my life now. If this means that I'll be a janitor the rest of my life to provide for you, I will! I will sacrifice whatever dreams I may have left to enable yours. It scares me to look at all the responsibility that you symbolize. I have next to no work experience, no education, and rely on my faith in something better. At times, I don't believe that there is a God personal to me. At times, I think that God's only job is to keep the planets in line, not to help men like me.

Here is a look at life through your father's eyes:

Repetition, daily repetition; a count on the hour, every hour. Chow, count, yard, chow, count, yard... We are issued clothes every third day, and we all dress alike because we are convicts. Personalities always surface; that can't be avoided. One man wears his pants saggy, another tight. To each his own. I am growing a beard to keep the cold off my face.

Most of my life, I've tried to fit some mold or category. Now I realize that I will never make everyone happy. It's most important for me to be happy, even if that takes all that I've got. Many people catch onto this at an early age. I seem to be a slow learner.

At night, I watch the sky burn brilliant before it dims into evening. When a man's freedom is taken away, he looks for ways to reclaim at least a portion of it. I've reclaimed some of my freedom in the evening sky and the southern mountains. Sadly, I have come to find comfort in the razor wire and cement that surrounds me as well. This is my third time to prison in five years. I am slowly becoming institutionalized, a process that's been in motion for the greater part of my life.

Baby girl, I am fighting this world that I've found myself in. Sometimes I feel like there's no fight left in me. Then I look at your picture and I am reminded of why I've emerged from a slow death and reentered this life. Your smiling face is my strength.

I need you to know that I love you no matter what happens to me. My life is very unpredictable, and I am sorry you were born into my reality and not the world of some other more successful person. You will have to be strong to love me. I am here voluntarily, doing time to earn my right to be in your life. I will fight with every ounce of strength I have. I've realized that through surrender, I can win the battle. Always remember that. Victory takes on many different forms. If no one has told you today that they love you, please know that I do and I always will—no matter what happens.

October 5, 2002
Mom and Mick,

I am no longer in denial about going home in three months. I don't know why I was fighting it so hard. It *probably has to do with the fear that I didn't know I felt until I said so aloud during our last call. Life scares me; it always has. As I get older, I realize how unprepared I am to face what's in store for me on the outside. Although freedom is what I want most in this world, I am not sure I am capable of working, paying bills, making restitution, raising a child, and so on.*

I was hoping for pre-release so I wouldn't have to ask anyone for help. I've disrespected such gestures in the past. This system makes as much sense as the book I am recording for the Montana State Library. It's a driver's manual for the blind. Why would a blind person need to learn how to drive? Why would they release a convict with one hundred dollars in the middle of winter, with no job, and no home, and then expect them to be successful?

I recognized my fear of the world into which I was about to be released, and I recognized that I didn't have everything figured out. These might have been the two most important realizations I had ever made before being released from an institution. I didn't believe that my success was a given, as I had so many times before. My success could not be guaranteed by my desire to remain clean. With humility, I could build upon my spirit of willingness and surrender. The world seems to tell us that surrender is a bad thing; that in recognizing our weaknesses, we become less significant. In fact, the opposite is true for the addict. In surrender, I became better able to follow the guidance of those who had come before me. I could find a way out of the depths of addiction and depression, and discover a solution that has worked for so many addicts before me. For the addict, surrender means victory.

28

THE PRISON'S METAL DETECTOR LOOKED LIKE A picture frame, boxing in the smiles that met me as I walked out of the prison doors for the last time. There was no way to contain my joy. I had walked through fear and emerged on the other side into the arms of a woman I had come to love and respect over my months in confinement. In her arms, looking curious, and a bit unsure, was my precious Taylor. As I looked at her, I realized that I would have to take things slow; I could not push her to warm up to me. She knew me as well as I knew her, and our visits through the glass of the jailhouse visiting room did little to further our relationship. Her intimidation of me was minuscule compared to the intimidation I felt towards her. For a split second, I considered turning to run back through the prison doors.

"I am so glad you made it out," Jenny exclaimed as she placed a measured kiss on my cheek. "We didn't know if they would ever let you go." She winked then began to lead me into the free world. In several of her letters, she had stated very clearly that she was uncertain about our relationship. She was as hesitant as Taylor. I, too, longed to both hold and push them away. I couldn't blame them for looking at me as if, at any moment, I might steal their hearts and leave again. Instead of pushing, I allowed them to set the pace. I would follow wherever they might lead me—taming the wind that had blown me away so many times before.

"Are you ready to go home?" Her words came as a long-awaited promise. "I've been ready since the cell door closed behind me," I told her. I felt blessed beyond measure as I had people supporting and standing behind me despite my track record. The odds were against me. Most men released to parole walked out alone with a check for a bus ticket, a parole order, and fear of what the future held. Even the most well-intentioned people returned through prison's revolving door. Some in society hinder rather than support such men. I felt humbled by those who continued to support me, and I silently prayed that I could live up to their expectations. I was very lucky to have support from my mother and Mick, as well as Jenny and her family. Without their support, I would have been checking into a mission. Instead, I would soon be entering a one-bedroom apartment in Butte with a job and a recovery support system already in place.

Thank the Creator for those who look beyond the records of prisoners being released from our penal system. Thank the Creator for those who don't turn their gaze from the men searching for redemption. Thank the Creator for those who see within all of humanity the right to a better life regardless of their current circumstances or past afflictions. Some provide opportunity rather than turning their backs and dismissing others as unredeemable.

Butte welcomed me back with open arms, much as they had when I had arrived years before. The recovering community surrounded me and brought me back in as if I had never left. The restaurant where I had worked as a dishwasher hired me back as well. It seemed like I had been dropped back into my previous life with greater understanding and a sincere willingness to remain clean. In time, Jenny began to warm up to me again and we eventually moved in together. She'd taken a job as a manager and accountant in a local bar and casino. She spent her evenings running the business while I worked my way up the chain at the restaurant, and then went home to be with the kids.

"Eric, how do you feel about management?" I could not believe my ears. It had been just six months since my release and Jeff, the general manager, was offering me a position that seemed unattainable when I had started. "Well," I said slowly, "I'll have to talk to Jenny about it, but I am honored to be considered." There was a great deal to consider as we now had Jenny's son, who was seven, his cousin, who Jenny had taken in when her mother could no longer care for her, and Taylor. "Please consider it," Jeff said. "It would mean a temporary move to Missoula for training and then, after a few weeks, you'd return here to work under me."

Jenny and I both knew that opportunities like this didn't happen every day for ex-felons. In order to regain the credibility I had lost, I needed to begin rebuilding my life outside of the prison walls. For the next six months, I bounced between Missoula and Bozeman, training and working. I was not able to come home as quickly as we would have liked. In the restaurant world, the word "management" is used like a whore in the red light district. Managers are thrown every which way and are paid just enough to keep them coming back for more. "Jeff, you promised I would only be gone for a few weeks." Jeff had me in several respects: I was ambitious, desperate, and grateful for the opportunity. "Eric," Jeff said after my pleading had stopped, "we are perfect for each other. You need me and I don't need you nearly as much." That was, in fact, the truth, and although he laughed while he spoke, I knew that he meant every word. Despite my irritation, I knew that I had very little leverage. After a time—and without further protests—I finally returned home to the position I had been promised months before.

Shortly thereafter, Jenny and I began making plans for our wedding. With the salaries from both of our management positions, we were able to buy a family sized home in town. My dreams were finally becoming realities, and the thought of using didn't even register in the family world I had created. The thought of trading in my new life seemed impossible. My family meant more to me than anything. The images from the photographs I had so delicately taped to my cell walls were now living and breathing, framed by our days together. For the first time in many years, I felt at least partially complete. Though I could hear the fingers of depression tapping against the front door, I paid them no heed. I was able to hold it at bay by working extra hours. I avoided the many signs that my life was not as perfect as I had convinced myself that it was. I believed that if I ran hard enough and long enough, I could outrun my old nemesis. This seemed rational to a mind willing to face addiction superficially but not at the core. I was blinded by my fear of facing whatever prowled outside my door in the dark hours of the night. Something sought to drag me back into the misery of my former life.

In my attempts to make up for lost time through job advancement, I became blind to the needs of the very people I worked to support. A long time after the warmth of our bed had diminished, I realized that Jenny found what had been lost in our bed in the bed of another.

When I made the hesitant drive to Jenny's work at 3 am to face my fear, her words repeated in my head as if in torment: "My hours have changed at work." I found what had been scratching at my door. Jenny was not at work. The text she'd sent just minutes before had been a lie. "I am just about done, just finishing the tills."

I had never experienced anything as intense as the upheaval of everything I held precious and sacred. The notion of karma came to me as waves of emotion, emotion that would not leave me for many months. The actions of my past had returned to collect payment again. It began with the sharp pain of betrayal and ended in a rage that ultimately brought me back to her workplace to find the man she had chosen over me. Bartender's schedules are predictable, and I knew that if I waited in my truck, I could catch him as he walked to his car. I was no longer afraid of what lay behind the penitentiary walls. In many ways, I was better suited for prison than I was for the intense emotions I experienced without the aid of any chemicals.

"Where the fuck is he?" I asked as the workers streamed out of the bar. The look on my face and my tone of voice caused several of his coworkers to turn around, grab him by the arm, and drag him into the bar before I could get to him. I had decided that I wouldn't go back to prison alive. Although it no longer scared me, I understood that I would not be capable of living with myself if I took the life of another human being, even one involved in the destruction of my own life. The words, "When I get at you, I will kill you," followed him inside, less of a threat than a promise. His retreat into the casino saved him and me from a permanent solution, one born of passion, regret, deep sorrow, and rage. I was alone again, experiencing the emotions that Jenny had endured in my absence through her pregnancy. I believed that through aggression, I could somehow alleviate the pain from which I suffered. It didn't register that violence only enflamed pain, setting one on a course of self-destruction.

When I returned home that morning, I told my old lawyer of my plans to find and kill the man. Thomas, the same attorney who had been my court counsel for the escape charge, became my counsel in grief. He spoke to me as one who had also experienced great pain. His words would become my saving grace in the months to come.

"Go and hold your daughter before you make the decision to throw your life away. Get out of yourself and understand that it isn't about you anymore. It's about others. Are you so selfish that you'll willingly throw away all that you've worked for to satisfy an emotion that's only temporary?" I heard his words. Taylor's eyes held the promise of a different kind of life. Even though my dreams included a family different from the one I now had, I realized that Taylor was my family. I could not allow myself to give in so easily. As she had done before, simply by existing, my daughter brought me back to reason in a world that seemed so unreasonable.

Really, that was the conflict. My mind conspired against my conscience. As a result, I was left with a conflicted spirit, one that went from compassion to aggression, repeatedly. Reason became an afterthought as emotional upheaval began to rule through the ego, feeding off of each other like an abusive relationship. When I looked at my daughter, I could not do to others what my ego told me I must do. When I looked through eyes of pride and anger, anything seemed possible. Thomas was brilliant. He knew that in the innocence of my daughter and through the love that I felt for her, I could find a compromise within. I would remain in the land of the living and find a way to survive my great loss for one more day.

Betrayal is a gong that hammers at the soul, leaving a reverberation that lingers far beyond the initial impact. "I am leaving you." "I don't love you." "I am taking Taylor." I heard these words among many others. Some were spoken in hushed voices behind closed doors, and others were shouted, threats as we both fought for ourselves through the separation. All the resentment that Jenny felt as a result of my betrayal surfaced in a rage. I felt all the desperation she felt when I left her as I watched my dreams, formulated in incarceration deteriorating–our roles had reversed–karma. As the moving van pulled away from our empty home, the sound of the slamming door seemed magnified by the silence. I sat on the floor and sobbed until there was no feeling left. Then I sought oblivion.

Oblivion wears many different guises, all in shades of black. The tink of casino machines; the thrill of driving a truck at high speeds on curving country roads while drinking liquor; the flesh of a stranger pressed against my own; the feel of another's fist against my jaw; the fullness that comes of eating several day's worth of food in one sitting. These are only a few examples of the thousands of ways to avoid being present in one's life. My avoidance brought more misery, the opposite of what I believed it would do. I had no idea that what I did to myself was far worse than the feelings and the lessons that come with living one's life. Somewhere deep within, I knew that I would repeat this same experience repeatedly until I learned from it, and even that horror could not change my course. Chemically, my mind was altered again, and when this happened, tragedy ensued.

Work provided another place where I could avoid my circumstances, but the tears found me there. The silent head shakes of those who would rather look away than embrace confirmed that I was truly alone. Emotion is uncomfortable, especially if it stinks of decay from going unresolved. Could I blame others for not wanting to be a part of the darkness of my spirit? My daughter's professions of love when we were together broke up my sadness. "I love you daddy," she told me every time, followed by kisses that seemed to bruise as much as they soothed. I had returned to the world of the shadow walkers. It was a place where depression mingled with sin, and I stood on the precipice cursing the strings attached to my heart that kept me from jumping. Not only did the love for my daughter keep me in the land of the living, so did the love for my family. While I was an active participant in life, this love acted as a mortar for the foundation of the life I had been rebuilding. While seeking oblivion, it seemed like the steel and cement of a prison, far more oppressive than the one I had come out of only months before. I had only two options: seek help or use drugs again. Sadly, I chose the latter.

It was only a matter of time. I had quit going to recovery meetings and I stopped calling those who'd given me so much support throughout my incarceration. I stopped being honest with probation and parole, no longer attended mental health counseling, and stopped exercising, being in nature, and taking photos. I even stopped taking my daughter on the weekends. I was posturing for the end, and when this happened, my course was set. When my mother started to call due to my absence from her life, I was well on my way; the syringe had already drawn first blood. I had sought relief in the shadows, felt the relief of the initial rush, and then the misery returned tenfold. Death was near. I could smell it in my flesh again.

Ring, ring, ring, ring...Ring, ring, ring, ring...The calls would not stop, continuing hour after hour until I finally picked up the phone.

"I don't want to talk to you," I exclaimed irritably, holding the phone to my ear, shaking from the last shot of meth I had taken.

"That's fine, but you don't get to throw your life away this easily." Her words held very little emotion.

"Well, it's not your life. I can throw it away if I choose to." I felt like a six-year-old, arguing about having to clean my room.

"Actually, it's not your life. You gave up your right to be selfish the day your daughter came into this world and again when you told your loved ones you were committed to recovery."

I couldn't reply. My mother was just speaking aloud what I knew in my heart to be true. My self-destruction took place more out of habit than any belief system. Recovery had changed how I viewed the world; I could no longer fully invest in my total destruction. My heart was no longer in it. It took very little for my mom to convince me she should come spend time with me, to help me detox and get right again.

"I'll be there in three days. I need you to pick me up at the airport."

I promised I would be there as I hung up the phone and loaded another shot into the syringe. Quitting always seemed easier when I was loaded.

Even though I had made the decision to clean up again, my body protested, and I was not at the airport to meet my mother as promised. Three days later, I walked through the back door of my house to find her reading a twelve-step book, looking as calm as she ever had. She showed no reproach, although she was irritated. More, she stared as a mother seeing her sick child ravaged from a disease over which he had very little control. Compassion quickly replaced her frustration, and I felt safe falling into her arms numb from the months of use that had beaten me down and the pain in my heart left by a woman I loved who did not feel the same.

Because I had money in the bank, I had been able to fill my veins with numerous substances for months prior to my mother's arrival. Although I used meth daily, I also used opiates, barbiturates, cocaine, and anything else I could get my hands on. It was as though my addictive body sought some bizarre chemical equilibrium to make up for the many months I had been clean. This was especially dangerous as my head told me to use the same amounts I had used before. My mother spent the first day rubbing the dozens of knots out of my body, the result of dehydration and a lack of nourishment. I could barely move as a result of the lumps in my legs, back, neck, and arms. Chicken broth followed and I was only able to get down several spoonfuls at a time before I became sick. After food and vomiting, I took a bath then returned to address the knots. For hours, we repeated this process until my mother's exhaustion forced her to bed. First, she shared with me a section of the book she'd been reading.

"God, I offer myself to thee to build with me and to do with me as thou wilt. Relieve me of the bondage of self, that I may better do thy will. Take away my difficulties, that victory over them may bear witness to those I would help of thy power, thy will, and thy way of life. May I do thy will always."

With that, she turned to go to bed. Several minutes later, my mother walked out and said, "I will never come here again to help you get clean. I can't, for the sake of my own health. You know where to go to get the help that you need. All you have to do is ask and people will help you—preferably before you use, not after." Her kiss was light, as she left my room once more.

I spent the night alternating between groaning and standing on my kitchen counter, looking for shadow walkers and law enforcement in the night. Although reason told me that nothing was there, my paranoia prevailed. I spent a sixth consecutive night awake in terror before the sun rose and chased the shadows away. The shadows of the daytime never held the terror for me that the nighttime shadows held. For this reason, the warmth of the sun's rays coming through the living room curtains cloaked me in white as I faded into unconsciousness. I am not sure how long I slept, but when I came to, I felt hungry and showed some semblance of sanity.

The days that followed were filled with recovery meetings, bowls of homemade soup, and daily readings from recovery books that my mom seemed to pull from thin air. As I began to heal, both physically and mentally, she began to take the form of just another recovering person helping the next sick addict. She did very little for me, allowing me to return gradually to the responsibility of my life.

I couldn't remember the last time I had seen my daughter. Jenny, knowing how I acted when I used, refused to let me see her. Taylor was lucky to have one reasonable parent. I don't know how parents who are actively addicted take care of their children. I was incapable of keeping even a pet fed.

Shame and depression found me again. I would reenter recovery knowing what I had done and sacrificed as a result of my use and extreme selfishness. These were the burdens of use and recovery, and I had no idea how I could ever relieve myself of them. My mind told me that they were mine to bear as penance for the negativity I created in use. Recovery groups told me that I must be rid of them or I would eventually use again. Who was right? In my mind, I felt as though carrying this shame somehow repaid my debt—a lie perpetrated in order to abuse myself as though more pain meant I would feel better about it. Shame told me that there was no separation between my actions and who I am as a person.

The Creator told me that I was a precious child of earth and that the weight of the world did not rest on my shoulders. There was a difference between taking responsibility for one's actions and using ones action's to continue further self-abuse. True penance comes through realization, changing one's actions, and not repeating the same mistakes. The lesson lies not in the mistake itself but in taking responsibility for doing so without the weight of shame. I need to mix responsibility with humility and a compassion for myself, despite what my head tells me.

That is how I built myself back up despite society's rebukes. That is how I began to regain respect for myself and for others around me. I faced the wreckage and I began to sweep it into piles so that others could help me remove the debris from my life. In my spiritual work, I saw the devastation as an active participant in my own renewal; it was through this insight that I rebuked addiction's byproducts. I found value in the process and when I realized that I, myself, was the process, my self-esteem returned. It doesn't pay to shame those who struggle, even when their actions are deplorable. Shame ushers the injured along in their spiritual sickness. By building them up, helping them to take responsibility, we bring light into the universe and help to ensure that others don't fall prey to the same negative actions in the future. By showing compassion to even the most deplorable of humanity, we show compassion to all of humanity.

This approach doesn't take the addict off the hook. Instead, the addict is held more accountable to both themselves and their community. I took responsibility by creating a personal inventory with someone in the recovery program I attended. It resembled the one I had done years before with Laire on the beach and the one I had created in Montana's backcountry. In this inventory, I didn't explore the many years leading up to the present. Instead, we explored my choice to use, and the resentments and fears that allowed use to become an option again. I realized many things simply by looking at myself instead of others. My relationships took on a different meaning as I considered my own actions with respect to feeling resentment and fear.

Jenny's departure did not begin when she decided to pursue a physical and emotional relationship with another man. It began when I decided to pursue chemicals and another woman while she was pregnant. The gong that had hammered at my spirit hammered at hers as well, and the rising sound must have grown over the months leading her to seek her own remedy to its torment. Resentment is bread from anger and fear. How could I have expected her to simply bring me back into her life without putting a great deal of work into healing the damage I had created? She was only human.

With the realization that I had played the biggest part in our separation, the rage dissipated into sadness. In place of the emotion I tried to repress through drugs rested a compassion for the women who had given so much for a second chance. I should have thanked Jenny instead of blaming her. Her character brought me from the bonds of addiction to a world where I could participate in my daughter's life. For that, I will always be in indebted to Jenny, whether we're together or not.

I am not quite sure if it was during this process or after that my mother left. I do know that she and I sat next to each other in a recovery meeting and I watched her cry as she described how many family members she had buried as a result of addiction.

"I am giving my son to the people of Butte in recovery because I can no longer do for him what you can do. Actually, I've never been able to, and when I try, I become sicker than he is. If I could take five years of my recovery and give it to him, I would, but I know that in doing so I would rob him of the process that *is* recovery."

All eyes fell on us and I felt as though a contract had been signed in tears, honesty, and emotion.

"I will fly home tomorrow," my mother told those to whom she'd entrusted my care. "My faith will remain in the Creator who speaks through the men and women of these meetings. Please, love my son as I do."

With that, I stood and walked toward the door. I am not sure why love was so much harder to take than reproach, but it was. Before I could leave the meeting hall, a biker named Jimmy stood and cut off my exit with a tender hug. I had nowhere to go but into his arms. I had found home again and a family that would never turn their back on me. My mother passed my care to the recovery community in Butte, and in so doing she passed down an age-old tradition of wisdom and compassion through experience, strength, hope.

29

ADMITTING I HAD BEEN USING TO PEOPLE in recovery was one thing, but going to probation and parole was quite another. Taking responsibility went beyond simply acknowledging that I had gone astray to those who held very little sway over my future. For years, I pounded the idea into my consciousness that the state of Montana was against me. This belief had been punctuated by the slamming of doors and absurd sentencing guidelines. My experience taught me that outright honesty led to greater punishment with no promise of reward.

"Eric, your reward is not in whether or not you're sent back to prison. Your reward is a clear conscience and knowing that you've done everything in your power to amend the wrongs you've committed." This was shocking to hear, especially when it came from the mouth of a fellow recovering addict who'd also been in trouble with the law. "Facing our fears in complete faith is the objective of those who seek recovery from addiction through spiritual means." Tom had supported me through my incarceration by visiting, writing letters, and making phone calls. Again, he sat willing to walk me through yet another test of my faith in the judicial system, the Creator, and those who promised that taking responsibility would bring me the results I couldn't currently see.

Tom's comment "Facing our fears in complete faith..." echoed in my mind as I climbed the stairs to the probation and parole office. I had little choice. I could tempt fate and lie through my meeting with Michelle, or I could be completely honest and test this new hypothesis of faith.

"I relapsed." The words fell from my lips quicker than I would have liked. "I've been clean again for eight days and I've been working with my recovery mentor." Her face remained expressionless; a silence means to encourage more confession. "I lost my job, but I've been cutting firewood to make some money and I am looking for work every spare moment I can find." Jeff had been forced to fire me when I refused to come in for my shift during a binge. "I am very sorry that I've gone against the expectations of parole. I am prepared for whatever you decide." Did I really just say that?

"Eric, I am not just going to throw in the towel on you yet. You've shown me that you're willing to work hard at rebuilding your life. Your honesty today is an example of that continued commitment. I've known you were using for quite some time. I just wondered if you would lie to me or come clean. This town is small and the people here obviously care for you or I would never have found out the way that I did."

With that, Michelle established a clear cut set of expectations intended to hold me accountable for the things I had committed. Could this be real? Was I actually leaving her office without cuffs and a one-way ticket back to prison? Maybe faith in action wasn't just a theory; maybe it was more solid than the physical world around me even though I couldn't see it or touch it. Faith had existed to me as a philosophy until I experienced it firsthand; then I understood why it could not be quantified. Faith encompassed everything around me. It was the energy source of the Creator. The Creator existed through faith and faith alone. Consequently, faith was also the lens through which I could see a world free from ego's glare. Faith bonded me to the Creator. I needed to see faith applied to my life through something of consequence to realize as much. Faith as a philosophy made for great lip service, but it did little to build upon the foundation I so desperately needed. It wasn't until I practiced faith that I believed, without question, that making the right choice through action trumped all else—including fear and past experience.

As I stood to leave the office, I realized that Michelle's expectations weren't that different from the one's suggested by others in my recovery meetings: go to group meetings, don't use, find a job, make appropriate choices, and ask for help when help is needed. Michelle believed in me. That faith gave me a new respect for those working in the penal system. Michelle put a human face to the system I had rebelled against for so long. The monster that loomed over me, my suspended time, no longer looked so scary. Instead, it looked fair and compassionate, especially in my sincere and honest desire for change. Faith had paid off in ways that fear could not have. If I had gone in and lied, there is no doubt that I would have returned to prison. I had finally seen the payoff of complete disclosure. My paradigm shifted knowing that the system was on my side.

Butte is full of fiery Irish women whose sense of independence supersedes all else. When I saw Sue for the first time she intimidated me, and her flirtation made me blush, a rare occurrence. Sue was new to recovery, about six months in when we began to date. I had about thirty days clean, which should have been an indicator that I had more pressing things to address than pursuing a new love affair. Sue and I were perfect for each other. She needed a place to live and I had one. At once, I found myself in another intense relationship before I had given myself a chance to breathe after the last one.

Being in a relationship in early recovery was not intrinsically bad. The problem was my focus on issues around recovery was of paramount importance when coming back from a relapse. Relationships can take focus away from other, unresolved issues, which carried those issues forward into the new relationship. It was not a new lesson. I was in no position to be opening my heart to another woman before I had fully grieved the loss of Jenny. It was unfair to both of us. As was generally the case, I was able to justify anything to satisfy my base nature. The idea of healing from a previous relationship in the arms of another woman did little to respect the fragility of my own being, let alone the woman I was using in my rebound. Sexual healing sounds great in a Marvin Gaye song, but in real life, it just made my issues worse. Unfortunately, I often learned the same lesson a second or a third time before the information settled in. This was a natural spiritual progression, set in place for people who needed to understand further or who were simply slow learners.

On top of my physical attraction to Sue, I felt drawn in by her sense of humor, which bordered on profane. On many occasions, Sue's comments after too much coffee left those who knew her gasping for breath and fanning their blushing faces. She was an easy person to fall for, and in time, I felt as though my heart had rebounded. It was only a month after meeting that she moved in. Five months after that, our future together was sealed. "I am pregnant," she told me, as I walked in the door from work. We claimed to have planned it, but in reality, I am not sure either of us was ready for the consequence of our impulsive behavior.

Sometimes, the greatest gifts in life are the result of impulse and indiscretion. What was now forming in Sue was my next great blessing, and no less important than the first. In her pregnancy existed the possibility that I could live up to the promise I had made years before when I missed Taylor's birth. In recovery, I had the opportunity to be present in the lives of those for whom I was now responsible. In some ways, this action was an amends to my daughter, to her mother, and to me. Even though I could not pull back the hands on the clock, or change the rotation of the planets, I could prove that I was capable of being the man that I said I could and would be. Sue's fingers began to swell around her engagement ring and I understood the taste of bittersweet tears. In the growth of the human being within her body came the understanding that I had missed this stage before. This lesson felt so profound and I promised myself, sealing it in prayer, that I would never again be absent in the lives of either of my children, or their mothers, no matter what happened.

I cut firewood deep in the mountains surrounding Butte as a getaway. The separation from society gave me an opportunity to evaluate which direction I wanted my professional life to take. With faith as the catalyst and my Creator as the foundation, I hoped to build a family. My internal connection with the Creator multiplied as the beauty of creation surrounded me. The Creator filled my senses with every breath and glance. I found balance again, if only for the moment. Truly, I only had the moment. To prepare for the birth of my son and the wedding, I began to roof houses and do carpentry work along with logging firewood. In time, I received a job offer through a friend of a friend for work, which promised more money, and a better future than I currently had. I had built upon my circumstances, catapulting from one job to the next until I found the one that fit me best. Roofing in Big Sky, Montana proved to be the next ladder rung on my climb to success.

Many changes took place and my life transformed. My new job brought stability, and because both Sue and I were working, I was able to get another loan for a house. Our new home brought rekindled dreams of family and rosy-cheeked children climbing into bed with us. I had a good job, Sue was in her last stages of pregnancy, and we shared in the joy of seemingly endless possibilities. The illusion was complete.

"Would you like to cut the umbilical cord?" The nurse's words were lost in the moment as I lovingly stared at the woman who had endured so much to bring our child into this world. The nurse offered me a seat before I could pass out. I felt as if I would burst with joy. For the first time in my life, I was speechless. Through the birth of my son BJ, came my rebirth. In that moment, I experienced the most profound expression of love that the Creator could ever have given humankind.

Is it possible to fall in love with five different people all at once? In that moment, my love was redefined, realized, and redistributed. For Sue, I felt an intimate love. My love for Jenny shifted, erasing past conflicts and replacing them with admiration and compassion for a woman who had sacrificed so much for so many. Toward BJ and Taylor, my love radiated in its perfect form: unconditional in every sense of the word. The fifth was yet more profound, and in this reformation, I felt love for myself, an expression that had been lost over my many years of abuse. Self-love, no matter the interpretation, transformed a previously callous man into a soft spirit, one who acquiesced to the beautiful things in life. For once, I believed that I deserved the blessings of my life, not based on merit, but by simply participating as a spiritual being. Karma worked both ways, and at some point a scale tipped and I began to reap light from the light I had begun to bring into the world. My past mistakes were not wiped away. Rather, in the moment, I radiated that which I had finally given to the world.

I looked at myself in the same way that I looked at my son and my daughter, as they looked at their father, as my parents looked at me, and as the Creator looked upon all of its creation. I experienced balance. I existed free from attachment, yet fully attached. BJ came into the world at around 6 pm on March 22, 2006. In that miracle, faith bolstered what had already been building. Nothing could have diminished my elation.

After BJ's birth, my life began to lose its equilibrium again. My work required a four-hour commute in addition to the eight-to ten-hour workday. I woke at 4 am, left the house at 5 am, only to return home at 7 pm for dinner and bed. I had quickly risen to number three in the company thanks to my consistency and strong work ethic. As the work multiplied, so did my responsibilities. In no time, I had set aside the things that had ensured my emotional and spiritual balance in favor of my new obsessions: production and productivity. I was good at what I did and I had a mind for business. We had over twenty employees and a large portion of the management fell under my control. The pay was good, but with more money came more compromise in other areas of my life. Weekends became my recovery time while children ran loose in the house. I slept the weekends away in an attempt to be fully charged for the workweek. Depression was ever present, and instead of its usual manifestation, it appeared as bursts of anger, frustration, anxiety, and emotional disassociation.

"Eric, I am taking BJ and I am moving in with Julianne." Julianne was BJ's godmother and a mutual friend of ours. "I don't want to be with you anymore. I don't want to get married." I was in shock. Sue's words were the exact words I had heard from Jenny on the day that I confronted her about her affair. In my pursuit to better our circumstances and provide for our family, I had failed to realize that our relationship was suffering. Her words came swifter than any punch to the gut, and my only response was silence. She left the house with my six-month-old son on her hip. The grand illusion fell to pieces as I realized that I failed in another relationship, largely due to my inability to develop deep emotional bonds with others. Such bonds did exist, yet demonstrating them beyond sexual acts had been one of my great failings. Due to abuse, trauma, and betrayal, I failed to warm up to those closest to me. As a result, I watched another love walk through the door never to return.

The immature often find ways to make villains of those that they leave to justify such a decision. I believed every word that Sue said, as I had often been the cause of such discord. I took full blame for being unavailable given work and my melancholy spirit when I was home. Her complaints were reasonable and I had hoped they could be resolved. Considering our children, our home, and the love we had professed, it seemed a shame to simply give up without a fight. The several sessions in counseling we did before she left did very little to change the outcome.

My hopes were dashed when the man she left me for got out of her father's truck to pick up her belongings a week later. "I'll be taking the TV," he demanded, pushing his way through me and into my living room. "If you don't leave my house right now, I will hurt you." I intended to assault him without my kids' knowledge. Taylor was staying with me and the last thing I wanted to do was bring her into any violence. I asked Sue's father to take my kids and remove them from the scene. Sue's father didn't move. The people who had been my friends now became neutral. I couldn't understand how in the course of a couple of months, love could diminish and be replaced by bitterness. Tears were fought back as threats were exchanged. The man threatened to slit my throat in the darkness of night. This elevated an already tense situation.

My saving grace was my daughter's confused looks as she worked to make sense of the madness taking place in front of her. She, too, loved Sue, so the separation had touched her gentle spirit in much the same way it had touched my own. My rage magnified a deep sorrow within, and the gong that had been the pounding of my spirit not three years before with Jenny, began to sound again. I understood that rather than resolving our conflict maturely, Sue had run to another man, a choice that rubbed salt into my emotional wounds. What hurt the most was the knowledge that Sue knew how profoundly affected I had been by the betrayal I had experienced before. Despite that fact, she had chosen to exit through the same door.

Sue's boyfriend was a biker club "hang around"; as such, he was affiliated with a group of men who would back their people to the end. I had to think out a measured response. Although I had Taylor to care for, threats had been exchanged. My experience had taught me that it was better to act first than to be caught unaware, especially when children were involved. The fact that he was in a club didn't intimidate me. I had my own affiliations and knew the biker world quite well. My prison mentality had slowly been slipping away but in the moment flashed back in full force.

Jimmy, from my recovery group, had always been a sympathetic ear. I knew that I could talk to him and that he would hold in confidence to his dying breath whatever I chose to share. I trusted him like no other. He was also a member of a well-known outlaw biker club; he understood their politics. "I am going to hunt him down and kill him," I told Jimmy. "I will dump his body where no one will ever find it." I was not the type to make threats lightly and these threats didn't come in a rush of emotion; this made the situation even more critical. I had removed emotion and reason from the equation, and then reentered a world where numbness prevailed. I had decided that I would try to cover up the crime for the sake of my children, but if I failed, God help anyone who tried to take me from them. Sanity departed with the trauma of betrayal. I still loved Sue and I would not harm her. Both the best and the worst gift she had given me in her betrayal was a man towards whom I could direct all of my rage.

"Eric, I am not going to try to change your mind," Jimmy responded. "A man has a right to avenge a wrong in whatever way he sees fit, but let's have a talk about this first. I am glad you found me because this can be delicate, especially when dealing with bike clubs." I understood full well what I was getting into. I had fallen victim to a group of bikers many years before, and the rage that I felt for the men back then fed what I now experienced. Every betrayal to which I had been a victim played out in my head repeatedly, reinforcing a belief that I was a flawed human being, unworthy of love and fidelity. Shame led me to take full responsibility for her poor choices. This did not come from a spirit of taking responsibility for one's own actions. It came from blaming myself for the shortcomings of others and believing that I deserved to be treated with irreverence

Jimmy tried to warn me. "If you do this, you are inviting the same kind of retaliation upon yourself. You have children to consider. What Sue did was not your fault. She chose her own path. I am sorry you had to go through that. Throwing your life away over this is foolish. There are better ways of paying those back that have done you wrong. Do right and love your children. Help others and respect yourself. If you wake up in the morning and still decide you want to do this, there are ways to make it happen. Promise me this, though. Talk to the Creator and maybe you will wake up in the morning with a clearer perspective." I promised to follow Jimmy's advice then went to a recovery meeting uncertain of what the following day might bring.

"Creator, forgive me for I have been resentful, selfish, dishonest, and afraid today. Help me to not keep things to myself, but to discuss my issues openly with another person. Show me when I owe an apology and help me to make it. Help me to be kind and loving to all people. Use me in the mainstream of life. Remove worry, remorse, and morbid reflections so that I may be of use to others."

These were the reluctant words I offered up to my Creator as I entered my empty bed. By going to the meeting, I had set myself up to purge my soul despite myself. Everyone there knew both Sue and me. No sides were taken; only suggestions were given regarding how to keep my side of the street in order. These people understood the tragedy and triumph of the human condition. They knew that when dealing with such intense emotion, life was ultimately held in the balance. The addict who chose to use chose to die. Resentment left unresolved would fester and, in time, it would create a spiritual cancer that would eat away at the bond between the Creator and me. My spiritual realm would cease to exist and I would fade into the shadows again, at the mercy of whatever horrors awaited me.

When my eyes opened to take in the world around me, I followed through with my promise. I didn't know where my day would take me but this was my prayer. "Creator, make me a channel of thy peace, that where there is hatred, I may bring love; that where there is discord, I may bring harmony; that were there is error, I may bring truth; that where there is doubt, I may bring faith; and that where there are shadows, I may bring light." The words reverberated through my soul until nothing was left but a humming. Had my prayer described the shadows and the light? Had I just described my solution to the world of the shadow walker? Was it possible that by simply asking my Creator, I could avoid walking in the world of the shadow once more? Words hold great power, and when they are humbly offered to the Creator of our understanding, their power is magnified and etched into our being. "...That where there is sadness, I may bring joy. Creator, grant that I may seek to comfort, and then to be comforted; to understand, and then to be understood; to love, and then to be loved. For it is by forgetting oneself that one finds. It is by forgiving that one is forgiven. It is by dying that one awakens to eternal life."

I was not only responsible for my own well-being; I was responsible for showing compassion towards those against who I felt bitterness. I could not find all that I sought in life unless I was willing to place all others ahead of myself. This did not mean putting others ahead of me when it was easy to do so; it meant doing so when things became difficult. I was experiencing great difficulty. To forgive meant trading vengeance for compassion. It meant forgiving that which brought about the most painful experiences in my life. I no longer looked at Sue as the victimizer; instead I saw her as the victim of her own selfishness and my inability relate to her on an emotional level. She had done more damage to herself than she could ever have done to me. The shame of betrayal was now her burden; I shed that burden through the realization that what had been done was not done to me.

I felt a compassion for Sue that resembled the compassion I felt for Jenny in the wake of our separation. How could I love someone then simply turn it off? I could not. It was only natural to follow the words of the prayer of Saint Francis and show love, forgiveness, and compassion, not only to Sue but also to the man I had been blaming for my own misgivings. Was it possible that in one night of prayer I could have gone from homicidal to compassionate? It had less to do with me, and more to do with a simple willingness to do as others suggested, trusting in their wisdom when I had no confidence in my own. How could I ever wish to be forgiven my faults if I was unwilling to forgive the faults of others in my life? The world of the spirit seemed to be a world of opposites, yet they were opposites that worked. By pushing my ego aside and placing the well-being of others ahead of my own, it allowed me to take care of my own. I had been sent here to give to others. That was the promise I had made prior to my own birth, and I had inadvertently recited its truth through prayer just moments before.

Truth cannot easily be argued away. Instead, truth embeds itself and then dictates our path in life, stronger than any wind or whim. I was sealed to my truth. I felt freed from anger and I no longer wished ill will towards anyone, including myself. The promise of a life well-lived came into existence at a time when it appeared that I had lost everything. I had finally learned the one lesson I had been missing: Place the needs of others ahead of my own in the spirit of love and compassion. In so doing, the Creator's grace will spill forth and touch the lives of all who I encounter. As such, I will enter the world of light over the world of shadows. I will become a part of a world of sentient beings, expressing love through action and transforming shadow walkers into bearers of light.

It was a choice. I had made the choice to change the course of my life for good. This did not mean that I could avoid addressing the pain of rejection. It meant that I was willing to address the things that scared me most through intense work. As with all transformations, timelines are never set in stone, and where one lesson is learned, two more take the place of the previous. In time, Sue and I were able to come to an agreement regarding our son. What had been bitterness became a desire to work out our differences. We both had the guidance of a trusted recovery community who would help us do so with civility and dignity. As is human nature, we were not perfect in this endeavor, but we worked for the benefit of our child. In so doing, we healed wounds that might otherwise have continued to fester.

Instead of building upon this spiritual experience, I returned to the path I had been following before our separation. Spiritual experiences and insight thrive only within those who practice them. I had an understanding of the things that had helped me navigate through difficult experiences in my life; but once those experiences passed, I returned to a belief system that seemed to pay greater dividends in the physical realm than hard work would in the spiritual realm. For some, the physical realm is a safer place because it requires less internal exploration, freeing them from the difficult emotional work required in such a commitment. I could not live comfortably in the physical without the spiritual. Without the emotional exploration that came through spiritual living, and without proper medication, I repeatedly fell into a cycle of deep depression, short relapse, and emotional ostracism.

Depression seemed to throw a blanket over my spirit, causing the things that filled my soul to diminish. It made me feel as though I had been left with a hole that used to be filled with the things that made life worth living. The sound of my children's laughter no longer touched my heart as it once had. The beauty of a sunset bursting behind the mountains no longer sparked my spirit the way it once had. Because I had once felt in awe of such things, their absence felt like lashes against my flesh and soul. This was my affliction.

When depression worked me over, the force of God diminished. Instead of being filled with life's driving force, my body became a void. When I reached this point of despair, the shadows of life became my comfort. Sleeping for long periods of time; isolating myself from a world that frightened me; pouring in chemicals until all feeling dissolved; watching in the mirror as weight accumulated on my bones. These were all byproducts of a search for comfort. Sadly, my solutions further fractured my soul rather than soothing it. Giggles became torment instead of bliss. Nature's promise became a place out of reach, as I could not leave the darkness of my despair. I had entered a different kind of wilderness. The subtle irritability that grew to become a dark spiral of rage surfaced in ways that pushed those I loved away. This made my feelings of shame greater, which forced me further from the very people who held the key to my relief.

The scolding voices rattled in my head. *What is wrong with him...If only he would try harder...If he would just open up...He's missing the point...What an asshole...He needs more Jesus in his life...He knows where the solution is...Depression is all in your head...Man up...He's so dramatic...He's nothing but damaged goods...* The echoes added to the shame of a man possessed by a disorder dictated by his brain. The disease blocked my drive to do the very things that would have lifted me from my torture and delivered me to reality.

I lived in a constant state of guilt. Despite doing all the things that recovery suggested—meetings, service work, prayer, school, being a father, abiding the law, showing kindness, feeling compassion, expressing love—I continued to suffer emotionally and spiritually. This guilt was made worse when people around me said or insinuated that I was therefore doing something incorrectly. Some believed that if I did something differently, I could eliminate a condition that was etched into the very fabric of my being. This condition formed a pattern so complex that healers puzzled over how to create relief for the multitudes of people who pleaded for some sort of reprieve. Then I was punished for finding my own relief and then losing control. Using chemicals, I numbed all of my symptoms of depression such that affliction knocked but failed to come in.

As adolescence gave way to adulthood, the shadows grew larger, the struggle amplified, and the solution seemed frozen below the surface of an ice-covered pool; I could see it, but I could not reach it. The stakes became much higher as tiny souls looked up with their innocent eyes, a daily reminder that I had to hold on. Their rays of love became my beacon shining through the haze of a mind that distorted reality. When I wanted to cry out, I retreated within to a place that was not comfortable but which I knew well. I believed that retreat sheltered me and helped me to survive my sordid past.

When my soul emptied itself, I felt renewed for a time, and then the darkness would again descend. For some who suffer from depression, emotion flows like a river, growing stronger all the time. In my case, emotion roiled in the depths, agitating, festering, and then surfacing only when the pain grew so severe that it had to release. It exploded to the surface in the confines of my isolation, in the anonymity of late hours.

My loved ones saw me in the grip of my depression, but because of my silence, they were unaware of my daily struggle. The same despair that many addicts endure at the end of their addiction is the despair with which I lived with no bottle or drugs to blame it on. Instead, my depression manifested itself during times of its own choosing, uninvited and unwanted, ravaging the life I had rebuilt over and over. My hands ached from remolding the sands into castle walls to protect my heart from the unseen conqueror.

I am not the only one who suffered from this. I could see it reflected in the eyes of many people around me, and I empathize because there were so many out there who endured the same things that I did. Their voices were also muted, wanting to reach out but propelled by an internal force far more powerful than their desire to be understood.

For me, living with mental health conditions required applying holistic approach. This necessity stacked the odds against me. Small windows of opportunity revealed themselves between the bouts of depression, use, and overworking that allowed me to begin the difficult work of creating balance. Seizing the opportunities was especially difficult as doing so went against the depressive episodes to which I often succumbed. This where the spiritual component entered the equation. The world of the spirit has the force and the ability to cross the physical restraints of this world to effect change in the willing. Time in the spiritual plane does not follow the same rules to which it must adhere in the physical realm. This is why prayers may be answered years later.

My connection to the spiritual world could only be possible by living in the present. Presence of mind and focus on the now allowed the flow of the spirit within me to transcend in any direction. The past encompassed regret, sadness, anger, and resentment. The future held fear and apprehension. The world of the spirit could not live in such inhospitable environments. It needed faith, hope, forgiveness, and compassion to work its "miracle" in my ravaged life. These things did not come of pounding a nail or completing of the next project. They were the result of time taken to stop, breathe, and place importance on things beyond sight, smell, touch, and taste. I could only effect change by being in the physical present, allowing the world of the spirit to flow through me and into the streams of a spiritual past, present, and future.

My last relapse forced open a window of opportunity, and when I saw it, I felt ready and willing to jump through. The window opened neither out of regret, nor out of fear. Opportunity presented itself in a moment of intense emotion for which I happened to be present. My life had always consisted of putting out fires, rather than preventing them. I never seemed to be able to get ahead of the depression curve, and when I came close to seeking a solution, mania would emerge, telling me everything I had ever been told was a lie. Not only did I tell myself I was not afflicted, society told me the same. I could justify my own denial using the denial of the world around me, a world that believed that people like me created their own difficulties. This was a world that swore that biological and genetic components—though eventually proven—did not exist.

"Please, help me. I can't do this any longer and I am afraid I will end my life if there is no resolution to my affliction." When my denial dissipated in the face of acute depression, I lost all control. Only those who have experienced this can understand. I did not have a solution. When it came to drug addiction, I had learned to set aside my ego to acknowledge defeat; this allowed me to receive and accept the insight and wisdom of others who had gotten clean before me. When it came to mental health issues, I had not come to the place where I could set aside my shame of being a "flawed" human being, tainted in the Creator's failed design. I did not see perfection in myself and in this, shame multiplied.

The psychologist sat quietly listening to me as I verbalized the last secrets I had kept in my life. The acknowledgment of my self-hatred brought long awaited answers. By facing my great nemesis—self—I would be able to come to terms with the conditions from which I suffered and over which I had little to no control. My only means of control was to be honest, willing to learn, and complicit in following the directions of doctors who placed as much stock in my case as the Creator who had brought me to this point. Somehow science and faith had to merge; and in that union, a miraculous reaction could occur, destroying even the strongest argument made by those who would chastise the relevance of such claims. The doctor described my previous cycles.

"Your history has been to take the medication until you feel good and then to stop taking them. In so doing, you've created more problems than you've solved. Not only do you become emotionally confused, your brain's balance is in a constant state of disarray. Just when there is hope to achieve balance, you cut your knees out from under you, finding justification in a flawed belief system and societal pressures. Listen to me. You will never fully recover unless you accept the fact that you have severe chemical imbalances. The proper medications can alleviate the torturous mental and emotional deficiencies you've endured throughout your lifetime."

The psychologist wasn't telling me that I was a bad person. She was telling me that I had a set of issues that must be addressed in order for me to find relief. I could live on the perpetual emotional roller coaster, or I could medicate my brain to give it what it needed for balance. The latter would give me a chance at survival. This approach did not address my issues with relapse; it simply allowed me the same chances of success as the rest of the addicted world. She was not giving me a cure to anything; she was simply giving me my legs back, a fighting chance to finish the race. The rest of the work would be up to me.

It was not until I embraced surrender over my addiction that I found victory. It was not until I experienced complete hopelessness that I experienced hope. Each experience in my life provided a new spiritual truth, allowing me to grow. All I needed was to remain willing. This did not mean that my life became a picture of perfection—far from it. Even in the throes of use, I moved down a victorious path, willingness being my only necessity to remain. When hope was gone and willingness dissolved, the shadow walkers entered and my light diminished.

The man on the street with soiled clothing and a bottle of whiskey is not at a lower spiritual level than the guru speaking to millions; this falsehood diverts the masses from a true understanding of the spiritual world. This lie is the very thing that keeps people from realizing their true spiritual potential. The whiskey in the bottle is every bit as necessary to the spiritual experience as the holy water sprinkled on a newborn. Truth is everywhere—on a flower petal, in a doodle on the bathroom wall, or amid a plea for help to the stars above.

The day I placed the two medications that the doctor had prescribed into my mouth, swallowing with a prayer, my life began to change. I felt as though I had been given a new pair of eyes through which to see. I had no idea how severe my mental health issues had become until I had a taste of life without the extremes I had experienced from depression, PTSD, and ADD was like. The medication was designed to address particular symptoms. The first medication was an anti-seizure medication used to treat mixed episodes and mania in those who suffer from bipolar disorder. The intensity of the mania I experienced varied. When it surfaced, evidence could be seen in delusions of grandeur, suspiciousness, catatonic behavior, aggression, and a preoccupation with thoughts and schemes that led to compromised states such as illicit drug use, gambling, and heightened sexual behavior. When these bouts occurred, my life crumbled. Further, my mania often manifested as intense agitation, another form of aggression.

The second medication I used, which offered some of the greatest relief, was used to treat numerous mental health issues including depression, PTSD, and ADD. Within three months, I experienced improvements in almost all areas. Hyper-focus, mood swings, agitation, nightmares, flashbacks, and many other issues that had plagued me at different times throughout my life became non-existent. Since beginning to take these medications, I have not experienced a single severe depressive or manic episode. I have also avoided any return to active use. This does not mean that I am immune to the pitfalls of being a human in recovery. It simply means that I am balanced enough to remain clean due, in part, to the use of medications designed to address the very issues with which I was diagnosed.

The holistic approach went far beyond mental health counseling and medication. In my first six months of recovery, I quit smoking and have not picked up a cigarette in over five years. My previous attempts and prayers to quit had all been unsuccessful. Then one morning between sleep and consciousness I heard a clear, non-gendered voice tell me, "You are done." I knew immediately what the voice was referring to, and from that moment on, I've been smoke-free. The entity that answered my prayers eliminated any cravings or withdrawals. As the balance of one area in my life began to improve, so did the balance of other areas; they all seemed reliant on the others like a spiritual ballast. Health begets health, and as I began to feel better emotionally, I became empowered to improve in other aspects of my life. This is also true in reverse, as poor choices and bad health combine to create a downward spiral as well.

Over the years, I have slowly begun to address the issues that led me down that long and tortuous road. Each resolution provides the strength to tackle the next issue. This is how the light has begun to manifest, and when light permeates the spirit, it becomes increasingly difficult for darkness to take root. Poor choices have given way to good choices. Shame has given way to self-forgiveness and a renewal of my spirit. Now I am both content and willing to do the hard work to ensure my continued growth. I face my feelings and confront the things that scare me most, knowing that the shadows have lost their power.

30

MY SELF-ESTEEM AND SELF-RESPECT ARE NOT products of the material world. They are the result of the hard work that I've put into rebuilding and redefining who I am as a person. A nice vehicle, a large house, and the dollar amount of my paychecks have never done for me what acting with selflessness and improving the world has. Sure, the material things are a nice byproduct of hard work, but they are not the channels for change that I've needed to continue on the path of recovery. That's why placing emphasis on career advancement actually made me sicker mentally, emotionally, and spiritually. The belief that more hard work can solve most problems did not apply in my case. My life challenges went far beyond anything that a job or money could fix.

I believe that it's important for me to be as specific as possible about the things I've done to remain clean, to stay out of prison, and to function as an active participant in the lives of my loved ones. My path may not be the path taken by others. I respect that difference because I understand there are many paths to the top of the mountain. Following a holistic approach to life, I needed to address four areas of my life on a daily basis to remain emotionally, spiritually, mentally, and physically in balance. For years, I didn't understand that deficiencies in one area affected the other areas in profound ways. I found that when my weight slowly began to increase, I made no connection to my poor sleeping habits, lowered self-esteem, lack of exercise, poor nutrition, lowered inhibition, and lack of spiritual motivation. In fact, deficiency in one area created a snowball effect, which made achieving total balance across all areas of my life much more difficult. As time went by, I could not address the precipitating factors because deficiencies in other areas had become so critical. My attention shifted to addressing the symptoms rather than the issues that triggered those symptoms.

I had reached a point in my recovery where not using drugs or alcohol was simply not enough to keep me excited about abstinence. There had to be more. In many ways, coming into recovery beaten and deficient in all areas was easier than being in recovery and realizing that I was not much better off than when I first got clean. Staying clean simply wasn't enough for me to continue moving forward. To rest on my laurels, even for one day, could have a negative impact on my behavior that would affect me months down the road. For a recovering addict also battling mental health issues, this ripple effect could become a recipe for catastrophe.

In the years I've been living on my own, I've become overwhelmed by the realization that my relapses, issues with food, weight, and mental health all needed to be addressed at the same time.

My broken relationships with Jenny and Sue served as catalysts for this change. I drew upon the pain of their leaving as motivation to move forward with my life. In time, pain didn't provide the necessary motivation for long-term, consistent change either. That was a problem. I needed another motivator. Fear and pain worked in small bursts, but the things that proved to be the most powerful sources for continued success remained my hope for the future, a love for myself and others, and my compassion for all things in the physical and spiritual realm. I knew very little about such things. As always, I relied upon myself to produce that which comes from the world of the spirit. I fooled myself into believing that spiritual manifestations came from outside of me.

Some of the religions I had investigated taught that the manifestation of spirit came as a result of turning one's will over to their version of the Creator. This line of thinking seemed to require very little footwork and a lot of lip movement. They seemed more concerned about my souls' departure and where it might end up then the hands on reparation of a life lived in self-will. I was interested in the spiritual light produced by internal work that could be used to become more selfless and compassionate here on Earth.

When I came into recovery, I found it easiest to relate to the negative experiences of others, as the positive experiences seemed so foreign to me. I trusted them because the stories they told proved that they had endured what I had endured. Relying on that trust, many would try to convince me that there was another way to live. These people didn't do so to gain money, fame, or even to gain dominance over others. They did it because they knew that helping others would ensure their own recovery. It is a spiritual truth that in doing for others, we also do for ourselves. This magic elixir had staying power for me. In the success of others, my success grew. I simply needed to reframe what success meant to me. I was no longer taking from the world—I was giving back to it.

The idea of giving began to take on many forms. The more compassion I gave, the more compassion I received. It fed itself and I enmeshed myself in a community of recovering addicts who placed others before themselves. As I watched others around me grow away from their defects of character, I gained trust in the recovery process and an enthusiasm for my own potential as a human being. I was like a child again in many ways. Dewdrops on flower petals regained the magic they'd held when I was young. My life experience only added to my appreciation for the amazing beauty visible around every turn.

I was finally willing to take action, fueled by my love of the Creator, my children and my family, the beauty of the world around me, and my improved self-esteem. Every time I made a healthy choice, I improved myself in all aspects. Every time I chose to help someone rather than fulfilling my own selfish desires, the balance shifted, and the world of the spirit and the world of the physical converged. I could feel the union and it began to reflect in how I treated others and myself.

When I wanted to sleep my life away, I got up, called a friend, and participated in life despite my personal desire. When I wanted to use chemicals, I went to a meeting and allowed the experiences of others to strengthen me, exchanging hopelessness for hope. Every time I had to walk into probation and parole on Main Street, I held my head up knowing that I was no less of a person for entering those doors. In fact, I was a better person for being honest and sincere.

This change of character and spiritual way of living became critical. In balancing the four areas of my life, I placed the greatest emphasis on spirituality. I believed that in the spiritual world, perfect balance always exists, whether that spiritual balance registers in my life or not.

The book of life had already been written, and in it, I was a spiritual being even when I wasn't aware of that fact. My spiritual needs were always taken care of; even when I chose to do things that destroy the spirit, I was always protected. My spirit may have faded, but my soul had not changed. My presence in the realm of the spirit was whole and unaltered—it was my spirit that had been bruised and battered, emitting a dimmer light. Nothing could damage my soul, not even the lie of eternal damnation; the Creator was too full of love and compassion to allow such a thing. I had been told lies for too long; trying to initiate change through fear only creates more fear and less faith. My spiritual growth erased those lies as I came to understand that I would always be a part of the great union between the Creator and the universe that it created—they were one and the same. This meant that the Creator lived within me as well.

My admission of faith resulted in a variety of work to be done: work on myself through therapy, working with others who suffer, changes of diet, setting aside time for exercise, doing that which fills my spirit, eliminating damaging substances from my life, taking medication for my mental imbalances, and above all else, loving myself and others around me to the best of my ability. Perfection exists in the imperfections of this world. When I quit expecting perfection from others or from myself, I discovered this to be so. In the eyes of the Creator, I am on equal ground with the rest of humanity; I am no better and no worse than anyone else. I am simply a part of the whole. This came as a great relief and enabled me to find a niche in society in which I can be successful.

Daughters are amazing, and through Taylor, I have learned to respect women in a way that I hadn't for many years. Ultimately, every woman is someone's daughter. I began to see reflections of my daughter in the women around me. Instead of sexual objects, they became living, breathing, complex individuals that had more to give than physical pleasure. Would I want my daughter to be treated the way that I had treated many women in my life? Would I want men to look at her as an object rather than a sensitive, unique, and precious being? No! Forming a relationship with Taylor put me on the hook to be emotionally available to her and to others, the intimacy of which scared me. I had always run from emotional intimacy. I couldn't run from Taylor; I have a responsibility to be a father to her.

I had been given the opportunity to heal through the people in my life. Guidance doesn't always come in verbal form. Watching my children grow and develop has given me the privilege to review my own life. In respecting them, I walk back in time and show myself compassion when I needed it the most. As mentioned previously, prayer and positive thinking travel through time, eliminating the notion of past and future. Through the love I feel for my own children, I also love the small boy in me who lived in fear and could not turn to others because he'd learned that honesty would not help him. My healing took place retroactively. I began to understand that the acts of those in my past could not affect my present any longer. By showing compassion to my children, I reached back in time and held myself closely, stroking the head of a child who sought relief from a nightmare. Every hug I gave to my children was also an embrace for my childhood self.

I've had many allies in my life and without them I never would have made it this far. Probation and parole deserve credit for willingly walking me through some of the most difficult times in my life. They never gave up on my potential. The people who work within the system rarely receive the credit they deserve from the people they work with. Rather than being thanked for the support they provide for ex-cons, they are often blamed when the ex-con makes a poor choice that could result in their return to prison. The men and women with whom I have worked clearly do not enjoy this part of their job. It is never easy to take mothers and fathers, sons and daughter, and family members from their loved ones. Their recompense comes from the understanding that their difficult choices protect others from the potential dangers of those who have victimized in the past, including themselves.

I've never been thrown back in jail for remaining abstinent or going to my daughter's ballet practice. I have never been disciplined for being active in recovery and being a responsible member of society. Every time I blamed "the man" I did so because I had not acted in accordance with my release conditions. I learned to make probation and parole my allies, and in so doing, I took responsibility for my own life rather than living as a victim of my choices.

I decided to abandon the code of ethics that existed within the walls of prison. I no longer remained silent when I saw people victimizing others. I no longer stood on the sidelines when victimizers took advantage of those unable to fend for themselves. In silence, I had been a mute participant through inaction. The convict code ensured a return to its nightmare, lying by telling me the system was against me. It said silence is critical and that includes allowing others to know who I was as a person. In truth, the more people who knew and understood me, the more solutions they could offer when I needed their help the most.

Today, my thoughts and my behavior must reflect my current environment; this will keep me out of prison. Now,

I must remain calm and humble when my former self would have reacted in retaliation. If or when issues arise, I call the police and allow them to address issues. More importantly, I do not remain quiet when the actions of others could hurt those incapable of taking care of themselves. I will no longer remain silent in the face of abuse.

I learned these lessons from probation and parole as well as others who remained outside of the system despite all odds. They experienced a complete shift in how they viewed the prison system; as a result, they never returned to it. Instead of ruining my life, prison saved my life. Had I not been separated from use, I would have died like so many of my friends.

Leaf provides a good example of this. Several years ago, I received a call from my old friend. Since the night of our incarceration, he'd continued to use. He wanted to know how I had remained clean from heroin and meth for so long. He asked if I would be willing to help him get clean. I made my way up to Whitefish, excited that a friendship I had formed through use might lead to his recovery. We went to several recovery meetings together and discussed how I had managed to remain on the right path for so long. We laughed till we cried. I shared stories of my children and described the many reasons why recovery became far more valuable than anything I could've put into a syringe.

I understood Leaf's torture as he drank glass after glass in the bar while we discussed how wrong it was to do so. I understood his desire to show his family the person they once knew. Beyond his rough exterior, Leaf still had hopes and dreams. In those beliefs, anything was possible. We created an action plan that entailed detox, treatment, or recovery meetings. We discussed our days together and laughed about how we'd barely made it through alive. We hugged and called each other brother, knowing that we'd experienced life in a way that few ever would. I saw worth in Leaf that others don't possess. His heart was much bigger than the addiction that threatened to stop its beat.

Although Leaf knew I was clean, he asked if I would like to use. He'd scored some china white and planned on using it one last time before pursuing recovery. The "I'll quit tomorrow" myth affects every addict at one point or another. Leaf didn't offer out of spite; he offered out of respect. His definition of respect had not changed, and although I now viewed respect differently, I understood that his came from the same place. He didn't know any other way. For a moment, I considered his request, as most junkies do, but instead of using, memories of my life came to mind that were more important than any need to escape. I sat in his driveway listening to Bob Marley's "Three Little Birds" and thinking about how life had made its way back into his eyes overnight. It was the beginning of the miracle. "If you can make it Eric, I can." With those words, I watched as he danced to his front door, shrinking in my mirror, until I could no longer see him. I loved him. He was my brother.

It seemed cruel that death would find a man who had endured so much for so long, only to have the opportunity to get clean snatched from him. Emotion hit me so powerfully that the tears took minutes to catch up. Leaf was gone. He didn't quit the following day. Fentanyl had taken his life. He died alone on his couch with his dogs at his feet. The joy of the previous weekend died away as I realized I could not reach back into our past to bring him out of the darkness we'd shared. Hope died with a needle buried in his arm, his dreams of tomorrow lost in a disease that forced him to pursue relief in chemicals.

The same day I received word of Leaf's death, my son asked if I would put a movie in for him to watch. I told him to choose one so we could sit and watch it together. Halfway into the movie, the song "Three Little Birds" began to play. Before hearing it in Leaf's driveway, I had not heard that song in years and now it seemed to be playing every time I turned on music. My son, unsure of what was happening, reached up much like Christian had so many years before and offered me comfort between looks of concern. Though this may seem like coincidence to some, I believe otherwise. Had I turned the music off, I would have been turning away the workings of the spiritual realm. Leaf found a way to reach across the boundaries of death and life to touch my heart. For over a week, the same song played whenever I turned on music.

"Some die so that others may live," is a saying that I believe attempts to explain the senseless death of those who could not stay clean. With Leaf's death, that saying became truth. His passing reinvigorated my desire to help others in any way that I could, especially those who, like Leaf, wanted to get clean but didn't know how. I swore that I would use his story to help others as he had helped me both in life and death.

I decided to return to school. With that decision came the same lies I had been telling myself my whole life: *I am a stupid person incapable of amounting to anything academically or otherwise.* I left my scholastic self-confidence in the last class I attended in the ninth grade. My emotional maturity stopped when my drug and alcohol use began. Credibility is far easier to loose than it is to gain. I understood that if I wanted to have a voice in the professional world, I had to have an education. Laire's words from so long before rang true and I knew that if he could do it, I could, too. Of course there are obstacles for those who wish to return to school after being gone for so long. I had more obstacles than most, and for that reason I almost allowed fear to defeat me before I had even begun.

In order for a person with little more than an eighth-grade education to succeed in college, they must start at the very bottom. My journey into education started with adult education classes. Pushing aside my pride to walk through those doors was difficult. I left my previous job as part owner and boss. Now, I was a thirty-two-year-old man sitting next to fourteen- and fifteen-year-olds studying for their GED. Instead of being scared off, I reached deep within and drew from the experience of those who had gone before me. My mother and Laire provided examples of those who had traveled the road of uncertainty and reached the other side, emerging far better people as a result. If they could do it given their own life circumstances, then I could as well.

When a person asks for help, false pride falls away and is replaced by something far more powerful. My admission that I didn't know all the answers allowed others to teach me. This was my experience returning to school. I used every resource available to me—from the learning centers in the library to the tutors available for those in need of extra help. At first, I didn't see the importance of beginning at the lowest levels at the community college. Yet in time, it became apparent that following the advice of my advisors would pay off. I needed the successes of each class to create the momentum required to enter the university system. The memory of my friends attending the University of Washington while I walked the streets searching for a fix came back to me. I realized that they had created their own opportunity through hard work and commitment. This realization propelled me down the same path and in time, I was on the Dean's List with a 4.0 GPA.

Surprisingly, my self-esteem didn't reflect my academic success. When I earned A's my head continued telling me that I was stupid and incapable of finishing what I had started. Thankfully, more voices told me that I could finish otherwise I may have listened to the lies of a mind conditioned through failure. What I told myself was still crucial to my success—even if I didn't appear to believe in the possibility of success. I began to tell myself the opposite of what I had believed the majority of my life. If I wanted to be a success in school, I would have to act the part and quit believing that everyone saw my life in print. I had become actively involved in writing new chapters in my own story. I didn't want to leave this world regretting that I had not taken the hand of opportunity when it appeared. All I had to do was let that hand lead me to my own success.

For a while, I questioned my academic direction, wondering if I had what it takes to be a drug and alcohol counselor. Could I remain stable long enough to apply what I had learned through my own recovery and my education to help those who suffered from addiction? Every time I tried to change my major, roadblocks appeared, making the transition difficult, and finally pushing me back to the agreement I had made with my Creator. I had agreed to sacrifice my life for the betterment of others. I sought to give back to a world from which I had taken so much for so long. The Creator has a way of holding us to promises, especially when they're made in sincerity. When I began my counseling degree, doors began to open in ways that I never would have imagined.

Shifting from the past and present creates a seam that doesn't really exist. I can't point a finger at one thing and give it credit for the spiritual and emotional shifts that have occurred throughout my life. From the very beginning, I've seen the workings of the divine. Even in my darkest moments, I've felt the touch of the Creator. Every prayer and every curse was necessary for my transformation from light to darkness and back to light again. I finally understood what my teachers meant when they spoke of trusting the process of transformation.

The willingness to sacrifice bliss for others despite separation from the divine, and to enter the physical world to work with the multitudes of spiritual beings here to create love, compassion, and healing, are the very sacrifices that ensure a reunion with the life force. I do not fear it, but instead have total faith. This belief system has placed me in a position to share my miracle with others. I am not attempting to make others think as I do; instead, I am trying to bring myself to a better way of life. I must be the best human that I can be, rather than simply making a vow then believing it is enough. As I write these words, both of my children sleep comfortably in their rooms knowing that I am here and have been for the majority of their lives. A warmth keeps away the chill of the night, and that warmth does not radiate from any heat source. I think about how this used to be the time of night when I would walk the streets feeding a hunger far more powerful than even the love I have for my children—or so it seemed at the time. Now, I send out a silent prayer to the shadow walkers, knowing that many would love to be in the chair in which I now sit. This humbles me and propels me to continue doing the things that have kept me out of prison for the past eleven years.

A year or so ago, I was approached by one of my professors.

"Would you like to create and implement a college mentoring program here at the college for nontraditional students? I've been watching your success and I believe you'd be the perfect person for this project."

After the shock wore off, I gratefully accepted the offer and began my research to create the program. Before it even kicked off, I was given the opportunity to work with several people in the same position that I had been in and who needed the same kind of help I had needed when I began. The universe had placed me in a position to share my successes with others to help them succeed. For the first time, I felt that I was fulfilling my promise to give back through my education and experience. All I had to do was ask and opportunities would make themselves available in my life. These opportunities seemed contingent on my own humility. When I sought to put a feather in my own cap, rather than commend others, opportunities faded. I learned as such through my own selfish search for praise in the years' prior.

Recovery has taught me that I create my own destiny through hard work and my availability to the Creator. Last spring, I wrote letters to treatment programs all over the United States seeking a summer internship. After waiting several weeks, I received an email from Wilderness Treatment Center here in Montana asking me to come and intern for them. I knew that this was a time in my life when I was on the right path. Their invitation confirmed that I was headed in the right direction. I had passed by similar spiritual markers at other points in my life, ultimately learning that going in my own direction was futile and could only lead to a life of misery run on selfishness.

The night before I left for my internship, I began to write the chapter in this book about being put on a train and sent to Wilderness Treatment twenty years before. I started writing the book several weeks before sending out internship requests. I had not planned it that way; things just fell into place exactly as they were supposed to—yet another marker. Sitting in the hotel room in Missoula, my life had come full circle. This sort of experience is what has kept me on this course. The union of my life with the Creator's plan is a mind- and spirit-altering experience. I could not have chosen the day or the place for such to occur, but the ingredients were there for it to happen. Many miracles have transpired in this manner. Full circles are inevitable after entering the world of the spirit and learning from the lessons that present themselves. These lessons are like the healing of a wound that's been festering for years. A relief comes of knowing that I will never have to repeat the same mistakes again if I choose not to do so. In place of these mistakes, a life beyond my wildest imagination exists for my taking.

When I arrived at Wilderness Treatment Center, I sat down with the clinical director, Mark, and spoke honestly. I felt concerned that I wouldn't be allowed to work there if they knew that I was an ex-felon. I had been turned away more times than I could count for this very reason, and I knew that honesty would save everyone time and heartache in the long run.

"I am a convicted felon and have four felonies all stemming from my drug use. None of them are sexual, assault related, or heinous, but I would rather be turned away now than get going then find out in a month that I have to leave because of my past mistakes."

Mark's facial expression was unlike most I had seen under similar circumstances.

"Eric, if I turned away everyone with a history that they regretted or was criminal in nature, I would lose half of my staff. Your credentials speak for themselves and we're happy to have you."

My relief was palpable. It became evident that the place that had given me this chance also lived by the principles that they taught: forgiveness, hope, faith, redemption, and compassion. With Mark's encouraging words, I felt a freedom I had not felt before. I had finally passed the point of living a life in which my past dictated my future. In reality, I had always been a good human being. I just hadn't put in the work necessary to earn the trust of those in positions that required such a relationship.

Fifteen years ago, I sat before a judge with a prosecutor eager to send me away for a long period of time. What I perceived to be one man's arrogance was actually society's stance against men like me who had chosen to victimize the world rather than participate as responsible human beings. At that time, I deeply resented the men who sent me away as I didn't understand that I held the key to my freedom. I had been given the opportunities to remain out of prison and instead I chose to continue to use and in so doing proved them right.

At the beginning of September 2011, one week after I returned from my internship in Montana, a letter was sent to the prosecutor and sentencing judge, signed by Butte Probation and Parole. The envelope included numerous letters of reference from members in the community in support of a petition to the county attorney and sentencing judge for the termination of my sentence several years before my scheduled release. The letter stated, *We believe it to be in the best interest of society that the defendant has his sentence terminated early.*

This letter was the second of its kind. A year ago to the month, I was released from supervision and the courts were given jurisdiction over my sentence. This was the first step in the process of completing one of my debts to society. I had worked for this day for fifteen years, and it is not the finish line, just another marker along the path I've chosen. I have no idea what the return letter from the judge and prosecutor will say. I do know that I walk to the mailbox with sun on my face, no longer afraid of the shadows that once existed, continuing to do the things that have afforded me these opportunities. I live my life one day at a time, offering up prayers and knowing that what will be, will be. Despite the inevitability of life, I will do my best to honor those I love—including myself—by turning towards the light and away from the shadows.

While waiting for this manuscript to be edited for distribution I received notice from the Flathead County Attorney's Office that my sentence had been terminated. The Probation Department's appeal to have it rescinded two years early had been granted. Interestingly enough, the two signatures that had sealed my fate sixteen years earlier were the two I needed to be released from the State of Montana Correction's system. The two men I believed were against me when I was sentenced were simply waiting for me to reach my full potential as a human being. The world, its characters and its dynamics have changed. Not because the world has changed–because I have.

"Be the change you wish to see in the world." Gandhi

1847629R00287

Made in the USA
San Bernardino, CA
08 February 2013